Past and Present Publications

The Brenner Debate

Past and Present Publications

General Editor: PAUL SLACK, *Exeter College, Oxford*

Past and Present Publications comprise books similar in character to the articles in the journal *Past and Present*. Whether the volumes in the series are collections of essays – some previously published, others new studies – or monographs, they encompass a wide variety of scholarly and original works primarily concerned with social, economic and cultural changes, and their causes and consequences. They will appeal to both specialists and non-specialists and will endeavour to communicate the results of historical and allied research in readable and lively form.

For a list of titles in Past and Present Publications, see end of book.

The Brenner Debate

Agrarian Class Structure and Economic Development in Pre-Industrial Europe

Edited by

T. H. ASTON

and

C. H. E. PHILPIN

Published in South Asia by

Foundation Books Pvt. Ltd.
CAMBRIDGE HOUSE
4381/4 Ansari Road
Daryaganj, New Delhi – 110002

First South Asian Edition 2005

ISBN 81-7596-261-5
Special edition for sale in South Asia only, not for export elsewhere.

This edition of *T.H. Aston and C.H.E. Philpin / The Brenner Debate: Agrarian Class Structure and Economic Development in Pre-Industrial Europe* is published by arrangement with Cambridge University Press, The Edinburgh Building, Shaftesbury Road, Cambridge CB2 2RU, UK.

Published by Manas Saikia for Foundation Books Pvt. Ltd.
and printed & bound at Raj Press, R-3 Inderpuri, New Delhi - 110 012

Exclusively distributed by
AAKAR BOOKS
28-E, Pocket-IV, Mayur Vihar Phase-I, Delhi-110 091
Phone: 011-22795505, Telefax: 011-22795641
Email: aakarb@del2.vsnl.net.in

Contents

Preface

The Brenner debate, as it has come to be called, may justifiably lay claim to being one of the most important historical debates of recent years, and goes back, in one form or another, to at least the time of Marx. In general terms, it bears witness to the continuing interest among historians and scholars in allied fields in the epoch-making theme of the transition from feudalism to capitalism. More specifically, it maintains the tradition of *Past and Present* in fostering and stimulating discussion and debate on the fundamental issues of the past of which *Crisis in Europe, 1560–1660* (published by Routledge and Kegan Paul in 1965) was the first and perhaps the most catalytic. The debate now reprinted from the journal has been long in the making, from Robert Brenner's original article, published in *Past and Present* in 1976 but stemming from an earlier version given as a paper to the social science seminar of the Institute for Advanced Study, Princeton, in April 1974, until his response published in 1982. Regrettably two of the contributors, Professor Sir Michael Postan and Mr J. P. Cooper, died before the debate was concluded, but their contributions stand as outstanding examples of their own different but equally stimulating approaches to the question. Doubtless they and some of the other authors would now put their points in slightly different form, but it was decided, if only to preserve the structure of the debate, that the essays should be reprinted as they originally appeared in the journal, save only for minor corrections and alterations.

The debate has already aroused a most widespread interest among academics in many fields, as well as among ordinary readers, whether they are concerned with social, economic or demographic history, with the medieval or early modern periods, or whether their interests are directed to England, France or other countries of western and central Europe; it has also had a most welcome readership among sociologists, historians of ideas, historiographers and students of peasant societies and indeed of western civilization as a whole. But it cannot aspire to be definitive and we would not wish it to be seen in that light. Rather it is our hope and belief that it will advance discussion of the great issue with which it is concerned in a most material way and that it will be essential reading for all historians and scholars in allied fields whatever the period with which they are specifically concerned.

We are most grateful to all those at the Cambridge University Press who have assisted in the preparation of the volume, and especially to Mrs Fiona Barr for kindly compiling the index.

T.H.A.
C.H.E.P.

Introduction

R. H. HILTON

Robert Brenner's challenging article, "Agrarian Class Structure and Economic Development in Pre-Industrial Europe", published in issue no. 70 of *Past and Present* (February 1976), initiated a debate of intense interest, not only to historians, but to all concerned with the causes behind transitions between successive social formations. In some respects it might be regarded as a continuation of that other well-known debate concerning the transition from feudalism to capitalism, which had been sparked off by the criticism by the American economist Paul Sweezy of the analysis given by Maurice Dobb in his *Studies in the Development of Capitalism*. That debate, however, which began in the American journal *Science and Society* in 1950, was largely conducted between Marxists.[1] And although it undoubtedly had a resonance beyond them, it was inevitable that it should be seen as a debate within Marxism rather than one addressed to a wider public. This so-called "Transition debate" is hardly referred to in the "Brenner debate", even though there is considerable overlap in subject-matter, and even though Brenner himself, in a critique of Paul Sweezy, André Gunder Frank and Immanuel Wallerstein, referred extensively to the Transition debate in the pages of the *New Left Review* in 1977.[2] Nevertheless, those interested by the discussion in the pages of this volume would find much of interest in the Dobb–Sweezy controversy.

The responses to Brenner's article were of varying character. Since Brenner was attacking what he considered to be a form of demographic determinism in the interpretation of the development

[1] M. Dobb, *Studies in the Development of Capitalism* (London, 1946; repr. London, 1963, 1972). The *Science and Society* debate was republished, with supplementary material, as *The Transition from Feudalism to Capitalism*, introd. R. H. Hilton (London, 1976).

[2] R. Brenner, "The Origins of Capitalist Development: A Critique of Neo-Smithian Marxism", *New Left Rev.*, no. 104 (1977).

of the pre-industrial European agrarian economies (and to a lesser extent a commercial interpretation), some of the earliest responses were from historians whom he designated as "neo-Malthusians". Whatever these historians may have said about the deficiencies or otherwise of Brenner's factual basis, the main conflict was between rival explanatory theories concerning historical development. This seems to have been the principal motivation behind the responses of M. M. Postan and John Hatcher and of Emmanuel Le Roy Ladurie. Another weighty theoretical critique of Brenner's thesis came, however, not from a neo-Malthusian but from as severe a critic of neo-Malthusianism as Brenner himself. This was Guy Bois, whose then recently published *Crise du féodalisme*, a detailed study of late medieval Normandy, had paid particular attention to population movements between the thirteenth and sixteenth centuries.[3]

Somewhat different reactions came from historians who did not concern themselves so much with overarching theoretical interpretations as with the factual underpinning of Brenner's argument. Patricia Croot and David Parker questioned Brenner's perception of agrarian structures and developments in early modern France and England. Heide Wunder expressed doubts about his appreciation of the agrarian histories of western and trans-Elbian Germany. The remaining contributors were not in fact so locked into the argument with Brenner as were those historians already mentioned. My own essay was based on a lecture given in Germany in 1977 and was unrelated to the Brenner debate, but included in the symposium because of the relevance of its theme. J. P. Cooper's article, unrevised because of his death, was, no doubt, influenced by the debate but was a development of his own particular interests in the economic and social history of early modern Europe. It would seem too that Arnošt Klíma's article is similarly a development of his own preoccupation with the early history of Bohemian capitalism rather than a specific response to Brenner.

As will be seen, then, the contributions to the symposium relate to issues raised by Brenner but in rather different ways. Brenner's long and comprehensive summing up brings together most of these rather disparate contributions, absorbing and synthesizing, and, it must be said, giving no ground to his critics as far as his original

[3] G. Bois, *Crise du féodalisme* (Paris, 1976); Eng. trans., *The Crisis of Feudalism* (Cambridge, 1984).

position is concerned. It would seem that the gap between the opponents has much more to do with their theoretical starting-points than with the evidence adduced.

Brenner has some justification in referring to neo-Malthusianism (or demographic determinism) as the prevailing orthodoxy in historical studies of pre-industrial economic development. This orthodoxy should not, of course, be regarded merely as something imposed by academic mandarins. It is linked with the development of historical demography since the 1950s as an indispensable contribution to historical studies (though not, as some seem to think, as a separate discipline in itself).[4] It is true that M. M. Postan, who could be regarded as an early standard-bearer of this orthodoxy in medieval studies, hardly mentions Malthus in his many writings on medieval economic history. Nevertheless, he gives pride of place to population expansion and decline. His seminal contribution, as Brenner remarks in his first article,[5] was in his report on medieval economic history to the Tenth International Congress of Historical Sciences at Paris in 1950,[6] in which he rejected, *inter alia*, a monetarist explanation of long-term price movements and firmly asserted the primacy of the demographic factor. It is interesting, however, that he confessed that his definition of the "economic base" of society[7] "carries with it a certain early-Marxist implication".[8] Nevertheless, the theme of "population and land settlement", without concern for "the working of legal and social institutions" or "relations of class to class", recurs in his subsequent work, whether as a background to writings on trade, or more specifically in relation to demographic problems, as in his well-known article "Some Economic Evidence of Declining Population in the Later Middle Ages".[9]

[4] About which, many general works. For example, T. H. Hollingsworth, *Historical Demography* (London, 1969); E. A. Wrigley, *Population and History* (London, 1969).

[5] Below, p. 15.

[6] M. M. Postan, "[Section 3, Histoire économique:] Moyen âge", in *IXe Congrès international des sciences historiques, Paris, 1950*, 2 vols. (Paris, 1950–1), i, *Rapports*; repr. in his *Essays on Medieval Agriculture and General Problems of the Medieval Economy* (Cambridge, 1973).

[7] Quoted by Brenner, below, p. 15.

[8] Postan, "Moyen âge", p. 225 (p. 3).

[9] M. M. Postan, "Some Economic Evidence of Declining Population in the Later Middle Ages", *Econ. Hist. Rev.*, 2nd ser., ii (1949–50); repr. in his *Essays on Medieval Agriculture and General Problems of the Medieval Economy*.

Emmanuel Le Roy Ladurie on the other hand was, early on in his career, firmly attached to the Malthusian model of population expansion beyond the means of subsistence with inevitable regression as famine, plague and war brought population back to its "proper" relationship with resources. He built this model into his major and formidable work *Les paysans de Languedoc*,[10] whose second section was subtitled "Renaissance malthusienne", the whole work ending with an evocation of Malthus. This work did not ignore the social and political dimensions of peasant existence. In fact, its third section was subtitled "Prises de conscience et luttes sociales". However, by the time of his inaugural lecture to the Collège de France, "L'histoire immobile", in 1973, his Malthusianism was more pronounced – "it is in the economy, in social relations and, even more fundamentally, in biological facts, rather than in the class struggle, that we must seek the motive force of history".[11] And again, "from the fourteenth to the seventeenth centuries inclusive, the economy is servant rather than master, led rather than leading . . . in the last analysis it is meek enough before the great forces of life and death. And as for politics or the class struggle, their moment of power is still to come".[12]

It should not be assumed that Postan, at any rate, was totally hostile to Marxist historical interpretations. In spite of evident clashes of opinion, the Soviet historian E. A. Kosminsky thanked him for his help to him at the Public Record Office and for introducing him to English historians. Postan welcomed Kosminsky when he visited England in the 1950s, a by no means propitious period for such contacts. Postan used to refer to Marx as "that universal genius"[13] and in 1977 reviewed in a very friendly fashion for the *New Left Review* the work of the Polish Marxist historian, Witold Kula.[14]

It is not suggested that Brenner has, as a Marxist, for polemical reasons, exaggerated the distance between the neo-Malthusian (or neo-Ricardian) and his own position. But then, the reader of this debate needs to understand that there are different ways of under-

[10] E. Le Roy Ladurie, *Les paysans de Languedoc*, 2 vols. (S.E.V.P.E.N. edn, Paris, 1966).

[11] E. Le Roy Ladurie, "L'histoire immobile", *Annales E.S.C.*, xxix (1974), p. 675.

[12] *Ibid.*, p. 689.

[13] Personal communication with the author.

[14] M. M. Postan, "The Feudal Economy", *New Left Rev.*, no. 103 (1977), review of W. Kula, *An Economic Theory of the Feudal System* (London, 1976).

standing the Marxist position. As will be clear from the ensuing articles, what most clearly differentiates Postan and those of his school from Brenner is the exclusion of the "relations of class and class" from the subject-matter of economic history. For Brenner, and for many Marxist historians, the issue of class exploitation and class struggle is fundamental for understanding essential aspects of the medieval economy.

In medieval society, as in all pre-capitalist economies, agricultural predominated over industrial production. The peasants, who were overwhelmingly the principal producers, certainly put some of their product on to the market in order to acquire cash to buy industrial goods and products like salt, and especially to be able to pay rent and tax. But most of their production was for self-subsistence and economic reproduction. The luxury goods of international trade; the cathedrals, castles and other massive building enterprises; arms and armour for war and plunder; and all cultural artefacts, depended primarily on upper-class demand. Variations in the demand for non-agricultural products by the peasant majority of the population only minimally affected the upper reaches of the economy. It was variations in the incomes of the landed ruling class and its states which were crucial. But what determined these fluctuations? Since the principal component of these incomes was rent, one must enquire what determined the level of rent. It is here that the Marxist contribution becomes relevant. Medieval peasants were not free agents in a market for land which they could take up or leave as they wished. Most of them lived in traditional communities which probably pre-dated feudal lordship. A high proportion were legally servile or, if free in status, were nonetheless dependent on the power of the landlord. For Marxist historians, whatever may have been the influence of the land/labour ratio or of the technological level of agrarian production, the power of the landlord was a crucial element in determining the level of rent. The relationship between landlord and tenant was "political" rather than "economic", hence the use of the term "non-economic compulsion" – contrasted by Marx with the free bargaining between capitalist and wage-worker in a capitalist economy. Non-economic compulsion was not, however, uniformly successful. The exaction of rent, whether as labour service, in kind or in cash, would be seen by the peasant producer as an open appropriation of his product. It was resisted more or less strongly and in many different ways, ranging from labour service inadequately performed to open rebellion. This was the conflict of classes, central to Marxist theory.

Central, but not exclusively so. The contribution of Guy Bois to this debate reminds us that there are important divergences between historians working in the Marxist tradition. To understand these divergences, it is necessary to be aware of the principal tenets of historical materialism. This is by no means a fixed canon: there is debate within Marxism as well as between Marxists and non-Marxists. Nevertheless, the concept of the "mode of production" is accepted by all Marxist historians as an essential tool in undertaking historical investigation. Since Marxism is a materialism, a mode of production is understood as being based, first, on what Marx called the "forces of production", that is, natural resources, technology and labour power – the relations between humanity and nature in the struggle to exist and to reproduce. The second element in the definition is the "relations of production". This brief term essentially describes the relationships between the owners of the means of production and those who, through their labour, provide not only their own subsistence but the income of the owners. The relations of production naturally vary considerably according to the level of development of the forces of production. In what Marxists call the feudal mode of production, this is essentially the relationship between peasants and landlords – or perhaps one should say that it begins with that relationship, for historical development produces other classes and other relationships, in particular with the development of markets and urbanization.

"Modes of production" are simply the bare bones of a Marxist analysis of the historical process. The mode of production is simply the infrastructure of a society, whose laws, religions, state forms and cultures are superstructural features closely related to or developed from the economic structure. Nothing is simple: a given social formation, though primarily shaped by a dominant mode of production, can contain elements of other modes and their superstructural forms. One need only consider survivals of feudalism in capitalist societies from the eighteenth century to the present day. Nor is there necessarily agreement among Marxists as to what is infrastructure and what belongs to superstructure. Is law always superstructural? Some would argue that in feudal society the laws of serfdom entered so deeply into the process of "surplus extraction" that they should be regarded as part of the relations of production rather than as part of the legal, political and ideological superstructure. It could be argued perhaps even more strongly that the law of slavery, in making men and women simply instruments of production, was unquestionably an element in the economic infrastructure.

This sketchy presentation of some of the problems of Marxist historiography is meant to provide background to an important element in the Brenner debate. What caused movement in history? For Brenner, the class struggle has primacy. But his Marxist critics are aware that Marx himself, as well as many working in his intellectual domain, emphasize that developments in the *forces* of production – new technology, new means by which labour is organized, the economic success of new social classes – come into conflict with the existing *relations* of production, and, of course, with the legal, political and ideological superstructure. So, to which element in the mode of production do we ascribe primacy in causing movement from one social formation to another? It is possible, somewhat crudely, to give primacy to technological development ("The hand-mill gives you society with the feudal lord, the steam-mill society with the industrial capitalist" to quote an early formulation of Marx).[15] But it is also clear that those who would give primacy to class conflict must recognize that, however crucial in feudal society was the determination of ruling-class incomes through the struggle over rent, this struggle by no means occurred in an unchanging context. In particular, as Maurice Dobb suggested many years ago, the land/labour ratio is of crucial importance in a society where peasant production predominates. It can hardly be doubted that the conflict over rent will result in different outcomes where there is an abundance of land and a shortage of tenants as compared with the situation characteristic of western Europe around 1300, where land was over-occupied to such a degree that with a shortage of pasture and an overcrowding of infertile arable, the productivity of agriculture was severely reduced. These contradictions cannot be understood without appreciating that labour power is crucially affected by the essential elements in the demographic profile of a society – birth, fertility and mortality. This, above all, in a society where the basic

[15] Frequently cited by G. A. Cohen, *Karl Marx's Theory of History* (Oxford, 1978), e.g. pp. 41, 144, quoting Marx, *The Poverty of Philosophy* [1847] (Moscow, n.d.), p. 122. Cohen argues that Marx gave primacy to the forces of production.

units of production – the peasant holdings and the artisan workshops – had a labour force based on the family.

Brenner, as will be perceived by readers of the debate, strongly emphasizes the class struggle rather than developments in the forces of production as being the determinant of the various historical developments in the countries of late medieval and early modern Europe. This leads, among other things, to the conclusion that a successful struggle by peasants to protect the integrity of the tenancy of their holdings led to a sort of historical regression. This was because small-scale production was by its nature incapable of technological innovation and that this had to be left to proto-capitalist landowners and well-to-do yeomen, who would lay the basis for fully fledged capitalist agriculture. Whether small-scale agricultural production was incapable of innovation is a matter for debate not only among historians but also among those concerned with surviving modern (especially Third World) peasantries. One might suggest that the question is not necessarily blocked by the fact that England, pioneer of industrial capitalism, did happen to develop, to begin with, an agrarian capitalism based on the destruction of the peasantry.

As has been indicated, there are Marxist historians who, without denying the importance of class conflict in feudal society, lay more emphasis than does Brenner on economic factors, which (in Marxist terminology) would privilege the "forces of production" rather than the "relations of production". Some of them, in fact, see an inner logic in the feudal mode of production analogous to an argument of Marx about modern capitalist development which was not linked to class conflict. Marx suggested that capitalist technological progress in large-scale factory production brought about a changing organic composition of capital (an increasing amount of capital invested in machinery and raw material as against labour power), a falling rate of profit and periodic crises of over-production. Both Bois and Kula lay stress (though inevitably in different ways)[16] on a structural contradiction within feudalism between large-scale feudal landownership and the smallholding peasant unit of production. In medieval feudalism there was a long-term fall in the rate of feudal levy, beginning (according to Bois) during the expansion phase, when increas-

[16] Kula's *Economic Theory of the Feudal System* is concerned with early modern Poland.

ing numbers of peasant families were forced into the sub-class of smallholders without adequate subsistence. This economic logic was by no means identical to that perceived by Marx in capitalist production, but it was not, at any rate totally, determined by the conflict between lord and peasant at the political level (in Brenner's meaning of the term).

It may be of interest that the divergence between Marxists who particularly emphasize the role of class conflict and those who rather look at the whole mode of production without privileging the class struggle is not peculiar to this debate. It has, for instance, arisen in discussion among French Marxist historians concerning the crisis of the ancient world. Some accept a view also held by some non-Marxists that the mode of production based on slavery was becoming less and less profitable because of the shortage of slaves and because of the technological backwardness which was a legacy of reliance on cheap slave labour. Others insist that ancient slavery was itself profitable, provided that the control of slave labour could be assured – but that this failed because of the increasing success of slave rebellions in the later Roman empire.[17] Those emphasizing class struggle accuse their Marxist critics of "economism", and these in turn accuse their opponents of "politicism". It goes without saying, of course, that each tendency denies the overemphasis of which it is accused. In the same way, the neo-Malthusians deny that they neglect social structure, class divisions and the realities of exploitation. The readers of this volume will have plenty of opportunity to judge these matters and to retread the paths cleared by Robert Brenner and his critics.

[17] See P. Dockès, *La libération médiévale* (Paris, 1979); Eng. trans., *Medieval Slavery and Liberation* (London, 1982), and the discussion in the *comptes-rendus* of the *Séances de la Société de l'étude du féodalisme* for December 1979.

1. *Agrarian Class Structure and Economic Development in Pre-Industrial Europe**

ROBERT BRENNER

General interpretations of the processes of long-term economic change in late medieval and early modern Europe have continued to be constructed almost exclusively in terms of what might loosely be called "objective" economic forces – in particular, demographic fluctuations and the growth of trade and markets. A variety of models have been constructed centring on these forces. But whatever the exact nature of the model, and whether the pressure for change is seen to arise from urbanization and the growth of trade or an autonomous demographic development, a market supply/demand mechanism is usually assumed to provide the elementary theoretical underpinnings. So, the response of the agrarian economy to economic pressures, whatever their source, is more or less taken for granted, viewed as occurring more or less automatically, in a direction economically determined by the "laws of supply and demand".

In the construction of these economic models, the question of class structure tends to be treated in a variety of ways. Typically, there is the statement that one is abstracting (for the moment) from the social or class structure for certain analytical purposes.[1] The fact remains that in the actual process of explanation, that is in the application of the model to specific economic historical developments, class structure tends, almost inevitably, to creep back in. Some-

* This paper was originally presented at the annual convention of the American Historical Association, December 1974. An earlier version was given at the social science seminar of the Institute for Advanced Study, Princeton, April 1974. I wish to thank Franklin Mendels, T. K. Rabb, Eleanor Searle and Lawrence Stone for the substantial time and effort they gave in commenting on and criticizing this paper. I owe a special debt to Joel Singer for the great amount of help he gave me, including both information and analysis, in trying to understand German developments.

[1] See for example below, p. 15. M. M. Postan, "[Section 3, Histoire économique:] Moyen âge", in *Xe Congrès international des sciences historiques, Paris, 1950*, 2 vols. (Paris, 1950–1), i, *Rapports*.

times, it is inserted, in an *ad hoc* way, to comprehend a historical trend which the model cannot cover. More often, however, consciously or unconsciously, class structure is simply integrated within the model itself, and seen as essentially shaped by, or changeable in terms of, the objective economic forces around which the model has been constructed in the first place. In the most consistent formulations the very fact of class structure is implicitly or explicitly denied. Long-term economic development is understood in terms of changing institutionalized relationships of "equal exchange" between contracting individuals trading different, relatively scarce factors under changing market conditions.[2]

It is the purpose of this article to argue that such attempts at economic model-building are necessarily doomed from the start precisely because, most crudely stated, it is the structure of class relations, of class power, which will determine the manner and degree to which particular demographic and commercial changes will affect long-term trends in the distribution of income and economic growth – and not vice versa. Class structure, as I wish here to use the term, has two analytically distinct, but historically unified, aspects.[3] First, the relations of the direct producers to one another, to their tools and to the land in the immediate process of production – what has been called the "labour process" or the "social forces of production". Second, the inherently conflictive relations of property – always guaranteed directly or indirectly, in the last analysis, by force – by which an unpaid-for part of the product is extracted from the direct producers by a class of non-producers – which might be called the "property relationship" or the "surplus-extraction relationship". It is around the property or surplus-extraction relationship that one defines the fundamental classes in a society – the class(es) of direct producers on the one han[illegible] the surplus-extracting, or ruling, class(es) on the other.[4] It

[2] For a recent attempt to apply this sort of approach to the interpretation of socio-economic change in the medieval and early modern period, see D. C. North and R. P. Thomas, *The Rise of the Western World* (Cambridge, 1973).

[3] The following definitions derive, of course, from the work of Karl Marx, especially the preface to *A Contribution to the Critique of Political Economy* (New York, 1970 edn); "The Genesis of Capitalist Ground Rent" and "Distribution Relations and Production Relations", in *Capital*, 3 vols. (New York, 1967 edn), iii, chs. 47, 51; and the introduction to *Grundrisse* (London, 1973 edn).

[4] This is not necessarily to imply that classes exist or have existed in all societies. Classes, in my view, may be said to exist only where there is a surplus-extraction

would be my argument then that different class structures, specifically property relations or surplus-extraction relations, once established, tend to impose rather strict limits and possibilities, indeed rather specific long-term patterns, on a society's economic development. At the same time, I would contend, class structures tend to be highly resilient in relation to the impact of economic forces; as a rule, they are not shaped by, or alterable in terms of, changes in demographic or commercial trends. It follows therefore that long-term economic changes, and most crucially economic growth, cannot be analysed adequately in terms of the emergence of any particular constellation of relatively scarce factors unless the class relationships have first been specified; indeed, the opposite outcomes may accompany the impact of apparently similar economic conditions. In sum, fully to comprehend long-term economic developments, growth and/or retrogression in the late medieval and early modern period, it is critical to analyse the relatively autonomous processes by which particular class structures, especially property or surplus-extraction relations, are established, and in particular the class conflicts to which they do (or do not) give rise. For it is in the outcome of such class conflicts – the reaffirmation of the old property relations or their destruction and the consequent establishment of a new structure – that is to be found perhaps the key to the problem of long-term economic development in late medieval and early modern Europe, and more generally of the transition from feudalism to capitalism.

Put in such general terms, the foregoing propositions and definitions likely appear vague. What I should like to do is to try to give them substance by relating them to a critique of certain major explanatory motifs in the economic historiography of late medieval and early modern Europe, where they have hardly been taken for granted, and where it seems to me that economic/determinist model-building holds an overwhelmingly dominant position. Thus, I will focus on two different overarching interpretations of long-term economic change in medieval and early modern Europe, one of which might be called the "demographic model", the other of which might be called the "commercialization model". The former

or property relationship in the specific sense implied here – that is, in the last analysis non-consensual and guaranteed either directly or indirectly by force.

grew out of a critique of the latter, but I shall try to show that both are subject to analogous problems.

I THE DEMOGRAPHIC MODEL

The emerging dominance of the so-called demographic factor in the economic historiography of Europe even through the age of industrialization was recognized as early as 1958 by H. J. Habakkuk in his well-known article "The Economic History of Modern Britain". As Habakkuk wrote, "For those who care for the overmastering pattern, the elements are evidently there for a heroically simplified version of English history before the nineteenth century in which the long-term movements in prices, in income distribution, in investment, in real wages, and in migration are dominated by changes in the growth of population. Rising population: rising prices, rising agricultural profits, low real incomes for the mass of the population, unfavorable terms of trade for industry – with variations depending on changes in social institutions, this might stand for a description of the thirteenth century, the sixteenth century and the early seventeenth, and the period 1750–1815. Falling or stationary population with depressed agricultural profits but higher mass incomes might be said to be characteristic of the intervening periods".[5] Well before Habakkuk's article, M. M. Postan had presented the basic contours of what has become the standard interpretation of long-term socio-economic change in the medieval period; and his demographic approach was filled out and codified in his chapter on "Medieval Agrarian Society in its Prime: England" in the *Cambridge Economic History of Europe*.[6] Roughly the same line of argument has, moreover, now been carried through the sixteenth and seventeenth centuries by Peter Bowden in the *Agrarian History of England and Wales*.[7] Nor has this approach been confined to English economic history, where it is now more or less standard. It has been rigorously applied in what is perhaps the most influential work on French socio-economic history of the pre-industrial period,

[5] H. J. Habakkuk, "The Economic History of Modern Britain", *Jl Econ. Hist.*, xviii (1958), pp. 487–8.

[6] M. M. Postan, "Medieval Agrarian Society in its Prime: England", in *Cambridge Economic History of Europe*, i, 2nd edn.

[7] P. Bowden, "Agricultural Prices, Farm Profits, and Rents", in J. Thirsk (ed.), *The Agrarian History of England and Wales*, iv, *1500–1640* (Cambridge, 1967).

Emmanuel Le Roy Ladurie's classic monograph, *Les paysans de Languedoc*.[8] With such eminent exponents, it is hardly surprising that what might be termed secular Malthusianism has attained something of the level of orthodoxy. Its cyclical dynamic has replaced the unilineal "rise of the market" as the key to long-term economic and social change in pre-industrial society.

Nor can there be any question but that the Malthusian model, in its own terms, has a certain compelling logic. If one takes as *assumptions* first an economy's inability to make improvements in agricultural productivity, and second a natural tendency for population to increase on a limited supply of land, a theory of income distribution seems naturally to follow. With diminishing returns in agriculture due to declining fertility of the soil and the occupation of increasingly marginal land, we can logically expect demand to outrun supply: thus terms of trade running against industry in favour of agriculture, falling wages, rising food prices and, perhaps most crucially in a society composed largely of landlords and peasants, rising rents. Moreover, the model has a built-in mechanism of self-correction which determines automatically its own change of direction and a long-term dynamic. Thus the ever greater subdivision or overcrowding of holdings and the exhaustion of resources means over-population, which leads to Malthusian checks, especially famine/starvation; this results in demographic decline or collapse and the opposite trends in income distribution from the first phase. As Habakkuk pointed out, this two-phase model has now been applied to the entire period between roughly 1050 and 1800. Indeed, the very essence of "traditional economy" has seemed to be captured in this centuries-long *motion biséculaire* (two-phase movement). As Le Roy Ladurie succinctly states, "Malthus came too late": ironically, Malthus's model was correct not for the emergent industrial economy he was analysing, but for the stagnant backward society from which this had arisen. Indeed, for Le Roy Ladurie the pattern seemed so inescapable as to invite analogies from biology or physiology. The history of rural Languedoc over six hundred years should be seen, he says, as "the immense respiration of a social structure".[9]

[8] E. Le Roy Ladurie, *Les paysans de Languedoc*, 2 vols. (S.E.V.P.E.N. edn, Paris, 1966).

[9] *Ibid.*, introduction, esp. i, p. 8; also conclusion, esp. pp. 652–4.

(A) DEMOGRAPHY, INCOME DISTRIBUTION AND ECONOMIC GROWTH

In terms of its special premises and the small number of variables it entails, secular Malthusianism seems almost foolproof. Yet what must be questioned is its relevance to the explanation of actual historical change. Do the model's assumptions and constants, indeed its very dynamic, illuminate or actually obscure the crucial conditions and processes underlying the varying patterns of long-term economic change in late medieval and early modern Europe? In his classic article of 1950 which set out his demographic model for medieval European economic development, Postan made sure to specify that he was concerned only with what he termed the "economic base" of medieval society. He defined the "economic base" as "population and land settlement, technique of production and the general trends of economic activity: in short, all those economic facts which can be discussed without concentrating on the working of legal and social institutions and upon relations of class to class".[10] Postan argued that what made it "necessary and possible to deal with this group of subjects together", and in abstraction from class relations, was that "they have all been recently drawn into the discussion of general trends of economic activity, or, to use a more fashionable term, into the 'long-term movements' of social income".[11] But the question which must immediately be posed precisely when one is attempting to interpret "long-term movements" of social income – that is, long-term trends of income distribution and economic growth – is whether it is at all admissible to abstract them from "the working of legal and social institutions". Can the problems of the development of Postan's so-called "economic base" be very meaningfully considered apart from the "relations of class to class"?

With respect to long-term trends in income distribution, I shall try to argue that the Malthusian model runs into particularly intractable problems in relation to the always ambiguous and contested character of medieval and early modern landholding arrangements. On the one hand, the very distribution of ownership of the land between landlord and peasant was continually in question throughout the period. Could the peasantry move to establish heritability

[10] Postan, "Moyen âge", p. 225. [11] *Ibid.*

and fixed rents – that is, essentially freehold rights on the land? If so, the very significance of rent would be transformed, and the viability of the landlord class put in jeopardy. On the other hand, in situations where the landlords had established ownership of the land, a further question might be raised: could the landlords gain extra-economic power over the person of their tenants, control marriage, and in particular land transfers and peasant mobility? If so, the possibility would emerge of imposing extra-economic or arbitrary payments upon the peasantry – payments beyond custom or beyond what the relative scarcity of factors might dictate. Any explanation of the progress of income distribution in the late medieval and early modern period must therefore be able to interpret not merely the changing distribution of the immediate product of the land, but the prior questions of the distribution of property between lord and peasant and of the direct applicability of force in the rent relationship. Some economic historians have attempted to deal with this problem by denying or ignoring its existence, in particular by describing the economy in terms of contractual relationships among individual holders of scarce resources, such as military skill and weaponry, land, agricultural labour power and so on.[12] Others have

[12] See for example North and Thomas, who argue that "Serfdom in Western Europe was essentially a contractual arrangement where labor services were exchanged for the public good of protection and justice": D. C. North and R. P. Thomas, "The Rise and Fall of the Manorial System: A Theoretical Model", *Jl Econ. Hist.*, xxxi (1971), p. 778. North and Thomas can make this argument because they assume: (a) that the serf was essentially "protected from arbitrary charges" and (b) that because there was an absence of "a central coercive authority" the serfs were essentially free, especially to move, and that as a result there was a "rudimentary labor market". In my view, these assumptions are consistent with one another but inconsistent with the realities of serfdom precisely because serfdom was in its essence non-contractual. There was no "mutual agreement" between lord and serf – according to North and Thomas a defining feature of contract. On the contrary, it is precisely the interrelated characteristics of arbitrary exactions by the lords from the peasants and control by landlords over peasant mobility that gave the medieval serf economy its special traits: surplus extraction through the direct application of force rather than equal exchange via contract, as North and Thomas would have it. The sort of problems entailed in the approach of North and Thomas are evident in their account of the origins of serfdom. Thus: "Individuals with superior military skills and equipment were urgently needed to protect the peasants who were unskilled in warfare and otherwise helpless. Here was the classic example of a public good, since it was impossible to protect one peasant family without also protecting their neighbors. In such cases *coercion was necessary* to overcome each peasant's incentive to let his neighbor pay the costs, and *the military power of the lord provided the needed force*". North and Thomas, *Rise of the Western World*, pp. 29–30 (my italics). This

attempted to meet the problem by assimilating it to their basic economic models: by insisting, directly or indirectly, that in the long run the distribution of property and the successful applicability of force in the rent relationship will be subject to essentially the same sorts of supply/demand pressures as the distribution of the product itself, and will move in roughly the same direction. I shall try to show empirically that this is not the case and argue instead that these are fundamentally questions of class relations and class power, determined relatively autonomously from economic forces.

The demographic interpreters of late medieval and early modern economies run into even more serious problems in attempting to explain general trends of total production, economic growth or stagnation, than they do with regard to the distribution of income. Certainly, their assumption of declining productivity in agriculture is a reasonable one for most, though not all, pre-industrial European economies. Indeed, these economic historians have been able to specify clearly some of the technical and economic roots of long-term falling yields through their researches into the problems of maintaining soil fertility in the face of a shortage of animals and fertilizer, especially under conditions of backward agricultural organization and technique and low levels of investment.[13] Nevertheless, specifying in this manner the conditions conducive to long-term stagnation is not really explaining this phenomenon, for no real account is provided of why such conditions persisted. Thus, to explain economic "rigidity" as does Le Roy Ladurie as the "fruit of technical stagnation, of lack of capital, of absence of the spirit of enterprise and of innovation" is, in fact, to beg the question.[14] It is

explanation not only begs the fundamental question of class: how do we explain, in the first place, the distribution of land, of the instruments of force, and of military skill within the society. It also undermines their own argument for the essentially contractual nature of serfdom, for it is here explicitly admitted that the serf is coerced. To go on to say that the "lord's power to exploit his serfs . . . was not unlimited, but constrained (in the extreme case) by the serf's ability to steal away" (p. 30) does not eliminate the fundamental difficulty – that is, attempting to treat serfdom as contractual, while admitting its essentially coercive nature.

13 Postan, "Medieval Agrarian Society in its Prime: England", pp. 548–70; M. M. Postan, "Village Livestock in the Thirteenth Century", *Econ. Hist. Rev.*, 2nd ser., xv (1962–3); J. Z. Titow, *English Rural Society, 1200–1350* (London, 1969).

14 Le Roy Ladurie, *Paysans de Languedoc*, i, p. 634. Le Roy Ladurie seems at times to want to view economic development as essentially the direct result of apparently autonomous processes of technical innovation. Thus, he says, "it was the technological weakness of the society . . . its inability to increase productivity, and lastingly and definitively raise production, which created the barrier which,

analogous to attempting to explain economic growth merely as a result of the introduction of new organizations of production, new techniques and new levels of investment. These factors do not, of course, explain economic development: they merely describe what economic development is. The continuing stagnation of most of the traditional European economies in the late medieval and early modern period cannot be fully explained without accounting for the real economic growth experienced by the few of these economies which actually developed. More generally, economic backwardness cannot be fully comprehended without an adequate theory of economic development. In describing the specific two-stage agrarian/economic cycle set in motion in a number of medieval and early modern European economies by declining agricultural productivity, the Malthusian theorists have indeed isolated an important pattern of long-term economic development and stability. But this dramatic two-phase movement is not universal even for traditional societies;[15] and besides, it still needs an interpretation. I shall argue that the Malthusian cycle of long-term stagnation, as well as other forms of economic backwardness, can only be fully understood as the product of established structures of class relations (particularly surplus-extraction relations), just as economic development can only be fully understood as the outcome of the emergence of new class relations more favourable to new organizations of production, technical innovations, and increasing levels of productive investment. These new class relations were themselves the result of previous, relatively autonomous processes of class conflict.

(B) THE DEMOGRAPHIC MODEL IN COMPARATIVE PERSPECTIVE

I hope the force of these objections will appear more compelling as they are specified in particular historical cases. My concrete method of critique is exceedingly simple and obvious: it is to observe the prevalence of similar demographic trends throughout Europe over the six- or seven-hundred-year period between the twelfth and the

at the end of the period, stopped its quasi-two-phase (*quasi-biséculaire*) growth of population and of small peasant proprietorship" (p. 639); see also below, pp. 28–9, n. 37.

[15] Cf. C. Geertz, *Agricultural Involution* (Berkeley, 1963).

eighteenth centuries and to show the very different outcomes in terms of agrarian structure, in particular the patterns of distribution of income and economic development, with which they were associated. In this way, I may begin to expose the problems inherent in the complementary and connected demographic-deterministic models of Postan (for the twelfth to fifteenth centuries) and Le Roy Ladurie (for the sixteenth to eighteenth centuries).

Demographic growth, according to Postan, characterizes the twelfth and thirteenth centuries. It leads to the occupation of marginal lands and the decreasing fertility of the soil: in short, a rising demand for a relatively inflexible supply of food and land; thus, rising food prices and rising rents. However, as Postan is of course aware, we are dealing in this period with a very peculiar form of rent. There is very little in the way of direct lease and contract. We have instead a theoretically fixed, but actually fluctuating, structure of customary rights and obligations that define landholding arrangements. These specify in the first place the regular (ostensibly fixed) payments to be made by the peasant to the lord in order to retain his land. But they often lay down, in addition, a further set of conditions of landholding: the lord's right to impose additional extraordinary levies (tallages and fines); the peasant's right to use, transfer and inherit the land; and finally, the very disposition of the peasant's own person, in particular his freedom of mobility. Now it is Postan's argument that these latter conditions, which together defined the peasant's customary status – his freedom or unfreedom – in so far as they are relevant to long-term economic trends, can be more or less directly assimilated to his supply/demand demographic model. Thus the central point for Postan is that, due to developing pressure of population, the thirteenth century is a period in which the landlords' position improves *vis-à-vis* the peasants not only in those few areas where what might be termed modern leaseholding has emerged, but also in the so-called customary sector. Thus competition for land induces the peasantry to accept a serious degradation of their personal/tenurial status in order to hold on to their plots and this, in turn, exacerbates the generally deteriorating economic situation to which they are being subjected simply by forces of supply and demand. So, in order to retain their land, the peasants must submit in particular to (1) increasing arbitrary taxes (fines, tallages), levied above and beyond the traditional rent; and (2) increasing labour services on the lord's demesne. These increased payments are part and parcel of the generally increasing ability of the lord to control the peasants and determine their condition. In other words, for Postan, the extra-economic relationships between lord and peasant – specifically, those payments which are associated with increasing peasant unfreedom – can be understood in terms of the same form of "relative scarcity of factors" argument that would apply to purely market contractual arrangements, and indeed conduced to the same effect in terms of income distribution between lord and peasant. As Postan says, for example, at one point: "the fluctuation of labour services requires no other explanation than that which is provided by the ordinary interplay of supply and demand – demand for villein service and supply of villein labour".[16]

The fourteenth and fifteenth centuries witnessed a decline in population as a result of falling productivity, famine and plague. Ultimately, demographic catastrophe led to a drastic reversal of the man/land ratio. Postan thus argues, consistently enough, that this demographic change brought about precisely the opposite conditions to those which had prevailed in the thirteenth century. Scarcity of peasants meant a decline not only in the level of rent, but equally in the lord's ability to restrict peasant mobility, and peasant freedom in general. With competition among lords to obtain scarce peasant tenants, one gets according to the laws of supply and demand, not only declining rents in general, and labour services in particular, but the giving up by the lords of their rights to control the peasantry. Demographic catastrophe determines the fall of serfdom.[17]

Le Roy Ladurie takes up the cycle from the point where Postan leaves it – that is, at the end of the fifteenth century. Serfdom is now no longer extant in either England or most of France. We have instead a society of free peasants in both England and France, some holding their land on a roughly contractual basis from the landlords, others having achieved the status of something like freeholders. (I

[16] M. M. Postan, "The Chronology of Labour Services", *Trans. Roy. Hist. Soc.*, 4th ser., xx (1937), p. 171. For this paragraph, Postan, "Medieval Agrarian Society in its Prime: England", pp. 552–3, 607–9.

[17] Postan, "Medieval Agrarian Society in its Prime: England", pp. 608–10. "In the end economic forces asserted themselves, and the lords and employers found that the most effective way of retaining labour was to pay higher wages, just as the most effective way of retaining tenants was to lower rents and release servile obligations" (p. 609).

shall return to this a little later.) At any rate, as has been noted, we get a repetition of the two-phase movement Postan charted for the twelfth and thirteenth centuries and then the fourteenth and fifteenth centuries: that is, first an upward push in population during the "long sixteenth century" leading to rising rents, falling wages and the disintegration of peasant holdings. Drastically declining productivity then leads to demographic catastrophes during the seventeenth century, a turning of the trend, and the opposite configuration in terms of the distribution of income and of land.[18]

The obvious difficulty with this whole massive structure is that it simply breaks down in the face of comparative analysis. Different outcomes proceeded from similar demographic trends at different times and in different areas of Europe. Thus we may ask if demographic change can be legitimately treated as a cause, let alone the key variable. So it is true that in the thirteenth century the increase in population was accompanied by increasing rents and, more generally, increasing seigneurial controls over the peasantry, not only in England but in parts of France (especially to the north and east of the Paris region: Vermandois, Laonnais, Burgundy).[19] Yet it is also the case that in other parts of France (Normandy, Picardy) no counter-tendency developed in this era to the long-term trend which had resulted in the previous disappearance of serfdom.[20] Moreover, in still other French regions (especially the area around Paris) a process of deterioration in peasant status was at just this time abruptly terminated and an opposite movement set in motion which had decisively established peasant freedom (as well as nearly full peasant property) by the end of the thirteenth century.[21] These contrasting developments obviously had a powerful effect on trends of income distribution. As Postan himself points out, landlords were able to extract far greater rents from serfs (villeins) than from free tenants – and were able to increase these significantly in the course

[18] Le Roy Ladurie, *Paysans de Languedoc*.

[19] P. Petot, "L'évolution du servage dans la France coutumière du XIe au XIVe siècle", *Recueils de la Société Jean Bodin*, ii (1937); C.-E. Perrin, "Le servage en France et en Allemagne", in *X Congresso internazionale di scienze storiche, Rome, 1955*, 7 vols. (Florence, 1955), iii, pp. 227–8; G. Fourquin, *Les campagnes de la région parisienne à la fin du moyen âge* (Paris, 1970), pp. 175–9; R. Fossier, *Histoire sociale de l'Occident médiévale* (Paris, 1970), pp. 161–3.

[20] R. Fossier, *La terre et les hommes en Picardie jusqu'à la fin du XIIIe siècle*, 2 vols. (Paris, 1968), ii, pp. 555–60. See also the references cited in the preceding note.

[21] Fourquin, *Campagnes de la région parisienne*, pp. 160–72, 189–90.

of the thirteenth century.[22] Postan contends, however, that "The reason why landlords were now not only desirous to increase the weight of labour dues but also 'got away with it' are not difficult to guess. With the growing scarcity of land and with the lengthening queues of men waiting for it, the *economic* powers of a landowner over his tenants were more difficult to resist".[23]

Clearly, a growth of population leading to rising demand for land would tend to increase a lord's power to extract rent, in whatever form, from the peasantry – but only if the lord had successfully established his right to charge more than a fixed rent. However, the point is that by and large in the medieval period the only tenants subject to the exercise of this sort of "economic" power on the part of the lord – that is, to the imposition of additional labour services, as well as additional arbitrary payments of other kinds above the customary rent, in particular entry fines and tallages – were unfree and held by villein tenure. The very status of free tenant in the thirteenth century (which incidentally included a significant section of the population) generally carried with it precisely freedom from heavy (or increasing) labour service on the lord's demesne, and freedom from tallages, entry fines and other similar payments.[24]

So the determination of the impact of the pressure of population on the land – who was to gain and who to lose from a growing demand for land and rising land prices and rent – was subject to the prior determination of the qualitative character of landlord/peasant class relations. Thus during the thirteenth century in the Paris region the trend towards increasing tallaging of the peasantry by landlords was directly aborted by a counter-trend towards peasant enfranchisement. The point, here as in England, was that, once free, peasants paid only a fixed customary rent; they could not be forced to pay additional, arbitrary rents. It is notable, moreover, that this trend towards restricting rent and establishing free tenure

[22] Postan, "Medieval Agrarian Society in its Prime: England", pp. 552–3, 603, 607–8, 611, and esp. p. 603: "the money charges incumbent upon customary, i.e. villein, holdings were heavy beyond all comparison . . . even with those of substantial peasant freeholders".

[23] *Ibid.*, p. 608 (my italics).

[24] See above, nn. 22, 23, and p. 20, n. 16; R. H. Hilton, *The Decline of Serfdom in Medieval England* (London, 1969), pp. 18–19, 24, 29–31. For graphic illustrations of the ability of established free peasants to resist the most determined (and desperate) efforts of rent-gouging landlords even during the thirteenth-century increase in population, see E. Searle, *Lordship and Community* (Toronto, 1974), pp. 163–6.

in the Paris region took place in the most heavily populated region in all of France.[25] Thus the same upward pressure of population could, and did, lead to changes in the distribution of income favourable to the lords *or* to the peasants – opposite outcomes – depending on the social-property relationships and balances of class forces.

The demographic decline experienced throughout Europe which began at various points during the fourteenth century poses analogous problems. In the long run the parallel trends of declining rents and the rise of peasant freedom did dominate this period in England, certainly by the fifteenth century. But, by contrast, the late fourteenth and fifteenth centuries also witnessed a sharpening of landlord controls over the peasantry in Catalonia; and this was also the case, at least temporarily, in parts of France (Bordelais, the centre).[26] It is true that in these areas and in most of western Europe serfdom was dead by the early sixteenth century. On the other hand, in eastern Europe, in particular Pomerania, Brandenburg, East Prussia and Poland, decline in population from the late fourteenth century onwards was accompanied by an ultimately successful movement towards imposing extra-economic controls, that is serfdom, over what had been, until then, one of Europe's freest peasantries.[27] By 1500 the same Europe-wide trends had gone a long way towards establishing one of the great divides in European history, the emergence of an almost totally free peasant population in western Europe, the debasement of the peasantry to unfreedom in eastern Europe.

But the period from 1500 to 1750 marked another great divide which puts in question once more the explanatory value of the Malthusian model. This time what is left unexplained is not merely the question of income distribution but the whole problem of dramatically contrasting trends of economic development: continuing long-term stagnation accompanying the increase of population

[25] Fourquin, *Campagnes de la région parisienne*, esp. pp. 170ff.

[26] P. Vilar, *La Catalogne dans l'Espagne moderne*, 3 vols. (Paris, 1962), i, pp. 466ff.; J. Vicens Vives, *Historia de los remensas en el siglo XV* (Barcelona, 1945), pp. 23–4ff.; R. Boutruche, *La crise d'une société* (Paris, 1963 edn), pp. 321ff.; I. Guérin, *La vie rurale en Sologne aux XIVe et XVe siècles* (Paris, 1960), pp. 202–15ff.

[27] F. L. Carsten, *The Origins of Prussia* (London, 1954), pp. 80–4, 101–16; M. Malowist, "Le commerce de la Baltique et le problème des luttes sociales en Pologne aux XVe et XVIe siècles", in *La Pologne au Xe Congrès international des sciences historiques à Rome* (Warsaw, 1955), pp. 131–6, 145–6; J. Blum, "The Rise of Serfdom in Eastern Europe", *Amer. Hist. Rev.*, lxii (1957), pp. 820–2.

in some areas, the spectacular emergence of an entirely new pattern of relatively self-sustaining growth accompanying the increase of population in other areas. Thus, as Le Roy Ladurie would lead us to expect, in much of France during the sixteenth and seventeenth centuries increasing population did lead to fragmentation of holdings, rising rents and declining productivity. And at different points in time in different regions we do get the classic crises of subsistence, demographic disaster and ultimately a "turning of the trend".[28] Nevertheless, ironically, the parallel growth of population in England in this same period has been used to explain precisely opposite developments. Thus, according to Bowden, "Under the stimulus of growing population, rising agricultural prices, and mounting land values, the demand for land became more intense and *its use more efficient*. The area under cultivation was extended. *Large estates were built up at the expense of small-holdings*".[29] So, in France, as population increased, there was extreme fragmentation of holdings and declining productivity. But in England, by contrast, the dominant tendency was to build up larger and larger units; to consolidate holdings and to farm them out to a large tenant farmer who in turn cultivated them with the aid of wage labour. Accompanying this change in the organization of production were major increases in agricultural productivity, with truly epoch-making results. By the end of the seventeenth century, English population had returned to its high, late thirteenth-century levels, but there was nothing like the demographic pattern of seventeenth-century France, no "phase B" following inescapably from "phase A". Instead, we have the final disruption of the Malthusian pattern and the introduction of a strikingly novel form of continued economic development.[30]

[28] See, for example, P. Goubert, "Le milieu démographique", in his *L'ancien régime*, 2 vols. (Paris, 1969–73), i, ch. 2; also P. Goubert, *Beauvais et le Beauvaisis de 1600 à 1730* (Paris, 1960); J. Meuvret, *Etudes d'histoire économique* (Paris, 1971); F. Braudel and E. Labrousse (eds.), *Histoire économique et sociale de la France*, 4 vols. in 7 (Paris, 1970–80), ii.

[29] Bowden, "Agricultural Prices, Farm Profits, and Rents", p. 593 (my italics).

[30] On English agrarian change, its causes and consequences, see for example R. H. Tawney, *The Agrarian Problem in the Sixteenth Century* (London, 1912; New York, 1967 edn); E. Kerridge, *The Agricultural Revolution* (London, 1967); E. Kerridge, *Agrarian Problems in the Sixteenth Century and After* (London, 1969), esp. ch. 6; W. G. Hoskins, "The Leicestershire Farmer in the Seventeenth Century", *Agric. Hist.*, xxv (1951); Thirsk (ed.), *Agrarian History of England and Wales*, iv. See also below, pp. 46ff.

II THE COMMERCIALIZATION MODEL

Before I present the alternative which I think follows from the foregoing comparative analysis, it should be noted that both of the two most prominent exponents of the population-centred approaches to economic change in pre-industrial society, Postan and Le Roy Ladurie, originally constructed their models in opposition to a prevailing historiographical orthodoxy which assigned to the growth of trade and the market a role somewhat analogous to that which they were ultimately to assign to population. Thus Postan and Le Roy Ladurie made powerful attacks on the simple unilineal conceptions which had held that the force of the market determines: first, the decline of serfdom, which was often simply identified as the change from labour rents to money rents and *ipso facto* the emergence of a free contractual tenantry; and second, the rise of capitalist agriculture, classically large-scale tenant farming on the basis of capital improvements and wage labour.

(A) TRADE AND SERFDOM

Postan was, in particular, concerned to show that in the medieval period the force of the market, far from automatically bringing about the dissolution of serfdom, might actually coincide with its intensification. He demonstrated, for example, that in some areas most accessible to the London market the trend towards increased labour services and the seigneurial reaction of the thirteenth century was most intense. Perhaps an even clearer illustration of Postan's point is provided in the areas under the influence of the Paris market during the same period. Thus, as one proceeded along the Seine through a series of different regions, all of which produced for Parisian consumption, one passed through regions of peasant freedom, peasant semi-freedom and peasant serfdom. Most spectacular, as Postan pointed out, was the case of eastern Europe, where during the late medieval and early modern period the powerful impact of the world market for grain gave a major impetus to the tightening of peasant bondage at the same time as it was stimulating the development of capitalism in the west.[31]

[31] Postan, "Chronology of Labour Services", esp. pp. 192–3; Fourquin, *Campagnes de la région parisienne*, pp. 169–70 (and n. 71). See also M. M. Postan, "The Rise of a Money Economy", *Econ. Hist. Rev.*, xiv (1944).

Still, Postan never really specified the fatal flaw of the trade-centred approach to European development; this, in my view, is its tendency to ignore the fact that serfdom denoted not merely, nor even primarily, labour dues as opposed to money dues, but, fundamentally, powerful landlord rights to arbitrary exactions and a greater or lesser degree of peasant unfreedom. Thus serfdom involved the landlord's ability to control his tenant's person, in particular his movements, so as to be able to determine the *level* of the rent in excess of custom or what might be dictated by the simple play of forces of supply and demand. For this reason the decline of serfdom could not be achieved, as is sometimes implied, through simple commutation, the "equal exchange" of money rent for labour rent which might be transacted in the interest of greater efficiency for both parties.[32] What would remain after commutation was still the lord's power over the peasant. Indeed, it is notable that commutation could be unilaterally dictated – and reversed – at the lord's will. Thus, as Postan points out, commutation was an extremely widespread development in twelfth-century England; but this trend did not signify the emancipation of the peasants, for in the thirteenth century they were once again made subject to the landlords' demands for services. Indeed, even where the lord did not decide to take labour services, the peasant was still required to pay money fees to buy off his labour dues and moreover remained subject to those arbitrary exactions (tallages, entry fines and so on) which were bound up with his status as a bondsman.[33] What therefore had to be eliminated to bring about the end of serfdom was the type of "unequal exchange" which was manifested in the direct, forceful, extra-economic controls exerted by the lord over the peasant. Since the essence of serfdom was the lord's ability to bring extra-market pressure to bear upon the peasants in determining the level of rent, in particular by preventing peasant mobility and thus a free market in tenants, it is hardly surprising that fluctuations in trade, indeed of

[32] For a recent restatement of this view, see North and Thomas, *Rise of the Western World*, pp. 39–40. It is of course a corollary of their view of serfdom as an essentially contractual, rather than coercive and exploitative, relationship. See above, pp. 16–17, n. 12.

[33] Postan, "Medieval Agrarian Society in its Prime: England", pp. 604–8, 611. For an analysis of the reasons why commutation is misunderstood if it is taken to mean a relaxation of serfdom, see especially Hilton, *Decline of Serfdom in Medieval England*, pp. 29–31, and R. H. Hilton, "Freedom and Villeinage in England", *Past and Present*, no. 31 (July 1965), p. 11.

market factors of any type, were not in themselves enough to determine the dissolution of serfdom. Serfdom was a relationship of power which could be reversed, as it were, only in its own terms, through a change in the balance of class forces.

Obviously, there might be periods when the enormous demand for land, and thus for tenancies, deriving in particular from the rising pressure of population, would allow the lords to take a very relaxed attitude towards peasant mobility (voluntarily easing restrictions on their villein tenants' movements) since they could always get replacements, quite often indeed on better terms. The latter part of the thirteenth century, as noted, was probably just this sort of period. But evidence from such a period cannot legitimately be used to argue for the end, or the essential irrelevance, of peasant unfreedom.[34] Serfdom can be said to end only when the lords' right and ability to control the peasantry, *should they desire to do so*, has been terminated. It is significant that, even throughout the thirteenth century, peasants wishing to leave the manor were required to obtain licences to depart and had to return each year for the one or two views of frank-pledge. In this period, as Raftis says, "the manorial court was usually only concerned to keep the villein under the lord's jurisdiction, not to have him back on the lord's demesne". What is telling, however, is the sudden change in the lords' approach to villein mobility which followed immediately upon the Black Death and the sudden shortage (as opposed to plethora) of tenants. For this period there is ample evidence for the distraining of villeins to become tenants and take over obligations; for much heavier fines for licence to leave the lord's manor; for a remarkable increase in the number of pledges required for those permitted to leave the manor; for a sharper attitude concerning fugitives from the domain; and for limitations on the number of years the villein was allowed to be away from the manor.[35] Certainly, from the lords' point of view, serfdom was still the order of the day, and they had every intention of enforcing it. Whether or not they would be able to was a question that was resolved only in the conflicts of the following period.

[34] As does, for example, Titow, *English Rural Society, 1200–1350*, pp. 59–60.
[35] J. A. Raftis, *Tenure and Mo[illegible]v* (Toronto, 1964), pp. 139–44.

(B) COMMERCIALIZATION AND AGRICULTURAL CAPITALISM

In a manner analogous to Postan's, Le Roy Ladurie carried forward the critique of the trade-centred approach to European economic development by showing that even following the downfall of serfdom a tendency towards capitalism (large, consolidated holdings farmed on the basis of capital improvement with wage labour) could not necessarily be assumed, even under the impact of the market. Thus Le Roy Ladurie's study of rural Languedoc was designed in part to qualify the earlier conception of historians like Raveau, Bloch and others that during the early modern period, under the stimulus of the market, there was a universal tendency towards the development of large holdings, cultivated often by farmers of bourgeois origin with a strong orientation towards improvement and efficient production for the market. By contrast, as we have seen, Le Roy Ladurie showed that the emergence of "capitalist rent" (based on increases in the productivity of the land due to capital investment) as opposed to the simple squeezing of the peasant (on the basis of rising demand for land stimulated by increased demographic pressure) was far from inevitable; that fragmentation of holdings was just as likely as consolidation.

Still, the fact remains that, like Postan, Le Roy Ladurie does not get to the root of the difficulties of the trade-centred approach to agrarian change in this period for he does not attempt to specify why, in fact, during the sixteenth and seventeenth centuries, a new cycle of fragmentation and declining productivity was set off in some places, while consolidation and improvement took place in others. He does imply that *morcellement* (fragmentation) and *rassemblement* (consolidation) were in some sense competitive trends, and shows that the "mercilessly pursued dismemberment" of holdings "rendered derisory the efforts of the consolidators of the land". The result, he says, was that the economic history of rural Languedoc ended up as "pure peasant history . . . far from the 'origins of capitalism' . . . ".[36]

But Le Roy Ladurie never really poses the question (not only for rural Languedoc but for all of western Europe) of why the victory of one trend rather than another occurred.[37] Nor does he search for an

[36] Le Roy Ladurie, *Paysans de Languedoc*; the quotations are at i, p. 8.

[37] *Ibid.*, pp. 8ff. To explain the failure of agrarian capitalism in France, Le Roy Ladurie falls back, in the last analysis, upon the prevalence of backward

answer, as I am inclined to do, in the emergence of a structure of ownership of land which provided the peasantry in most of France (in contrast to England and elsewhere) with relatively powerful property rights over comparatively large areas of the land. This presented a powerful barrier to those who wished to concentrate land. For whatever the market situation or the price of land, the peasantry would not in general easily relinquish their holdings, the bases of their existence and that of their heirs. It was thus, I will argue, the predominance of petty proprietorship in France in the early modern period which ensured long-term agricultural backwardness.[38] This was not only because of the technical barriers to improvement built into the structure of smallholdings, especially within the common fields. It was, as I shall try to demonstrate, because peasant proprietorship in France came to be bound up historically with the development of an overall property or surplus-extraction structure which tended to discourage agricultural investment and development – in particular, the heavy taxation by the monarchical state; the squeezing of peasant tenants (leaseholders) by the landlords; and, finally, the subdivision of holdings by the peasants themselves.[39]

mentalités. Thus, "technological stagnation (*immobilisme*) was enveloped in, supported by, a whole series of . . . cultural blockages" (pp. 640–1). For Le Roy Ladurie, it was the "invisible spiritual frontiers" which were "the most constraining of all" on the economy (p. 11). And consistently enough, he appears to find the germs of true economic growth in the *mentalités nouvelles* of the epoch of the Enlightenment (p. 652).

[38] For the difficulties (not of course the impossibility, especially under certain conditions and over a relatively long term) of consolidating large holdings in the face of widespread and entrenched peasant proprietorship, see L. Merle, *La métairie et l'évolution agraire de la Gâtine poitevine de la fin du moyen âge à la Révolution* (Paris, 1953), pp. 70–2; A. Plaisse, *La baronnie du Neubourg* (Paris, 1961), pp. 583–5; also Le Roy Ladurie, *Paysans de Languedoc*, i, p. 327. Roger Dion enunciated the following general rule concerning the powerful limiting impact of the French peasant community on the development of large farms: "The regions of large farms are defined negatively: they are those which largely escaped the grip of the village communities": quoted in J. Meuvret, "L'agriculture en Europe aux XVIIe et XVIIIe siècles", in his *Etudes d'histoire économique*, p. 177. Of course, as Meuvret points out (agreeing with Dion), large farms tended to develop in France only to a very small extent, and even then generally on the worst lands – precisely because they were prevented from doing so by the widespread strength of the "strongly rooted peasant collectivities".

[39] For the full arguments, see below, pp. 46ff.

III CLASS CONFLICT AND ECONOMIC DEVELOPMENT

In sum, despite the destructive force of their attacks upon the unilineal trade-centred theories of economic change, it may be doubted that either Postan or Le Roy Ladurie has carried his critique quite far enough. For, rather than searching for underlying differences which might account for contrasting lines of development in different places under similar constellations of economic forces, both Postan and Le Roy Ladurie have chosen to construct new models largely by substituting a different objective variable, population, for the old, discredited one, commerce. Because, in my view, they have failed to place the development of class structure and its effects at the centre of their analyses, their own cyclical Malthusian models encounter, as we have seen, precisely the same sorts of difficulties in the face of comparative history that they themselves exposed in their criticisms of the trade-centred unilineal approaches. In particular, their methods prevent them from posing what in my view are perhaps the two fundamental problems for the analysis of long-term economic development in late medieval and early modern Europe, or more generally, the "transition from feudalism to capitalism": (1) the decline versus the persistence of serfdom and its effects; (2) the emergence and predominance of secure small peasant property versus the rise of landlord / large tenant farmer relations on the land. In historical terms this means, at the very least: (1) a comparative analysis of the intensification of serfdom in eastern Europe in relation to its process of decline in the west; (2) a comparative analysis of the rise of agrarian capitalism and the growth of agricultural productivity in England in relation to their failure in France. Simply stated, it will be my contention that the breakthrough from "traditional economy" to relatively self-sustaining economic development was predicated upon the emergence of a specific set of class or social-property relations in the countryside – that is, capitalist class relations. This outcome depended, in turn, upon the previous success of a two-sided process of class development and class conflict: on the one hand, the destruction of serfdom; on the other, the short-circuiting of the emerging predominance of small peasant property.[40]

[40] This view obviously derives from Marx's arguments on the barriers to and the class structural bases for the development of capitalism, especially as presented

(A) THE DECLINE OF SERFDOM

One can begin by agreeing with Postan that there was a long-term tendency to demographic crisis inherent in the medieval economy. But this tendency to crisis was not a natural fact, explicable solely by reference to available human and natural resources in relation to an ostensibly given level of technique. It was, rather, built into the interrelated structure of peasant organization of production on the one hand, and, on the other, the institutionalized relationships of serfdom by which the lord was able to extract a feudal rent. Thus the inability of the serf-based agrarian economy to innovate in agriculture even under extreme market incentives to do so is understandable in view of the interrelated facts, first, of heavy surplus extraction by the lord from the peasant and, second, the barriers to mobility of men and land which were themselves part and parcel of the unfree surplus-extraction relationship.

Thus the lord's surplus extraction (rent) tended to confiscate not merely the peasant's income above subsistence (and potentially even beyond) but at the same time to threaten the funds necessary to refurbish the peasant's holding and to prevent the long-term decline of its productivity. Postan has estimated that on average something like 50 per cent of the unfree peasant's total product was extracted by the lord.[41] This was entirely unproductive profit, for hardly any of it was ploughed back into production; most was squandered in military expenditure and conspicuous consumption.[42]

At the same time, given his unfree peasants, the lord's most obvious mode of increasing income from his lands was not through capital investment and the introduction of new techniques, but through squeezing the peasants, by increasing either money rents or labour services. In particular, the availability of unfree rent-paying tenants militated against the tendency to expel or buy out peasants

in "The So-Called Primitive Accumulation of Capital", in *Capital*, i, pt 8, and *Pre-Capitalist Economic Formations*, ed. E. J. Hobsbawm (London, 1964), pp. 67–120.

41 Postan, "Medieval Agrarian Society in its Prime: England", pp. 603–4.

42 M. M. Postan, "Investment in Medieval Agriculture", *Jl Econ. Hist.*, xxvii (1967); R. H. Hilton, "Rent and Capital Formation in Feudal Society", in *Second International Conference of Economic History, Aix-en-Provence, 1962*, 2 vols. (Paris, 1965), ii, esp. pp. 41–53. Hilton estimates that no more than 5 per cent of total income was ploughed back into productive investment by landlords in the thirteenth century (p. 53).

in order to construct a consolidated demesne and introduce improvements on this basis. Revenues could be raised through increasing rents via tallages, entry fines and other levies, so there was little need to engage in the difficult and costly processes of building up large holdings and investing, of removing customary peasants and bringing in new techniques. Thus the argument sometimes advanced that the medieval landlords' agricultural investments were adequate to the requirements of their estates begs the question, for it takes as given the landlords' class position and the agrarian structure bound up with it.[43]

There were, in fact, known and available agricultural improvements – including the ultimately revolutionary "convertible husbandry" – which could have brought significant improvements in demesne output.[44] Indeed, as Eleanor Searle has demonstrated, fully fledged convertible husbandry was systematically adopted on Battle Abbey's manor of Marley from the early fourteenth century. It is most significant that this manor consisted entirely of a single consolidated demesne (with no customary tenancies) and was farmed entirely with wage labour, marking a total break from feudal organization of production and class relations. It is notable, moreover, that the manor of Marley had been constructed by buying out free tenants. Because these tenants were freeholders, Battle Abbey had not been able to increase its rents, although it had tried to do so. Indeed, Battle Abbey had waged an extended struggle to force its tenants into unfree status, precisely in order to open them up to the imposition of additional levies. However, in the end this had been unsuccessful and, as a result, the only alternative for raising the revenue from these lands was to buy up the peasants' holdings. The abbey could then farm these itself as a consolidated demesne – and this, in fact, is the solution it hit upon.[45]

Of course, the methods used on the manor of Marley by Battle

[43] Titow, *English Rural Society, 1200–1350*, pp. 49–50. If I properly understand his argument, Titow is asserting that the failure to improve was by and large the result of the lack of technical knowledge, the unavailability of new techniques. Thus, he says, "the technical limitations of medieval husbandry seem to me to have imposed their own ceiling on what could be usefully spent on an estate" (p. 50).

[44] See, for example, the use of convertible husbandry in Flanders in the early fourteenth century: B. H. Slicher van Bath, *The Agrarian History of Western Europe, A.D. 500–1850* (London, 1963; repr. London, 1966), pp. 178–9.

[45] Searle, *Lordship and Community*, pp. 147, 174–5, 183–94, 267–329.

Abbey were almost totally ignored by English landlords. They generally did not have to improve – to raise labour productivity, efficiency and output – in order to increase income. This was because they had an alternative, "exploitative" mode available to them: the use of their position of power over the peasants to increase their share of the product.

At the same time, because of lack of funds – due to landlords' extraction of rent and the extreme maldistribution of both land and capital, especially livestock – the peasantry were by and large unable to use the land they held in a free and rational manner. They could not, so to speak, put back what they took out of it. Thus the surplus-extraction relations of serfdom tended to lead to the exhaustion of peasant production *per se*; in particular, the inability to invest in animals for ploughing and as a source of manure led to deterioration of the soil, which in turn led to the extension of cultivation to land formerly reserved for the support of animals. This meant the cultivation of worse soils and at the same time fewer animals – and thus in the end a vicious cycle of the destruction of the peasants' means of support. The crisis of productivity led to demographic crisis, pushing the population over the edge of subsistence.[46]

On the other hand, the lords' property relationships to that small group of peasants who had enough land to produce a marketable surplus and thus the potential to accumulate – that is, to concentrate land, assemble a labour force and introduce improvement – was also a barrier to the development of productivity.[47] First, of course, feudal rent itself limited the funds available for accumulation. Second, restrictions on peasant mobility not only prevented peasant movement to areas of greater potential opportunity, but tended to limit the development of a free market in labour.[48] Finally, feudal restrictions on the mobility of land tended to prevent its concen-

[46] Hilton, "Rent and Capital Formation in Feudal Society", pp. 53–5; Postan, "Medieval Agrarian Society in its Prime: England", pp. 548–70. The net product of at least one-third of all the land, including a disproportionate share of the best land, was directly in the hands of the tiny landlord class (that is, in demesne): E. A. Kosminsky, "Services and Money Rents in the Thirteenth Century", *Econ. Hist. Rev.*, v (1934–5); Postan, "Medieval Agrarian Society in its Prime: England", pp. 601–2. See also above, p. 31 and n. 41.

[47] See Hilton, *Decline of Serfdom in Medieval England*, pp. 30–1, and *passim*.

[48] Admittedly, in the thirteenth century, given the extreme over-population, the availability of wage labour was not a problem. On the supply of wage labour in

tration. Unfree peasants were not allowed to convey their land to other peasants without the lord's permission. Yet it was often in the lord's interest to prevent large accumulating tenants from receiving more land, because they might find it harder to collect the rent from such tenants, especially if they had free status.[49]

Given these property or surplus-extraction relationships, productivity crisis leading to demographic crisis was more or less to be expected, sooner or later.[50] The question, however, which must be asked concerns the economic and social results of the demographic catastrophe, in particular that of the later fourteenth and fifteenth centuries. Postan showed one logic: that the peasants apparently used their economic position, their scarcity, to win their freedom. As B. H. Slicher van Bath argues for western Europe in general, "the lord of the manor was forced to offer good conditions or see all his villeins vanish from the land".[51] Yet, curiously, quite another logic has sometimes been invoked to explain the intensification of serfdom in eastern Europe: viz., that the crisis in seigneurial revenues which followed upon the decline in population and the disappearance of tenants led the lords to assert their control over the peasants and bind them to their lands in order to protect their incomes and their very existence.[52] Obviously, both logics are unassailable from different class viewpoints. It was the logic of the peasant to try to use his apparently improved bargaining position to

the thirteenth century, see E. A. Kosminsky, *Studies in the Agrarian History of England in the Thirteenth Century* (Oxford, 1956), ch. 6.

49 See especially Raftis, *Tenure and Mobility*, pp. 66–8, for evidence concerning lords' actions to prevent customary tenants from concentrating too much land or to prevent customary tenants from conveying land to freemen. Searle suggests that a key motivation for Battle Abbey's continuing attempts from the mid-thirteenth century to depress its tenants from free to unfree status was to be better able to control the peasant land market in order to assure rent: Searle, *Lordship and Community*, pp. 185ff. See also M. M. Postan, "The Charters of the Villeins", in M. M. Postan and C. N. L. Brooke (eds.), *Carte nativorum* (Northants. Rec. Soc., xx, Northampton, 1960), pp. xxxi–xxxiiff.

50 Especially relevant here is Postan's remark that the peasants' feudal rents "had to be treated as prior charges. They could not be reduced to suit the harvest or the tenant's personal circumstances . . . In fact the tenant's need of food and fodder had to be covered by what was left after the obligatory charges had been met": Postan, "Medieval Agrarian Society in its Prime: England", p. 604.

51 Slicher van Bath, *Agrarian History of Western Europe*, p. 145.

52 Carsten, *Origins of Prussia*, pp. 103ff.; Malowist, "Commerce de la Baltique et le problème des luttes sociales en Pologne aux XVe et XVIe siècles", pp. 132–3ff.; G. Fourquin, *Seigneurie et féodalité au moyen âge* (Paris, 1970), pp. 215–16.

get his freedom. It was the logic of the landlord to protect his position by reducing the peasants' freedom. The result simply cannot be explained in terms of demographic/economic supply and demand. It obviously came down to a question of power, indeed of force, and in fact there was intense Europe-wide lord/peasant conflict throughout the later fourteenth, fifteenth and early sixteenth centuries, almost everywhere over the same general issues: first, of course, serfdom; second, whether lords or peasants were to gain ultimate control over landed property, in particular the vast areas left vacant after the demographic collapse.

In England after 1349 and the Black Death there was a seigneurial reaction: attempts to control peasant mobility by forcing peasants to pay impossible fees for permission to move; legislation to control wages; an actual increase in rents in some places. But by 1400 it was clear that the landlords' offensive had failed; revolt and flight, which continued throughout the fifteenth century, led to the end of serfdom.[53] In Catalonia, a particularly revealing case, one also finds increased legislation by the *Corts* – the representative body of the landlords, the clergy and the urban patriciate – to limit peasant movement and decrease personal freedom. By the early fifteenth century this legislation had proceeded a good distance, apparently with significant success. But, correlatively, it provoked in response a high level of peasant organization and, in particular, the assembling of mass peasant armies. Well after the mid-fifteenth century it appeared quite possible that the seigneurial reaction would succeed. Only a series of violent and bloody confrontations ultimately assured peasant victory. Armed warfare ended finally in 1486 with the Sentence of Guadalupe by which the peasantry were granted in full their personal freedom, full right in perpetuity to their property (while remaining obligated to the payment of certain fixed dues) and, perhaps equally important, full right to those vacant holdings (*masos ronecs*) which they had annexed in the period following the demographic catastrophes.[54] Finally, in Europe east of the Elbe we have the familiar story of the lords entirely overwhelming the peasantry, gradually reducing through

[53] For the seigneurial reaction and its failure, see Hilton, *Decline of Serfdom in Medieval England*, pp. 36–59. For a detailed case study, see Raftis, *Tenure and Mobility*, esp. pp. 143–4ff.

[54] Vicens Vives, *Historia de los remensas en el siglo XV*, pp. 23ff.; Vilar, *Catalogne dans l'Espagne moderne*, i, pp. 466–71, 506–9.

legislation peasant personal freedom, and ultimately confiscating an important part of peasant land and attaching it to their demesnes. In short, the question of serfdom in Europe can not be reduced to a question of economics. Its long-term rise in the east corresponded first to a fall in population and stagnation in trade and then to a rise in population and a rise in trade (1400–1600). In the west serfdom declined during a period first of rising population and growing commerce, then of declining population and reduced trade (1200–1500).

In sum, the contradictions between the development of peasant production and the relations of surplus extraction which defined the class relations of serfdom tended to lead to a crisis of peasant accumulation, of peasant productivity and ultimately of peasant subsistence. This crisis was accompanied by an intensification of the class conflict inherent in the existing structure, but with different outcomes in different places – the breakdown of the old structure or its restrengthening – depending on the balance of forces between the contending classes. Thus in the end the serf-based or feudal class structure opened up certain limited patterns of development, gave rise to certain predictable crises and, especially, tended to the outbreak of certain immanent class conflicts. The element of indeterminacy emerges in relation to the different character and results of these conflicts in different regions. This is not to say that such outcomes were somehow arbitrary, but rather that they tended to be bound up with certain *historically specific* patterns of the development of the contending agrarian classes and their relative strength in the different European societies: their relative levels of internal solidarity, their self-consciousness and organization, and their general political resources – especially their relationships to the non-agricultural classes (in particular, potential urban class allies) and to the state (in particular, whether or not the state developed as a class-like competitor of the lords for the peasants' surplus).

Obviously, it is not possible in this compass adequately to account for the differential strengths of lords *vis-à-vis* peasants and the different patterns of class conflict between them across Europe in the late medieval period. It is necessary, however, at least to pose this problem in order to confront the fundamental question of the success or failure of the seigneurial reaction which was nearly universal throughout medieval Europe, and thus, especially, the question of the differential outcomes of the later medieval agrarian crises and class confrontations in eastern and western Europe, which resulted in totally divergent paths of subsequent social and economic development. It should at least be clear that we cannot find an explanation in the direct impact of forces of supply and demand, whether commercial or demographic in origin, no matter how powerful. Serfdom began its rise in the east (and its definitive downfall in the west) in the period of late medieval demographic decline; it was consolidated during the trans-European increase in population of the sixteenth and seventeenth centuries; and it was further sharpened at the time of the demographic disasters of the later seventeenth century.

Nor will the pressure of trade provide a more convincing answer although, ironically, the rise of large-scale export commerce has sometimes been invoked to explain the rise of serfdom in the east[55] (as it has, analogously, the rise of capitalism in the west). It is not, of course, my point to deny the relevance of economic conditions, especially the growth of trade, to the development of class relations and the strength of contending classes. No doubt, in this instance, the income from grain produced by serf-based agriculture and sold by export from the Baltic to the west enhanced the class power of the eastern lords, helping them to sustain their seigneurial offensive. But the control of grain production (and thus the grain trade), secured through their successful enserfment of the peasantry, was by no means assured by the mere fact of the emergence of the grain markets themselves. In the rich, grain-producing areas of north-western Germany the peasants were largely successful in gaining command of grain output in precisely the period of developing enserfment in north-eastern Germany – and they appear to have done so after a prolonged period of anti-landlord resistance. In fact, the peasants' ability in this region to control the commerce in agricultural commodities (a share of the Baltic export trade, as well as the inland routes) appears to have been a factor in helping them to consolidate their power and property against the landlords.[56]

Indeed, on a more general plane, the precocious growth of com-

[55] For a recent version of this position, see I. Wallerstein, *The Modern World System*, 2 vols. (New York, 1974–80), i, pp. 90–6.

[56] F. Lütge, *Deutsche Sozial- und Wirtschaftsgeschichte* (Berlin, 1966), pp. 232–5. See the interesting material on the emergence in the regions of Dithmarschen and Fehmarn of a highly commercialized free peasantry with large holdings deeply involved in the Baltic export trade in the late medieval and early modern period, in C. Reuter, *Ostseehandel und Landwirtschaft im sechzehnten und siebzehnten Jahrhundert* (Berlin, 1912), pp. 18–29.

merce in the medieval west has often been taken to explain in large measure the relative strength of the peasantry in western Europe and thus the decline of serfdom. The growth of the market, it is argued, made possible the emergence of a significant layer of large peasants who, through the sale of agricultural surpluses, were able to accumulate large holdings and, on this basis, to amass power and to play a pivotal role in organizing peasant resistance.[57] So the argument for the disintegrating impact of trade on landlord power appears prima facie to be as convincing as the counter-case for its enhancing effects. We are therefore brought back to our point of departure: the need to interpret the significance of changing economic and demographic forces in terms of historically evolved structures of class relations and, especially, differing balances of class power.

Perhaps the most widely accepted explanation of the divergence between east and west European development, in particular the rise of serfdom in eastern Europe, has been found in the weaker development of the towns in this region which made the entire area more vulnerable to seigneurial reaction.[58] Because the towns were smaller and less developed they could be more easily overwhelmed by the nobility, thus shutting off a key outlet for peasant flight and depriving the peasants of significant allies. However, this classic line of reasoning remains difficult to accept fully because the actual mechanisms by which the towns had their reputedly dissolving effects on landlord control over the peasantry in western Europe have still to be precisely specified.

The viability of the towns as a potential alternative for the mass of unfree peasantry must be called into question simply in terms of their gross demographic weight. Could the relatively tiny urban entres – which could have surpassed 10 per cent of the total population in only a few European regions – have exerted sufficient attractive power on the rural masses to account for the collapse of serfdom almost everywhere in western Europe by 1500?[59] The real

[57] See, for example, R. H. Hilton, "Peasant Movements in England before 1381", in E. M. Carus-Wilson (ed.), *Essays in Economic History*, 3 vols. (London, 1954–62), ii, pp. 85–90; E. A. Kosminsky, "The Evolution of Feudal Rent in England from the XIth to the XVth Centuries", *Past and Present*, no. 7 (April 1955), pp. 24–7.

[58] See Carsten, *Origins of Prussia*, esp. pp. 115–16, 135; Blum, "Rise of Serfdom in Eastern Europe", pp. 833–5.

[59] For an indication of the very small relative size of the urban population in later

economic opportunities offered by the towns to rural migrants are also questionable. Few runaway serfs could have had the capital or skill to enter the ranks of urban craftsmen or shopkeepers, let alone merchants. At the same time the essence of urban economy, based on luxury production for a limited market, was economic restriction – in particular, control of the labour market. Certainly, few of the established citizens of the medieval towns, typically organized in closed corporations, could have welcomed rural immigrants. Admittedly, the urban freemen often constituted only a minority of the urban population; but they were often in a position to place real limits on opportunities in the towns.[60] It is in fact a historical commonplace that the strength of the guilds was a significant factor in forcing potential industrial capital into the countryside to find free labour.

Finally, it is far from obvious that the medieval towns housed the natural allies of the unfree peasantry. For many reasons, the urban patriciate would tend to align themselves with the nobility against the peasantry. Both of these classes had a common interest in maintaining social order and the defence of property and in protecting their mutually beneficial relationships of commercial exchange (raw materials for luxury products). Moreover, the urban patricians were often themselves landowners and, as such, opponents of the peasants in the same nexus of rural class relations as the nobility.[61] It is true that, in contrast, the urban artisans tended to be anti-aristocratic. But this would not necessarily lead them to support the struggles of the peasants; for, again, freeing the peasantry posed a threat to urban controls over the labour market and invited increased competition.

In truth, the historical record of urban support for the aspirations to freedom of the medieval European peasantry is not impressive. The large towns of Brandenburg, Pomerania and Prussia, which were the scene of chronic social conflict throughout the later middle ages, offered no apparent objection to the nobility's demands that they legislate against fleeing serfs.[62] Nor did the townsmen of

medieval England, see R. H. Hilton, *A Medieval Society* (London, 1966; repr. Cambridge, 1983), pp. 167–8.

[60] For a survey of urban organization in the medieval period, see *Cambridge Economic History of Europe*, iii, esp. chs. 4–5.

[61] See, for example, Vilar, *Catalogne dans l'Espagne moderne*, i, pp. 490–3.

[62] Carsten, *Origins of Prussia*, p. 111 (see also pp. 83–8).

Königsberg come to the aid of the peasant revolt in East Prussia in 1525 – the one really large-scale rural rising of this period in north-eastern Europe. The town's patriciate positively opposed the revolt. Meanwhile, the remainder of the citizenry – despite their own engagement at this time in fierce struggles against the patriciate – failed to come forth with the material aid which was requested by the rebellious peasants who were threatened by encroaching enserf-ment.[63] Correlatively, in the large-scale revolt of the later medieval period in which urban/rural ties were perhaps most pronounced – that of maritime Flanders between 1323 and 1328 – the peasant element was already free (or had never been enserfed), so there was never a question here of urban opposition to a rural social order of unfreedom.[64] Finally, in perhaps the most significant of the late medieval revolts against serfdom – that of the Catalan *remensas* from the later fourteenth century – there were no significant link-ups between rural and urban lower classes; and this despite the fact that in Catalonia rural rebellion was accompanied by serious out-breaks of urban class conflict over an extended period. The Catalan peasant revolt was probably the best organized and, despite the lack of support from the urban classes, the most successful in all of Europe: it brought about the downfall of serfdom in Catalonia.[65] In sum, the towns rarely aided peasant resistance to serfdom, nor was the success of such resistance apparently dependent upon such aid.

If the significance of differing levels of urban development has been overstated in some explanations of the divergent socio-economic paths taken by eastern and western Europe from the later middle ages, the importance of the previous evolutions of rural society itself in these contrasting regions has been correspondingly neglected. The development of peasant solidarity and strength in western Europe – especially as this was manifested in the peasants' organization at the level of the village – appears to have been far greater in western than in eastern Europe; and this superior

[63] F. L. Carsten, "Der Bauernkrieg in Ostpreussen, 1525", *Internat. Rev. Social Hist.*, iii (1938), pp. 400–1, 405–7; G. Franz, *Der deutsche Bauernkrieg* (Munich, 1933), p. 287; A. Seraphim, "Soziale Bewegungen in Altpreussen im Jahre 1525", *Altpreussische Monatsschrift*, lviii (1921), esp. pp. 74, 82–3, 87, 92.

[64] R. H. Hilton, *Bond Men Made Free* (London, 1973), pp. 114–15, 125–7; H. Pirenne, *Le soulèvement de la Flandre maritime de 1323–1328* (Brussels, 1900), pp. i–v, and *passim*.

[65] Vilar, *Catalogne dans l'Espagne moderne*, i, pp. 448–521, esp. pp. 449, 492–3, 497–9, 508–9.

institutionalization of the peasants' class power in the west may have been central to its superior ability to resist seigneurial reaction. The divergent evolution of peasant class organization is clearest in what is probably the pivotal comparative case – east versus west Elbian Germany; and the divergent developments in these two regions provide important clues to the disparate development patterns of the far broader spheres of which they were a part.

Thus, throughout much of western Germany by the later middle ages the peasantry had succeeded, through protracted struggle on a piecemeal village-by-village basis, in constituting for themselves an impressive network of village institutions for economic regulation and political self-government. These provided a powerful line of defence against the incursions of landlords. In the first instance, peasant organization and peasant resistance to the lords appear to have emerged out of the quasi-communal character of peasant economy. Most fundamental was the need to regulate co-operatively the village commons and to struggle against the lords to establish and to protect commons rights – common lands (for grazing and so on) and the common-field organization of agricultural rotation (in which the post-harvest stubble played an important role in the support of animals). Sooner or later, however, issues of a more general economic and political character tended to be raised. The peasants organized themselves in order to fix rents and to ensure rights of inheritance. Perhaps most significantly, in many places they fought successfully to replace the old landlord-installed village mayor (*Schultheiss*) by their own elected village magistrates. In some villages they even won the right to choose the village priest. All these gains the peasants forced the lords to recognize in countless village charters (*Weistümer*) – through which the specific conquests of the peasantry were formally institutionalized.[66]

The contrasting evolution in eastern Germany is most striking. Here peasant economic co-operation and, in particular, the self-government of peasant villages appear to have developed only to a relatively small extent. As a result the east German peasants appear to have been much less prepared to resist seigneurial attacks and the imposition of seigneurial controls leading to serfdom than were their counterparts in the west. Probably most telling in this respect

[66] G. Franz, *Geschichte des deutschen Bauernstandes vom frühen Mittelalter bis zum 19. Jahrhundert* (Stuttgart, 1970), pp. 48–66.

was the relative failure to develop independent political institutions in the village, and this is perhaps most clearly indicated by the apparent inability of the eastern peasantry to displace the *Lokator* or *Schultheiss*, the village officer who originally organized the settlement as the representative of the lord and who retained his directing political role in the village (either as the lord's representative or as hereditary office-holder) throughout the medieval period. It is remarkable, moreover, that the numerous *Weistümer* which clearly marked the step-by-step establishment of village rights against the lord in the west are very rarely found in late medieval eastern Germany.[67]

The relative absence of village solidarity in the east, despite the formally similar character of village settlement (the so-called "Germanic" type), appears to have been connected with the entire evolution of the region as a colonial society – its relatively late formation, the "rational" and "artificial" character of its settlement, and especially the leadership of the landlords in the colonizing process. Thus, in the first place, the communal aspects of the village economy appear to have been comparatively underdeveloped. In general there were no common lands. Moreover, the common-field agriculture itself appears to have been less highly evolved, a consequence, it seems, of the original organization of the fields at the time of settlement – in particular, the tendency of the colonists to lay out holdings within the fields in rather large, relatively consolidated strips (often stretching directly behind the peasants' houses) in contrast to the tiny, scattered parcels characteristic of the "natural" and "chaotic" development in the west. There seems, then, to have been more of a tendency to individualistic farming; less developed organization of collaborative agricultural practices at the level of the village or between villages (for example, inter-commoning); and little tradition of the "struggle for commons rights" against the lords which was so characteristic of western development.[68]

At the same time, the planned, landlord-led organization of settlement in the east tended to place major barriers in the way of

[67] *Ibid.*, pp. 50, 53, 58, 62. See the correlative failure of the peasantry of eastern Germany to win the right to appoint village priests (pp. 62–3).

[68] H. Aubin, "Medieval Agrarian Society in its Prime: The Lands East of the Elbe and German Colonization Eastwards", in *Cambridge Economic History of Europe*, i, 2nd edn, pp. 464–5, 468–9.

the emergence of peasant power and peasant self-government.[69] East German villages were generally smaller and less densely populated than their western counterparts; they tended, moreover, to have but a single lord. As a result, they were less difficult for the lords to control than were the villages of the west, where the more concentrated population and, in particular, the tendency of the villages to be divided between two or more lordships, gave the peasants more room to manoeuvre, making *Gemeinbildung* that much easier.[70]

As one historian of the German peasantry has stated, "without the strong development of communal life in [western] Germany, the peasant wars [of 1525] are unthinkable". From this point of view, it is notable that the only east German region which experienced peasant revolt in 1525 – that is, East Prussia – was marked by unusually strong peasant communities, as well as an (apparently) weak ruling nobility. Thus, on the one hand, the East Prussian peasant revolt originated and remained centred in the Samland, an area characterized not only by an extraordinarily high density of population, comparable to that of western Europe, but also by the persistence of well-entrenched and relatively powerful forms of peasant organization. The Samland was one of the few east Elbian areas to escape the process of colonization and thus the imposition of the "Germanic" agrarian and political forms of settlement. In consequence, its original Prussian peasant communities were left largely undisturbed and were allowed to retain their own apparently ancient and distinctive socio-political structures.[71] On the other

[69] Note the following comment on the late medieval east German village community (*Gemeinde*) in accounting for its weakness: "The village lord was there first, then came the village members. In the area of older settlement the *Gemeinde*, whose beginnings are mostly lost in the dark, distant past, was primary": H. Patze, "Die deutsche bäuerliche Gemeinde im Ordensstaat Preussen", in *Die Anfänge der Landgemeinde und ihr Wesen*, 2 vols. (Konstanzer Arbeitskreis für mittelalterliche Geschichte, Vorträge und Forschungen, vii–viii, Stuttgart, 1964), ii, p. 151. For a suggestive case study of a locality where landlord-led colonization left the peasantry in a position of weakness, open to expropriation, see Searle, *Lordship and Community*, pt 1, ch. 3, esp. pp. 62–8.

[70] Aubin, "Medieval Agrarian Society in its Prime: The Lands East of the Elbe and German Colonization Eastwards", p. 469; Franz, *Geschichte des deutschen Bauernstandes*, pp. 49, 53, 56–7.

[71] The quotation is to be found in Franz, *Geschichte des deutschen Bauernstandes*, p. 63. On the development of the Samland region, and the special social, political and demographic characteristics of its Prussian communities, see R. Wenskus, "Kleinverbände und Kleinräume bei den Prussen des Samlandes", in *Anfänge*

hand, the East Prussian nobility was perhaps the least well established of any in the entire region. The colonization of the area had been, of course, largely carried out under the bureaucratic administration of the Teutonic Order. At the time of the peasant revolt of 1525 the new *Junker* ruling aristocracy was only just completing its take-over from the Order's disintegrating state.[72]

Of course, the peasant wars in both western and eastern Germany were largely a failure, as were most of the really large-scale peasant revolts of the later medieval period in Europe. What was successful, however, not only in western Germany, but throughout most of western Europe, was the less spectacular but ultimately more significant process of stubborn resistance, village by village, through which the peasantry developed their solidarity and village institutions. It was by this means that the peasants of western Europe were able to limit considerably the claims of the aristocracy and, ultimately, to dissolve serfdom and forestall seigneurial reaction.[73] Lacking the strength that the western peasantry had developed in constructing the instruments of village co-operation and resistance, the peasantry of colonized eastern

der Landgemeinde und ihr Wesen, ii, pp. 202–32ff. See Wenskus's comment (p. 232): "In north-west Samland, the centre of resistance against the Order, the native dominant classes had disappeared. Precisely because of this, the old associations appear to have been maintained for an especially long time". See also H. H. Wächter, *Ostpreussische Domänenvorwerke im 16. und 17. Jahrhundert* (Würzburg, 1958), p. 7. Note also the apparent interrelationship of unusually dense population and distinctively powerful village communities with successful peasant revolt on the lands of the bishopric of Ermland (East Prussia) in 1440: Carsten, *Origins of Prussia*, pp. 60–1, 104–5; Patze, "Deutsche bäuerliche Gemeinde im Ordensstaat Preussen", pp. 164–5.

[72] On the decline of the Teutonic Order and the rise of the Prussian nobility, especially in relation to the revolt of 1525, see Carsten, "Bauernkrieg in Ostpreussen, 1525", pp. 398–9; Seraphim, "Soziale Bewegungen in Altpreussen im Jahre 1525", pp. 2–3. Note also Seraphim's interesting suggestion that the Order frequently attempted to defend the peasantry, and its customary position, against the growing incursions of an emergent nobility which was, of course, simultaneously undermining the Order itself (pp. 9–11). Cf. Carsten, *Origins of Prussia*, pt 2, "The Rise of the Junkers", esp. pp. 111ff. See also below, pp. 54–7.

[73] For a meticulous reconstruction of these processes in one French region, see Fossier's section on "Les conquêtes paysannes", in his *Terre et hommes en Picardie*, ii, pp. 708–28. See Fossier's comment (p. 708): "The progressive elevation of the living standard of the peasants and the progress achieved in the sphere of their social condition are rightly considered as fundamental phenomena of medieval history . . . In the face of an aristocratic world on the defensive, that of the peasants was strengthened, was emancipated little by little"

Europe were less prepared to hold out; and in consequence they succumbed to seigneurial reaction and the imposition of serfdom.

The social-property settlements which emerged from the breakdowns and conflicts of the late medieval period had momentous consequences for subsequent European social change. For the pattern of economic development imposed by the now-intensified class structure of serfdom in the east, under the impact of the world market, was very different from that which prevailed in the free conditions of the west. Specifically, the newly emergent structure of class relations in the east had as its outcome the "development of underdevelopment", the preclusion of increased productivity in general, and of industrialization in particular. First of all, the availability of forced labourers whose services could be incessantly intensified by the lord discouraged the introduction of agricultural improvements. Second, the lord's increasing surplus extraction from the peasantry continually limited the emergence of a home market for industrial goods. Third, the fact of direct and powerful controls over peasant mobility meant the constriction of the industrial labour force, resulting in the suffocation of industry and the decline of the towns. Finally, the landlords, as a ruling class which dominated their states, pursued a policy of what has been called "anti-mercantilism"; they attempted to usurp the merchants' function as middlemen and encouraged industrial imports from the west, in this way undermining much of what was left of urban and industrial organization.[74] Thus the possibility of balanced economic growth was destroyed and eastern Europe consigned to backwardness for centuries.

Economic backwardness in eastern Europe cannot therefore be regarded as economically determined, the result of dependence upon trade in primary products to the west, as is sometimes

[74] Some of the most important recent analyses of the rise of serfdom in eastern Europe, its causes and consequences, may be found in the writings of Marian Malowist. A number of these are collected in his *Croissance et régression en Europe XIVe–XVIIe siècles* (Paris, 1972). See also Malowist, "Commerce de la Baltique et le problème des luttes sociales en Pologne aux XVe et XVIe siècles". See, in addition, Carsten, *Origins of Prussia*; A. Maczak, "Export of Grain and the Problem of Distribution of National Income in the Years 1550–1650", *Acta Poloniae historica*, xviii (1968); J. Topolski, "La régression économique en Pologne du XVIe au XVIIIe siècle", *Acta Poloniae historica*, vii (1962); L. Zytkowicz, "An Investigation into Agricultural Production in Masovia in the First Half of the 17th Century", *Acta Poloniae historica*, xviii (1968).

asserted. Indeed, it would be more correct to state that dependence upon grain exports was a result of backwardness – of the failure of the home market (the terribly reduced purchasing power of the mass of the population) which was the result of the dismal productivity and the vastly unequal distribution of income in agriculture, rooted in the last analysis in the class structure of serfdom.

(B) THE EMERGENCE AND CHECK OF AGRARIAN CAPITALISM

Finally, however, it needs to be remembered that even in the west the collapse of serfdom did not lead in any automatic way to capitalism or successful economic development. From the late fifteenth century there was Europe-wide pressure of population, development of the market and rise in grain prices. In England we find the landlords consolidating holdings and leasing them out to large capitalist tenants who would in turn farm them on the basis of wage labour and agricultural improvement. But in France we find comparatively little consolidation. Even the land controlled directly by the landlords – that is, the demesnes farmed out on terminable contractual leases – was generally let in small parcels and cultivated by small peasant tenants. At the same time, of course, fragmentation dominated the sector of peasant proprietorship. These different class structures determined substantially different results in terms of changes in agricultural productivity and, indeed, wholly disparate overall patterns of economic development – and I shall return to these shortly. But it is necessary first to account for the class structures themselves – the rise of capitalism in England in contrast with the maintenance of peasant possession and production in France. Once again I would argue that these can only be understood as the legacy of the previous epoch of historical development, in particular the different processes of class conflicts which brought about and issued from the dissolution of serfdom in each country.

In England, as throughout most of western Europe, the peasantry were able by the mid-fifteenth century, through flight and resistance, definitively to break feudal controls over their mobility and to win full freedom. Indeed, peasant tenants at this time were striving hard for full and essentially freehold control over their customary tenements, and were not far from achieving it. The elimination of unfreedom meant the end of labour services and of arbitrary tallages. Moreover, rent *per se* (*redditus*) was fixed by custom, and subject to declining long-term value in the face of inflation. There were in the long run, however, two major strategies available to the landlord to prevent the loss of the land to peasant freehold.

In the first place, the demographic collapse of the late fourteenth and fifteenth centuries left vacant many former customary peasant holdings. It appears often to have been possible for the landlords simply to appropriate these and add them to their demesnes.[75] In this way a great deal of land was simply removed from the "customary sector" and added to the "leasehold sector", thus thwarting in advance a possible evolution towards freehold, and substantially reducing the area of land which potentially could be subjected to essentially peasant proprietorship. Significantly, as we shall see, this alternative was not easily available to the landlords in France under similar conditions in the same period.

In the second place, one crucial loophole often remained open to those landlords who sought to undermine the freehold-tending claims of the customary tenants who still remained on their lands and clung to their holdings. They could insist on the right to charge fines at will whenever peasant land was conveyed – that is, in sales or on inheritance. Indeed, in the end entry fines often appear to have provided the landlords with the lever they needed to dispose of customary peasant tenants, for in the long run fines could be substituted for competitive commercial rents.[76]

[75] Raftis, *Tenure and Mobility*, pp. 197–8; Hilton, *Decline of Serfdom in Medieval England*, pp. 44ff.; R. H. Hilton, "A Study in the Pre-History of English Enclosure in the Fifteenth Century", in *Studi in onore di Armando Sapori*, 2 vols. (Milan, 1957), i; M. W. Beresford, "A Review of Historical Research (to 1968)", in M. W. Beresford and J. G. Hurst (eds.), *Deserted Medieval Villages* (London, 1971).

[76] Tawney, *Agrarian Problem in the Sixteenth Century*, pp. 287–310; L. Stone, *The Crisis of the Aristocracy, 1558–1641* (Oxford, 1965), pp. 306–10. The significance of the use of fines "at will" as a mechanism by which the lord could gain economic control of the land remains controversial. It appears to hinge on two questions in particular: (1) the amount of copyhold land subject to variable fines; (2) the right of the lord to charge truly arbitrary fines where the tenant's copyhold was otherwise held by inheritance. For some estimates of the amount of land subject to variable fines, see Tawney, *Agrarian Problem in the Sixteenth Century*, pp. 297–300; Kerridge, *Agrarian Problems in the Sixteenth Century and After*, pp. 35–46. Kerridge has argued that copyhold by inheritance generally ensured "reasonable fines" – that is, that fines had to be set at a level that would not defeat the tenant's right of inheritance. Still, the date from which this doctrine of "reasonableness"

The landlords' claim to the right to raise fines was not, at the start however, an open-and-shut question, nor did it go uncontested. Throughout the fifteenth century there were widespread and apparently quite successful refusals by peasants to pay fines. And this sort of resistance continued into the sixteenth century when an increasing labour/land ratio should, ostensibly, have induced the peasant to accept a deteriorating condition and to pay a higher rent.[77] Ultimately, the peasants took to open revolt to enforce their claims. As is well known, the first half of the sixteenth century was in England a period of major agrarian risings which threatened the entire social order. And a major theme of the most serious of these – especially the revolt in the north in the mid-1530s and Kett's rebellion in 1549 – was the security of peasant tenure, in particular the question of arbitrary fines.[78]

If successful, the peasant revolts of the sixteenth century, as one historian has put it, might have "clipped the wings of rural capitalism".[79] But they did not succeed. Indeed, by the end of the seventeenth century, English landlords controlled an overwhelming proportion of the cultivable land – perhaps 70–75 per cent[80] – and

vis-à-vis fines on heritable copyholds was recognized and enforced by the king's courts is unclear. Kerridge appears to produce no case of this sort earlier than 1586: Kerridge, *Agrarian Problems in the Sixteenth Century and After*, pp. 38–9. See also Tawney, *Agrarian Problem in the Sixteenth Century*, pp. 296 (and n. 3), 307; Stone, *Crisis of the Aristocracy*, pp. 306–10.

77 C. Dyer, "A Redistribution of Incomes in Fifteenth-Century England?", *Past and Present*, no. 39 (April 1968); Raftis, *Tenure and Mobility*, pp. 198–9. On the early sixteenth century, see B. J. Harris, "Landlords and Tenants in England in the Later Middle Ages", *Past and Present*, no. 43 (May 1969).

78 Tawney, *Agrarian Problem in the Sixteenth Century*, p. 307; S. T. Bindoff, *Ket's Rebellion, 1549* (Hist. Assoc. pamphlet, gen. ser., G.12, London, 1949; repr. London, 1968), pp. 7–9.

79 Bindoff, *Ket's Rebellion, 1549*, p. 9.

80 G. E. Mingay, *English Landed Society in the Eighteenth Century* (London, 1963), p. 24, gives a figure of 80–85 per cent for the proportion of land held by the landlord classes (that is, the "great landlords" and the "gentry") in 1790 (an additional, uncertain proportion was held by "freeholders of a better sort", a category which presumably included a significant number of capitalist owner-cultivators). He goes on to say that the "figures for the proportion of land owned probably did not change very significantly over the hundred years before 1790, but there was certainly a shift in favour of the great landlords at the expense of the other two groups [that is, the gentry and freeholders]". F. M. L. Thompson has estimated that freeholders (large and small) owned about one-third of the land at the end of the seventeenth century: "The Social Distribution of Landed Property in England since the Sixteenth Century", *Econ. Hist. Rev.*, 2nd ser., xix (1966), p. 513.

capitalist class relations were developing as nowhere else, with momentous consequences for economic development. In my view, it was the emergence of the "classic" landlord / capitalist tenant / wage-labourer structure which made possible the transformation of agricultural production in England,[81] and this, in turn, was the key to England's uniquely successful overall economic development. With the peasants' failure to establish essentially freehold control over the land, the landlords were able to engross, consolidate and enclose, to create large farms and to lease them to capitalist tenants who could afford to make capital investments. This was the indispensable pre-condition for significant agrarian advance, since agricultural development was predicated upon significant inputs of capital, involving the introduction of new technologies and a larger scale of operation. Such higher levels of agricultural investment were made feasible through the development of a variety of different leaseholding arrangements, which embodied a novel form of landlord/tenant relationship. By virtue of these arrangements the capitalist tenants entered into essential partnership with landlords. They were assured that they could take a reasonable share of the increased revenue resulting from their capital investments and not have them confiscated by the landlords' rent increases.[82] They were therefore set free to bring in those key technological innovations, most especially convertible husbandry systems and the floating of the water-meadows, as well as to make sizeable investments in farm

[81] This is not to say that *precisely* these arrangements were necessary for real agricultural breakthrough leading to economic development in this period; it is to say that some form of larger-scale capitalist farming was required. Thus the only real alternative to the "classic English" landlord / large tenant / wage-labourer form of capitalist agriculture seems to have been an equally capitalist system based on large-scale owner-cultivators also generally using wage labour. The latter was the structure which in fact emerged in Catalonia at the end of the fifteenth century out of the previous period of agrarian struggle in which the large peasants had been able to win not only essentially freehold rights over their land: but, in addition, the proprietorship of large areas of land (*masos ronecs*) which had been left vacant by demographic disaster in the later fourteenth century. Thus the characteristic unit of agricultural ownership and production in sixteenth-century Catalonia, the *masia*, was typically a very large but compact farm. And this structure did in fact provide the basis for significant and continuing agricultural advance throughout the early modern period. Vilar, *Catalogne dans l'Espagne moderne*, i, pp. 575–8, 584, 586, 588. See also above, p. 35, and below, p. 52, n. 88.

[82] Kerridge, *Agrarian Problems in the Sixteenth Century and After*, p. 46; E. L. Jones, "Agriculture and Economic Growth in England, 1660–1750: Agricultural Change", *Jl Econ. Hist.*, xxv (1965).

facilities, which were generally far less practicable on small unenclosed farms operated by peasants.[83]

That is not to say, of course, that peasant production was incapable of improvement. The point is that it could not provide the agrarian basis for economic development. Thus small-scale farming could be especially effective with certain industrial crops (for example, flax) as well as in viticulture, dairying and horticulture. But this sort of agriculture generally brought about increased yields through the intensification of labour rather than through the greater efficiency of a given unit of labour input. It did not, therefore, produce "development", except in a restricted, indeed misleading, use of the term. Of course, the very spread of this type of husbandry in non-basic agricultural commodities was, as in industry, predicated upon the growth (elsewhere) of basic food (grain) production. And improvements in the productivity of grain were, in fact, best achieved on large consolidated farms with major capital inputs.[84]

[83] On the strong advantages of large "capital" farms with respect to agricultural improvement, investment and general efficiency, see Kerridge, *Agrarian Problems in the Sixteenth Century and After*, pp. 121–6; G. E. Mingay, "The Size of Farms in the Eighteenth Century", *Econ. Hist. Rev.*, 2nd ser., xiv (1962). It should be noted that some of the most important works of synthesis dwell on the advantages of English agrarian class relations for agricultural development, but in the end tend to play down their significance. Thus, in his "Editor's Introduction" to *Agriculture and Economic Growth in England, 1650–1815* (London, 1967), E. L. Jones argues that the key to English agricultural development was the introduction of new techniques rather than changing institutional arrangements, apparently dismissing the idea that these were indissolubly linked. He states at one point (p. 12): "Novel systems of husbandry thus account much more for the new 'responsiveness' of agricultural supply than do improvements in agrarian organization". Nevertheless, Jones himself at other points emphasizes the crucial advantages of large-scale capitalist farming for agricultural advance and, moreover, provides the key intra- and international comparisons which would tend to demonstrate the saliency of this connection and, correlatively, the barriers to improvement built into peasant-dominated agricultural systems. Thus, he says (p. 17), "The pattern of the countryside and the agrarian organization which evolved in England made production more flexible and far more responsive to the market than a peasant system could have been". He also gives the following case in point (p. 43): "In parts of the Midlands where the land had belonged to a few proprietors enclosure had come early, the 'new' crops had been sown and farmers specialized in fatstock breeding. More usually the 'peasant' farming of the Midland clays defied any change except the pungent expedient of parliamentary enclosure".

[84] B. H. Slicher van Bath, "The Rise of Intensive Husbandry in the Low Countries", in J. S. Bromley and E. H. Kossman (eds.), *Britain and the Netherlands* [i] (London, 1960), esp. pp. 135–7, 148–9, 153. As Slicher van Bath con-

Even the emergence of large-scale units of farming did not, in itself, guarantee agricultural improvement. As we shall see, in those (relatively restricted) areas where large farms emerged in France, they did not generally bring major increases in agricultural productivity. What proved, therefore, most significant for English agricultural development was the particularly productive use of the agricultural surplus promoted by the special character of its rural class relations – in particular, the displacement of the traditionally antagonistic relationship in which landlord squeezing undermined tenant initiative, by an emergent landlord/tenant symbiosis which brought mutual co-operation in investment and improvement.[85]

That agricultural improvement was already having a significant effect on English economic development by the end of the seventeenth century can be seen in a number of ways: most immediately in the striking pattern of relatively stable prices and (at least) maintenance of population of the latter part of the century; in the long run in the interrelated phenomena of continuing industrial development and growth in the home market. Thus although English population in this period reached the very high levels of the early fourteenth century (which at that time had meant demographic crisis) there were not the same sort of violent fluctuations in prices nor the crises of subsistence which gripped France and much of the Continent in this period.[86] Nor was there the marked demographic decline which came to dominate most of Europe at this time, the famous Malthusian "phase B".[87] In short, England remained largely exempt from the "general economic crisis of the

cludes of the Flemish region of intensive husbandry (p. 153): "It is not a picture of wealth, but of scarcely controlled poverty".

[85] See Jones, "Agriculture and Economic Growth in England, 1660–1750: Agricultural Change". On large-scale farming in early modern France, see below, pp. 62–3, n. 111.

[86] For the avoidance of crises of subsistence in late seventeenth-century England, see A. B. Appleby, "Disease or Famine?", *Econ. Hist. Rev.*, 2nd ser., xxvi (1973), esp. pp. 403, 430–1. For a comparison of fluctuations in prices between France and England in the later seventeenth and early eighteenth centuries, stressing England's avoidance of the "violent fluctuations" which characterized much of France, see J. Meuvret, "Les oscillations des prix des céréals aux XVIIe et XVIIIe siècles en Angleterre et dans les pays du bassin parisien", in his *Etudes d'histoire économique*.

[87] G. S. L. Tucker, "English Pre-Industrial Population Trends", *Econ. Hist. Rev.*, 2nd ser., xvi (1963–4). This is not to deny the possibility that there was some slowing down in the rate of growth of population, even perhaps a temporary halt, in the late seventeenth and/or early eighteenth centuries.

seventeenth century" which sooner or later struck most of the Continent.[88] This crisis, much like the previous "general economic crisis of the fourteenth century", was in the last analysis a crisis of agricultural production, resulting as had its predecessor from the maintenance of relationships of property or surplus extraction which prevented advances in productivity. By contrast, it was the transformation of the agrarian class structure which had taken place over the period since the later fourteenth century that allowed England to increase substantially its agricultural productivity and thus to avoid a repetition of the previous crisis.

It seems, moreover, that agricultural improvement was at the root of those developmental processes which, according to E. L. Jones, had allowed some 40 per cent of the English population to move out of agricultural employment by the end of the seventeenth century, much of it into industrial pursuits.[89] Obviously, English industrial growth, predominantly in cloth, was in the first instance based on exports, spurred by overseas demand. Yet such export-based spurts were common in Europe throughout the middle ages and the early modern period; but previously none had been able to sustain itself. The inelasticity of agricultural output, it seems, had always set strict limits on the development of industrial production. Rising food prices, if not a total failure of food supply, resulting from declining agricultural productivity might directly stifle industry by limiting the proportion of the population which could devote itself to non-agricultural pursuits. Otherwise, they would undermine the markets for industrial goods either by forcing up wages (the cost of subsistence) and thus industrial prices or by cutting into the proportion of the population's income which was available for non-food purchases. These mechanisms meant, in particular, that the general agricultural/demographic crisis of the seventeenth century would also mean, for most of Europe, a long-term crisis of industry. This has been shown most clearly for seventeenth-century France by Goubert, who directly links the long-term decline of the

[88] It is notable that Catalonia, one of the few areas to achieve agrarian transformation with a concomitant increase in agricultural productivity in this era, was also one of the few areas to escape the general economic crisis of the seventeenth century and, like England, to avoid demographic catastrophe while achieving continued economic development: Vilar, *Catalogne dans l'Espagne moderne*, i, pt 3, esp. pp. 586, 588. See also above, p. 49, n. 81.

[89] Jones, "Editor's Introduction", *Agriculture and Economic Growth in England, 1650–1815*, p. 2.

extensive textile industry of Beauvais in this period to underlying problems in the production of food.[90] But a similar case seemingly could be made for the decline of Italian industry in the early seventeenth century. In Italy drastically rising food prices seem, as much as any other factor, to have been responsible for the enhanced (subsistence) wage costs which ostensibly priced Italian goods out of their European and especially their eastern Mediterranean markets. Correlatively, the backward, largely peasant agriculture appears to have largely cut off the possibility of developing a significant market in Italy itself.[91] Finally, although Dutch industry appears to have escaped the seventeenth-century crisis with relatively minor damage, its failure to sustain continued development through the eighteenth century appears to have been bound up to an important extent with an overwhelming dependence on overseas grain imports, which rose precipitately in price after 1750.[92]

Thus what distinguished the English industrial development of the early modern period was its continuous character, its ability to sustain itself and to provide its own self-perpetuating dynamic. Here, once again, the key was to be found in the capitalist structure of agriculture. Agricultural improvement not only made it possible for an ever greater proportion of the population to leave the land to enter industry; equally important, it provided, directly and indirectly, the growing home market which was an essential ingredient in England's continued industrial growth throughout the entire period of the general economic crisis of the seventeenth century in

[90] Goubert, *Beauvais et le Beauvaisis de 1600 à 1730*, pp. 585–7.

[91] On high wages as a basic cause of the decline of export-centred Italian industry from the early seventeenth century onwards, see C. M. Cipolla, "The Economic Decline of Italy", in B. Pullan (ed.), *Crisis and Change in the Venetian Economy in the Sixteenth and Seventeenth Centuries* (London, 1968), pp. 139–42. On problems of food supply and high food prices leading to higher wages (subsistence), see B. Pullan, "Introduction" and "Wage-Earners and the Venetian Economy, 1550–1630", *ibid.*, esp. pp. 12–14. On the structural roots of problems of food supply and the home market in the small-tenant, rent-squeezing organization of the Venetian mainland, see S. J. Woolf, "Venice and the Terraferma", *ibid.*, esp. pp. 179–87. For the general problem of food supply in Italy and the Mediterranean, which intensified sharply in the latter part of the sixteenth century, see C. T. Smith, *An Historical Geography of Western Europe before 1800* (New York, 1967), pp. 416–18.

[92] This is suggested in Jones, "Editor's Introduction", *Agriculture and Economic Growth in England, 1650–1815*, p. 21.

Europe.[93] Thus, during the sixteenth and seventeenth centuries, the prosperous class of tenant farmers, as well as landlords, appears to have offered significant outlets for English industrial goods.[94] At the same time, and in the long run, especially from the later seventeenth and early eighteenth centuries, continuing improvements in agricultural productivity combined with low food prices to give an extra margin of spending power to significant elements throughout the middle and perhaps even the lower class so as to expand the home market and fuel the steady growth of industry into the period of the industrial revolution.[95] English economic development thus depended upon a nearly unique symbiotic relationship between agriculture and industry. It was indeed, in the last analysis, an agricultural revolution, based on the emergence of capitalist class relations in the countryside, which made it possible for England to become the first nation to experience industrialization.

The contrasting failure in France of agrarian transformation seems to have followed directly from the continuing strength of peasant landholding into the early modern period, while it was disintegrating in England. Reference has already been made to the relative success with which peasant communities throughout western Europe were able to resist landlord power in the medieval period. In particular, the long-term process by which village after

[93] For continued English industrial growth into the later seventeenth century, and the important role of the home market in this process, see L. A. Clarkson, *The Pre-Industrial Economy in England, 1500–1750* (London, 1971), ch. 4, esp. pp. 114–15. See also "The Origins of the Industrial Revolution" (Conference Report), *Past and Present*, no. 17 (April 1960); C. Wilson, *England's Apprenticeship, 1603–1763* (London, 1965), ch. 9, esp. pp. 185ff.; F. J. Fisher, "The Sixteenth and Seventeenth Centuries: The Dark Ages of English Economic History", *Economica*, new ser., xxiv (1957).

[94] W. G. Hoskins, "The Leicestershire Farmer in the Sixteenth Century", in his *Essays in Leicestershire History* (Leicester, 1950); F. J. Fisher, "London as an Engine of Economic Growth", in J. S. Bromley and E. H. Kossman (eds.), *Britain and the Netherlands*, iv (The Hague, 1971); Fisher, "Sixteenth and Seventeenth Centuries".

[95] For this argument, see Jones, "Editor's Introduction", *Agriculture and Economic Growth in England, 1650–1815*; Jones, "Agriculture and Economic Growth in England, 1660–1750: Agricultural Change"; E. L. Jones, "Agricultural Origins of Industry", *Past and Present*, no. 40 (July 1968); A. H. John, "Agricultural Productivity and Economic Growth in England, 1700–1750", *Jl Econ. Hist.*, xxv (1965); A. H. John, "Aspects of English Economic Growth in the First Half of the Eighteenth Century", *Economica*, new ser., xxviii (1961); D. E. C. Eversley, "The Home Market and Economic Growth in England, 1750–1780", in E. L. Jones and G. E. Mingay (eds.), *Land, Labour and Population in the Industrial Revolution* (London, 1967).

village in various French regions was able to win certain important economic and political rights – to use the commons, to fix rents and secure hereditability, and to replace the old village *maires* with its own elected representatives – has been traced with special care by historians, who have remarked upon its historical significance.[96] What still requires explanation, however, is the ability of the French peasants not only to establish certain freedoms and property rights *vis-à-vis* the landlords in the first place, but to retain them over an extraordinarily long historical epoch – in particular, during the period in which their English counterparts ceased to be able to do so. Any answer must be very tentative. But in the light of English developments, what appears to lie behind the striking persistence of peasant proprietorship in France is its close interconnection with the particular *form* of evolution of the French monarchical state.

Thus in France, unlike England, the centralized state appears to have developed (at least in large part) as a class-like phenomenon – that is, as an *independent* extractor of the surplus, in particular on the basis of its arbitrary power to tax the land. To the extent that the peasants were able to unite against the landlords, to win their freedom from serfdom and to gain the essentials of freehold property – and they did so, as noted, to a significant degree – they tended to expose themselves to potential exploitation as a financial base for the monarchy. For if the peasants' locally based organization – which was the essential source, and effective limit, of their power – might at times be adequate to withstand the claims of the local landlord, it was far less effective against the pretensions of the centralizing state, at least in the long run. Correlatively, the state could develop, as it ultimately did, as a competitor with the lords, largely to the extent to which it could establish rights to extract the surplus of peasant production. It therefore had an interest in limiting the landlords' rents so as to enable the peasants to pay more in taxes – and thus in intervening against the landlords to end peasant unfreedom and to establish and secure peasant property.

Probably the archetypal case of the state actually developing in this manner as an independent class-like surplus-extractor in relation to the emergence of an entrenched landholding peasantry

[96] See especially Fossier, *Terre et hommes en Picardie*, ii, pp. 708–28. Also above, p. 44, n. 73, and Fourquin, *Campagnes de la région parisienne*, pt 1, ch. 3, esp. p. 190.

can be found in the rise of the "mini-absolutisms" of the west German princes in the early modern period. In these states the princes pursued a conscious policy of protecting a peasant proprietorship which, emerging from the medieval period, was already relatively well ensconced. In particular, the princes sought to defend the security and extent of peasant landholding, with the aim of providing their own independent tax base (*Bauernschutzpolitik*). Thus peasant dues were fixed in law; peasant hereditability was retained or restored; and in some cases land which had formerly been in peasant hands but had then been lost to the nobility was returned to the peasants. At the same time the princes did what they could to reconstitute the scattered parcels of peasant land into unified tenements and, on the other hand, acted to prevent the peasants from subdividing their holdings. In the end the princes succeeded in turning the peasant holding into a unified fiscal unit for taxation.[97] But, correlatively, by the seventeenth century the west German peasantry appears to have been able to gain control of up to 90 per cent of the land.[98]

The stages in the corresponding process in France by which the peasantry were able to consolidate their own powerful (if far less extensive) grip on the land in relationship to monarchical development are far from clear. One turning-point does seem to have occurred, at least in the Paris region, during the middle part of the thirteenth century in what turned out to be decisive conflicts between peasants and landlords over the landlords' attempts to extend the seigneurial *taille* (tallage). It was around the question of the *taille*, as we have noted, that the question of peasant unfreedom in this region came to be decided. The lords aimed to consolidate their right to tax their customary peasants at will. Their success would have established the peasants' unfree status, exposing them to further arbitrary seigneurial levies. However, the peasants of the Paris region resisted with force and in great number. What seems to

[97] F. Lütge, *Geschichte der deutschen Agrarverfassung* (Stuttgart, 1963), pp. 100–2, 134–54. For the foregoing discussion of west German developments, I am deeply indebted to Joel Singer.

[98] E. Weis, "Ergebnisse eines Vergleichs der grundherrschaftlichen Strukturen Deutschlands und Frankreichs vom 13. bis zum Ausgang des 18. Jahrhunderts", *Vierteljahrschrift für Sozial- und Wirtschaftsgeschichte*, lvii (1970), esp. p. 13. As a result, the German nobility appears to have been forced into an extraordinary degree of dependence upon the princes, becoming the administrative aristocracy *par excellence*.

have turned the tide in their favour was the intervention of the monarchical state against the landlords. When the crown agreed to consider the case, it recognized by implication the peasants' free legal status, paving the way for fixed rents and effective proprietorship.[99] Perhaps even more decisive in the long run were certain actions taken by the state during the fifteenth century. At this time the monarchy seems to have generally confirmed the integrity of the *cens* (peasant hereditary tenure). It thus remained legally difficult for the landlords to appropriate to their own demesnes the large number of holdings subject to this tenure which had been abandoned as a consequence of war and demographic decline. The result was the preservation of the area of land under peasant proprietorship. It is notable that it was at just this time that the monarchy also was taking decisive steps formally to organize the peasant community around village assemblies with elected syndics, in order to administer and collect the dramatically increasing royal taxes.[100]

Certainly, by the early modern period the consolidation of peasant property in relationship to the development of the French state had created a very different sort of class structure in the French countryside from that which had emerged in England. And there is no better index of these contrasting structures than the dramatically different sorts of peasant revolts which marked the early modern era in both countries. In England, of course, peasant revolt was directed against the landlords, in a vain last-ditch struggle to defend disintegrating peasant proprietorship against advancing capitalist encroachment. In France the target of peasant revolt was, typically, the crushing taxation of the absolutist state, which ironically had been instrumental in securing and protecting peasant proprietorship (and thus impeding capitalist development).[101]

[99] M. Bloch, "Blanche de Castille et les serfs du chapitre de Paris", in his *Melanges historiques*, 2 vols. (Paris, 1963), i; Fourquin, *Campagnes de la région parisienne*, pt 1, ch. 3.

[100] Fourquin, *Campagnes de la région parisienne*, pp. 180, 377, 382, 430–2ff., 514–15; J. F. Lemarignier, *La France médiévale* (Paris, 1970), p. 318; M. Bloch, *French Rural History* (London, 1966), pp. 128–9.

[101] For the English revolts, see above, p. 48. On peasant revolts in France, see the review article by J. H. M. Salmon, "Venality of Office and Popular Sedition in Seventeenth-Century France", *Past and Present*, no. 37 (July 1967). Although there is sharp debate on many aspects of these revolts, virtually all parties to the argument, including the leading protagonists Boris Porchnev and Roland Mousnier, agree that the opposition to state taxation was central. See B.

Thus in France strong peasant property and the absolutist state developed in mutual dependence upon one another. The state increased its own power by virtue of its ability to get between the landlords and the peasants, to ensure peasant freedom, heredit-ability and fixed rents, and thus to use peasant production, via non-parliamentary taxation, as the direct source of revenue for royal strength and autonomy. As Marc Bloch pointed out, in the seventeenth century – the high point of absolutist development in France – a key function of the *intendants*, the direct administrative representatives of the monarchy in the provinces, was "to protect rural communities, ripe material for taxation, from intemperate exploitation by their landlords".[102] Correlatively, the landlords waged a fierce defensive struggle throughout the period to protect their peasants from the encroachments of a royal fiscal machine which sought systematically to extend its scope within the countryside.[103]

In England, by contrast, monarchical centralization developed, especially from the later fifteenth century, in relationship to and with ultimate dependence upon the landlord classes, as was most dramatically evidenced in the contemporaneous growth of parliamentary institutions (while they decayed in France). The English peasantry, as we have seen, through flight and resistance were able to win their freedom from serfdom by the fifteenth century. Their relative failure, however, to establish freehold rights over much of the land (as had their French counterparts at a far earlier date) deprived the monarchy of a potential financial base in the peasantry for developing its independence of the landlords. Thus monarchical centralization could not take an absolutist and peasant-based form. By the same token; the monarchy's reliance upon the landlords in its drive towards centralization in the later fifteenth and early sixteenth centuries prevented its playing a decisive role in aiding the peasants in their abortive struggle for freehold, which occurred in precisely

Porchnev, *Les soulèvements populaires en France de 1623 à 1648* (Paris, 1963); R. Mousnier, "Recherches sur les soulèvements populaires en France avant la Fronde", *Revue d'histoire moderne et contemporaine*, v (1958).

102 Bloch, *French Rural History*, p. 134.

103 For a revealing account of the struggle between the French monarchy and the French nobility to protect the peasantry in order to exploit it for themselves, focusing especially on the attempts to extend royal land-taxation and on noble resistance to these attempts in the name of their peasants, see P. Deyon, "A propos des rapports entre la noblesse française et la monarchie absolue pendant la première moitié du XVIIe siècle", *Revue historique*, ccxxxi (1964).

this period. Important sections of the English nobility and gentry were willing to support the monarchy's centralizing political battle against the disruptive activities of the magnate-warlords in the interest of achieving order and stable conditions for economic development. But it was precisely these same landlord elements who were most concerned to undermine peasant property in the interests of enclosure and consolidation – and agricultural capitalism.[104]

It cannot be said that the French landlords did not wish to consolidate holdings. But in order to do so they could not, as in England, merely raise rents or fines to impossible levels and thus evict the small tenant on the expiry of his lease or copyhold. Throughout most of France, state-supported law assured heredit-ability and fixed fines (*lods et ventes*) for customary tenures. Thus the landlord might have to *buy up* countless small peasant holdings in order to amass a consolidated unit. And this was rarely easy to accomplish. On the one hand, the peasant had every positive incentive to hold on to his holding, for it formed the basis for his existence, and that of his family and heirs. On the other, purely economic forces seem to have worked to undermine the peasants' property only in the very long term.

The point is, then, that the peasant proprietor was under relatively little pressure to operate his plot as profitably or effectively as his potential competitors in order to survive, for there were no direct means for such competitors to "defeat" him. In other words, the

[104] For the process of centralization under the Tudors, especially the interrelationship between the crown and those sections of the landed class (noble and non-noble) who supported centralization against the magnate-warlords, see Stone, "Power", in his *Crisis of the Aristocracy*, ch. 5; as well as the series of works by M. E. James: *A Tudor Magnate and the Tudor State* (Borthwick Papers, no. 30, York, 1966); *Change and Continuity in the Tudor North* (Borthwick Papers, no. 27, York, 1965); "The First Earl of Cumberland and the Decline of Northern Feudalism", *Northern Hist.*, i (1966); "The Concept of Order and the Northern Rising, 1569", *Past and Present*, no. 60 (Aug. 1973). The researches of Lawrence Stone and Mervyn James provide detailed case studies which demonstrate the important overlap between those landlord elements, both noble and non-noble, who supported royal centralization in the interests of social peace and public order, and those who wished to pursue highly commercial and progressive policies with regard to their land – consolidation, enclosure, agricultural improvement. On this point, I have benefited from reading an unpublished essay by E. Searle, "The Jack Cade Rebellion: Social Unrest in England, 1450–1460". On the development of parliament in this period, the fundamental works are the writings of G. R. Elton and J. E. Neale.

peasant did not have to be competitive, because he did not really have to be able to "hold his place" in the world of the market, either the market for tenants or the market for goods. Unlike a tenant, the peasant proprietor did not have to provide a level of rent equal to what the landlord might get from any other tenant – or else be evicted on the expiry of his lease. Unlike the independent artisan, he did not have to be able to produce cheaply enough to sell his goods profitably at the market price – or else go out of business. All that was necessary for survival for the peasant proprietor (assuming of course that he was a food producer) was sufficient output to provide for his family's subsistence and to pay his taxes (and generally fixed customary rents); and this could often be supplemented through wage labour.

Of course, merely maintaining subsistence was rarely easy for the peasantry, especially the large numbers with relatively small holdings. Demographic growth and the subdivision of holdings diminished the size of the peasant's productive base, either relatively or absolutely. Meanwhile, the growth of taxation, especially consequent upon war, meant that greater production was necessary merely to survive (thus, ironically, the state which in the first instance provided the primary support for peasant proprietorship was indirectly perhaps also the major source of its disintegration). Finally, rising prices throughout the period lowered the value of the supplementary wage often required to make the peasant's holding viable. Throughout the early modern period many peasants were indeed forced deeply into debt and were ultimately obliged to sell their holdings.[105] It was no accident, moreover, that the greatest number of casualties appears to have occurred in times of war (especially the wars of religion and the Fronde) and of dearth (particularly the subsistence crises of the later seventeenth century) and to have been concentrated in the zones immediately affected by military action (for example, the Paris region and Burgundy).[106] Yet even such long-term pressures and short-term catastrophes seem to

[105] See P. Goubert, "The French Peasantry of the Seventeenth Century", *Past and Present*, no. 10 (Nov. 1956), p. 75.

[106] For case studies of the destruction of peasant proprietorship, see especially J. Jacquart, *La crise rurale en Ile-de-France, 1550–1670* (Paris, 1974); M. Venard, *Bourgeois et paysans au XVIIe siècle* (Paris, 1957); P. de Saint-Jacob, "Mutations économiques et sociales dans les campagnes bourguignonnes à la fin du XVIe siècle", *Etudes rurales*, i (1961).

have worked their undermining effects on peasant proprietorship relatively sporadically and slowly over the whole of France. The continuing strength of the French peasant community and French peasant proprietorship even at the end of the seventeenth century is shown by the fact that some 45–50 per cent of the cultivated land was still in peasant possession, often scattered throughout the open fields.[107] In England, by contrast, the owner-occupiers at this time held no more than 25–30 per cent of the land.[108]

Given the French property structure, it is hardly surprising that the rising population, markets and grain prices of the sixteenth and seventeenth centuries did not lead in France to agricultural improvement, but merely to a renewal of the old Malthusian cycle of underdevelopment. Given the strength of peasant property, supported by the exploitative state, the landlord could not usually take advantage of increasing prices for land and agricultural products by improving and by increasing output, because this usually entailed the very difficult task of consolidation. The landlords therefore took the only course generally open to them: to try to obtain an ever greater share of a constant or even declining total product. On their demesne land, composed generally of small separated plots, they imposed short-term leases on draconian terms, designed to squeeze the peasant tenants by raising their rents and lowering their level of subsistence by taking advantage of the growing demand for holdings arising from demographic pressure. This procedure, of course, reduced the possibility of agricultural improvement by the tenants, since they would rarely have sufficient funds for investment left over after paying the rent.[109] The difference from the situation in England – where landlords would obtain increases in rent by co-operating with their tenants in capital improvements on large farms and thereby increasing total output, rather than by simply taking a larger share of a constant or declining output at the expense of the

107 P. Goubert, "Le paysan et la terre: seigneurie, tenure, exploitation", in Labrousse and Braudel (eds.), *Histoire économique et sociale de la France*, ii, pp. 135–9: "It is commonly admitted that the peasants of France were able to 'possess' . . . a mere half of the French soil" (p. 135).

108 See above, p. 48, n. 80.

109 For a good account of this procedure of squeezing the leaseholding tenants and its economic effects, see Merle, *Métairie et l'évolution agraire de la Gâtine poitevine*.

tenants[110] – could not have been more stark.[111] At the same time, in the sector of free peasant proprietors, to repeat, the holdings were divided and subdivided. This too naturally reduced the general level of peasant income, the surplus available for potential investment in agriculture, and the slim hope of agricultural innovation. Meanwhile, of course, the state, which had helped to maintain the peasants on the land, now helped to reduce their enjoyment of it by confiscating much of what was left of the peasants' product through ever higher taxes.

In sum, it is not difficult to comprehend the dismal pattern of economic development imposed by this class structure in France. Not only was there a long-term failure of agricultural productivity, but a corresponding inability to develop the home market. Thus, ironically, the most complete freedom and property rights for the rural population meant poverty and a self-perpetuating cycle of backwardness. In England, it was precisely the absence of such rights that facilitated the onset of real economic development.

110 See Adam Smith's analogous observations: "Rent anciently formed a larger proportion of the produce of agriculture than now . . . In the progress of improvement, rent, though it increases in proportion to the extent, diminishes in proportion to the produce of the land": Smith, *Wealth of Nations*, bk ii, ch. 3, ed. E. Cannan, 2 vols. in 1 (Chicago, 1976), i, p. 355.

111 It is striking in this respect that, in those relatively restricted areas where large consolidated holdings were created in France, the landlords generally applied the same squeezing policy to their large tenants, with the result that even on the relatively small number of large farms few improvements were adopted. See Jacquart, *Crise rurale en Ile-de-France*, pp. 289–91, 326–30, and esp. pp. 747–8, 756–7. Also Venard, *Bourgeois et paysans au XVIIe siècle*, esp. pp. 117–18. Why French landlords adopted this approach, rather than opting for the "English system" of landlord/tenant co-operation, is uncertain. But the reason may once again be bound up with an overall structure of landholding in France which was still heavily dominated by peasant proprietorship – and with the generally stagnant economy which this landholding structure tended to produce. Most especially, in comparison with England, French agriculture had at its disposal a great pool of agricultural labour without alternative opportunities for employment – that is, at relatively very low wages – and this naturally encouraged labour-intensive methods of cultivation, and the neglect of capital-using and labour-saving techniques. With no apparent incentive to promote capital improvement of his land, the lord had no reason to refrain from squeezing his tenant. Thus even where large, consolidated farms dominated considerable portions of the surface area, they still tended to be surrounded by a sea of petty proprietors who needed to hire themselves out as wage-labourers in order to make ends meet. See Jacquart, *Crise rurale en Ile-de-France*, pp. 332–48, esp. pp. 341, 348; Venard, *Bourgeois et paysans au XVIIe siecle*, pp. 27–9. It was not merely that strong peasant rights in the land tended to be bound up with subdivision of holdings

(partible inheritance) and the rapid concentration of the peasant population on tiny plots. Probably more significant, due to the lack of economic development elsewhere in the economy (industry, the towns), which was itself the result of the established peasant-dominated agrarian structure, this rural semi-peasantry/semi-proletariat, unlike the English agricultural labourers, had virtually nowhere else to go (increasing pressure on the land meant downward pressure on wages). Their natural tendency to remain on their mini-holdings was thus greatly intensified by the economic necessity to do so. Thus peasant agriculture set up yet another vicious cycle of backwardness thwarting agricultural capitalism even where its outward forms (large consolidated holdings farmed by big tenants using wage labour) were present.

2. *Population and Class Relations in Feudal Society*

M. M. POSTAN and JOHN HATCHER

The essentials of Robert Brenner's argument have been put forward many times before by a long and distinguished line of proponents. The counter-argument is also securely placed in historiography. Consequently, there is much to be said for simply referring readers to previous publications. Yet Brenner's thesis warrants a comment, if only because it harbours a number of widespread misconceptions. In dealing with these misconceptions we will also take the opportunity of dissipating the doctrinal, or rather the nomenclatural, confusion which has for years befogged the controversies over the role of demographic factors in history. Lack of space and expertise has compelled us to restrict ourselves to western Europe, mainly England, in the middle ages. Brenner's notions of post-medieval developments in western Europe mainly attach to Le Roy Ladurie's writings, and had better be left to the latter's superior competence.

I

In his article Brenner sets himself a double task – to discredit the so-called "demographic" or "cyclical" Malthusian model, and to offer in its stead the class-oriented model. He makes the first of the two tasks far less arduous than it might otherwise have proved by misrepresenting the views of the historians he holds responsible for it. These misrepresentations are exemplified in his double accusation that the erring historians have assigned to demographic factors an all-determining role in the medieval economy and society and that, in so doing, they have disregarded or minimized the importance of social factors, above all the feudal class system and the exploitation of villeins inherent in it. Both imputations are groundless. The historians in question do not present demographic factors as an omnipresent and omnipotent force behind every economic and social activity or every feature of economic and social organization. With respect to demographic factors, their aim is far more limited:

namely, to relate periodic movements or economic fluctuations – repeat fluctuations – to concomitant demographic changes – repeat changes – over time. The imputation of neglect of social factors, which was originally formulated by Kosminsky, reiterated by such reputable Marxist medievalists as Malowist and Barg, and recently given official sanction in the Soviet historical encyclopaedia, is equally unwarranted.[1] The erring historians have not attempted to account for the abiding features of the medieval economy and society, its structure, institutions or attitudes, by demographic factors alone.[2] In fact, when examining or describing an economic situation, they have almost invariably tried to fit it into its social situation. More particularly, they have attached to feudal rent much of the blame for the villeins' impoverishment and for their inability to

[1] E. A. Kosminsky, *Studies in the Agrarian History of England in the Thirteenth Century* (Oxford, 1956), pp. vii–xiv, 178, 327 n.; E. A. Kosminsky, "Byli li XIV n XV veka vremenem upadka evropeiskoi ekonomii" [Were the Fourteenth and Fifteenth Centuries a Period of Decline in the European Economy?], *Srednie veka*, no. 10 (1957); M. A. Barg, *Issledovaniya po istorii angliiskogo feodalizma* [Research on English Feudalism] (Moscow, 1962), pp. 9–11; M. A. Barg, "K voprosu o . . . krizise feodalizma v XIV–XV v." [On the Crisis of Feudalism in the Fourteenth and Fifteenth Centuries], *Voprosi istorii*, no. 8 (1960); also the note on M. M. Postan in the *Sovetskaya istoricheskaya entsiklopediya*, 16 vols. (Moscow, 1961–76), vi.

[2] It would be invidious to expose other historians to Brenner's criticisms, but the vast majority of specialized studies published in recent years stress or assume the primary importance of demographic factors. So do such general studies as J. Z. Titow, *English Rural Society, 1200–1350* (London, 1969), and E. Miller, "The English Economy in the Thirteenth Century", *Past and Present*, no. 28 (July 1964). In none of these studies does population figure as the sole determinant of economic change but, *pari passu*, some modern works devoted to non-demographic factors nevertheless assign to demographic and economic factors a great, even the leading, role in the historical process. For example, R. H. Hilton concludes his *Bond Men Made Free* with the following remarks: "There was a long-term, though occasionally reversed, trend away from labour rent towards money rent. There were periods when the general level of rents declined. It could be argued, and of course it is argued, that these trends had nothing to do with the organized and deliberate action of peasant communities but depended simply on such impersonal factors as the supply of land, population trend, the demand for agricultural products and so on. Of course these factors were most important and perhaps the most that one could claim for peasant actions, in the long run, was that they followed, perhaps reinforced, the existing currents of historical change": R. H. Hilton, *Bond Men Made Free* (London, 1973), pp. 234–5. Not surprisingly, such orthodox Soviet Marxists as Academician Skazkin bracket Hilton and Postan together as two representatives of the "economist view of medieval history": S. D. Skazkin, "K voprosu o genezise kapitalizma v sel'skom khozyaistve zapadnoi Evropy" [On the Genesis of Capitalism in West European Agriculture], *Ezhegodnik po agrarnoi istorii vostochnoi Evropy* (1959).

invest in their holdings or even to keep their land in good heart.[3] This, however, is not the only social factor they have commonly invoked. Family structure, inheritance customs, attitudes to technological discovery and innovation, communal facilities and restraints, the prevailing hierarchy of economic objectives and consumption needs, the special rank which the possession of land occupied in that hierarchy, the burdens and penalties of war, the vicissitudes of government and the rules of law – all these and many other realities of medieval life have been commonly drawn by the same historians into their general view of economic and social processes in the middle ages.[4] In this view, there is more in the middle ages than the feudal system, and more to the feudal system than the class relations within it. In other words, where the historians in question differ from Brenner is not in their neglect of social factors but in their range of social reference – a range too wide to be squeezed into the old-Marxist concept of class conflict.

So much for the twofold accusation. This accusation, however, does not exhaust Brenner's case, since he also tries to dispose of the demographic hypothesis in substance. His argument against the demographic hypothesis is largely based on instances of "different outcomes" proceeding "from similar demographic trends at different times and in different areas of Europe".[5] Does Brenner mean that no causal factor can be proved true unless it can be shown to produce identical results in totally different circumstances?

The deficiencies in Brenner's argument are not confined to its logic, but overflow into its historical evidence. The major example he cites of similar "cause" and dissimilar "effect" is that of eastern Europe. Whereas, he argues, serfdom declined in many western

[3] Titow, *English Rural Society, 1200–1350*, p. 81; M. M. Postan, *The Medieval Economy and Society* (London, 1972), pp. 124–6; M. M. Postan, "Medieval Agrarian Society in its Prime: England", in *Cambridge Economic History of Europe*, i, 2nd edn, pp. 602ff.; and several of M. M. Postan's other medieval studies.

[4] The *locus classicus* for the invocation of social environment in its totality is G. C. Homans, *English Villagers of the Thirteenth Century* (Cambridge, Mass., 1942). Views sympathetic to those of Homans on the importance of inheritance rules, family structures and patterns of landholding are widely held by historians, however "Malthusian" – especially by those dealing with East Anglia, Danelaw and Kent: for example, H. E. Hallam, *Settlement and Society* (Cambridge, 1965); H. E. Hallam, "Population Density in Medieval Fenland", *Econ. Hist. Rev.*, 2nd ser., xiv (1961–2).

[5] Above, pp. 21–2.

countries when population was falling, eastern Europe at the same time and with the same demographic situation experienced the rise and spread of serfdom. This is not the right place and we are not the right persons to deal in full with Brenner's east European references, but they loom so large in his critique that some comment is unavoidable. So we shall confine ourselves merely to reminding the reader that the rise of serfdom beyond the Elbe largely post-dates the late medieval fall in population. It was, in the main, a post-medieval development, spreading widest in the sixteenth and seventeenth centuries and culminating in rather different circumstances in eighteenth-century Russia. For Hungary this chronology is clearly demonstrated in the work of Z. P. Pach, who has maintained that until the end of the fifteenth century "labour dues played a merely subsidiary role", and that "in Hungary, until the end of the fifteenth century, the trend of development of medieval rural economy was fundamentally concordant with that of the west European countries". Similar conclusions have emerged from Bohemian and Polish sources, and are contained in the works of Kula, Graus, Małowist and others.[6]

However, the main weakness of Brenner's east European example is its conceptual confusion of declining population with scarcity of manpower relative to the other factors. The inducement behind the action of east German governments and nobles in their expropriation of peasant holders (*Bauernlegen*) and compulsory recruitment of labourers (*Gesindezwang*) was not the absolute decline in population (the decline had begun at the turn of the thirteenth and the fourteenth centuries and was eventually arrested by the sixteenth and seventeenth centuries), but the expansion of the international market for grain between the fifteenth century and the eighteenth, and the stimulus which it gave to large-scale grain production. The consequent demand for labour, which the population of peasants well provided with land could not and would not meet, induced landlords to seek a solution in the expropriation of peasant

[6] Z. P. Pach, "The Development of Feudal Rent in Hungary in the Fifteenth Century", *Econ. Hist. Rev.*, 2nd ser., xix (1966), p. 13. Brief summaries of east European agrarian history and its divergence from western development will be found in F. Lütge, *Deutsche Sozial- und Wirtschaftsgeschichte*, 3rd edn (Berlin, 1966), pp. 215–18; M. M. Postan, "Economic Relations between Eastern and Western Europe", in G. Barraclough (ed.), *Eastern and Western Europe in the Middle Ages* (London, 1970), pp. 170–4. The latter study lays great stress on the post-medieval chronology of feudalism in the east.

land and obligatory labour services. Needless to say, this solution could not have been imposed had the *Junkers'* position in the east German states been less powerful than it was; but it was also powerful in the earlier centuries, when the east European peasantry were still prosperous and free.

The use which Brenner makes of this particular example is mistaken in both fact and sense. He could have found better examples of "contradictory" processes: the lessening of servile burdens in twelfth-century England and the purchase of charters of enfranchisement by French villages in the thirteenth century took place while population was increasing.[7] He might also have noted that the widespread post-plague seigneurial reaction was not everywhere doomed to failure. But even had he done so, Brenner would still have been tilting at windmills. Historians who attach importance to demographic factors have not maintained that a rising population invariably led to an intensification of serfdom and a falling population to its demise.

Last, but not least, Brenner's discussion of demographic factors displays a certain misconception as to the doctrinal origins and affiliations of the views he criticizes. The misconception is largely one of names, and the name in question is that of "Malthusianism". We do not regard the label as libellous as it may sometimes appear to old-fashioned Marxists. In the genealogy of economic theory, Malthus occupies the position of a father-founder, and his ideas still enter into the main body of modern development economics. Our quarrel with Brenner's use of the name is that the historical hypothesis he criticizes, more particularly the medieval one, cannot be described as Malthusian except in the sense in which all references to demographic factors are Malthusian. Had he taken a closer view of Malthus, he would have noticed how imperfectly the name fits the views of Postan and others of the same persuasion.

In the first place, the main preoccupation of these historians is not quite that of Malthus. Their concern is with economic activity and economic development as well as standards of life, whereas Malthus was interested not in economic development or economic activity in the aggregate, but almost entirely with the well-being or

[7] M. M. Postan, "The Chronology of Labour Services", repr. in his *Essays on Medieval Agriculture and General Problems of the Medieval Economy* (Cambridge, 1973); G. Duby, *Rural Economy and Country Life in the Medieval West* (London, 1968), pp. 242–4.

income per capita of individuals. Second, Malthus presented the link between population and economic well-being as an exclusive relationship – an equation into which other variables do not enter. In the third place, changes of population and well-being, as defined by Malthus, are intermittent, or reciprocating, in the engineering sense of the word. In this intermittent action, the phase of increasing population and falling incomes is automatically succeeded and counterbalanced by the phase of falling population and rising incomes. This two-phase rhythm of the Malthusian mechanism is the one feature of the doctrine Brenner takes into account, but in doing so he sadly misapplies it. It may superficially resemble the version of demographic change represented by Le Roy Ladurie, but it certainly differs from the demographic movements implied by the medievalists Brenner criticizes. One of their main propositions is that the fall of population in the fourteenth century did not wholly reverse the preceding trends, as it should have done in the Malthusian scheme, and that the higher per capita incomes of the later period did not lead to commensurate increases in population. Indeed the reason why the recovery was so belated and so sluggish is still one of the incompletely resolved difficulties inherent in the medieval hypotheses Brenner disagrees with.

Anyone anxious to fit these hypotheses with a doctrinal cap would be advised to look for it elsewhere, and in the first place to Ricardo. It will be remembered that the essence of the Ricardian theory of rent is the continuous trend of diminishing returns in agriculture which manifested itself in the declining productivity of older lands, the extension of cultivation to new lands of lower quality, and the consequent fall in output per head. In the course of subsequent discussion, Ricardo's theory was criticized and corrected by several people, more particularly by Carey, Mill and Marshall who argued or assumed that investment and technological progress could, and in fact did, reverse the tendency of diminishing returns.[8] Thus corrected and supplemented, the Ricardian system provides a better matrix than Malthusianism for the historical views Brenner criticizes. If we accepted that Ricardo's irreversible trend of diminishing returns operated only so long and so far as it remained

[8] The same argument about the compensating effect of investment and technological progress figures in most of present-day criticisms of the Malthusian approach to economic development.

unchecked by investment and innovation, then the absence of innovation and paucity of investment in medieval agriculture would go a long way to explain why the late medieval recovery was so slow and tardy. This is in fact the explanation implied in the views of medieval history which Brenner rejects. If nevertheless the historians holding these views have refrained from overtly invoking the name of Ricardo, they have done so mainly because no theoretical matrix, not even Ricardo's, will fit closely enough the infinite complexity of historical facts. The amended theory of rent is commended here in preference to Malthus's original theory of population merely in order to demonstrate how slipshod the imputations of Malthusian creed can sometimes be.

II

From seeking to minimize the role of population in the promotion of economic and social change, Brenner turns to the alternative thesis he prefers, that of class structure. Starting from the premise that "Serfdom was a relationship of power which could be reversed, as it were, only in its own terms, through a change in the balance of class forces", he is driven to find the cause of the early fourteenth-century "crisis" in the "surplus-extraction relations of serfdom [which] tended to lead to the exhaustion of peasant production *per se*".[9] In so doing, he goes badly astray. His aberrations are perhaps too many, and often too trivial, to be fully discussed here. Some of them nevertheless deserve attention, however brief.

If all the inadequacies of medieval husbandry had lain solely in feudalism and the "surplus-extraction relations of serfdom", poverty and economic backwardness would not have manifested themselves strongly, if at all, in situations in which feudal oppression was absent or weak. Were the regions of England outside its manorialized core exempt from the economic trends of the thirteenth century? Were the freeholders, the sokemen, *censuarii* and *molmen*, all of them partly or wholly relieved of the main burden of "manorial oppression", also immune from the economic malaise of the middle ages? Postan and others have, of course, argued that serfdom had a pauperizing effect on peasant existence, that personal freedom could carry with it economic advantages, and that consequently freeholders well provided with land could be

[9] Above, pp. 27, 31–3.

expected to do better than villeins with holdings of comparable size. This does not, however, mean that freeholders as a group were more prosperous and productive than the villeins. Free tenure brought its resulting dangers as well as rights. Freedom to alienate, often combined with partible inheritance, led to the multiplication of exiguous freeholdings.[10] As a Kentish charter of 1276 succinctly put it: "it often happens that lands and tenements which . . . , undivided, were accustomed decently to suffice for the subsistence of many men . . . afterwards are separated and divided into so many parts and parcels among coheirs, that to none of them does his part then suffice for his subsistence".[11] It was practices like these, combined of course with a sharply rising population, which made the predominantly free villages of the Lincolnshire fenland among the most densely populated parts of England, and reduced the average arable, meadow and pasture per head (excluding demesnes and fenland wastes) to somewhere around 1–1½ acres.[12]

Brenner draws our attention to the disappearance of serfdom in Normandy and the Paris region in the thirteenth century,[13] but neither case will bear the interpretation that he forces upon it. The movement towards freedom which took place in many parts of France in the twelfth and thirteenth centuries, and the consequent absence of the "surplus-extraction relations of serfdom", manifestly failed to provide immunity from the pressures of rising population and growing scarcity of land. The very regions upon which Brenner chooses to concentrate are well known for the signs of distress which they displayed at the turn of the thirteenth and fourteenth centuries. The multiplication of families and the short-term attractions of the cash which could be realized from alienations led to the fragmentation of holdings, often into pathetically small parcels. The

[10] In the broad sweep of midland counties covered by the Hundred Rolls of 1279, some 8 per cent of freeholders held more than a virgate and 47 per cent held less than five acres; the respective proportions for villeins were 1 per cent and 29 per cent: Kosminsky, *Studies in the Agrarian History of England in the Thirteenth Century*, esp. tables, pp. 216–23. The best and the fullest demonstration of economic differences among freeholders and the large number of poor smallholders among them will be found in M. A. Barg, "Frigold tsentral'noi Anglii v XII–XIII vv." [Freehold in the Midlands in the Twelfth and Thirteenth Centuries], *Srednie veka*, no. 9 (1957).

[11] Quoted in Homans, *English Villagers of the Thirteenth Century*, pp. 112–13.

[12] Hallam, *Settlement and Society*, pp. 197–222; Hallam, "Population Density in Medieval Fenland".

[13] Above, p. 21.

inadequacy of peasant incomes led to a massive growth of indebtedness and still further falls in income as many, and in some parts the great majority of, farmers were induced to cede an annual perpetual rent on their farms in return for a cash sum. But even if the new rent charges upon peasants' farms are disregarded and an impression is formed simply from the ratio of men to land, the conclusion must be that in Normandy and the Paris region around 1300 there was "a severe pressure on resources" and the prevalence of "near-famine conditions" even in years when the harvest did not fail.[14]

The fact is that in thirteenth-century Normandy and the Paris region, as in thirteenth-century England, peasants both free and servile suffered the consequences of the great and growing scarcity of land. The consequences as a rule expressed themselves in prices – the cost of land to buy and the burden of payments weighing upon it. On Titow's and Postan's showing, the payments borne by peasant holdings in the thirteenth century were crushingly heavy. The prior claims of landlords, the church and the state could, in combination, come to at least half of a holding's gross output. This share was frequently lower on ancient holdings of free land and on those of villeins whose dues had been anciently commuted for a fixed money rent. It was to be greatly reduced in most regions in the late fourteenth and the fifteenth centuries when land values slumped and charges for it correspondingly fell. But, by the same token, the persistently high level of charges during the preceding century and a half reflected the economic conditions at that time – the scarcity of land and the plethora of would-be tenants. That the high and mounting payments reflected market forces, and not mere excesses of feudal power, is also shown by the fact that in the thirteenth century as much as one half of the gross product or *métayage* was frequently demanded in freely negotiated contracts of lease, *ad campipartem*, *ad meditatem* or *pro media vestura*, even in cases where both the lessor and the lessee were villagers and villeins.[15]

[14] N. J. G. Pounds, "Overpopulation in France and the Low Countries in the Later Middle Ages", *Jl Social Hist.*, iii (1969–70), pp. 239, 246; J. R. Strayer, "Economic Conditions in the County of Beaumont-le-Roger, 1261–1313", *Speculum*, xxvi (1951); G. Fourquin, *Les campagnes de la région parisienne à la fin du moyen âge* (Paris, 1962); G. Fourquin, *Lordship and Feudalism in the Middle Ages* (London, 1976), pp. 173–99; Duby, *Rural Economy and Country Life in the Medieval West*, pp. 122–5, 255–9.

[15] M. M. Postan, "The Charters of the Villeins", repr. in his *Essays on Medieval*

III

Brenner's exclusive regard for the "surplus-extraction relations of serfdom" distorts his view of the landlord as well as that of the peasant. If, as he assumes, feudal exploitation was the sole morbid cause of medieval agriculture, why then should the exploiting lords themselves have been afflicted by it? And afflicted they certainly were. Needless to say, in this as in other respects, no two landlords were alike. Historians could easily cite the instances of progressive landlords busily improving their estates – Henry of Eastry of Christ Church Priory, Richard of London and one or two other abbots of Peterborough, Michael of Amesbury of Glastonbury, and the earl of Lacy. Most of these instances belong, of course, to the time in the thirteenth century when the very economic conditions Brenner disparages happened to favour the enterprising landowners. Yet, even on these estates, demesne husbandry was by comparison with other times and places exceedingly poor. Some demesnes may have had a larger share of the good soils than the holdings of villagers; some of them were better provided with pasture and could lay preferential claims to the village folds. Yet on many, perhaps most, of the demesnes, yields were abysmally low and falling.[16]

In our view, to be recapitulated later, the low standard of demesne husbandry reflected the backwardness and stagnation of prevailing technology and, above all, the insufficiency of manorial investment. In Brenner's view, the insufficiency of the lords' investment resulted from the lords' powers over their peasantry. Their unlimited ability to squeeze ever higher rents from their villeins relieved them of the necessity "to engage in the difficult and costly processes of building up large holdings and investing, of removing customary peasants and bringing in new techniques".[17] This proposition begs questions too numerous to be answered in a short contribution like this. However, some of the questions begged here by Brenner lie too near the crux of the problem to be left unanswered. In the first place, his theory carries the implication that rents invariably formed the main source of lords' revenues in the twelfth and the thirteenth centuries. No doubt some landlords, of whom the

Agriculture and General Problems of the Medieval Economy, pp. 135–43 *passim* (for example, pp. 135, 136, 140, nn. 62, 65, 73).

[16] J. Z. Titow, *Winchester Yields* (Cambridge, 1972).

[17] Above, p. 32.

earls of Cornwall or the Templars were the most notable, had by the thirteenth century transformed themselves almost completely into *rentiers*, but many others, more particularly the ecclesiastical ones, continued to derive a very substantial proportion of their revenues from the sale of demesne produce. In 1298–9 the demesne accounted for 40 per cent of the bishop of Ely's income, and in 1258, 1288 and 1317 the demesne accounted for 72 per cent, 47 per cent and 65 per cent respectively of the bishop of Winchester's income. And there were, of course, also very large "seigneurial" incomes from feudal jurisdiction and incidents.[18]

In the second place, Brenner greatly exaggerates not only the relative importance of rents, but also their elasticity. Elastic they sometimes were, but never to the extent imagined by Brenner. The core of rent payments, the customary rents, were by definition fixed. The lords were, of course, able to supplement the customary rents by additional impositions, but these impositions did not offer unlimited possibilities of expansion. The close definition of villein status and obligations in the late twelfth and the thirteenth centuries may have helped to harden the legal rigours of the villeins' condition, but it also helped to protect the villeins against arbitrary exactions. As Bracton somewhat ruefully remarked, "the authority of their lords . . . once extended to life and death, but is now restricted by the civil law".[19] In the thirteenth century, unfree peasants often resisted both by direct action and due legal processes the reimposition of old commuted labour services and the imposition of new. Where services were in fact increased in the thirteenth century, the increases were usually relatively small; the bishops of Ely, for example, managed to increase the total week-work due to them only by around 10 per cent between 1222 and 1251.[20] Tallage, theoretically arbitrary in incidence and amount, was on very many

[18] E. Miller, *The Abbey and Bishopric of Ely* (Cambridge, 1951), p. 93; J. Z. Titow, "Land and Population on the Bishopric of Winchester's Estates, 1208–1350" (Cambridge Univ. Ph.D. thesis, 1961), esp. pp. 10, 36–41, 55–8, 61–2. Demesnes with a lower proportion of manorial incomes are cited in R. H. Hilton, *The English Peasantry in the Later Middle Ages* (Oxford, 1975), pp. 232–3. But some of Hilton's figures for rents and profits of jurisdiction may have been swollen by payments of rents and fines of non-villeins.

[19] Bracton, *De legibus et consuetudinibus Angliae*, ed. G. E. Woodbine, rev. S. E. Thorne, 4 vols. (Cambridge, Mass., 1968), ii, p. 34.

[20] J. A. Raftis, *The Estates of Ramsey Abbey* (Toronto, 1957), p. 115, n. 68; Miller, *Abbey and Bishopric of Ely*, pp. 101–2.

manors converted into a regular impost. Where this happened, entry fines assumed a special significance, for they could reflect market forces more accurately than other charges; and this is why they increased in many parts of the country during the thirteenth and early fourteenth centuries. Yet even entry fines will not bear Brenner's interpretation of exploitation through the "surplus-extraction relations" of serfdom. The high fines seem to have been supported by market forces; in places where the fines happened to be low or stable they reflected, rather untypically, the customary restraints prevailing in some manors or the local abundance of rentable land.[21] Most significantly, we find that heirs within the family tended to be charged lower fines than outsiders, and that wealthier villagers, frequently freeholders, who took on additional holdings, tended to be charged the highest fines of all,[22] thus suggesting once again that it was market forces which lay behind the rising price of land. In general the fines paid by those over whom the lord could exercise in full his manorial compulsion were often lower than the fines paid by those who were under no such compulsion. In fact the high payments borne in the thirteenth and early fourteenth centuries by holdings leased without the constraints of manorial custom were usually higher than the payment from holdings in villeinage.[23]

Brenner's insistence on feudal relations as the prime mover behind higher rents also accounts for his misrepresenting the reasons why general increases in feudal rent incomes took place. Had these increases occurred mainly as a result of the lord's feudal power over his villein, we would expect them to have been largest and most widespread in earlier centuries when this power, and the manorial economy, were at their peak. In fact the proportion of seigneurial incomes derived from rent rose fastest in the later

[21] See the discussion in Titow, *English Rural Society, 1200–1350*, pp. 73–8.

[22] For an account of these processes at work, see E. King, *Peterborough Abbey, 1086–1310* (London, 1973), pp. 166–7, 182–8.

[23] Instances of recently established freeholds and leaseholds subject to rents or capital valuations higher than those of villein holdings of comparable size and quality will be found in large numbers of records of the thirteenth and fourteenth centuries and are well known to historians. The precise calculation of the total charges upon villein land is a difficult task but see *inter alia*: Miller, *Abbey and Bishopric of Ely*, pp. 109–11; R. H. Hilton, *A Medieval Society* (London, 1966; repr. Cambridge, 1983), pp. 144–5; *Ancient Petitions Relating to Northumberland*, ed. C. M. Fraser (Surtees Soc., clxxvi, Durham, 1966), nos. 96–7, pp. 119–21; H. P. R. Finberg, *Tavistock Abbey* (Cambridge, 1951), pp. 249–50; R. H. Britnell, "Production for the Market on a Small Fourteenth-Century Estate", *Econ. Hist. Rev.*, 2nd ser., xix (1966), p. 386.

middle ages when demesnes and labour services were in dissolution. In places where aggregate proceeds of rent also grew in earlier centuries, this growth came very often from new tenures, mostly additions to rentable land through reclamations or through leases of demesne lands. Undoubtedly, on many thirteenth-century estates rents or rent-like charges on older holdings also tended to rise, but the stimuli behind the rises and the conditions which made them possible did not come from the lords' increased powers as feudatories – since these were relatively constant – but from the economic changes of the pre-plague period which made it easier and more profitable for lords to make fuller use of their powers.[24]

Finally, even at their highest, these powers did not as a rule enable the landlords to add to their wealth or income by dispossessing their villeins, as the German *Junkers* were to do in the sixteenth and seventeenth centuries. Indeed Brenner betrays a certain lack of acquaintance with the age when he implies that mass eviction of villeins was a practice in which landlords could regularly engage. Apart from the well-known evictions by new Cistercian foundations, there were remarkably few instances of arbitrary dispossession. The usual punishment for a villein defaulting on his rent or services, or neglecting his house or holding, was a fine. Small wonder that villeins came to assume a hereditary interest in their holdings which rivalled that enjoyed by free tenants.

To sum up. In order to prove that the thirteenth- and early fourteenth-century subsistence crises were caused by the prevailing class structure, and in particular by the excessive exploitation of serfs by their lords, rather than by a shortage of land, Brenner would have to demonstrate *inter alia* that seigneurial power was greater in the thirteenth century than in the twelfth or the fourteenth, and that the personal or legal disabilities of peasant tenure were correspondingly worse. All in all it is probable that, even though serfdom exposed peasants to greater exploitation by landlords than that suffered by free men, villein tenure in the thirteenth century could often provide a measure of protection against the rigours of the market in a period of increasing inflation and land hunger – protection which many a sixteenth-century English peasant must have wished he possessed.

[24] Brenner wisely neglects to establish a causal link between feudal class relations and the coming of plague to Europe in the mid-fourteenth century.

IV

Exclusive preoccupation with the lord's supposedly unlimited powers over his villeins is also responsible for Brenner's confused view of manorial investment. He invites this confusion by his very formula of the "difficult and costly processes" of buying up land and investing, which lumps together purchase of land with productive investment. In the language of modern economics, purchases of land represent merely extensions "in width" of individual enterprises, whereas additions to productive capital or investment "in depth" come only from expenditures on improvements. What characterizes medieval landlords is not their reluctance to engage in the acquisition of land; greater landlords who disposed of investable funds (and not all of them did) were adding to their possessions throughout the thirteenth and early fourteenth centuries. What they did not as a rule do was to devote a comparable share of their resources to investment "in depth".[25] This failure was partly to be accounted for by the insufficient supply of new technological possibilities. Reclamations apart, the building of newer and better barns, or additions to livestock where pasture was sufficient for the purpose, were nearly the only forms of capital in which "net" investment "in depth" was possible. Even on the estates of the improving landlords of the thirteenth century, the improvements were, as a rule, brought about not by large productive investments of capital but by more efficient administration, better systems of accounts, more rational disposal of produce and, occasionally, by slight changes in crops and rotation. None of these improvements required or absorbed much capital. Some capital was, of course, employed by thirteenth-century landlords when adding to cultivated areas, either by reclamation or by purchase. But as we have already suggested, these additions could not be expected to raise the productivity of manorial cultivation, though they may have

[25] For discussions of landlords' investment, see R. H. Hilton, "Rent and Capital Formation in Feudal Society", repr. in his *English Peasantry in the Later Middle Ages*; M. M. Postan, "Investment in Medieval Agriculture", *Jl Econ. Hist.*, xxvii (1967). The activities of Adam of Stratton, analysed by Hilton, clearly demonstrate that when an upstart clerk, money-lender and associate of Jewish financiers – and Stratton was all of these – found himself in charge of a large estate, he was able to conduct himself like a true land-speculator and developer of our own age, even though the estate and the lordship he administered (those of the countess of Albemarle) were as "feudal" as any great estate of that period.

augmented the aggregate product of individual manors. The reason why they nevertheless attracted the bulk of their owners' investable savings is that in the middle ages acquisition of land was the one employment of capital which its owners preferred, indeed exalted, above all other employments.

This preference was deeply rooted in the mode of life and scale of values of feudal nobility. A gentleman's or a baron's standing in his region or in the country as a whole; the following he was able to recruit and the power he could mobilize in times of political and military stress; his ability to provide for daughters or to form family alliances, and even to ensure salvation by religious or charitable endowments – in effect, every benefit and privilege a feudal lord esteemed most – were best measured and secured by the size of his landed estate. It is for this reason that landlords failed to channel into productive use the bulk of the savings they were able to make. Many, perhaps most, of them also failed to save, and this double failure is one of the reasons why manorial landowners themselves failed to escape the economic malaise of the age.

3. *Agrarian Class Structure and the Development of Capitalism: France and England Compared*

PATRICIA CROOT and DAVID PARKER

Robert Brenner's exposure of the weakness of traditional explanations for the pattern of economic development in late medieval and early modern Europe is welcome and effective. His insistence on the necessity to examine in comparative fashion the class structures of different European countries is also to be applauded. But in the process of making a number of important observations he so telescopes long-term economic trends that crucial stages in them are obscured, and his explanation for the contrasting developments in England and France in particular is open to serious doubt.

The core of his argument is that it was the failure of the English peasant to establish secure property rights which made possible the concentration of estates in the hands of capitalist landlords who leased them to capitalist tenant farmers, whereas in France the success of the French peasantry in establishing complete freedom was an insuperable barrier to economic progress. Both halves of this argument are suspect. As far as England is concerned, it is based on generalization and a reading "backwards" of economic history from the end of the seventeenth century; as far as France is concerned, the position of the peasantry is misunderstood.

Brenner has succumbed to the general unwillingness to believe that agricultural development could take place anywhere except on *large* farms which made *large-scale* capital investment possible and profitable. Any examination of the development of capitalist farming from the point of view of "large, consolidated holdings farmed on the basis of capital improvement with wage labour",[1] besides

[1] Above, p. 28. These "large farms" are never defined – an idea of the acreage meant would probably save a good deal of unnecessary argument – and regional variations in viable farm sizes are ignored. Probably the "large" tenant farms formed a very small percentage of total farm area well into the eighteenth cen-

referring more to eighteenth-century developments, must necessarily concentrate on large landlords. This produces a circumscribed view of the real developments in England in the early modern period since it seems to eliminate the "peasantry" from participating in this development except by their disappearance. Because he believes that large-scale farms were a *sine qua non* of a "real agricultural breakthrough",[2] Brenner condenses three centuries of agricultural development and then generalizes from the existence of large farms. While important reclamation schemes and the floating of water-meadows did require heavy financial resources, other improvements, such as manuring, new crops and even convertible husbandry, could be undertaken on holdings of any size, financed by the farmer himself either from profits or by loans.[3] The real agricultural revolution was a long-continuing process of good husbandry, hard to detect where farmers left no records; but careful scrutiny of inventories left by the sheep-and-corn farmers in Sussex or those of open-field Oxfordshire has revealed significant improvements made with leys, a concern with increasing livestock to give more manure, and the introduction of clovers and pulses in a longer rotation to reduce fallowing and increase wheat production.[4] The object was plainly to take advantage of better prices, since grain gave a better return per acre than sheep, especially for the small farmer, and such an adaptation to market demands and an awareness of profit is apparent wherever farmers have left accounts or diaries.[5] While fundamental improvements were carried out by

tury. Even in 1830 two-thirds of English tenant farms were under 100 acres: L. A. Clarkson, *The Pre-Industrial Economy in England, 1500–1700* (London, 1971), p. 66; and this after the greatest period of consolidation in the eighteenth century.

2 Above, p. 49, n. 81.

3 The large numbers of bills and bonds in inventories show that a great deal of substantial borrowing went on, some of which may well have been used for this purpose. Clover seed was being sold in Exeter by 1668 for 2d. or 3d. a pound, so it would not have required much outlay to sow a few acres: R. V. Lennard, "English Agriculture under Charles II", in W. E. Minchinton (ed.), *Essays in Agrarian History*, 2 vols. (Newton Abbot, 1968), i, p. 176.

4 J. Cornwall, "Farming in Sussex, 1540–1640", *Sussex Archaeol. Colls.*, xcii (1954), p. 58; M. A. Havinden, "Agricultural Progress in Open-Field Oxfordshire", in Minchinton (ed.), *Essays in Agrarian History*, i.

5 Cornwall, "Farming in Sussex, 1540–1640", pp. 60–3; E. Kerridge, "Agriculture, c.1500–c.1793", in *V.C.H. Wiltshire*, iv, pp. 54–5; J. Thirsk, "Farming Techniques", in J. Thirsk (ed.), *The Agrarian History of England and Wales*, iv, *1500–1640* (Cambridge, 1967), pp. 197–8; M. Campbell, *The English Yeoman under Elizabeth and the Early Stuarts* (New Haven, 1942), pp. 171–6. The few

all levels of farmers,[6] they were vital for the survival of the small, vulnerable sheep-and-corn farmers who lacked the acreage or capital for large sheep flocks. In fact the overriding need for flexibility to permit the adoption of new crops could bring them into conflict with their landlords; in Norfolk tenants enclosed their strips and sowed turnips, thus interfering with the foldcourse system in which many landlords had a greater economic interest and which required extensive grazing.[7] The peasant, far from being an obstacle to economic development, may actually have supplied its impetus by adopting new practices or new crops or just by showing landlords the profits that good husbandry could bring.[8]

In the same way, the changes in landholding and agrarian structure in England are usually given a lord-centred explanation. Looked at from the manorial viewpoint, customary tenants are seen as the bottom rung of the farming ladder, destined to become wage-labourers if they fail, but little is said of the customary tenant as landlord, or the unknown number of landless husbandmen without the freehold interest of the customary tenant, who leased small parcels mainly on a very short-term basis. Customary tenants with fixed rents, even though fines might be increased, were in a position to capitalize on the demand for land and rising rents.[9] This subletting

farmers whose records survive can only be a fraction of those who worked out by experience how to get the best out of their particular soil type and conditions. For instance, the tenants of Mudford and Hinton in 1554 proposed to divide up the common fields because then "every man will use a further trayvale and dylygence with his londe to converte yt to the best use and purpose": *Tudor Economic Documents*, ed. R. H. Tawney and E. Power, 3 vols. (London, 1924), i, pp. 61–2.

6 J. Cornwall, "Agricultural Improvement, 1560–1640", *Sussex Archaeol. Colls.*, xcviii (1960), p. 123; W. G. Hoskins, *Devon* (London, 1954), pp. 93–4.

7 K. J. Allison, "The Sheep-Corn Husbandry of Norfolk in the Sixteenth and Seventeenth Centuries", *Agric. Hist. Rev.*, v (1957), pp. 26–8. It was the very rigidity of sheep-and-corn husbandry that made improvement so vital and so apparent in these areas, rather than the presence of large farms.

8 M. A. Havinden, "Lime as a Means of Agricultural Improvement", in C. W. Chalkin and M. A. Havinden (eds.), *Rural Change and Urban Growth, 1500–1800* (London, 1974), esp. pp. 127–8. Yeoman and tenant farmers actually appear to have antedated the landlords' interest in liming by a good hundred years. J. Thirsk, "New Crops and their Diffusion: Tobacco-Growing in Seventeenth-Century England", *ibid.*, p. 97, points out that peasants, using only family or minimum wage labour, were quick to adopt economically viable cash crops, and that the lack of success with other innovations should probably be attributed to causes other than the peasants' resistance to change.

9 For example, P. Bowden, "Agricultural Prices, Farm Profits, and Rents", in Thirsk (ed.), *Agrarian History of England and Wales*, iv, p. 689. It would prob-

was, of course, a purely economic relationship, with no elements of feudalism or "compulsion" in it, unlike customary tenure.[10] On the other hand, leasing of demesne sometimes still carried a feudal connection in the form of manorial perquisites and did not necessarily open up the capitalist perspective suggested by Brenner.

One reason why Brenner inflates the role of the large capitalist farmer at the expense of the part played by the peasant is that he correspondingly underestimates the latter's legal position. Though he admits that the ability of manorial lords to get rid of their customary tenants is still a matter of controversy,[11] he accepts wholesale Tawney's conclusions that variable fines were more common than fixed fines and that, unless custom of the manor prevented "unreasonably" high fines, the courts would not support the tenant's appeals against them.[12] In fact by the early seventeenth century the courts had developed principles concerning the admission of copyhold custom in common law courts, and an "unreasonable" custom was considered void;[13] the courts also developed their own idea of what constituted an unreasonable fine – manorial custom did not necessarily come into it. However, even if a manorial lord could raise the fines and, in fact, did so to a considerable degree, this does not in itself prove that the higher fines drove the peasants off the land. There is also a difficulty here in using the term "peasant" to refer to all customary tenants, or even all those who worked the land, since economic variations within these groups were very large. Consequently, however high fines became, there was usually someone with the capital to buy the copyhold; indeed in some manors

ably be more accurate, therefore, to regard surveys of customary tenants not so much as showing whether a tenant had enough acres for subsistence, but as an indication of an individual's capital assets. In any case the study of an individual manor can be misleading for, while a tenant may only have a miserable seven-acre holding in a given manor, he may well have broad acres in several other manors, making a mockery of attempts to calculate the number of subsistence peasants on random manors.

[10] R. H. Hilton, *The Decline of Serfdom in Medieval England* (London, 1969), p. 44. Subletting is largely ignored when surveys are analysed because evidence for it is so sparse and cannot be readily analysed statistically, though it is usually acknowledged that subletting may substantially alter the picture presented by the surveys.

[11] Above, pp. 47–8 and n. 76.

[12] R. H. Tawney, *The Agrarian Problem in the Sixteenth Century* (New York, 1967), p. 293.

[13] A. W. B. Simpson, *An Introduction to the History of the Land Law* (London, 1964), p. 161.

vacant holdings were open to the highest offer with the implication that the lord was obliged to accept the highest bid.[14] Brenner attributes the relative freedom of western peasants in the late medieval period to the strength of their communal village institutions in resisting their lords' encroachments. Why therefore does the same argument not apply in the sixteenth century when the institutions were still there in common-field manors? The cases that were taken beyond the manor to the central courts show that co-operative action was indeed being carried out, and with some success. Furthermore, the number of cases cited where action by manorial lords was responsible for removing most or all of the tenants, customary or otherwise, is rather small considering the number of manors, and seigneurial action does not seem to be the prime factor in the change in the agrarian structure and economic development.

Just as Brenner passes over the contribution of the English peasant and minimizes his independence, so he exaggerates the independence of the French peasantry. This is not to deny that the rights of the French peasantry were an obstacle to more rational farming, particularly communal rights, but these would not have been an insuperable obstacle if the economic incentives and determination to override them had existed. Indeed, during the course of the sixteenth and seventeenth centuries the majority of peasants were so squeezed that they could not survive on the income from their land alone and were forced to seek supplementary employment.[15] A significant minority became totally dispossessed and, if they could not find more than intermittent employment, joined the vagabonds that caused such problems for the urban authorities. This process did not only take place in regions devastated by warfare, but also in the vicinity of the great towns, where the urban bourgeoisie was buying up the estates of destitute peasantry and nobility alike, and in regions where transport facilities offered access to markets. It appears to have reached exceptional proportions in the Toulousain and Lauragais, where the *parlementaires*

[14] It is not always clear whether or not, when a tenant died leaving no widow, heirs or reversioners, the lord could take the land into his own hands and, if a fine was offered, lease it as he chose and without the consent of the homage (the body of the customary tenants of the manor).

[15] P. Goubert, *Cent mille provinciaux au dix-septième siècle* (Paris, 1968), pp. 210ff.; J. Jacquart, *La crise rurale en Ile-de-France, 1550–1670* (Paris, 1974), pp. 358ff.

were consolidating their grip on the land and where, by the eighteenth century, peasant "ownership" was reduced to something like 20 per cent of the land or less.[16] Here there was also a tendency to farm by using wage labour direct rather than through the intermediary of a *fermier*.[17] Around other towns it was apparently more common to lease the estate to a *fermier*, but the same steady expropriation of the peasantry occurred, with the less accessible, and frequently the less fertile, areas being left to them to cultivate.[18] The system of *métayage*, based on the payment of rent in kind and constituting the predominant form of exploitation, also contributed to the dispossession of the peasantry. The tenants became increasingly dependent on the landlord for material, equipment and finance. Most leases, both under the system of *métayage* and of *fermage*, were limited to between five and nine years, and (as Brenner somewhat contradictorily recognizes) could be renewed to the disadvantage of the peasant.[19] Whole communities were driven into debt, and evidence of a seigneurial reaction is to be found in more than one region of France.[20] Where rents tailed off, this was largely due to the inability of the peasants to pay, rather than to their capacity to resist.[21]

In fact, in both France and England economic rather than legal considerations were instrumental in determining the pattern of landholding. The legal rights of the small English freeholders, which went hand in hand with their economic independence down to 1650, did not save them from rapid decline in the more adverse economic conditions of the late seventeenth century. Equally in France the peasantry trembled on the verge of expropriation for perhaps three centuries; this process was most advanced around the towns and least so in areas where the market did not exert a strong

[16] G. Frèche, *Toulouse et la région Midi-Pyrénées au siècle des lumières vers 1670–1789* (Toulouse, 1974), p. 207.

[17] *Ibid.*, pp. 246–8.

[18] Jacquart, *Crise rurale en Ile-de-France*, pp. 107–8.

[19] Goubert, *Cent mille provinciaux*, p. 212; Jacquart, *Crise rurale en Ile-de-France*, pp. 129ff., 332ff.; Frèche, *Toulouse et la région Midi-Pyrénées*, p. 248.

[20] E. Le Roy Ladurie, *Les paysans de Languedoc* (Flammarion edn, Paris, 1969), pp. 311ff.; Jacquart, *Crise rurale en Ile-de-France*, pp. 630ff.; G. Roupnel, *Les populations de la ville et de la campagne dijonnaise au XVIIe siècle: bibliographie critique* (Paris, 1922), pp. 257ff.

[21] Le Roy Ladurie, *Paysans de Languedoc*, pp. 309–10.

influence.[22] Had economic incentives been greater and commercial attitudes more widespread, there is little reason to suppose that the peasantry had the means to resist their complete dispossession. Moreover, the economic stagnation of the non-agricultural sector meant that the peasant had no incentive to surrender even totally inadequate holdings to seek for better things, while the associated lack of a diversified market reduced the incentives for other members of the village community to take up the holdings of the less fortunate. In any event, as time passed, the number of peasant farmers who were in a position even to contemplate such expansion diminished sharply.

Brenner's lack of appreciation of this last point derives from his failure to discern what was in effect the most striking contrast between the agrarian structures of the two countries during the sixteenth and seventeenth centuries – that is, the lack of any equivalent in France to the celebrated class of English yeomanry, which was itself the product of a process of differentiation within the ranks of the peasantry, a process not experienced by their French counterparts. Of course, this differentiation could not and did not take place without a reduction in the number of copyholders;[23] but, as pointed out above, it was not principally action by manorial lords that led to the engrossing of holdings, but the copyholders themselves who were responsible.[24] Those who already held an above-average number of acres were, given reasonable economic fortune, able to take advantage of higher prices and take over further holdings as they became available through failure of heirs or economic misfortune. The significant point, however, is not that copyholders were forced through human or economic agency to give up their holdings, but that there were others both willing because of the rising profits of farming, and able because of the capital they could amass, to take up these holdings, whereas in the fifteenth century the lord was scratching around for tenants and half-heartedly trying

[22] Frèche observes also that: "In Armagnac, as in the Albigeois, non-peasant property was distributed in a precise relationship (*en fonction des*) to the possibilities of cheap exportation of agricultural produce": Frèche, *Toulouse et la région Midi-Pyrénées*, p. 193.

[23] Mainly in the sheep-and-corn areas where grain was the staple product for the market; pastoral areas seem to have been affected in the late seventeenth century and later, and in a slightly different way.

[24] See the discussion in M. Spufford, *Contrasting Communities* (Cambridge, 1974), pp. 76–85.

to fine those who left.[25] The increasing value of land is also reflected in the amounts men were prepared to pay for a copyhold, and meant that only villagers with resources, or wealthy outsiders, could take advantage of vacant holdings; landless husbandmen were prevented from acquiring a secure stake in the land they farmed.[26] The same applied to large leasehold farms: only a man with some capital could afford to take up the lease.

By contrast, in France this period is characterized not by a differentiation within the ranks of the peasantry but, on the one hand, by their depression into a uniform, poverty-stricken mass whose holdings grew ever smaller and, on the other, by the growth of some (by English standards) very large estates consolidated by those lay and ecclesiastical landlords in a position to take advantage of the peasants' desperate plight. The growth of substantial middle-sized holdings, which could be detected at the end of the fifteenth century, was arrested and never resumed.[27] Indeed in some regions the proportion of independent *laboureurs* to humble *manouvriers* continued to decline until 1789.[28] Those who did hold their heads above water were invariably receivers or *fermiers* but in many areas seigneurs had difficulty in finding *fermiers* who could afford to take on the demesne estates,[29] a problem which did not arise in England. To compare, as Brenner does, the peasantry who possessed 45–50 per cent of cultivable land in France with owner-occupiers who held about 25–30 per cent of the land in England, as though they were the same sort of animal, is quite misleading, as a comparison of the acreage of individual peasant holdings in the two countries shows. In Ile-de-France, for example, the vast majority of the rural peasants held less than 10 hectares, most less than 5 hectares, and similar figures from all the regional studies show that 90 per cent of

[25] J. A. Raftis, *Tenure and Mobility* (Toronto, 1964), pp. 34, 190ff.

[26] Court rolls do not often record the amount of the "consideration" for which copyholds changed hands, but in one Somerset manor a holding of 37 acres plus common rights was sold for £262 in 1631: Somerset Record Office, DD/CC 131911a/7. The fine received by the lord (the dean and chapter of Wells) was only £24. 10s. 0d., and the parliamentary survey of 1650 assessed the annual value of the holding at £28. 17s. 9d.: *ibid.*, DD/CC 110001/1. This was, incidentally, held by copy for three lives, which had equal attractions with inheritance copyhold in providing for the family or taking advantage of rising prices and rents.

[27] Le Roy Ladurie, *Paysans de Languedoc*, pp. 24ff., 97; Jacquart, *Crise rurale en Ile-de-France*, *passim*; Frèche, *Toulouse et la région Midi-Pyrénées*, pp. 147ff.

[28] Roupnel, *Populations de la ville et de la campagne dijonnaise*, p. 319.

[29] Jacquart, *Crise rurale en Ile-de-France*, p. 203.

the peasantry, after meeting the claims of church, state, landlord and seigneur, were left with insufficient for the sustenance of their families, let alone reinvestment.[30] In England on the other hand by the mid-seventeenth century, despite some regional variations, there was a far greater range of holdings with a significant proportion in the middle range[31] using some wage labour and producing a surplus for the market. In a very real sense, these enterprises were the economic heirs of the pioneering capitalist farmers who had begun to emerge in the fourteenth and fifteenth centuries.[32] Not until the last half of the seventeenth century did the concentration of landed property characteristic of the eighteenth century really get under way and by then agricultural capitalism was well established. The existence of substantial leasehold farmers also made possible a degree of economic co-operation between landlord and tenant which the depressed French peasant was less and less able to sustain.[33]

Merely describing the agrarian structure, however, does not explain *why* there was a movement towards capitalist farming in England, rather than just a squeezing of the peasantry as in France. Though the development of large consolidated holdings, in France ruthlessly exploited, has been seen perhaps rightly as a transitional form between feudal and capitalist farming,[34] their exploitation never managed to break out of the old seigneurial/*rentier* framework, despite the existence of a potential labour force and despite the way in which they cut across old jurisdictions: large estates did not necessarily lead to capitalist farming. Though it is hard to estimate what effect the presence of the yeomanry in England had on

[30] *Ibid.*, p. 119; Goubert, *Cent mille provinciaux*, pp. 210ff.

[31] For a few examples of sizes, see Clarkson, *Pre-Industrial Economy in England*, p. 66; J. Thirsk, "The Farming Regions of England", in Thirsk (ed.), *Agrarian History of England and Wales*, iv, pp. 30, 32; Spufford, *Contrasting Communities*, tables 3, 7, 9, at pp. 69, 100, 138–9.

[32] Tawney, *Agrarian Problem in the Sixteenth Century*, pp. 81–2, 136–7; Campbell, *English Yeoman*, pp. 104, 160ff.

[33] Clarkson, *Pre-Industrial Economy in England*, pp. 67–8; G. Batho, "Landlords in England: B, Noblemen, Gentlemen and Yeomen", in Thirsk (ed.), *Agrarian History of England and Wales*, iv, p. 304; H. J. Habakkuk, "Economic Functions of English Landowners in the Seventeenth and Eighteenth Centuries", in Minchinton (ed.), *Essays in Agrarian History*, i, p. 199.

[34] P. Goubert, "Le paysan et la terre: seigneurie, tenure, exploitation", in F. Braudel and E. Labrousse (eds.), *Histoire économique et sociale de la France*, 4 vols. in 7 (Paris, 1970–80), ii, p. 145; Jacquart, *Crise rurale en Ile-de-France*, pp. 348, 755ff.

economic development, it probably went further than the creation of a significant home market. Would it be too far-fetched to suggest that it was the example of substantial copyholders and the like, with their strictly commercial attitude to their land and produce, that gave lords the idea of adopting commercial rather than feudal relationships, when the former became more promising? As far as the peasantry were concerned, the leasing of demesne to one or two villagers in the fifteenth century, rather than its distribution among all the customary tenants,[35] broke up what uniformity medieval peasant communities had maintained and provided an encouraging example of individual wealth and enterprise, particularly when these farmers could take advantage of sixteenth-century price rises.

In France, on the other hand, the entrepreneurial attitudes of the middle peasantry, detectable here and there, succumbed to the *rentier* mentality of the bourgeois purchasers of the land. However ruthless they were in exploiting their estates, their attitudes were always tempered by a desire to bolster the seigneurial system and to become true seigneurs themselves. They extracted every ounce of profit from seigneurial justice and used it to retain their domination over the peasantry.[36]

Thus, while we agree with Brenner that the poor economic performance of France in the early modern period is directly related to the agrarian class structure and that conversely it was the development of capitalist relations in English agriculture which was the key to economic advance here, the explanation offered for the emergence or non-emergence of such relations is unconvincing. Indeed his concept of capitalist relations is narrow and cannot do justice to the perhaps decisive role played by the small capitalist farmer at least from the early sixteenth to the mid-seventeenth century. The root of the difficulty is the assumption that petty peasant tenure was in itself an obstacle to the development of capitalism and that this explains the French tragedy. For what a comparison with England in fact reveals is that petty proprietorship was a major element in capitalist relations in the period of their formation and "breakthrough". The real crime of the French monarchy was not

[35] Raftis, *Tenure and Mobility*, p. 219; Hilton, *Decline of Serfdom in Medieval England*, p. 45.

[36] Jacquart, *Crise rurale en Ile-de-France*, pp. 410ff., 755; Roupnel, *Populations de la ville et de la campagne dijonnaise*, p. 276.

that it bolstered up petty peasant ownership but that (together with the church, seigneurs and landowners) it depressed it so brutally. The consequence was that the countryside lost its most dynamic force – a class of truly independent peasants.

Lastly, although we concur with the view that a comparative analysis of class structures is a prerequisite for a full understanding of economic development, it is surely true that at any given moment the possibility of a change in class relations and the balance of forces is related to a plurality of factors ranging from the exigencies of foreign policy to social attitudes. It is difficult to deny, for instance, that the interminable warfare in which France was involved for most of the sixteenth and seventeenth centuries did not profoundly modify the balance of class forces to the disadvantage of both the peasantry and the bourgeoisie by virtue of the insupportable burdens which they were compelled to shoulder. The prodigious scale on which offices were sold by the crown as it endeavoured to finance its wars also diverted capital from productive investment and created a welcome channel of upward mobility for those who wished to flee the uncertainties of commercial life and integrate themselves into the existing social hierarchy. By contrast, the virtual immunity of the English people from taxation in the century or so before the civil war facilitated the emergence of an interdependent group of prosperous yeomen, artisans and traders, thus contributing to the formation of a domestic market whose resilience and dynamism the French, from the mid-sixteenth century, were unable to match. The sequence of foreign and civil wars in which France was involved also prolonged the survival of the military/feudal ethos which so inhibited the development of a capitalist one.

Of course, it is possible to see the warfare of this period as an aspect of the crisis of feudalism or as part of a wider European conflict of civilizations generated by the rise of capitalism, and thus incorporate it within a Marxist framework.[37] But this involves going beyond the theoretical position expressed in Brenner's formulation that "class structures . . . , once established, tend to impose rather strict limits and possibilities, indeed rather specific long-term

[37] See J. V. Polišenský, *The Thirty Years War* (Berkeley and Los Angeles, 1971); D. Parker, *Europe's Seventeenth Century Crisis: A Marxist Reappraisal* (Our History pamphlet, no. 56, London, 1973).

patterns, on a society's economic development" and that the processes by which the structures arise are "relatively autonomous".[38] As generalizations, such statements are not unreasonable; but the inclusion of the qualifying words "rather" and "relatively" immediately indicates the problem which is raised and Brenner does not come to grips with it. His basic contention that the impact of particular phenomena such as demographic change can produce radically different results depending on the character of the class structure is acceptable. But unless he wishes to take the unlikely step of claiming that the *conjuncture* of circumstances and relatively short-term phenomena cannot affect in any significant way the pre-existing *structure*, his recognition of their interaction, far from demonstrating the autonomous nature of the evolution of class structures, actually calls it into question. Brenner appears to skirt round this difficulty and to explain the balance of class forces in terms of itself, thus making himself vulnerable to the same sort of criticism with which he so effectively exposed the proponents of the "demographic" and "commercialization" models of economic development.

[38] Above, pp. 11–12.

4. *Peasant Organization and Class Conflict in Eastern and Western Germany**

HEIDE WUNDER

In his attempt to relate agrarian class structure and economic development in order to explain long-term economic development in pre-industrial Europe, Robert Brenner has made use of the German experience in several contexts. I, however, shall restrict myself here to discussing Brenner's thesis that the "divergent evolution of peasant class organization is clearest in what is probably the pivotal comparative case – east versus west Elbian Germany".[1]

Brenner gives only a brief sketch of peasant communities in western Germany, but goes on to depict their counterparts in east Elbia in greater detail to support his thesis that the failure of the east Elbian peasants to develop strong communal organization during the middle ages finally reduced them to serfdom in the early modern period. It is the lot of the comparative historian to have to rely on textbooks and secondary literature, but unfortunately Brenner has fallen victim to the Prussian myth (*Hohenzollernlegende*) with all its contradictions and inconsistencies. Though he obviously tried to avoid this pitfall by using some recent specialist studies, he has nevertheless reproduced the main weakness of the *Hohenzollernlegende* by projecting back to the middle ages the positive and negative aspects of more recent German history. Therefore, without going into too much detail, I wish, first, to examine the factual basis of Brenner's argument and, second, to discuss his concept of class structure in the light of the German experience.

* * *

Brenner maintains that the east Elbian peasant communities were comparatively weak because, as late colonial settlements domi-

* I am greatly indebted to E. Krause and R. Tamchina who took the trouble to correct my English.

[1] Above, pp. 40–6; quotation at p. 41.

nated by landlords and their agents, they had no communal tradition. Their sense of community was weak, because there were no common lands and little co-operative agriculture in the colonial type of *Waldhufen* or "ribbon" settlement and also because villages were small and sparsely populated. The lack of *Weistümer* (declarations of custom) is taken as additional proof of this. Nevertheless, Brenner has characterized the east Elbian peasants as "one of Europe's freest peasantries".[2]

It is now well established that from the twelfth century onwards independent peasant communities were founded in east Elbia in which interference by either landlord or territorial lord in the jurisdiction and economic affairs of the village was very limited.[3] While the basic elements of communal independence and personal freedom had been developed in western Germany, corporate peasant communities are first documented in east Elbia. The peasants' favourable position was surely no gracious gift offered by the landlord, but rather the result of economic efficiency, communal organization and a strong bargaining position. Such a degree of communal independence and individual freedom was only attained in some of the territories of western Germany. The expression of peasant and seigneurial interests in a dual set of institutions, which was typical of the early development of peasant organization, was transferred to the middle Elbe region by settlers from Thuringia and Lower Saxony and transformed in the process of planned colonization. The *Lokator* (contractor) who organized and often financed this colonization attained in the village he had founded a position of considerable privilege and influence, that of *Schulz*. The landholding of the *Schulz* was larger than that of the ordinary peasant and was exempt from seigneurial dues. He was granted rights of public authority (*banalité*) and also the hereditary office of *Schulz/Richter* (judge), which meant that he presided over the village court and received one-third of all fines exacted there. At the same time he acted as rent-collector, and also supervised the compulsory services performed for the landlord. However, it would be wrong to conclude that the *Schulz*, by combining communal and seigneurial authority, impeded the development of independent political insti-

[2] Above, p. 23.
[3] *Die Anfänge der Landgemeinde und ihr Wesen*, 2 vols. (Konstanzer Arbeitskreis für mittelalterliche Geschichte, Vorträge und Forschungen, vii–viii, Stuttgart, 1964).

tutions at village level. It was his hereditary status alone which enabled him to resist becoming a mere agent of the lord. On the contrary, *Schulz* and peasant community appear as a unit in which the *Schulz* acted as the spokesman of peasant interests and the leader of peasant protest, not only during the middle ages but also in the early modern period up to the age of reform.[4]

The lack of *Weistümer* in most parts of east Elbian Germany is easily explained. During the period of colonization, legal instruments had been developed which dispensed with the need for *Weistümer* to record local customs and usages and to declare peasant and seigneurial rights. The act of foundation was recorded in a document called the *Handfeste* (village charter) which defined the extent of the village, the legal status of the peasants in relation to their holdings, their dues and labour services, tithes, communal rights, the village court, and the position of both *Schulz* and parish priest. These village charters became the accepted point of reference in the event of any dispute between peasant community and lord. In those regions which were settled before the charter of foundation became common form, the first written document establishing the existence of a peasant community is frequently that recording the settlement of a dispute between lord and peasants or the community's acquisition of additional land for communal use. The second component of the *Weistümer*, village by-laws, did exist in east Elbian territories as well, but were there called by the alternative names of *Willküren*, *Beliebungen* and *Dreidingordnung*.[5]

The arguments drawn by Brenner from geographical and demographic evidence also need correction.[6] In fact, two regions with characteristic types of settlement should be distinguished in east Elbia – one which was restricted to parts of Saxony and Silesia where *Waldhufen* settlements predominated (and it is these Brenner seems to have in mind), and another of far greater extent where nucleated villages predominated. The nucleated villages had open fields whereas *Waldhufen* settlements had consolidated fields,

[4] J. Ziekursch, *Hundert Jahre schlesischer Agrargeschichte vom Hubertusburger Frieden bis zum Abschluss der Bauernbefreiung* (Breslau, 1915).

[5] For example, K. H. Quirin, *Herrschaft und Gemeinde nach mitteldeutschen Quellen des 12. bis 18. Jahrhunderts* (Göttingen, 1952).

[6] See C. T. Smith, *An Historical Geography of Western Europe before 1800* (London, 1967); A. Mayhew, *Rural Settlement and Farming in Germany* (London, 1973).

but both were generally organized on the lines of a three-course rotation system.[7] It is true that there were no common lands (*Allmende*) in *Waldhufen* settlements but nevertheless the peasants here had to organize the grazing of their animals on a communal basis because the *Schulz* and often the landlord enjoyed certain grazing rights. Even if close co-operation in the fields had not been essential, institutions existed which would have facilitated the development of a communal spirit, namely the village court and the church. In the open-field villages, peasant co-operation worked along the same lines as in western Germany, as is demonstrated by the existence of identical articles in the by-laws of both east and west Elbia.[8]

As to the size of villages, there were usually marked differences between the smaller villages of the indigenous Slavs and the larger German villages. In East Prussia the native Prussian peasants also lived in larger villages as a result of seigneurial administration, while the Prussian freemen preferred hamlets. Even allowing for the great local and regional variations in both eastern and western Germany, the latter was without doubt the more densely populated region, because more intensive forms of cultivation (horticulture and viticulture) could be practised there; also, more industrial production was possible because of the existence of natural resources not to be found on the plains of northern and eastern Germany.

The crucial test of peasant solidarity is, of course, the strength of peasant resistance to seigneurial influence and exploitation. The two best-known examples of peasant action in east Elbia – the "rising" of the Warmian peasants in 1440 and the Samland rising of 1525 – do not fit the "colonial" situation as conceived by Brenner. To him they appear exceptional and therefore to be regarded as deviations from the general pattern, explainable by the high density of population in both regions and, in the Samland, by the persistence of comparatively powerful forms of Prussian peasant community undisturbed by German colonization. This view requires modification. In the first place, the Warmian peasant "rising"[9] was

[7] W. Abel, *Geschichte der deutschen Landwirtschaft vom frühen Mittelalter bis zum 19. Jahrhundert* (Stuttgart, 1962), p. 200.

[8] There are also surprising similarities between German and English by-laws; see W. O. Ault, *Open-Field Farming in Medieval England* (London, 1972).

[9] V. Röhrich, "Ein Bauernaufruhr im Ermlande, 1440–42", *Königliches Gymnasium zu Rössel. Bericht über das Schuljahr Ostern 1893–4* (1894).

not a violent revolt of peasants. Upholding the rights embodied in their village charters, several peasant communities of the "colonial" type under the leadership of their *Schulz* protested against certain new forms of economic exploitation which the Warmian chapter had attempted to establish. As the dispute could be settled neither by the parties concerned nor through the arbitration of the bishop, it was treated by the territorial assembly as a legal process. Notwithstanding several attempts by deputies of the territorial assembly to mediate between the parties, the peasants proved unwilling to abandon their demands for the restitution of "old law" as laid down in their charters and finally, after two years of legal wrangling, the bishop arrested some of them. Only through the intervention of burghers from the town of Braunsberg were the peasants released, but they were heavily fined and had to make public submission. This "rising" demonstrates the power of the "colonial" peasant communities, the cohesion between community and *Schulz*, the comparative security afforded by village charters and the overarching legal system, and a degree of solidarity between the towns and the peasantry.

The second case is the Samland rising of 1525. The Samland is the northern part of East Prussia,[10] and formed part of the Baltic territories conquered by the crusading Teutonic Knights in the thirteenth century. It is true that this part of the Teutonic Knights' state was comparatively densely populated by indigenous Prussians and that German villages were only located in some wooded areas. The traditional Prussian pattern of dispersed settlement was transformed around 1400 by the policy of concentrating settlements. By 1525 the Samland had become the most densely populated part of Prussia, largely because of efforts made to secure it from the devastation of war and of mercenary troops in order to provide for the territorial lord who resided in nearby Königsberg. Yet the Prussian peasant rising of 1525 cannot by any means be regarded as the achievement of powerful Prussian peasant communities which had been substantially unaltered by German colonization. To make this very point, however, Brenner cites an article by Reinhard Wenskus,[11] not appreciating the fact that Wenskus was dealing primarily with Prussian freemen, and not with the majority of

[10] H. Mortensen, *Siedlungsgeographie des Samlandes* (Stuttgart, 1923).
[11] Above, pp. 43–4, n. 71.

Prussian peasants. The sources point to the fact that all sections of the peasantry in this multi-ethnic region took part in the rising – German peasants, Prussian peasants, and also Prussian freemen, who in view of their economic status can still be classed as peasants even though socially they belonged to a military "caste" promoted by the Teutonic Knights. As far as we can tell from the records, the leaders of the rising came from the privileged ranks of German villages and from the Prussian freemen, who had already provided the leaders of "peaceful" legal protest before 1525. Indeed, following Brenner's line of argument, it is difficult to explain why Prussian peasants joined the rising at all, and why moreover they seem to have comprised the major part of the peasant army. No doubt there were strong social and cultural links among the Prussian peasants but they had been unable to preserve or develop political institutions at the village level. It should be added that peasants from other regions of East Prussia also tried to join the Samland peasant army, but the speedy conclusion of a truce prevented the spread of the rising beyond the Samland and Natangen.[12] In spite of their defeat the peasants were not so completely broken as to desist from further protest against seigneurial encroachment. Sixteenth-century records are full of peasant actions, and the peasant problem constantly came before the territorial assembly of estates for debate.[13]

Brenner has tried to link the different routes towards capitalism with divergences in feudal class relationships which, as he would have it, already divided society in western and eastern Europe in the middle ages. He attempts to substantiate his case by comparing peasant (class) organization and peasant/landlord conflicts in Germany west and east of the Elbe. However, as I have tried to show, the factual basis of his argument does not stand the test of re-examination and therefore does not warrant his conclusions: neither essential divergences in peasant organization nor in the power of peasant protest in east as opposed to west Elbian Germany have been established for the middle ages. The modern geopolitical

[12] H. Wunder, "Zur Mentalität aufständischer Bauern", *Geschichte und Gesellschaft*, Sonderheft 1, *Der deutsche Bauernkrieg, 1524–1526* (1975); H. Wunder, "Der samländische Bauernaufstand von 1525", in R. Wohlfeil (ed.), *Der Bauernkrieg, 1524–26* (Munich, 1975).

[13] N. Ommler, "Die Landstände im Herzogtum Preussen, 1543–1561" (Univ. Bonn, Phil. Diss., 1966).

division between east and west Elbian Germany and more generally between eastern and western Europe simply does not apply to medieval Europe. In trying to explain the origin of this division Brenner hardly does justice to the Baltic area and its cultural and economic significance to northern and eastern Europe during the middle ages, which can be paralleled by that of the Mediterranean for southern Europe. This reflects the fact that central European historians have not been particularly successful in presenting their findings to their British and French colleagues. As perhaps the outstanding example of this failure the work of Wilhelm Abel may be cited: his *Agrarkrisen und Agrarkonjunktur* is not even mentioned by Brenner.[14]

* * *

It is also difficult to follow Brenner's argument on the more theoretical level because, first, he does not consider sufficiently seriously the two analytical aspects of class structure which he himself distinguishes at the very beginning of his article – namely, the "labour process" or the "social forces of production" and the "property relationship" or "surplus-extraction relationship" – and second, he obscures the distinction between "property relationship" (*Eigentumsverhältnisse*) and "surplus-extraction relationship" (*Ausbeutungsverhältnisse*).[15]

As to late medieval "property" relationships,[16] it has to be remembered that peasants all over Germany had gradually acquired long-term or even hereditary rights of land usage, landlords finding it more profitable to live on rents. These property relationships remained essentially unchanged up to the nineteenth century, even in large parts of east Elbia.[17] Economic changes, however, affected the surplus-extraction relationships and the labour process. Even if we accept that the whole system of surplus extraction was based on

[14] W. Abel, *Agrarkrisen und Agrarkonjunktur* (Berlin, 1935; 3rd edn, Hamburg and Berlin, 1978); Eng. trans., *Agricultural Fluctuations in Europe from the Thirteenth to the Twentieth Centuries* (London, 1980).

[15] Above, p. 11.

[16] According to German legal history, the term "property" (*Eigentum*) cannot be applied to medieval forms of possession.

[17] There were regions, of course, where manorial lordship (*Grundherrschaft*) had not been introduced – as in some areas bordering the North Sea – and also those where manorial lordship was almost totally abolished on the nobility's estates after the Thirty Years War – as in Mecklenburg.

non-economic coercion, it is nevertheless the case that changes in economic life deeply influenced the surplus-extraction relationship between peasant and lord. The commutation of rent in kind to a fixed money rent, for instance, which was significant for the status of the colonial peasantry of east Elbia, proved to be advantageous to them because it reduced the landlord's share in their surplus (*Mehrprodukt*). Yet long-term devaluation of customary money rent reduced the lords' income and made them look for new methods of surplus extraction. At first they tried to recompense themselves for the loss by using the labour services of the peasants to exploit their own rights of *banalité*. This is illustrated by the Warmian peasant rising of 1440–2, where the peasants were reacting to attempts to increase seigneurial income by the intensified exploitation of woods and lakes, which to them meant additional services in transporting honey, floating timber, and fishing.[18] It was only later, when seigneurial demesnes had been enlarged, that peasant labour services in the fields were also enforced.

While devaluation of rents occurred all over Germany, the precise nature of the seigneurial reaction differed widely from one area to another according to the varying options available to both landlords and peasants. Many knights were impoverished, many took to highway robbery, some survived as mercenaries, some were able to embark on diplomatic careers, some accumulated estates and squeezed their peasants, and some took to working their lands themselves (as in Brandenburg). In light of the impact of grain exports on the east Elbian gentry and the lack of any major agrarian incentives to the class of landlords in the more central parts of Germany, Brenner's statement that class structures were "highly resilient in relation to the impact of economic forces"[19] must be questioned. Already by the middle of the seventeenth century the traditional form of surplus extraction in many parts of east Elbia had changed from customary money rent (*Rentengrundherrschaft*) to compulsory labour service on the seigneurial estate (*Gutsherrschaft*). Thus the peasants lost control of their economic resources in addition to their financial independence. They had to adjust their labour force, their livestock and their equipment to the requirements of the east Elbian type of *Gutsherrschaft*. Peasant economy was reduced to a variable of seigneurial economy; and the urban

[18] Röhrich, "Bauernaufruhr im Ermlande", p. ii. [19] Above, p. 12.

economy contracted because both peasant and landlord either did not or could not use the local market. While serfdom (*Erbuntertänigkeit*) which was newly introduced into these territories must be regarded as a radical innovation in the relationship between peasant and landlord, the form of serfdom (*Leibeigenschaft*) which had long been established in many west and south-west German territories did not in general touch upon the labour process, but was used as a means to extract additional rent in money or kind.

As these brief remarks may have suggested, a major problem arises because Brenner does not consistently apply his analytical criteria of class structure to the different cases he wishes to compare. This applies also to his notion of "power". It was probably the Marxian concept of "class struggle" (*Klassenkampf*) as the main driving force of social progress that induced Brenner to restrict "power" to *class* power, be it the power of peasants or of landlords as a class, while *political* power – interrelated and interwoven as it may be with that of the class of landlords – is not conceived as a distinct entity. Wherever the state, being the most prominent representative of central political power, is mentioned it is only as the instrument of the ruling class or as a "class-like" competitor with the landlords for the peasants' surplus.[20] Useful as this contrasting of two classes may be to define the various stages of social evolution (*Gesellschaftsformationen*) it is not very helpful in analysing the historical process. For in fact the common interest of landlords and the state in the exploitation of the peasantry generated different attitudes towards them, the state being concerned to preserve the peasant class as its economic and military base, the landlords being interested only in an adequate labour force to secure the best possible profit for themselves. Besides, the state did not entirely rely on the peasants' surplus, as it could also dispose of such additional resources as mines and customs dues. The balance of class power therefore also depended on the strength or weakness of the central political power – that is, the relative strength of landlords as the *local* and the state as the *central* political power. In the west European context Brenner regards the west German "mini-absolutisms" as the "archetypal" case of the state developing as a "class-like surplus-extractor" using the instrument of *Bauernschutz* (protection of the peasantry by the state).[21] Yet he hardly touches upon this

[20] Above, pp. 36, 55–6. [21] Above, pp. 55–6.

subject when dealing with the development of peasant class power in Europe and its "pivotal comparative case of east versus west Elbian Germany", though it is precisely the Prussian experience which points to the relevance of political power for surplus-extraction relationships, and the Prussian absolutist sovereigns who are best known for the policy of *Bauernschutz*.

But the notion of class power has also to be enlarged with regard to the peasants. The class organization of the medieval peasantry was rooted in communal village institutions competent to exercise "public authority" in the village and its territory. Peasant communities participated in the system of "legitimate" power and were part and parcel of medieval political life.[22] This demonstrates that the medieval pattern of power distribution differed in its essentials from the modern pattern. Any attempt to explain the rise of *Junker* class power in east Elbia has therefore to evaluate a series of changes in the balance between central and local powers as well as the decline of the economic, social and political position of the peasantry.

[22] H. Wunder, *Die bäuerliche Gemeinde in Deutschland* (Göttingen, 1985).

5. *A Reply to Robert Brenner*

EMMANUEL LE ROY LADURIE

I wish to comment briefly on Robert Brenner's article, carefully following the thread of his argument, which is certainly very skilful and well informed but at times not only somewhat superficial but also extremely insular. For my part, I will speak of a "neo-Malthusian" and not a "Malthusian" model. This takes into account the fact that many new factors have appeared since the time of Malthus to make both the factual and the theoretical position more complicated. Here then are my reactions, numbered from one to thirteen.

* * *

1. Despite what Brenner suggests at the outset of his article,[1] the neo-Malthusian model in no way turns the class structure into an abstraction. On the contrary, it incorporates it, quite simply, by taking care to stress the role of concrete social groups (landowners, farmers, agricultural workers and the like) over and above abstract economic categories (ground rent, business profits, wages). In this connection – and I apologize for citing my own work but Brenner himself has put me in this position – see my *Paysans de Languedoc*.[2]

2. Brenner criticizes both Postan's work as well as my own, but he neglects to mention (and this is curious on the part of a scholar with such an impressive command of the sources) the extensive research into European, and particularly German, rural history undertaken many years ago by Wilhelm Abel.[3] Abel's conclusions fully support the neo-Malthusian thrust of the work of Postan and myself.

[1] Above, pp. 10–11.

[2] E. Le Roy Ladurie, *Les paysans de Languedoc*, 2 vols. (S.E.V.P.E.N. edn, Paris, 1966; Flammarion edn, Paris, 1969).

[3] W. Abel, *Die Wüstungen des ausgehenden Mittelalters*, 2nd edn (Stuttgart, 1955); W. Abel, *Agrarkrisen und Agrarkonjunktur* (Berlin, 1935; 3rd edn, Hamburg and Berlin, 1978); Eng. trans., *Agricultural Fluctuations in Europe from the Thirteenth to the Twentieth Centuries* (London, 1980).

3. Brenner talks about the "surplus-extracting, or ruling, class(es)".[4] It is perhaps surprising to find a talented historian making such a simplistic assimilation between power (political) and surplus value (economic). Would Engels himself, despite his lack of nuance, have risked so summary an equation? I hardly venture to think so.

4. The neo-Malthusian and neo-Ricardian model outlined by Habakkuk in 1958,[5] and since put forward by Postan and myself,[6] in effect postulates the existence of a homoeostatic system or ecosystem, with a built-in mechanism of self-correction. This model provides for major interrelations, with secular fluctuations, which bring into play population, production, land rent, industrial and agricultural prices, real wages, landownership (fragmented or concentrated to a greater or lesser degree) and so on. Now, this model has very recently been substantiated in every important respect by Guy Bois in his masterly and monumental study of Normandy from the fourteenth to the sixteenth centuries.[7] The fact that Guy Bois considers himself a Marxist only makes my own argument the stronger. I have explained my views on this point in some detail in a long article in *Annales*.[8] Moreover, I do not deny that this homoeostatic model also contains a certain unilinear drift in the direction of agrarian capitalism.

5. I think, and on this point I differ from Postan, that the idea of a declining fertility of the soil (though not necessarily wrong) is in no way indispensable to the formulation and multi-secular functioning of a neo-Malthusian model.

6. Side by side with properly and traditionally Malthusian factors

[4] Above, p. 11.
[5] H. J. Habakkuk, "The Economic History of Modern Britain", *Jl Econ. Hist.*, xviii (1958).
[6] M. M. Postan, *Essays on Medieval Agriculture and General Problems of the Medieval Economy* (Cambridge, 1973); M. M. Postan, *The Medieval Economy and Society* (London, 1972); E. Le Roy Ladurie, "L'histoire immobile", *Annales E.S.C.*, xxix (1974), repr. in E. Le Roy Ladurie, *Le territoire de l'historien*, 2 vols. (Paris, 1973–8), ii.
[7] G. Bois, *Crise du féodalisme* (Paris, 1976); Eng. trans., *The Crisis of Feudalism* (Cambridge, 1984).
[8] E. Le Roy Ladurie, "En Haute-Normandie: Malthus ou Marx?", *Annales E.S.C.*, xxxiii (1978).

(pauperization of the peasant and the masses by demographic expansion within the framework of limited cultivable space) I believe that history must give more and more room to specifically epidemic and therefore, one might say, "biological" factors in order to explain instances of neo-Malthusian "blockages" in the fourteenth or seventeenth centuries. I have outlined my views on this subject in various articles.[9] Brenner, however, in my view greatly underestimates epidemic factors (plagues and the like) when he seeks to explain the crisis of the fourteenth and fifteenth centuries primarily in terms of seigneurial exploitation.[10] This strictly epidemic causality is, indeed, the main reason for my preferring the more adequate term "neo-Malthusian" to the older words "Malthusianism" or "Malthusian" which Brenner employs when he characterizes my position.[11]

7. I have applied the term "two-phase movement" to the sixteenth and seventeenth centuries only and not, as Brenner seems to imply,[12] to the whole period 1050–1800. As far as this very long period is concerned, I prefer to talk in terms of a chronology of two large agrarian cycles, each with an ebb and flow: 1100–1450 for the first cycle; 1450–1720 for the second.

8. The intensification of labour services in thirteenth-century England is perhaps, as Postan thinks, partly due to the unfavourable position in which the local labour force was placed *vis-à-vis* lords and large employers, caused by the heavy demographic pressure and growth registered at this period in the English (and French) countryside. This increase of labour services was perhaps also caused by institutional and power factors, as Brenner believes: it is not for me to analyse these factors here. In this period the region around Paris was more "modern" than England (in the seventeenth century, of course, the lead would pass to the north of the Channel and constitutes during these two periods, medieval and modern, the element of unilinear drift mentioned above). Be that as it may, around Paris the economic effect of strong demographic pressure in the thirteenth century was not translated into any heavier incidence

[9] E. Le Roy Ladurie, "L'unification microbienne du monde", *Revue suisse d'histoire*, xxiii (1973), repr. in Le Roy Ladurie, *Territoire de l'historien*, ii; Le Roy Ladurie, "Histoire immobile".

[10] Above, pp. 36–7. [11] Above, p. 14. [12] Above, p. 14.

of serfdom (which actually diminished), but in fact, in a perfectly Ricardian and Malthusian manner, into a very marked rise in ground rent.[13]

9. Brenner is mistaken about the Bordelais, the Sologne and Catalonia. In these three regions the depopulation of the fourteenth and fifteenth centuries was accompanied after an interval by a weakening of "evil customs", labour services and share-cropping – three types of imposition which burdened the villagers in various ways. Sometimes a peasant war favoured these developments. This also arose, among other things, from a balance of forces which depopulation had made favourable to the peasant, who had himself become responsible for the declining supply of manpower. I do not, of course, say this in any way to minimize the importance of purely cultural, institutional and social factors, which frequently culminated in the extinction of serfdom in Renaissance and pre-Renaissance Europe.

10. The model I have suggested is regional in the broadest sense of the word (western Europe). And, in formulating it, I have not, for instance, taken into account the problems relating to what remained of serfdom in early modern France (in Burgundy and Franche-Comté, for example). It is therefore quite pointless to set a counter-argument apropos a "second serfdom" in eastern Europe against my theory, as Brenner does. This "second serfdom" took place in a demographic and institutional context quite different from the one I have analysed for France from the fifteenth to the eighteenth centuries. If it were absolutely necessary to make some sort of comparison between east and west, the "second serfdom" would rather suggest to me the rise of the colonate (a sort of "first serfdom") in Gaul in the period of the Later Roman Empire and the invasions (from the third to the fifth centuries).

11. I entirely agree with Brenner that England escaped the infernal cycle of agrarian-type Malthusian misfortunes from the seventeenth century onwards (in any case, England was for centuries less densely populated than France and from this point of view therefore in a far less unenviable position). France itself would begin to escape

[13] See in this context the very interesting article by G. Fourquin, "Les débuts du fermage", *Etudes rurales*, nos. 22–4 (1966).

the inflexibility of the great neo-Malthusian type of agrarian cycle in the course of the eighteenth century, after about 1720 – that is to say, slightly earlier than Brenner thinks. It would escape much more obviously in the course of the nineteenth century: on this particular point, I think I am in agreement with Brenner, despite the scorn he professes for the economic and especially the agricultural performance of France during this period.[14]

12. Brenner displays a sort of Augustinian, Calvinist or Jansenist view of history. He thinks that for "modernity" to emerge and to develop the peasant has to be overwhelmed, expropriated by the action of lords who then themselves become the agents of a capitalist triumph; that the peasant community has to disintegrate, and so on. But this is surely only one of many possible routes to "modernization". Brenner completely underestimates the remarkable potential of the peasant family economy, as described by Chayanov, Thorner and others.[15] Its performance was particularly impressive in Holland and Belgium, where it contributed efficiently to provisioning a working population created by the new industrial capitalism, and has also been more than creditable in several regions in northern and even southern France, in northern Italy, and Japan – and also in Catalonia, which in so many respects resembles eighteenth-century Languedoc. It is Catalonia which Brenner, who has perhaps not fully appreciated all the implications of the work of Pierre Vilar,[16] assimilates (I know not why) to his beloved English capitalist models, the only ones he considers valid to enable a nation to develop.

13. However, Brenner is justified in thinking that agricultural capitalism in the strict sense of the term very often originates on the great seigneurial demesnes, providing that a number of favourable conditions are also present. But this "favourable" evolution of seigneurialism towards capitalism is not confined to England. It is

[14] For a more objective appreciation, see R. Roehl, "French Industrialization", *Explorations in Econ. Hist.*, xiii (1976).

[15] A. V. Chayanov, *Organizatsiya krest'yanskogo khozyaistva* [Peasant Farm Organization] (Moscow, 1925); Eng. trans., *The Theory of Peasant Economy*, ed. D. Thorner, B. Kerblay and R. E. F. Smith (Homewood, Ill., 1966); D. Thorner, "Peasant Economy as a Category in Economic History", in T. Shanin (ed.), *Peasants and Peasant Societies: Selected Readings* (Harmondsworth, 1971).

[16] P. Vilar, *La Catalogne dans l'Espagne moderne*, 3 vols. (Paris, 1962).

also to be found in slightly different forms in the large, relatively modern farms of the Paris region, and also in Picardy in the seventeenth and eighteenth centuries – areas which have been studied both by the Physiocrats and, in recent years, by Jacquart, Venard, Postel-Vinay and their like.[17]

* * *

However, I would not like to end on a purely critical note. Like others, I have found Brenner's article both stimulating and provocative. But I hope I have outlined some of the reasons why I cannot accept his presentation either in general terms or in some of its more particular aspects.

[17] J. Jacquart, *La crise rurale en Ile-de-France, 1550–1670* (Paris, 1974); M. Venard, *Bourgeois et paysans au XVIIᵉ siècle* (Paris, 1957); G. Postel-Vinay, *La rente foncière dans le capitalisme agricole* (Paris, 1974).

6. *Against the Neo-Malthusian Orthodoxy*

GUY BOIS

Robert Brenner's article has a dual merit: first, it courageously attacks the Malthusian model; and second, it stresses the decisive role of the class struggle in long-term economic evolution, notably in the pre-industrial phase of European history. On these two points I would support him, but without agreeing with his reasoning and while radically disagreeing with his methodological orientation.

* * *

Let me first emphasize the points on which we agree. Like him, I deplore the fact that the Malthusian model should have become the orthodox one.[1] Served by the reputation of the historians who defend it, it is crushing our historiography in its tentacles. The majority of research workers in the medieval and modern periods draw their inspiration from it, either implicitly or explicitly, and no longer even feel it necessary to justify it. If perchance another analysis challenging this orthodoxy is advanced, efforts are immediately made to reintegrate the intruder into the Malthusian fold. In such a way has it been possible to represent my own *Crise du féodalisme*[2] as an illustration and confirmation of the work of Postan and Le Roy Ladurie.[3] And in this particular case, the "salvage"

[1] By the Malthusian (or neo-Malthusian) model I mean, in general terms, any model in which the principal determinants are in the last resort of a demographic order. It would naturally be desirable to elaborate on this definition in such a way as to take into account the distinctive positions of Wilhelm Abel, M. M. Postan and Emmanuel Le Roy Ladurie, but that is not my intention here.

[2] G. Bois, *Crise du féodalisme* (Paris, 1976); Eng. trans., *The Crisis of Feudalism* (Cambridge, 1984).

[3] See E. Le Roy Ladurie's review of my *Crise du féodalisme* in *Le Monde*, 11 Mar. 1977: this book, he claims, "is in the spirit of Postan and Abel, both of them pioneers of our agrarian history. In the spirit of the old masters too, who moulded the thought of Postan and Abel . . . I am thinking of Ricardo and Malthus".

attempt rests simply on the fact that I observed in Normandy secular fluctuations in population, production, prices, wages and the like, which closely approximated those recorded in England, Languedoc and Germany.

A second point of agreement between Brenner and myself lies in the importance given to social relationships in the evolution of medieval and modern Europe. It is here in fact that the shoe pinches in the Malthusian analysis. Not that Postan and Le Roy Ladurie want to turn the social dimension into an abstraction, as Brenne implies. In actual fact, their work abounds in discussions of, among other things, the patrimonies, incomes and levies of the various social groups, and indeed they have played a pioneering role in this area of research. But in the models that they have formulated, social and political considerations are ultimately subordinated to the demographic factor, to which they have assigned the determining role. Le Roy Ladurie's "ecosystem"[4] is based on the idea of a stable equilibrium between population and resources, an equilibrium which is maintained by "homoeostatic" control implying great durability and inertia in social relationships.[5] It can, with apparent accuracy, account for alternations of boom and slump, but is totally inadequate when it comes to understanding the genesis of capitalism within the old structures. There is nothing left for Le Roy Ladurie, conscious of the difficulty, to do but assign to his "ecosystem" a movement of "drift" towards agrarian capitalism, without further specifying the origins of this mysterious phenomenon. The formula is doubtless felicitous but the explanation thin.

To summarize: Brenner is right in thinking that demographic determinism tends to obscure the role of class relations and, on this specific point, I willingly place myself at his side.

* * *

Things are less simple as soon as we leave the critical aspects of the article and begin to consider Brenner's own preferred interpretation. And rather than attempting to examine his argument in its entirety, let us instead take one of his principal themes by way of

[4] See E. Le Roy Ladurie, "L'histoire immobile", *Annales E.S.C.*, xxix (1974).

[5] "As for politics or the class struggle", writes Le Roy Ladurie, "their moment of power is still to come . . . In the final perspective, the system contains its own destiny; the effect of conflict is purely superficial": *ibid.*, p. 689.

example: the comparison between the capitalist take-off in England as opposed to the relative inertia of France. He tells us that this is a question of the different balance of forces between classes. In sixteenth-century France the peasantry are too solidly rooted on the land to be expelled from it. Conversely, on the other side of the Channel, the peasantry prove incapable of resisting seigneurial pressure. Hence the movement of expropriation favouring the emergence of capitalist relationships in the countryside which, in their turn, create the conditions for a process of industrialization.

For the moment we may pass over the fact that it is not very clear from his analysis why the same upsurge of agrarian capitalism (though of variable intensity) appeared throughout western Europe at about the same time.[6] It remains true that the hypothesis put forward by Brenner is worthy of very serious consideration. What I was able to observe in Normandy fully accords with his analysis: from 1520–30 one can see the beginnings of a tendency towards the expulsion of tenant farmers (a faint echo of the British enclosure movement), which in the end encountered fierce peasant resistance, and the complex development of which would need to be followed right through the wars of religion. This is the same class struggle as occurred in England, but the result is different because the peasantry in France proved to be very strong.[7] Unfortunately, from this point on, Brenner's analysis deteriorates. Having at the outset presented the hypothesis of an inequality in the relationship of social forces in both France and England, he must then find a satisfactory explanation for this phenomenon. What does he suggest? First, a social origin (the long history of struggle on the part of the peasant communities on the Continent); second, a political one (the

[6] It is true that Brenner tells us that the decline of serfdom and of forced labour created a new situation, but this is unacceptable. The thesis on which this rests, unfortunately sanctioned by the classics of Marxism, is in conflict with all recent research. The economic bases of the system are in reality the various rent-paying holdings within the framework of the seigneurie. And when this system disintegrated in northern France in the fourteenth century, serfdom had long since ceased to play any role whatsoever. In seeking the origin of the rupture, Brenner would in my opinion be better advised to look to the fall in seigneurial income which drove the ruling class to seek new solutions.

[7] All the same, I gladly subscribe (without having the space to justify it) to Brenner's thesis whereby the decisive part in the transition from feudalism to capitalism is played out in the countryside. This is certainly one of the keys to the "mystery" of the transition, though not readily perceived when one is obsessed by the commercial and industrial manifestations of nascent capitalism.

connection between the strength of the peasant class and the development of the absolutist state in France). Naturally, here again, there can be no question of denying the reality and the importance of these two phenomena. There is no doubt that the role of the monarchical state in providing obstacles to the development of French society from the end of the middle ages was in fact considerable. But why should this factor be isolated? Why is it alone thus favoured?[8] And by virtue of what specific predisposition would French peasants have fought better than English peasants? Why did absolutism flourish in France and not in England? To be fair, Brenner does suggest an answer, but at best it can only be regarded as a partial explanation. The precision which characterizes the rest of his article shows strange signs of weakness here. Having started from hyper-theoretical premises (the synthesis of the capitalist advance on a Continental scale) he emerges with conclusions which touch on empiricism and positivism (one isolated political fact to account for the contrary fates of two societies). Simply a false step? I see it rather as the inevitable result of a misconceived or defective epistemological approach. Brenner's thought is, in fact, arranged around a single principle: theoretical generalization always precedes direct examination of historical source material.[9] The starting-point is the fundamental principle of historical materialism: the driving role of the class struggle. And he sets out to verify it through decreasing abstraction, by comparing it with the available empirical data. This is characteristic of a system of closed thought, where ideology triumphs over scientific rationalism. The various mechanisms by which the class struggle is dominant in the historical process are normally so complex and unpredictable that it is very rare that such a unilateral approach leads to anything other than ideological short-cuts. In the present case, it results in an imposing superstructure, impressive at first sight by virtue of its very scale, even acceptable in certain of its general characteristics (and precisely because they *are* general), but extremely fragile as soon as one begins to examine what should be its foundations.

This is no mere matter of detail. In order to demonstrate the repercussions of our methodological divergence, let me try to

[8] In its extreme form, we have here the same defect of method for which the Malthusian historians can be criticized when they surreptitiously introduce the primacy of the demographic factor.

[9] *A fortiori* when one utilizes material collected by others.

approach the same problem (the comparative fate of French and English societies) in a rather different way from Brenner.[10] This alternative approach may not lead me to a perspective as global as his, but at least it makes it possible, it seems to me, to establish a few foundations indispensable to the construction of any global model. I will here summarize the principal propositions resulting from an investigation which, starting with the example of Normandy, bears on the very functioning of feudalism as a socio-economic system or a mode of production.

In the first place, in the feudal system the rate of seigneurial levies shows a tendency to fall which originates in the structural contradiction of small-scale production and large-scale property. When economic expansion draws to an end (around the middle of the thirteenth century) the fall in the rate of levy is no longer offset by the establishment of new tenures, with the result that seigneurial income in its turn tends to decrease. The crisis of the feudal system is bound up with this phenomenon: the dominant class does not succeed in maintaining the economic basis of its hegemony. This takes place against a background of social and political confrontation the results of which are, on the one hand, the strengthening of the middling peasantry and, on the other, the hypertrophy of the machinery of the state (royal absolutism). The consequence is a radical rearrangement of the production relationship, characterized by the addition to direct seigneurial levies of a centralized levy organized by the royal administration to the almost exclusive advantage of the seigneurial class.[11]

Second, there are secular movements, specific to the feudal economy, causing the alternation of economic (or demographic) growth and stagnation or recession, and also originating from the

[10] In formulating this hypothesis, I have adhered to the following two precepts: first, "pre-eminence of the historical method by as heavily researched an investigation as possible of the economic facts, and by the continuous confrontation of the partial theoretical hypotheses with reality; this in order to save oneself from the risk of speculation"; second, "the maintenance of the direction of research towards its ultimate objective, the global comprehension of a socio-economic system, because as soon as one strays, however little, from this objective, the slide into empiricism is not long delayed": Bois, *Crise du féodalisme*, pp. 18–19.

[11] In this context it is not possible to accept the term "independent extractor of the surplus", which Brenner uses to describe the monarchical state (above, p. 55). The state remains, for the most part, the instrument of feudalism, even if the use to which this instrument was actually put served in the long run to weaken feudalism by competing with direct seigneurial extraction.

structure of feudalism (hegemony of small-scale production and extensive character of growth). Constant economic and social phenomena are linked to these movements: the upsurge of agricultural prices and the relative fall of industrial prices, wages and productivity during movements of growth, and vice versa. This is indispensable to an understanding of the origins of agrarian capitalism because every movement of growth creates economic conditions which are ever more favourable both to the expansion of the dimensions of the unit of production and also to a wider recourse to the wage-earning labour force, while at the same time it increases the pauperization of the day-labourers.

In short, there is an original dynamic of the long term, a dynamic which carries within itself, in each of its phases of growth, a movement of land accumulation opening the way to new production relationships, as in the twelfth to the thirteenth, and the sixteenth to the eighteenth centuries.

Third, the first half of the sixteenth century is marked by a sudden upsurge of agrarian capitalism in western Europe: this is the period when the seigneurial class, which had for centuries made great efforts to tie the peasantry to their plots, decided to increase the demesne at the expense of holdings and to recruit hired labour. Why? Because, quite simply, of the very low level of the various rents levied on those holdings – the long-term tendency referred to above had reached a critical point. The result was that the accumulation of landed property (associated with the onset of the Renaissance) was further increased.

These three propositions, which do not follow from any pre-established schema but purely from strict examination of the facts, in my opinion constitute the bases from which can be formulated a hypothesis – and I deliberately say hypothesis – on the divergent evolution of France and England. The hypothesis is as follows: it is inequalities in the world of feudal production (and not this or that political or social factor!) which are at the root of the divergence.

At the end of the thirteenth century, northern France was the region where feudalism was most advanced. By the density of its population, the volume of its agricultural production, and its place in international exchanges, it influenced the whole of western Europe in the way that any dominant economy does. But, above all, the feudal system can be seen there – where it had its origins – in its purest and most advanced forms: small-scale production had irresistibly established itself at the expense of seigneurial demesnes, and the erosion of seigneurial levies was most marked (decline or disappearance of forced labour, weakening of the real value of fixed money rent, and so on). At the same period England exhibits an evident backwardness in this respect. In England, where feudalism had come later (and was partly imported), there are numerous archaisms: the larger role of forced labour and of the manorial economy; the more recent and weaker assertion of the rights of landholders; finally, backwardness at the level of growth itself.

In these circumstances it can readily be appreciated that, generally speaking, the crisis of feudalism, though of course still having a European dimension, actually has its epicentre in the kingdom of France. It was there that the "blockage" to growth and the decline in seigneurial revenues took their most acute forms. Shaken to its very foundations, the system had to generate the remedies necessary to its survival, in the forefront of which figured royal taxation and the development of those monarchical or princely institutions which guaranteed both the functioning of fiscal extraction and the maintenance of the tottering social order. In England on the other hand, the effects of the crisis were less severe, and for two reasons: first, because, as a result of its relative backwardness, the English economy had run up against its ceiling of growth less brutally than the French; and second, because the English nobility was (at least temporarily) able to resolve some of its own difficulties at the expense of its French counterpart[12] by means of the convulsions attendant upon the Hundred Years War, which served to weaken and even exhaust the kingdom of France.

It is probably from that point that the origins of the divergence in the development of the two societies can be discerned. France, once the storm had passed and the restructuring of its feudalism had been accomplished (that is, by the middle of the fifteenth century), plunged, by means of the traditional mechanisms of the feudal economy, into a phase of new growth – or rather, recovery – which carried within itself (as has been said earlier) an upsurge of agrarian capitalism. Moreover, through the influence that it continued to exercise over the European economy,[13] it stimulated in regions

[12] Which worsened the French crisis accordingly.

[13] Note, for example, the significant fluctuation of cereal prices in fifteenth- and sixteenth-century Europe, which closely reflects changes in the level of population.

beyond its own frontiers developments in the direction of capitalism. But it had itself gone too far in the logic of feudalism for any such expansion in new capitalist relationships to attain within its own boundaries the critical threshold beyond which such a trend would become irreversible: the peasants resisted expropriation here better than elsewhere, because the tenants were already beginning to appear as proprietors (an effect, in the final analysis, of the long-term fall in the rate of levy); and the lords, who had found some measure of salvation in the service of the state, were less inclined than elsewhere to explore new economic avenues. All in all, French society fell victim to its own advanced level of development. By virtue of having, to a large degree, led the way in the formation of European feudalism and been the first to come up against a ceiling of growth, its own restructuring was impeded. It remained ultimately the main driving force of a capitalist evolution the effects of which, however, were more on its periphery than within itself.

England, by contrast, was in an ideal position to take advantage of these developments. Sufficiently near to the most advanced feudal societies to have a high level of technical resource at her disposal, she was also sufficiently undeveloped to have escaped the consequences of the fossilization of social relations which feudal reorganization induced. The persisting crisis in seigneurial incomes, exemplified during the Wars of the Roses, forced the nobility to look for new economic solutions to their difficulties, a tendency which the general European situation encouraged. And this nobility was faced with a peasantry whose rights had been too well established for a return to serfdom to be possible, but not sufficiently determined to enable it to maintain control of the land when faced with seigneurial pressure. In other words, the relative backwardness of England's social evolution as compared to that of France was to prove its trump card in the transition from feudalism to capitalism.

As can readily be seen, the hypothesis I have here put forward differs from Brenner's in two important respects. First, the birth of capitalism is treated as a by-product of the socio-economic functioning of the feudal system as a whole; it should not therefore be studied in isolation, but in the context of the overall development of European feudalism, the various elements of which are indissolubly linked.[14] Second, the idea of the inequality of development within

[14] This is why Brenner's comparative method does not seem very convincing to me:

this whole appears to be fundamental. Variations in both the age and the degree of maturity of the feudal system in one place as compared with another probably play a leading and certainly a very complex role in the rhythms which then affect the emergence and development of the capitalist structures.[15] This is moreover a phenomenon which is found again *mutatis mutandis* in the evolution of contemporary capitalist societies.

* * *

Finally, one or two more general conclusions remain to be drawn as to the significance and importance of the divergences of analysis which divide Brenner and myself. It might be tempting to minimize them by emphasizing the many points on which we agree, and where our two analyses coincide, and even to defend the idea that the two hypotheses, although proceeding by different methods, interlock and complement one another. This would, however, be misleading. It is surely of more value to direct attention to the differences in our overall approach and methodology and to examine and analyse the theoretical basis of each – the more so as they are in effect two different applications of the theory of historical materialism.

Brenner's Marxism is "political Marxism" – in reaction to the wave of economistic tendencies in contemporary historiography. As the role of the class struggle is widely underestimated, so he injects strong doses of it into his own historical interpretation. I do not question the motivation behind such a reaction, but rather the summary and purely ideological manner in which it is implemented. It amounts to a voluntarist vision of history in which the class struggle is divorced from all other objective contingencies and, in the first place, from such laws of development as may be peculiar to a specific mode of production. Could one, for instance, imagine trying to account for the nature of the development of capitalism in the nineteenth and twentieth centuries solely by reference to social factors, without bringing into the picture the law of capitalist accumulation and its mainspring, that is to say the mechanism of surplus value?

it ends up by retaining only the internal elements of differentiation within a particular society, at the expense of such external relationships as may exist between neighbouring societies.

15 Naturally, the same reasoning could be applied to eastern Europe, where the much later emergence and consolidation of the feudal system explain the particular vulnerability of the peasantry.

In fact, the result of Brenner's approach is to deprive the basic concept of historical materialism – that is, the mode of production – of any real substance. It is significant in this respect that the idea of feudalism is totally absent from his article. To characterize "pre-industrial" society solely by reference to serfdom is both limited and inaccurate. What are the modes of production characteristic of feudalism? Is there a political economy peculiar to that system? Is it either necessary or possible to investigate the laws of its development? Brenner's approach does not deal, even at a superficial level, with any of these questions.

No less significant is the fact that Brenner has kept silent about the work of the Polish historian Witold Kula, who was the first to cast a theoretical glance at the feudal system and who succeeded in opening a wide breach in the positions of empiricism and dogmatism.[16] As long as such an attitude as Brenner's persists, that is to say as long as there is a refusal to regard the feudal mode of production as in itself a valid object of study, and to recognize that the way in which it functions still remains to be fully understood, penetration of the mystery of the origins of capitalism is prevented and a tedious oscillation from empiricism to speculation will result.

The error of such "political Marxism" lies not only in its neglect of the most operative concept of historical materialism (the mode of production). It also lies in its abandonment of the field of economic realities – to the great advantage of the Malthusian school. It is not enough to undertake a theoretical critique of the neo-Malthusian position, or to blame its proponents for underestimating one or other level of analysis. To be convincing and decisive, the critique must attack the very kernel of Malthusian interpretation in order to separate with absolute precision the valid elements from the invalid. The whole strength of this model derives from the fact that it is amply confirmed by detailed research: the importance of the demographic factor, the succession of long-term trends, the existence of ceilings of growth, and so on. By what strange perversion of Marxism is it possible to refuse to take such firm data into account on the absurd pretext that another theoretical construction rests upon it? Let us take the example of the demographic factor. It is true that a tendency to determinism (with clear ideological adaptations) has

[16] Notably in his *Théorie économique du système féodal* (Paris and The Hague, 1970); Eng. trans., *An Economic Theory of the Feudal System* (London, 1976).

characterized many historical works. It is nonetheless true that demography is essential to an understanding of the development of feudal society as a whole, for reasons which are implicit in the very nature of the feudal mode of production, namely that small-scale family production is the basic economic unit and that "reproduction" takes place on that scale according to an economic/demographic process. Postan or Le Roy Ladurie should not be criticized for giving too much importance to the demographic factor. They should on the contrary be criticized for stopping themselves in midstream and for not integrating the demographic factor into the all-embracing whole that is the socio-economic system.

The same point applies also where secular trends are concerned. The Malthusian historians have cited in evidence a series of correlations (prices, population, product and the like). Their error, it seems to me, lies in not having followed this path still further in order to comprehend the functioning of another variable which, whatever the socio-economic system, profoundly impregnates the forms of growth, namely the productivity of labour. It would appear, here also, that a movement specific to the productivity of labour (it diminishes in phases of economic growth, and vice versa) necessarily corresponds to the structural characteristics of feudalism (hegemony of the small family producer on a stable technological base), and that this movement is capable of clarifying that of other variables (prices, wages, and so on).

Thus it is by the progressive elucidation of the mechanisms of the feudal economy according to a process of increasing abstraction and generalization that a global vision of the system can be achieved. And it is by this course alone that we will finally come to understand by what subtle mechanisms the class struggle plays a driving role in the development of feudal societies.

In other words, to avoid undue emphasis on economic aspects, it is necessary paradoxically to make not less of the economic factor, but more. The flight into politics resolves nothing; on the contrary, it simply allows economic or demographic determinism to occupy the field uncontested.

One final comment. The approach I offer as an alternative to that of Brenner leads me to integrate some elements of the Malthusian analysis, such as the concept of the population/resources scissors.[17]

[17] By linking it to the tendency of the productivity of labour to decline.

This can make the various demarcation lines between the Malthusian and Marxist approaches more difficult to discern; it can even – when temptation to polemic gains the upper hand – lay me open to the charge of neo-Malthusianism. This is, however, ultimately of little consequence – because sooner or later the integration of these elements into a global model, stripped of all demographic determinism, will deprive them of their former ideological weight.

* * *

Such, in brief, are some observations that Brenner's article suggests to me. His great virtue is to have revived discussion and to have challenged a large number of accepted ideas. In so doing, he has invited a frank response. I have therefore tried to show that, beyond the few points on which we are in agreement, there is a methodological gulf that divides us. The problem exceeds, and exceeds considerably, the subject dealt with in his article. It touches on the very nature of historical materialism.

7. A Crisis of Feudalism

R. H. HILTON

The view that the social system of late medieval western Europe was undergoing a crisis had already been suggested in 1931 by Marc Bloch in his *Les caractères originaux de l'histoire rurale française.*[1] From 1949, when Edouard Perroy wrote "Les crises du XIVe siècle" in *Annales*,[2] the usefulness of the concept as a means of explaining a stage in the history of that system became well established. Interpretations varied considerably. For some, this seemed to be a crisis resulting from a maladjustment of the factors of production. A demographic collapse, followed by an agricultural depression characterized by low grain prices, had already been presented in 1935 by Wilhelm Abel as the most fundamental element.[3] This view, or variations on it, has since become the prevailing orthodoxy, of which Robert Brenner is simply the latest critic.[4] Other historians and economists, while not disputing the importance of the demographic, monetary and other aspects of the crisis to which Perroy, Postan and others drew attention, considered that the crisis was one of a whole socio-economic system, This was primarily a Marxist view, already sketched by Maurice Dobb in his *Studies in the Development of Capitalism*.[5] It was further explored in the American journal *Science and Society* and became known as the

[1] M. Bloch, *Les caractères originaux de l'histoire rurale française* (Oslo, 1931); ch. 3 is entitled "La seigneurie jusqu'à la crise des XIVe et XVe siècles".

[2] E. Perroy, "A l'origine d'une économie contractée: les crises du XIVe siècle", *Annales E.S.C.*, iv (1949).

[3] W. Abel, *Agrarkrisen und Agrarkonjunktur* (Berlin, 1935; 3rd edn, Hamburg and Berlin, 1978); Eng. trans., *Agricultural Fluctuations in Europe from the Thirteenth to the Twentieth Centuries* (London, 1980).

[4] I do not address myself in this article specifically to Robert Brenner's arguments nor to those of his critics. It should be clear, however, that while I agree with Brenner's emphasis on the overall determining role of social relationships in the evolution of feudal society, I think there are complexities which he has ignored.

[5] M. Dobb, *Studies in the Development of Capitalism* (London, 1946).

debate on *The Transition from Feudalism to Capitalism*.[6] The latest contribution from the Marxist point of view is *Crise du féodalisme* by Guy Bois, a profound working-out of theoretical issues on the basis of detailed empirical research.[7]

The concept of a general crisis of a social system was, of course, by no means far removed from the experience of historians from about 1930 onwards. Many believed, feared or hoped that the various political, economic and social crises were all part of a single crisis from which capitalist civilization would not recover. The vision was somewhat apocalyptic and in this resembled some aspects of thought in late medieval Europe. However, as we now know, well-established social systems have considerable powers of survival through adaptation. Crises by definition are turning-points in the history of a social as well as of a natural organism. The organism may die; it may also survive, more or less intact; or it may survive having undergone sufficient changes to enable it to cope with changing circumstances. After the first crisis in the fourteenth and fifteenth centuries, feudalism had a long and tortured subsequent history with various suggested terminal dates – 1640, 1789, 1917. If the first crisis of the social system did not end in its demise, we need not therefore pretend that the crisis did not happen.

If we are to discuss intelligently the crisis, or crises, of a social system, we must know what we are talking about, not only in the sense of having the empirical data but in the sense of agreeing on the definition of the system. I do not mean simply a description of its apparent contours at any given time, but rather a definition of its fundamental structure. Having defined the structure, we must then establish what is its internal dynamic, if it has one. I say "if it has one" because, as is well known, some historians think that medieval feudalism was a stagnant system which required external stimuli to get it moving towards capitalism. It should be added too, that if we are able to establish the internal dynamic, we may well also be able to establish how that dynamic breaks down.[8]

[6] The *Science and Society* debate was republished as *The Transition from Feudalism to Capitalism* (London, 1976).

[7] G. Bois, *Crise du féodalisme* (Paris, 1976); Eng. trans., *The Crisis of Feudalism* (Cambridge, 1984).

[8] The following analysis develops a suggestion made by Kohachiro Takahashi in *The Transition from Feudalism to Capitalism*, pp. 72–3, but also owes much to Bois, *Crise du féodalisme*.

The analysis of the structure of feudalism must begin with the agrarian base. However great at any particular time was the degree of urbanization in medieval Europe, the vast majority of the population – 80–90 per cent – was engaged in arable or pastoral farming, and in terms of numbers those engaged primarily in tillage vastly outnumbered the pastoral specialists. In our analysis of structure, therefore, the basic unit of production is to be sought in the arable, or better, the mixed-farming sector of the economy, since arable production, at the stage reached in the middle ages, would have been impossible without a minimum number of animals. It is within the agrarian base, therefore, that we must seek that fundamental element in the structure of the feudal mode of production which determined its health, growth and decline.

It can hardly be doubted that the basis of the rural economy throughout the whole of the middle ages was the holding of the peasant family. No doubt it fluctuated considerably in size according to the prevailing land/labour ratio, according to geographical conditions, according to the level of technology, and according to the character of the family which constituted the basic labour force. Many of these questions are still under debate – in particular, family structure. It is also the case, of course, that at most times there was considerable inequality in the size of family holdings. The basic core of family farmers, those with enough land, equipment and labour to sustain the family and its helpers, to provide for the reproduction of the economy and to pay the rent, usually had above them a few more prosperous families – freeholders, *allodiarii* and the like. More important, there was below them a fluctuating periphery of smallholders inevitably thrown off from the main mass of peasant producers when births exceeded deaths and the surplus population was not absorbed by industrial occupations, urbanization or war.[9]

It hardly needs emphasizing that it was the product of this peasant economy, or rather that part of the product which the peasant household was not able to retain within the holding (whether in labour, kind or cash), which provided the necessary support for the whole social and political superstructure of nobles, clergy, towns and state. Consequently, this superstructure depended in the first place on the relationship at any given time of

[9] See R. H. Hilton, "Reasons for Inequalities among Medieval Peasants", *Jl Peasant Studies*, v (1978).

the peasant household economy to nature. But this was a changing relationship. At one stage the successful transfer of surplus from the peasant economy was no doubt aided by certain technical improvements, especially between the tenth and the thirteenth centuries. But, on the whole, agricultural technology did not keep pace with increasing population. Even with a population increase of ½ per cent per annum under conditions of stagnation or slow-moving technology, the only solution within the bounds of the peasant household economy was the lateral expansion of holdings into hitherto uncultivated land. This resulted in a decline in the average size of the main family holdings, an increase in the number of smallholdings, and almost certainly an overall decline in the productivity of labour. Given the enormous forest areas in most European countries which existed at the height of population growth, it might seem that the lateral extension of the peasant economy need not have resulted in any deterioration in conditions. But of course the peasant economy did not exist in a social vacuum. The institutional restraints (such as forest law) on the natural growth of this economy were decisive. Furthermore, the lack of technical development which could have improved yields was also socially determined.[10]

Can the fatal tendency of a peasant household economy to enter into a self-destructive cycle of demographic expansion and impoverishment give us the answer to our historical problem? Some historians have thought so and indeed we cannot ignore this feature of peasant economic history. But if we are to analyse, not a self-contained "peasant economy" (which has probably never existed) but the *feudal* economy of the middle ages, we must consider other elements in the social structure. After all, the economy of the peasant family household was incomplete. The individual arable holding with its family labour force was never an economically self-sufficient unit. It was not simply that there were various products which had to be acquired from outside (like salt, metal objects and so on), but that it depended for its existence on natural and human resources outside the boundaries of its house-plot and its cultivated land. Meadow, grazing land, wood and turfs for fuel and building,

[10] R. H. Hilton, "Rent and Capital Formation in Feudal Society", in *Second International Conference of Economic History, Aix-en-Provence, 1962*, 2 vols. (Paris, 1965), ii, repr. in his *The English Peasantry in the Later Middle Ages* (Oxford, 1975); M. M. Postan, "Investment in Medieval Agriculture", *Jl Econ. Hist.*, xxvii (1967).

stone from quarries, and fisheries were not normally individually appropriated. Mutual help between neighbours may seldom have involved co-aration, but family labour was normally supplemented by that of a full-time servant taken from the young of other households, not to speak of part-time supplementary labour at difficult periods, especially at hay-making and harvest. Access to these extra resources was organized through the agency of another element in the structure, at one stage above the individual household, namely the village community.

Village or hamlet communities varied considerably, of course, in the scope of their collective activities and control over the resources mentioned. Tightly integrated common-field arable communities had a greater range of collective powers and responsibilities than small hamlets or scattered pastoralists, but at the least organized level some degree of collective access to resources that were not individually appropriated had to be organized. Furthermore, when one considers the relations between the peasantry on the one hand, and other social classes (not to speak of the institutions of state and church) on the other, it was normally the village or other local community representatives (usually the richer heads of households), rather than individual peasants, who faced the outside world.

When we consider the peasant household economy, which was recognized as early as the eleventh century by the bishop of Laon as that without which "no free [that is, noble] man could live",[11] or as late as the fifteenth century by an anonymous poet as that which "maintains this world",[12] it is clear that a *necessary* part of the explanation of the dynamic of feudalism was located there. Given, too, the tendency of the household economy to over-reproduce itself in relation to available resources, we also have a *necessary* explanation of the weakness of the feudal economy. At the higher level in the structure, it is again clear that the solid articulation of peasant communities by the local élites, or on the contrary the disintegration of these communities, are *necessary* features of our analysis of the wider horizons of this peasant-based social order. But, of course, the individual household economy and the socio-economic unit represented by the village community were not *specific* to feudalism.

[11] Adalbero of Laon's *Carmen ad Robertum regem* appears in French translation in *L'an mil*, ed. G. Duby (Paris, 1967), pp. 71–5.

[12] "God Spede the Plough", ed. W. W. Skeat (Early Eng. Text Soc., old ser., xxx, London, 1867), p. 69.

They are found as parts of other social formations, more recent as well as more ancient than feudalism. And though they are *necessary* elements in a description of the dynamic of feudalism, they are not in themselves *sufficient*.

To provide a sufficient explanation of the feudal mode of production, we must analyse a further element of the socio-economic structure, namely the lordship – in one of its manifestations sometimes named the fief (*feodum*), hence the term "feudalism". It is the lordship which is specific to feudalism. Within its boundaries it embraces the separate holdings of the family-based households and the higher stage of peasant organization in the village community. It is within the lordship that the two main classes of feudal society meet for the transfer of the surplus (or rather the unretained portion of the product of the holding) and its conversion into landowner income. Owing to the limited competence of feudal officialdom and the problems of communication, the lordship even had an element of regularity in character in spite of much fragmentation and reconstitution of its territorial elements. Hence even the great landed estates of kings and magnates tended to be congeries of smaller lordships.

The transfer of surplus labour, or of the fruits of surplus labour, from peasants to lords assumed a variety of forms from time to time and from place to place. It could consist of regular work throughout the year on the demesne or of occasional labour at hay-making and harvest analogous to mutual aid among peasants. Rents could be paid in kind, sometimes as survivals of ancient forms of tribute, sometimes as a proportion of the crop on the holding. They could also be paid in money, which had the advantage for the lord that the obligation of marketing was placed on the peasant, but the disadvantage that money, like other rents, tended to become fixed and to be devalued as prices rose. Lords also received income in labour, kind and cash arising from rights of dominance, such as court fines and the monopoly rights attached to essential services (milling, baking, grape-pressing), sometimes known as *banalités*. Whatever the form of income transfer, it was legitimated and guaranteed by jurisdiction. Jurisdiction was the principal expression of power in feudal society, more so than mere armed force, though armed force was always there, as it were in the wings, but visible.

An additional form of legitimation of income transfer was, of course, serfdom, about which there can be much understandable ambiguity.[13] Fully fledged juridical serfdom, where the servile peasant was totally unfree in the eyes of the public law, was only the extreme pole of peasant dependence on a dominant landowning class. At the other extreme was the free peasant holding or allod. In between was a considerable range of obligations reflecting dependence, the most important of which purported to restrict personal mobility, to restrict the free alienation of product or land, and to control inheritance. The great variety of the specific forms of dependence naturally reflect as well as determine the many separate histories which go to make up the general history of feudal society. But the variety of experience should not blind us to certain general contradictions in that society.

The most striking of the contradictions in feudalism was one which was not completely grasped by contemporaries but which was nevertheless dimly seen by some writers who were by no means sympathetic to the peasantry. As far apart as Normandy and Italy, we have similar expressions of opinion. Wace, the twelfth-century Anglo-Norman writer of a verse history of the dukes of Normandy, puts into the mouths of peasants in revolt the following words: "Let us take an oath to defend ourselves and our goods and to stick together. If they [the lords] were to wage war on us, we are thirty or forty peasants to one knight".[14] The Italian writer, Tamassia, says of peasants: "United they could confound Charlemagne. When they are by themselves, they aren't worth so many chickens".[15] These lords, with their armed retainers and their far-reaching private or public jurisdictions, had by no means complete control even over the servile peasantry. In particular, their military and political power was not matched by their power to manage the agrarian economy. This was because of the great distance between them and the productive process. Nor was this simply the contrast between the vast scale of feudal landownership and the small scale of the family enterprise, for these distances applied to the petty lords of

[13] Marc Bloch's writings on serfdom, though criticized, cannot be ignored: M. Bloch, *Mélanges historiques*, 2 vols. (Paris, 1963), i, pt 4. See also G. Duby, *Rural Economy and Country Life in the Medieval West* (London, 1968), bk 3, chs. 1, 3

[14] Wace, "Roman de Rou", cited in L. Delisle, *Etudes sur la condition de la classe agricole et l'état de l'agriculture en Normandie au moyen âge* (Evreux, 1851), pp. 123–4.

[15] Cited in G. Salvemini, *Magnati e popolari in Firenze dal 1280 al 1295* (Florence, 1899), p. 215.

single villages as well as to magnates possessing hundreds. It was also because, on the whole, the effective intervention of the lord or his officials in the economy of the peasant holding was very limited. It is true that the lord could affect, usually in a negative sense, the resources of the peasant holding by his demands for rents and services. He could also (though never as much as he hoped) control the movement of the dependent population. But he was not able to determine the application of labour and other resources within the economy of the holding; nor, on the whole, was there much attempt in the terms of leases, even when customary tenure began to break down at the end of the middle ages, to specify good husbandry practices.

There was another factor distancing the lord from the peasants besides this seeming impenetrability of the household economy. As indicated above, between the lord and the individual peasant family holding stood the village community. In practice, this was represented by the village notables, the élite of well-to-do husbandmen without whose co-operation the lordship was unmanageable. For the lord not only needed coercive power, he needed intermediaries. Now, we have read many writings about the estate officialdom of stewards, bailiffs and the like, but in fact the management of rural communities was not in the hands of these lord's representatives. The manorial or seigneurial courts were largely in the hands of the well-to-do villagers, who declared custom, adjudicated in disputes, formulated communal regulations, promulgated by-laws, kept out strangers, and generally speaking provided the essential lines of communication between the estate officialdom, or the lord himself, and the community of peasant householders.

It must also be emphasized that the element of the agrarian economy over which the lord might seem to have complete control, namely the demesne, was also entangled in the customary practices of the peasant community. Although there might be a group of professional farm servants, free or servile, such as ploughmen, carters, herdsmen, dairymaids and the like, important labour resources on the demesne were transferred straight from the household economy, such as ploughmen and plough-teams, hay-makers, harvesters, smiths, even building-workers. The demesne, therefore, was reduced to the work rhythm of the peasant holding – or worse, since labour services were badly and unwillingly performed. In any case, the demesne was almost certainly a minority feature of the medieval agrarian economy. Its importance is to a certain extent a documentary illusion because the best records of rural life during the period are almost always those produced by the great estates, while great stretches of country not involved with the demesne economy but dominated by peasant farms remain relatively undocumented.

We therefore have a landowning class whose very existence depended on the transfer to it of the surplus labour and the fruits of surplus labour of a class which was potentially independent of it, over which it exercised political, military and juridical power, but in relation to which it fulfilled no entrepreneurial function. Given the scattering of the immobile rural communities (compared with the noble retinues, which could be relatively easily mobilized), the compulsion of agricultural routine, the domination of custom and the powerful ideological influences from the priests, monks and friars to accept the rightness of the social order, it is not surprising that politically the position of the ruling class was strong. Nevertheless, changes in the peasant economy at the base always had reverberations up to the top of the social structure, precisely because landowner income depended so intimately on the productivity and the exploitability of the peasant economy, and because it was in the nature of feudal landownership to be passive rather than active.

These reverberations from the base were felt not only in the agrarian sector of the economy. The landed aristocracy, whether lay or ecclesiastical, constituted at all times the principal market for a range of products, mainly luxuries, which entered into international trade. These were the spices, the fruits and the silks which were imported from the eastern Mediterranean westwards; the high-price luxury cloths which were the products of the Low Country and central Italian cloth industries; the wines of the Mediterranean, Bordeaux, the Rhineland, Burgundy and the Paris basin; and furs from eastern Europe. International trade, of course, dealt also in bulk commodities like grain and timber but the demand for these was mainly urban and probably depended ultimately on the health of the international trade in luxuries. The landed aristocrats also provided an important, if not the principal, demand for armaments and building. International trade was largely run by merchant-capitalist urban élites, to support whose activities and consumption needs there existed a considerable urban service sector. State and state-like formations existed on resources which came either from direct taxation (mainly of the rural producers) or indirect taxation, which fluctuated according to the volume of trade. In other words, the urban and commercial sectors of the economy largely and directly depended on the purchasing power of an aristocracy whose income was more or less directly derived from peasant production.

These contradictions of feudal society are at the heart of the crisis of the fourteenth and fifteenth centuries. It seems almost certain from the evidence at our disposal that the per capita productivity of agriculture was stationary or falling towards the end of the thirteenth century. This was not simply the result of the increasing population, which pressed on *institutionally* restricted landed resources, resulting in a reduction in the average size of the family subsistence holding, the proliferation of smallholders and landless labourers, and the reduction in the pasture/arable ratio. It was also the result of the pressure of landowners for rent, jurisdictional fines, death duties and entry fines, and of the state for taxation and purveyance – pressures which had been growing during the thirteenth century, which removed all cash surpluses and prevented even the most elementary investment. Not that the landowners gave much of a lead in the improvement of demesne agriculture. In spite of some interest in rational estate management, the diversion of aristocratic income into war and largess resulted in a low level of investment of profit in the estate with, as a consequence, low or stationary yields.[16]

This pessimistic interpretation of the trends of the agrarian sector of the economy at the end of the thirteenth century is not unchallenged. But from the point of view of landowner income there was another factor, social rather than economic in origin – the declining exploitability of the peasants. The struggles by peasant communities to retain as much as possible of the product of their holdings and to gain as much access as possible to common woods, pastures and fisheries date back many centuries. But there seems little doubt that in the thirteenth century, and especially in the second half of the century, this struggle had intensified and was by no means unsuccessful. The geographical distribution of these successes was of course uneven, as were the immediate aims. In northern and north-eastern France success went as far as the formation of rural communities with elements of self-government. In

[16] See above, p. 122, n. 10.

eastern France and western Germany, with the issue of *rapports de droits* and *Weistümer*, rents and services were stabilized, a fixity which in the long run benefited tenants rather than landowners. The same degree of success cannot be claimed for England. Conflicts about rents and services between lords and customary tenants raised the larger issue of free as against villein status. But these conflicts were quite frequent and even where the plaintiffs did not achieve free status, or prove the privileges of ancient demesne, the tendency here too was for the stabilization of labour services and arbitrary exactions such as tallage.[17]

The conflict over feudal rent must be understood as taking place within the framework of a society where production for the market was well developed, a society where simple commodity exchange was widespread, but where the bulk of the product, at any rate of grain, was consumed within the family economy. Quantitatively, it was the peasant family economy which held back most of the grain (and livestock) from the market for its own consumption, precisely because of the numerical superiority of the peasant producers. But it must be remembered that the family economy of the lords also retained large quantities of demesne produce even though, according to convenience, much might be bought and sold. The obligation on the part of the peasant producer to pay money rent, fines and taxes, and evidence of occasional cash accumulations by rich peasants, implies of course that they had to market a proportion of their product. We must not, however, imagine that these were small-scale capitalist farmers. Very little cash was retained after the payment of dues, and inputs of labour and materials were largely provided from within the family economy.

Nevertheless, that appropriated part of peasant production which became the income of the landowners (including the church) and the state was largely paid over in cash. Similarly, that transferred effort of peasant labour by which the demesnes were cultivated was, as we have mentioned, to a considerable extent realized in cash. Now, there are good reasons for supposing that the cash incomes of many estate owners were stationary or declining by the early decades of the fourteenth century, whether because of a crisis in demesne profits or because of difficulty in sustaining rent levels,

[17] I have attempted to summarize these conflicts and successes in my *Bond Men Made Free* (London, 1973).

or both. In spite of variations, this seems to be the general pattern over much of England as well as in such areas of France as Normandy, the Paris basin and the north. Yet this stationary or declining estate income had to sustain growing demands on it, unavoidable because they arose from the built-in tendencies of contemporary feudal society.[18]

Although difficult to quantify, like all medieval population distributions, it seems likely that during the century there had been a growth in the proportion of the population not engaged in food production. In the first place, this would comprise the urban population, not merely the established groups of wholesale merchants, retailers and artisans, but the mass of unskilled day-labourers and an unknowable proportion of marginal people, many of them recruited from the unsettled elements in the countryside. The increasing complexity of state and church administration resulted in a growth of officialdom, though admittedly most of these would come from families at the consuming rather than producing end of the food-chain. More important than a possible decrease in the proportion of food producers was, however, a general increase in the expenses of the political superstructure. Royal and seigneurial households laid out a large quantity of cash on display, largess and retinues – an expenditure which, given the aristocratic ethos and the competitive element in feudal politics, was likely constantly to increase and itself contribute to rising prices. War also was becom-

[18] See G. Fourquin, *Les campagnes de la région parisienne à la fin du moyen âge* (Paris, 1964), pp. 190–208; Bois, *Crise du féodalisme*, pp. 203ff.; R. Fossier, *La terre et les hommes en Picardie jusqu'à la fin du XIIIe siècle*, 2 vols. (Paris, 1968), ii, pp. 623–52; H. Neveux, "Déclin et reprise: la fluctuation biséculaire, 1330–1560", in G. Duby and A. Wallon (eds.), *Histoire de la France rurale*, 4 vols. (Paris, 1975–6), ii, pp. 35–9. Some English estate histories which illustrate the point include H. P. R. Finberg, *Tavistock Abbey* (Cambridge, 1951), pp. 261–2; J. A. Raftis, *The Estates of Ramsey Abbey* (Toronto, 1957), p. 228, "depressed agrarian returns"; I. Kershaw, *Bolton Priory* (Oxford, 1973), pp. 19–30, an income collapse in the 1320s; C. Dyer, *Lords and Peasants in a Changing Society* (Cambridge, 1980), pp. 79–83, a contraction of the estate from the 1280s. In spite of better agricultural conditions in early fourteenth-century Cornwall, the rents of the duchy stagnated for thirty years after 1287: J. Hatcher, *Rural Economy and Society in the Duchy of Cornwall, 1300–1500* (Cambridge, 1970), pp. 81ff. On the estates of the bishops of Ely and Winchester, while gross rents kept up or increased, demesne production severely declined: E. Miller, *The Abbey and Bishopric of Ely* (Cambridge, 1951), pp. 98–111; J. Z. Titow, "Land and Population on the Bishopric of Winchester's Estates, 1208–1350" (Cambridge Univ. Ph.D. thesis, 1961), pp. 22–42.

ing a heavier burden at this time. It was not because there was more actual fighting in the later middle ages than during earlier periods, but that it was becoming more costly. Campaigns tended to be longer and more sustained; more and more soldiers of all ranks were being paid cash wages; and the equipment, from horses to fortifications, was becoming more expensive. And given the slow cash flow in rents and taxes from the agrarian base, these costs were usually paid for out of high interest loans made by merchant bankers.

These were the principal uses of surplus derived from agricultural production. Apart from any other characteristics, it is to be noticed that from none of them was there any significant feedback in the form of investment which would increase production. There was no productive spin-off from military technology – elaborate armour, complicated fortifications or clever siege-machines provided no lessons which would help agricultural production or cheapen the costs of artisan production. Taxation was almost entirely absorbed by military expenses and the costs of government (including the largess and patronage provided by royal households). The profits of merchant capital, even though some might be spent on the purchase of lordships and feudal landed property, were certainly not invested in such a way as to improve agricultural production. Nor was there any significant investment in industrial production, largely because this was organized on the basis of the family enterprise, which was as impenetrable by merchant capital as the peasant family enterprise was impenetrable by the feudal landowner. Mercantile profits remained almost entirely in the sphere of circulation.

The crisis of feudal society in the fourteenth century is usually associated with the demographic collapse of the middle of the century – attributed, that is to say, to an outside force, the bubonic plague. It would be an utterly blind historian who would ignore the demographic factor in the shaping of the economic and social developments of the period, particularly since demographic movements are themselves by no means exempt from social determination. However, it is clear that the crisis of feudalism was already beginning before the arrival of the bubonic plague, even before the great famines of the second decade of the fourteenth century. The point is, of course, that the crisis of feudalism as a social order was not a crisis of subsistence or a crisis caused by the scissors effect of rising industrial and falling agricultural prices. However important these features of the situation might be – and there can be no disguising their significance – the central feature was a crisis of relationships between the two main classes of feudal society, which had begun before the demographic collapse and continued, even if in somewhat altered forms, during and after it.

If there had been a stagnation of landowner income derived from peasant rent before the demographic crisis, this became much more serious afterwards. Clearly, the drastically altered land/labour ratio provoked a considerable fall in the amount of labour rent, rent in kind and rent in cash which peasants paid to landowners. This fall in rent was not, however, *simply* determined by the increase in the amount of land available. As always, the level of rent was partly dependent upon the degree of non-economic compulsion which landowners could apply. Consequently, the varied experiences of peasant communities in conflict with their lords in the years before the demographic decline were by no means irrelevant. Rent income fell at an uneven rate, reflecting the changing balance of power in the countryside, as well as the supply of, and demand for, land. It has been suggested that the level of rents in England was maintained until the 1370s because of continued high grain prices. It is as likely that the strength and determination of the ruling class, reflected in the operation of labour legislation against high wage demands, was also responsible. The fact that peasant pressure for reduced rents was particularly successful after the revolt of 1381 must also be borne in mind.

The difficulty experienced by the western European aristocracies after 1348 in maintaining rent income is to be considered in the light of other difficulties which faced them. Wars continued, involving not only fiscal demands but an enhanced destruction of resources by official armies. Even if there were some temporary successes in maintaining rent income, the price scissors hit lords' demesne agriculture more seriously than it affected the peasants, especially those peasants mainly dependent on family labour. That once important supplement to rent income, demesne profits, was therefore disappearing very rapidly, especially after the 1370s. No wonder that in the second half of the fourteenth century we see not only the economic aspect of the crisis but its political consequences. These, taking the form of intensified factional struggles among the landed aristocracy, largely over the control of the state and its fund of patronage, are obviously connected with declining landed income.

Having looked at the broader picture, let us return to the peasant economy and lordship. The fall in feudal rent, as we have seen, meant a critical situation for the landowners, the state and the dependent urban/commercial sector. But, for the feudal mode of production to be utterly undermined, it would be necessary for developments among the basic producers to reach such a level that there would be viable alternatives to replace the previous socio-economic relationships. At the political level the old institutions of class dominance would have to be replaced for, as we have seen, the guarantee of seigneurial income was political and jurisdictional power rather than economic hegemony.

What in fact happened to the peasant economy? The English case is of particular interest, partly because of the good documentation for agrarian history, partly because of England's importance in the later development of capitalism. Let us emphasize again that one of the most striking features of English peasant history, especially after the 1380s, was the successes which manorial peasantries – customary tenants – had in pressing for reductions in rents, especially rents of an obviously "feudal" type. This success was reflected juridically in the virtual disappearance of servile villeinage. But equally important, it allowed the retention of surplus on the peasant holding.

The lightening of the burden of rent was accompanied by other developments which resulted in a considerable degree of prosperity in the peasant economy. It is clear that there was a regrouping of settlement, both within and between villages, so that the worst land from the point of view both of natural fertility and convenience of access (to the farm and to the market) would be abandoned to pasture. As is well known, this meant a considerable expansion of animal husbandry, and a bigger livestock element in arable farming, producing meat and wool for the market as well as dropping manure on the cultivated land. These favourable conditions for production were accompanied, as one would expect, by a considerable reduction in the proportion of smallholders and an increase in the average size of the arable holdings of the middle peasantry. At the top end of the peasant social scale, we see the appearance of holdings of considerable size, both for arable farming and for livestock.

Conditions were evidently favourable for increased production at a time when the rent charges on the producer were diminishing. There are obvious indications of this, including the fall in grain prices and rising real wages. No doubt demand factors were an element in both cases, but improvements in agricultural productivity must have played a significant part. Shortage of labour was obviously a factor in rising wages, but the fact that a high level of real wages was sustained for so long suggests a real increase in the productivity of labour. It must also be borne in mind that the amount of family labour was diminishing as replacement rates dropped,[19] so that indications of increased productivity when less labour was available overall are quite remarkable. Dare one suggest that this was an aspect of that opportunity for relatively untrammelled petty commodity production which was discussed in the Dobb–Sweezy debate in the 1950s?

Was England alone in these developments? The evolution of the French rural economy was similar, though the devastation caused by the English invasions held back parts of the country for many years. One fact is certain. The fall in rents which affected the revenues of the English landed aristocracy can also be traced in France. The need of landowners to restore devastated villages made it all the more necessary for them to offer advantageous terms to tenants, the flow of immigrants to the Entre-Deux-Mers being the classic example.[20] But since one of the most serious aspects of the war was the killing off of livestock, it is also certain that French agriculture did not enjoy, to the same extent as in England, the same improvements in the livestock component of arable farming. It is perhaps for this reason that real wages in France did not increase to the same extent as in England. Nevertheless, in spite of all the difficulties, the mid-fifteenth century in France has been seen as a favourable period for the middle peasantry, but always within the framework of the seigneurie, an institution which had recovered its strength by the end of the century.

[19] S. L. Thrupp, "The Problem of Replacement-Rates in Late Medieval English Population", *Econ. Hist. Rev.*, 2nd ser., xviii (1965), emphasized the fall in replacement rates in the fifteenth century. The phenomenon, if not Thrupp's explanation, has been confirmed by T. M. Lorcin, *Les campagnes de la région lyonnaise aux XIVe et XVe siècles* (Lyons, 1974); Z. Razi, *Life, Marriage and Death in a Medieval Parish* (Cambridge, 1980); Dyer, *Lords and Peasants in a Changing Society*.

[20] R. Boutruche, "Les courants de peuplement dans l'Entre-Deux-Mers", *Annales d'histoire économique et sociale*, vii (1935).

While it would be a mistake to exaggerate the decline of the manor in fifteenth-century England, readers of manorial court rolls cannot fail to be struck by the relative lack of life in the institution after the middle of the century. How significant was this apparent drainage of the powers of lordship as far as the relations between lords and peasants were concerned? How typical was that piece of extraordinary self-assertiveness by which the tenants of the powerful earl of Warwick, almost within the shadow of his castle on the river Avon, successfully insisted on a rent reduction which long outlasted the Beauchamp dynasty?[21] We will not know until more work has been done on the strangely obscure history of the lords and their customary tenants during this period. We can say, however, that even if the individual coercive power of manorial lords through the manor court was diminishing, the collective power of the county landowners was being strengthened through the nomination of their most active members as J.P.s. But although J.P.s dealt not only with law and order but operated labour legislation as well, did this give them a voice in the transfer of peasant surplus in the form of rent? Evidently not (and the assault on the security of copyhold was yet to come) but there were also developments independent of the will of the peasantry which deprived them of some of their previous powers of resistance and initiative over questions of rent. The decline of the manor court was accompanied by a decline in the cohesive force of the village community. This decline was partly the result of the shrinkage of the peasant population, partly due to its extreme mobility, and partly due to social differentiation. Rich peasant families, now graziers and demesne farmers holding largely by leasehold tenure, no longer stood as mediators between the lords and the communities of customary tenants. They were no longer potential leaders of the resistance.

Can we therefore say that by the end of the fifteenth century, if not before, the first crisis of feudalism was over? In France the seigneurial framework was restored; in England the ruling class, with characteristic flexibility, changed its local focus of power, from the manor court to the sessions of the peace, as lord/peasant relationships in any case changed in character. But these conclusions cover only one, perhaps two, exemplary countries of western Europe and have emerged primarily from a study of the agrarian

[21] Hilton, *English Peasantry in the Later Middle Ages*, pp. 66–7.

economy. What about the urban/commercial sector? How was *it* affected by the changing income distribution between the major classes, the landowning lords and the peasants?

It must be said that research has, on the whole, not provided any clear answers. This is not surprising, given the insufficiency of quantitative evidence about population, production and commerce. Given the general population decline, were the old-established urban centres growing or contracting? Was industry (especially the textile industry) moving from town to country? Was the country industry catering for a new market – that is, responding to the demand of those who benefited from the relaxation of seigneurial pressures and whose incomes, we have suggested, were relatively buoyant during this period? War and other political factors affected many aspects of the economy, whether we look at the wine production of the Bordelais or the cloth trade from west of the Sound into the Baltic. Old centres and old trading currents shrank (for instance, the Italian–Flemish connection); others boomed (for instance, the Brabant–Frankfurt–Danube and south German axes). The complexity and variety of events in this sector defy generalization to a much greater extent than the agrarian, but some impressions nevertheless remain. First, that established towns with elaborate municipal and guild hierarchies were liable, in depressed conditions, to founder under the weight of institutional superstructures (as in the case of Coventry and many other English provincial towns). Others however (like Nuremberg) which were in a developing region preserved or even expanded the same superstructural elements. These are extreme cases. But by and large the shift towards cheaper textiles was manifested in the relocation of the industry in small towns and villages, taking advantage of, and at the same time strengthening, the growth of small-scale commodity production in the countryside. Other growing industrial sectors too, such as metallurgy and, of course, mining, tended to develop away from established towns. Shifts from textiles to the production of luxuries saved only a few of the established urban economies. Many of the once industrialized English provincial towns were, by the late fifteenth century, simply becoming regional markets for agricultural produce and food-processing centres for local institutional buyers.

Whatever might be the long-term implications of these developments in the rural and urban sectors of the late medieval economy, it is clear that feudalism, as a social formation based ultimately on the transfer of the surplus from a peasant economy to the landed aristocracy and its states, had recovered from its crisis by a process of shifts and adjustments. There was plenty of fight in the system yet, though it had had to undergo considerable changes. Most important of these were the changes in the character of small-scale commodity production, especially in agriculture, but also in industrial crafts – far more important, one suspects, than the spectacular accumulations of money capital by merchants, bankers and colonizers which tend to occupy the front of the stage.

8. *In Search of Agrarian Capitalism**

J. P. COOPER

In his article "Agrarian Class Structure and Economic Development in Pre-Industrial Europe", Robert Brenner has addressed himself to major historical problems about agrarian change and the modernization of societies. The effects on peasantries of such processes are of more than historiographical and methodological interest and have political and social reverberations among today's debates about strategies for development. Besides offering a general critique of neo-Malthusian accounts of European social and economic development since the twelfth century, Brenner also joins a long line of expositors beginning with the Physiocrats. These found the essential cause of differences in growth between France and England in differences in agrarian structures and productivity, due mainly to the dominance of large farms in England.

In so far as Brenner's argument suggests that demographic constraints and cycles have often been taken as the main determinants of economic and social developments, or at least have occupied so much attention and exposition as to have left little room for consideration of other factors, I sympathize with him. It has become a favourite axiom of French historians that a population of some twenty millions provided a ceiling in medieval and early modern France beyond which it was impossible to go, given existing agrarian techniques. Braudel believes that this figure around 1600 meant that France was too densely populated and had become "a vast emigration zone". Yet on his own figures Italy, with a far greater area of mountain, had a population density of forty-four persons to

[J. P. Cooper was finalizing this article for publication in *Past and Present* at the time of his premature death in 1978. Doubtless had he lived he would have made various alterations to the text. Nonetheless, with the kind consent of his widow, we were pleased to publish, as we are now pleased to reprint, this important contribution to historical studies as it stood when the author died.]

the square kilometre against France's thirty-four.[1] As a quarter or more of France was forest,[2] it is not immediately apparent why the cultivated area could not have been increased, even if agricultural techniques were unchanging. Some explanation might still be sought in the nature of the prevailing political and social arrangements. In wanting to pursue such analysis, it is not necessary to be committed in advance, as Brenner apparently is, to using Marxist terminology, but I would agree with him that the effects of power and constraint in society do seem to be relatively neglected in expositions of what he terms "the demographic model".

Both Goubert and Le Roy Ladurie invoke the image of a system in equilibrium, oscillating within determined limits, a balance between "the economy and size of population which changed little in the two centuries between 1550 and 1750, forty inhabitants to the square kilometre being what France could support given its physical and mental habits of living".[3] According to Le Roy Ladurie, "The Malthusian curse had fallen on Languedoc in the sixteenth and seventeenth centuries . . . it had invested a great agrarian cycle, after a vigorous starting phase, with the character of an inexorable fluctuation". It was a society without growth, because no one was interested in economics. This is symbolized or demonstrated by the failure of Protestantism in France to reach the peasants and the countryside. The "capital of human energy" in the sixteenth century "was not invested in the economy"; it was dissipated in the religious wars. "After 1600, the victory of Catholicism became more and more inseparable from a certain revival of 'feudal' society (. . . in the broad sense in which the philosophers of the eighteenth century used the term)". The military, social and theological objectives of Bourbon absolutism were approved by the French élites and

[1] F. Braudel, *Capitalism and Material Life, 1400–1800* (London, 1973), pp. 23, 29.

[2] M. Devèze, *La vie de la forêt française au XVIe siècle*, 2 vols. (Paris, 1961), i, pp. 268–9, estimates that thirty-one northern and western *départements* which had 9 per cent of their area as forest in 1912 (when 18.6 per cent of the national area was forest) had 16.3 per cent forest in 1550. Extrapolating from this percentage, Le Roy Ladurie has suggested 18 million hectares of forest in 1550, which would be a third or more of the total area: E. Le Roy Ladurie, "Les masses profondes: la paysannerie", in F. Braudel and E. Labrousse (eds.), *Histoire économique et sociale de la France* [4 vols. in 7 (Paris, 1970–80)], i, pt 2, pp. 594–5. In 1789 it was about 9 million hectares.

[3] P. Goubert, *L'ancien régime*, 2 vols. (Paris, 1969–73), i, p. 39. Although Goubert agrees that France could only sustain a population of twenty millions, he arrives at a different density from Braudel.

imposed fiscal burdens which made economic recovery and true growth impossible. Such general conclusions, and still more the invocation of feudalism, seem similar to Brenner's; the system invoked excludes increased production and the "bringing about of agrarian capitalism on a large scale",[4] and so would presumably exclude the emergence of capitalist class relations in the countryside which Brenner believes distinguished English from French developments.[5] However, Le Roy Ladurie has further claimed that, when real economic growth began in the eighteenth century, it produced "a rural France where the majority had been proletarianized" and where seigneurs were the temporary allies of capitalism.[6]

Thus Brenner's objections are less to Le Roy Ladurie's categorization of the French economy and society than to his attempt to explain their nature as the product of *mentalités* and of cultural blockages which could only be changed when the *mentalités* changed, a change which Brenner would presumably prefer to see arising from changing class relationships and conflicts.

The whole conception of *mentalités* as inherited from Febvre stresses the absence or impossibility of certain concepts and attitudes existing in given periods. In so doing, it tends to create a uniformity which hides or denies the capacity of individuals and societies to hold contradictory and incompatible ideas and ideals simultaneously. It also implies that change must come as some total mental and psychological transformation – which Le Roy Ladurie locates in the Enlightenment, with the peasants becoming political and religious nonconformists after 1760.[7] One may still wonder how agricultural progress and rises in productivity were possible in Flanders, Lodigiano, Catalonia or Brescia before any trans-

[4] E. Le Roy Ladurie, "A Long Agrarian Cycle: Languedoc, 1500–1700", in P. Earle (ed.), *Essays in European Economic History, 1500–1800* (Oxford, 1974), pp. 162, 151–2, 144–5; cf. E. Le Roy Ladurie, "Les paysans français du XVIe siècle", in *Conjoncture économique, structures sociales: Hommage à Ernest Labrousse* (Paris, 1974), pp. 350–1. Here the sixteenth century is seen as "reconstituting a rural ecosystem" disturbed by the negative fluctuations of the fourteenth and fifteenth centuries; "these tendencies towards 'restoration' were scarcely compatible with a readiness to accept cultural innovation".

[5] Above, pp. 28–9.

[6] E. Le Roy Ladurie, "Pour un modèle de l'économie rurale française au XVIIIe siècle", *Cahiers d'histoire*, xix (1974), p. 24; E. Le Roy Ladurie, "De la crise ultime à la vraie croissance, 1660–1789", in G. Duby and A. Wallon (eds.), *Histoire de la France rurale*, 4 vols. (Paris, 1975–6), ii, pp. 568–70.

[7] Le Roy Ladurie, "De la crise ultime à la vraie croissance", p. 544.

mutation of *mentalités*. The great strength of Le Roy Ladurie's work on Languedoc was the demonstration of the impact of war through fiscal pressures, instead of treating these as secondary to the long-term trends of *conjoncture*; yet in explaining them as the result of cultural blockages or attitudes, he seems to make them epiphenomena of the long-term trend of the *mentalités* of those who willed them. An acceptance of inevitability prevails, comparable to Mousnier's sense of the nation- and state-building mission of absolutism to which no viable alternative existed.

Brenner would base his explanation of the differences between French and English development on the absence of capitalist class relationships in the French countryside. The amount of reification involved might seem as great as in Le Roy Ladurie's invocation of *mentalités*. If all explanations which attempt more than mere description involve some degree of abstraction and reification, they need not become a glass darkening the analysis of actual developments. At least it may be worth trying to examine what Brenner means by capitalist farming, how it differs from peasant farming in efficiency and productivity, and how French and English agrarian structures were affected during the crucial periods of Le Roy Ladurie's cycles from 1400 to 1750, so far as present knowledge permits.

Although a long tradition since Quesnay has extolled the productivity of English agriculture by comparison with French, could this be an illusion to be explained away rather than a crux needing explanation? P. K. O'Brien has recently argued that English agriculture did not have such an outstanding record of growth in output as has been generally assumed. While it may have been more efficient and productive than French agriculture around 1700, its growth rate in the eighteenth century was much the same as the French, and was only marginally better in the first half of the nineteenth century. Moreover, for the crucial period 1650–1745, comparison of the long-term trend of prices shows that English prices did not fall as much as Continental ones. "But if the new husbandry had spread more extensively in Britain and if total factor productivity increased more rapidly here than it did in European agriculture, *ceteris paribus*, the fall in the prices of food and raw materials should have been more marked in Britain than elsewhere in Europe". This conclusion, like the estimates of agricultural production (taken from Deane and Cole), depends on the Brownlee-

Rickman estimates of English population growth from 1700 to 1750.[8]

However, the Cambridge Group's data from four hundred parish registers give a much greater rate of growth from 1695 than these estimates.[9] As the index of agricultural production is dominated by an assumed constant per capita consumption of grain, this means that the output of grain, instead of being virtually static between 1700 and 1740 (with a rise of 4 per cent) and rising under 12 per cent between 1700 and 1750, actually rose by nearly 24 per cent (to 1750). Although this would not change the overall rate of growth for 1700 to 1800, it does make the rate of growth much greater for the first half of the century, and particularly great between 1695 and 1720, when it was 11.4 per cent, whereas it was 10.1 per cent between 1720 and 1750.[10] Thus there probably was appreciable growth of agricultural output in the late seventeenth and early eighteenth centuries when French output was stagnant or falling, and the English rate of growth would have been much faster than the French until 1750.[11]

Almost simultaneously with O'Brien's reflections on statistical trends, Eugen Weber apparently confirmed Brenner's views that

[8] P. K. O'Brien, "Agriculture and the Industrial Revolution", *Econ. Hist. Rev.*, 2nd ser., xxx (1977), esp. p. 174.

[9] The crude data are displayed graphically for 1540–1750 in D. C. Coleman, *The Economy of England, 1450–1750* (Oxford, 1977), p. 16. The population estimates used are the preliminary ones made by R. D. Lee in a paper entitled "British Population in the Eighteenth Century" circulated for a conference on a projected new economic history of Britain 1700–1970s, sponsored by the S.S.R.C. and held at Emmanuel College, Cambridge, in December 1976. The estimates, giving a growth rate of 0.37 per cent per annum for 1700–40, are in table 1, p. 8. [A revised version of this paper appeared under the joint authorship of R. D. Lee and R. S. Schofield in R. Floud and D. McCloskey (eds.), *The Economic History of Britain since 1700*, 2 vols. (Cambridge, 1981), i, with table 2.1 at p. 21.] N. F. R. Crafts, "English Economic Growth in the Eighteenth Century", *Econ. Hist. Rev.*, 2nd ser., xxix (1976), pp. 226–7, 235, argues that a growth rate of 0.7 per cent per annum in 1710–40 would fit the price data better than the Brownlee estimates.

[10] Revised from P. Deane and W. A. Cole, *British Economic Growth, 1688–1959* (Cambridge, 1962), pp. 62–8.

[11] O'Brien's growth rate for French agriculture of 0.6 per cent per annum derives from J.-C. Toutain's global estimate of 60 per cent, but Le Roy Ladurie regards this as impossibly high and would reduce it to 25 to 40 per cent, making the average for the century between 0.25 and 0.4 per cent per annum: O'Brien, "Agriculture and the Industrial Revolution", p. 173; Le Roy Ladurie, "De la crise ultime à la vraie croissance", p. 395; J. Goy and E. Le Roy Ladurie (eds.), *Les fluctuations du produit de la dîme* (Paris, 1972), introduction, pp. 23–4.

peasant production "could not provide the agrarian basis for economic development", that "for real agricultural breakthrough leading to economic development . . . some form of larger-scale capitalist farming was required".[12] Weber holds that not until late in the nineteenth century had a significant proportion of most Frenchmen who worked the land "tied their production to the needs of the market"; for "Virtually all of the center, the south, and the west . . . the great survey of 1848 suggests that eighteenth-century advances accounted for whatever progress there was, and that methods of work on the whole remained those of the Ancien Régime", while in the poor regions between 1860 and 1880 the peasants' way of life was close to that of "the late Stone Age".[13] This might be thought to support Brenner to the extent of overkill. If French agriculture was still so backward in 1880, how had any economic development and industrialization come about? But Weber's observations do not apply to northern France: it was the northern plains, upper Normandy, Ile-de-France, Picardy and Champagne which were dominated by grain production and large farms. South and east of this area, farms were smaller and pastoral farming was more important. The northern area was the one in which there was the greatest loss of peasant property and engrossment of holdings into larger farms in the sixteenth and seventeenth centuries, thus resembling the arable-farming areas of lowland England.

Of course, Brenner is aware of France's diversity, even if he is not very explicit about the farming regions. He mentions "those relatively restricted areas where large consolidated holdings were created" and refers to Jacquart's and Venard's works on the Paris region.[14] He allows that large farms were consolidated where village communities were weakened, but he seems to underestimate the extent to which they were weakened from the time of the religious wars onwards.[15] His assumption that large farms only existed in gaps left by communities is clearly not true of regions like Beauce, where

[12] Above, p. 50, and p. 49, n. 81.

[13] E. Weber, *Peasants into Frenchmen* (London, 1977), pp. 117–18.

[14] Above, pp. 62–3, n. 111.

[15] J. Jacquart, "Immobilisme et catastrophes, 1560–1660", in Duby and Wallon (eds.), *Histoire de la France rurale*, ii, pp. 294–6; P. de Saint-Jacob, "Mutations économiques et sociales dans les campagnes bourguignonnes à la fin du XVIe siècle", *Etudes rurales*, i (1961).

large farmers dominated the village communities.[16] In some areas, what were by English standards very large farms of over 400 acres dominated the landscape.[17] Obviously, size is by itself no indication of either efficiency or value.[18]

Nevertheless, in their advocacy of large farms as the only effective means to improvement the Physiocrats thought they were imitating the example of England. Brenner shares their assumption that England was dominated by large capitalist farms dependent on a mass of wage labour. However, Mingay has shown that this requires modification. Although he believes that the number of farms between 20 and 100 acres declined from 1660 to 1750, he points out that even in 1891 the number of holdings of this size was still 55 per cent greater than those with over 100 acres. In 1878 Caird believed that 70 per cent of tenanted farms were under 50 acres and only 18 per cent over 100 acres.[19] Regional variations were great; population growth and intensification of exploitation led to fragmentation of holdings over much of Lancashire in the late eighteenth and early nineteenth centuries.[20] Industrialization led to

[16] J.-M. Constant, "La propriété et le problème de la constitution des fermes sur les censives en Beauce aux XVIe et XVIIe siècles", *Revue historique*, ccxlix (1973), esp. pp. 372–6; G. Lefebvre, *Etudes orléanaises*, 2 vols. (Paris, 1962–3), i, pp. 25–6. To the north of Paris the great farms were in the villages: C. Devitry, "Recherches sur quelques grandes fermes dans la plaine de France, XVIe–XVIIIe siècle", *Ecole Nationale des Chartes: Positions des thèses* (1967).

[17] Or 162 hectares (one acre = 0.405 hectares; one hectare = 2.471 acres). For the Norman Vexin, see G. Bois, *Crise du féodalisme* (Paris, 1976), p. 216 [Eng. trans., *The Crisis of Feudalism* (Cambridge, 1984)]; for the Soissonnais, see G. Postel-Vinay, *La rente foncière dans le capitalisme agricole* (Paris, 1974), pp. 26–9; for Brie, see E. Mireaux, *Une province française au temps du Grand Roi* (Paris, 1958), pp. 97–116, 137–52. For a spectacular example of the engrossing of farms and the domination of a village by a family of great farmers, see C. Brunet, *Une communauté rurale au XVIIIe siècle* (Paris, 1964).

[18] The seventeenth and eighteenth centuries saw the increase of large farms at the expense of small ones in the Sologne, accompanied by the growth of numbers of semi-proletarianized *locaturiers* (lessees) and the increasing degradation of some of the poorest soils in France: B. Edeine, *La Sologne*, 2 vols. (Paris, 1974), i, pp. 173, 186–207; G. Bouchard, *Le village immobile* (Paris, 1971).

[19] G. E. Mingay, "The Size of Farms in the Eighteenth Century", *Econ. Hist. Rev.*, 2nd ser., xiv (1961–2); Sir J. Caird, *The Landed Interest and the Supply of Food* (London, 1878), p. 58; "In 1800 England was in the main still a country of small farms": Mingay, "Size of Farms in the Eighteenth Century", p. 488.

[20] T. W. Fletcher, "The Agrarian Revolution in Arable Lancashire", *Trans. Lancs. and Cheshire Antiq. Soc.*, lxxii (1962), pp. 93–6, 100, 119–21; T. W. Fletcher, "Lancashire Livestock Farming during the Great Depression", *Agric. Hist. Rev.*, ix (1961), p. 19. In 1871, 70 per cent of the country's agricultural acreage was in farms under 100 acres, worked predominantly by family labour.

growth in the numbers of dwarf holdings in Shropshire, Staffordshire and parts of the West Riding,[21] while in the light soil regions of East Anglia the size of farms grew.[22] More generally, in 1831 the number of family "peasant" farmers without wage-labourers was only 10 per cent less than that of farmers who employed labour.[23] Colquhoun in 1801 thought that there were 160,000 farmers in England and Wales, 10,000 more than King's estimate for 1688, and put their average income at £120, implying an average farm nearer 100 than 200 acres.[24]

It was Cantillon who first claimed that English farmers were "generally more prosperous than in other Countries where the Farms are small". He also saw the farmer as a risk-bearing entrepreneur using capital.[25] Quesnay, inspired by English examples, saw "large-scale cultivation carried on by rich farmers", able to make advances from capital, as the only way to ensure increased production, while poor peasants and "small-scale cultivation" will produce a "net product which is almost zero".[26] Turgot generalized

[21] J. R. Wordie, "Social Change on the Leveson-Gower Estates, 1714–1832", *Econ. Hist. Rev.*, 2nd ser., xxvii (1974); in 1759–79 the number of tenants with under 5 acres was 537; in 1809–13 it was 1,014, and in 1829–33, 1,528; while the percentage of land in farms over 200 acres increased from 34 in the first period to 55 in the last: B. Jennings (ed.), *A History of Nidderdale* (Huddersfield, 1967), pp. 337–9.

[22] However, the proportion of farms over 500 acres in Norfolk in 1851 was lower than in Berkshire, Wiltshire, Hampshire and Dorset: D. B. Grigg, "Small and Large Farms in England and Wales", *Geography*, xlviii (1963), p. 278, table 2. Grigg concludes: "The distribution of large and small farms of the present day [1958] has been inherited from the early nineteenth century, and indeed may date from a much earlier period" (pp. 278–9).

[23] J. H. Clapham, "The Growth of an Agrarian Proletariat, 1688–1832", *Cambridge Hist. Jl*, i (1923–5). These figures are for Great Britain; the ratio of 2.5 to 1 between the number of labouring families and that of farming entrepreneurs is probably representative for England and Wales.

[24] P. Colquhoun, *A Treatise on Indigence, Exhibiting a General View of the National Resources for Productive Labour* (London, 1806), pp. 23–4. Their income is greater than that of the lesser freeholders, which is put at £90, whereas King had given them a slightly greater income than the farmers, £55 against £42. 10s. in the version used by Colquhoun, £50 against £44 in the original. This seems to imply that Colquhoun thought the average farmer's income and farm had increased relatively to those of the lesser freeholder since 1688.

[25] R. Cantillon, *Essai sur la nature du commerce en général*, ed. H. Higgs (London, 1931), pp. 122–3, 46–9; written before 1734. However, Cantillon also speaks of "undertakers of their own labour who need no capital to establish themselves" (pp. 52–3).

[26] *Quesnay's Tableau économique*, ed. M. Kuczynski and R. L. Meek (London, 1972), pp. 8 n. (a), 17–18 n. (a), 19–21 n. (a).

the notion of capitalism by clarifying Quesnay's conception of advances in agriculture and extending it to commerce and manufacturing. For the present occasion, Turgot's enunciation of historical stages of social, economic and tenurial evolution is even more important.

He sees societies in general passing from the hunting to the pastoral and then to the agricultural stage. Primitive societies cultivate land with slave labour; they are succeeded by serfs tied to the land, who become free proprietors owing dues in money and kind. *Métayage* (share-cropping) is a transitional form found in poor countries. The final stage, found in wealthy countries, is leasehold tenant farming, where the advances are made by the tenant. The farmer's advances and the payment of his rent are made possible by his possession of a stock of capital. The competition of these capitalist entrepreneurs "establishes the current price of leases" and efficient cultivation; the lack of such entrepreneurs means small-scale cultivation and *métayage*. "Hence . . . the Class of Cultivators, like that of Manufacturers, is divided into two orders of men, that of the Entrepreneurs or Capitalists . . . and that of the ordinary Workmen on wages . . . it is capitals alone which establish and maintain great Agricultural enterprises". Thus large-scale capitalist farming with wage labour is the means to economic growth. Turgot contrasts the regions of large farms in northern France with the poor share-croppers of central France (Limousin, Angoumois, Bourbonnais), whereas Quesnay had contrasted France in general with England and had emphasized the superior efficiency of horses over oxen.[27]

This view of the efficiency of very large capitalist farms was transmitted to Marx, who saw an "agricultural revolution" in which enclosures, sheep farming, rising prices and long leases created "a class of capitalist farmers" and expropriated labourers by the end of the sixteenth century.[28] This in turn derives from panegyrics on the uniqueness of the English yeoman[29] transmitted through

[27] *Turgot on Progress, Sociology and Economics*, ed. R. L. Meek (Cambridge, 1973), pp. 128–32, 145–56.

[28] K. Marx, *Capital*, 2 vols. (Everyman edn, London, 1934), ii, pp. 794–801, 823–5, 844–5; K. Marx, *Capital*, iii (Moscow, 1972 edn), pp. 798–9, 801.

[29] The contrast with the misery of French peasants goes back at least to Sir John Fortescue. [T. Gainsford], *The Glory of England* (London, 1618), pp. 304–9, surveys the oppression of peasants in Germany, Hungary, Spain and Italy as well, in order to illuminate the prosperity of the English yeoman and the "happy life of our Countrey-man and common people". Thomas Fuller makes the same point,

Harrington[30] and the political economists. The Reverend Richard Jones (Malthus's successor at Haileybury) described the rebellions of 1549 as due to enclosures, but: "The enterprising spirit of English aristocrats quailed not before these alarms, or their hopes of gain prevailed over their fears . . . before long the progress of manufactures brought employment to those whom at first it had made beggars and vagabonds . . . we date the rise of a body of capitalists in England, like our modern farmers, in whose hands nearly the whole country is found, in the reign of James the First".[31] Marx's chronology is somewhat more vague; the numbers of English peasants fluctuated, but declined in the long run: "Not until large-scale industry, based on machinery, comes, does there arise a permanent foundation for capitalist agriculture" with the destruction of domestic rural industry and the expropriation of "the enormous

seeing the yeomanry as "a fortunate condition . . . betwixt greatnesse and want, an estate of people almost peculiar to England", "a Gentleman in Ore, whom the next age may see refined", who "improveth his land to a double value by his good husbandry", and calls Bacon's interpretation of Henry VII's statute on enclosures in evidence: T. Fuller, *The Holy State* (Cambridge, 1642), pp. 116–19.

30 Harrington also invoked Bacon on the statute of 1488 which did "amortize a great part of the Lands to the hold and possession of the Yeomanry or middle People . . . unlink'd from dependence upon their Lords", stressing the change from seeking manpower to seeking money as the new aim of great landowners in the sixteenth century, while trade in land was helped by the freedom of alienation, supposed to have come in under Henry VII and Henry VIII: *The Oceana and Other Works of James Harrington* (London, 1737 edn), pp. 69–70, 457. This last was combined with the rise of commerce by his successors; thus John Dalrymple explained the failure of the commons to rise in Scotland as follows: "England was a trading country, and though originally the land property was ingrossed by the great nobles, yet in the progress of trade, the commons bought from those nobles, great part of their lands: but power follows property . . . In Scotland . . . we had little or no commerce; the land property was ingrossed by the nobility, and it continued to remain so, as long as we had parliaments": J. Dalrymple, *An Essay towards a General History of Feudal Property in Great Britain*, 2nd edn (London, 1758), p. 272.

31 *Literary Remains, Consisting of Lectures and Tracts on Political Economy, of the Late Rev. Richard Jones*, ed. W. Whewell (London, 1859), "A Short Tract on Political Economy", p. 224. The ingredients of a similar version of economic history can be found in Sir F. M. Eden, *The State of the Poor*, 3 vols. (London, 1797), i, pp. 73, 96, 107, 112, 115; "The language of the statute [again the 1488 act against enclosures] is a clear proof, that the business of agriculture began now to be carried on by persons of capital"; the abbeys were "indulgent landlords"; the period saw the advance of "middling ranks" and of arable production, a small acreage needing fewer hands, while the transfer of "a great portion of the estates of the church and the nobility into the hands of country gentlemen" meant improved agriculture, the decay of "the race of cottagers" and the increasing size of farms.

majority of the rural population". Large landownership with tenant farmers is "a prerequisite and condition of capitalist production". Capital as a leading force in agriculture appears gradually and sporadically.[32]

Yet manifestly in Scandinavia and most of western Europe industrialization had still not brought large farms by 1950. At that time the predominant holdings were under 50 hectares, except in lowland England, parts of northern France, parts of northern Italy, southern Italy and central and southern Spain where holdings of over 100 hectares predominated, while between a third and a quarter of the arable in western Europe was still held in scattered parcels.[33] While the verifiability of Marx's prophecies was a burning question for socialist parties before 1914,[34] it need not detain us. But Marx's or Turgot's scheme of tenurial evolution towards money rent and capitalist farming have been implicitly accepted by many historians, who have not concerned themselves with explicitly Marxist debates about the transition from feudalism to capitalism.

Marx's system belonged consciously to a well-established tradition whose model was a unilinear evolution by stages towards a commercialized market-dominated economy. Marx himself saw industrial capitalism as a higher stage, but denied that it was the highest stage of this evolution. Nonetheless, he accepted it as culturally and economically progressive: "It is one of the civilising aspects of capital that it enforces this surplus labour in a manner and under conditions which are more advantageous to the development of production forces, social relations and the creation of elements for a new and higher form than under the preceding forms of slavery, serfdom, etc.".[35] Private property in land necessarily made agricultural production inefficient; its abolition was the final stage of an evolution in which farming by capitalist tenants was necessarily more progressive and productive than peasant farming, which "created a class of barbarians . . . combining all the crudeness of

[32] Marx, *Capital* (Everyman edn, London, 1934), ii, p. 830; Marx, *Capital*, iii (Moscow, 1972 edn), pp. 801–2, 821.

[33] E. E. Evans, "The Ecology of Peasant Life in Western Europe", and G. Pfeifer, "The Quality of Peasant Living in Central Europe", in W. L. Thomas (ed.), *Man's Role in Changing the Face of the Earth*, 2 vols. (Chicago, 1970 edn), figs. 71(a), 72, pp. 235, 243; cf. fig. 74, p. 248.

[34] D. Mitrany, "Marx v. the Peasant", in T. E. Gregory and H. Dalton (eds.), *London Essays in Economics in Honour of Edwin Cannan* (London, 1927).

[35] Marx, *Capital*, iii (Moscow, 1972 edn), p. 819.

primitive forms of society with the anguish and misery of civilised countries". Both fail to achieve "conscious rational cultivation", because both depend on the mechanism of market prices.[36] But it is precisely these mechanisms and their evolution, the basis of Marx's model, which Brenner finds so unsatisfactory in what he terms the "commercialization model" of economic change.[37] If this is conceived as a unilinear model, contradictions appear, with the growth of international trade encouraging serfdom east of the Elbe and capitalism in western Europe: the stages appear in the wrong order. But few historians since Pirenne have favoured such unilinear models of explanation.

Brenner complains that in treating medieval serfdom as a contractual relationship in a rudimentary labour market North and Thomas ignore the functioning of power and coercion. Yet he himself argues that small-scale farming "could not provide the agrarian basis for economic development", because it could not increase basic grain production, which needed capital inputs. Peasant farmers could only provide intensification of labour, which would be effective solely for industrial crops, such as flax, and "in viticulture, dairying and horticulture". It did not increase yields "through the greater efficiency of a given unit of labour input. It did not . . . produce 'development', except in a restricted, indeed misleading, use of the term".[38] Here the criterion of efficiency must be determined by relative labour costs. Quite apart from the question of whether market and credit mechanisms might be rigged against peasants, not all economists would accept that labour inputs are qualitatively different from capital inputs in the way that Brenner's argument requires.[39] Even within a fully commercialized agricul-

36 *Ibid.*, pp. 802–13. 37 Above, pp. 25–9. 38 Above, p. 50.

39 Only very small holdings in Flanders turned over exclusively to industrial crops; the larger ones (middling peasant farms) were mixed farms with higher productivity of cereals than the great farms beloved of the Physiocrats; see the analysis of the output of a farm of 22.3 hectares near Lille in 1776: C. Le Clerc de Montlinot, in O. de Serres, *Le théâtre d'agriculture, et mesnage des champs*, 2 vols. (Paris, 1804–5 edn), i, pp. 185–6, 193–4. Despite the development of sugar beet, the small farms of French Flanders increased their yields of grain in the nineteenth century: M. L. de Lavergne, *Economie rurale de la France depuis 1789*, 4th edn (Paris, 1877), pp. 75–7. For Belgian Flanders, see E. de Lavelaye, *Essai sur l'économie rurale de la Belgique*, 2nd edn (Paris, 1875), pp. 44–58; capital employed and productivity per hectare were higher than anywhere else in Europe, except parts of Lombardy. See also below, p. 188 and n. 163. Brenner himself gives an example of peasant grain production for the international market

ture, small units could compete successfully with large-scale ones, as the example of late nineteenth-century France shows.[40] Despite its impeccable Physiocratic and Marxist ancestry, the application of Brenner's proposition to the early modern period is yet more doubtful, even as an economic model, abstracted from all considerations of social and political power, or of how peasants costed their own labour.

Brenner's views on the nature of the differences between French and English agricultural developments might seem to be confirmed by George Taylor's thesis on the dominance of proprietary non-capitalist wealth in France before 1789. This wealth was "investments in land, urban property, venal office, and annuities", yielding a constant but modest 1–5 per cent, "realized not by entrepreneurial effort, which was degrading, but by mere ownership . . . Risk was negligible . . . investments were almost fully secure". French landowners avoided risks; unlike merchants and industrialists, they were not interested in productivity, but only in raising rents. This is demonstrated by the fact that rent "was at the center of all calculations . . . was what determined the value of property".[41] Yet in England investment in land was certainly a form of risk avoidance for many buyers, while the thousands of investors in annuities, government stock and mortgages were hardly risk-taking entrepreneurs. The view that rent determines the price of land is not a quirk of non-capitalist psychology, but a still valid observation of fact.[42] The very greatest French landowners did invest in industry and mining,[43] but the view that their relations with tenants inhibited productive investment and the development of capitalist tenant farmers is supported by Robert Forster. Unlike Brenner, he admits that experience in the nineteenth and twentieth centuries by no

(above, p. 37, n. 56). For an example of the treatment of labour inputs which differs from the classical economists' distinction between labour and capital as the source of improvements, see S. N. S. Cheung, *The Theory of Share Tenancy* (Chicago, 1969), pp. 37–9.

[40] G. W. Grantham, "Scale and Organization in French Farming, 1840–1880", in W. N. Parker and E. L. Jones (eds.), *European Peasants and their Markets* (Princeton, 1975).

[41] G. V. Taylor, "Noncapitalist Wealth and the Origins of the French Revolution", *Amer. Hist. Rev.*, lxxii (1966–7), pp. 471, 474; cf. G. V. Taylor, "Types of Capitalism in Eighteenth-Century France", *Eng. Hist. Rev.*, lxxix (1964).

[42] C. Clark and M. Haswell, *The Economics of Subsistence Agriculture*, 3rd edn (London, 1967), pp. 117–18.

[43] G. Richard, *La noblesse d'affaires au XVIIIe siècle* (Paris, 1974), pp. 121–269.

means demonstrates the inefficiency and unproductiveness of small farms, but he argues that French landowners were not interested in investment for improvements, but in raising their rents. Though he may well be right about the way French landowners kept their accounts and expected their stewards to act, he undoubtedly exaggerates the extent to which English landowners invested in capital improvements, so that his contrast with his French examples is invalid.[44] On the other hand Lavoisier, though lamenting the lack of tenants' working capital in France, which on large farms he puts at a half or a third the amount used in England, believed that the landlords' capital invested in buildings was far greater in France.[45]

If Forster is right that in France only "the *gros fermiers*, supported by a sprinkling of middling resident landlords and independent peasant owners", possessed the values and attitudes appropriate to maximizing production for the market,[46] whatever the extent of the contrast with England, we need to try to analyse how this had come about. First, we might try to see how the distribution of landownership differed in eighteenth-century France and England. A currently accepted estimate for France is that some 40 per cent of the land belonged to the peasants around 1780, but that in the north

[44] R. Forster, "Obstacles to Agricultural Growth in Eighteenth-Century France", *Amer. Hist. Rev.*, lxxv (1970), pp. 1600–3, 1610–12; R. Forster, *The House of Saulx-Tavanes, Versailles and Burgundy, 1700–1830* (Baltimore, 1971), pp. 86–92. In the 1780s the duke of Saulx-Tavanes spent nothing on improvements and 4.3 per cent of his gross income on repairs; before this, "net investment in the land had surely never exceeded five per cent" (p. 91). But B. A. Holderness shows that the expenditure on repairs and improvements on a group of middling estates in Norfolk and Suffolk ranged from 8.6 to 12.4 per cent of gross rental between 1746 and 1780, the average for the whole period being 10.7, the greater part of which consisted of repairs. But on the great estates "the average rarely exceeded 5 per cent before the 1780s". Allowances were sometimes made to tenants for repairs, but they were also often charged interest on improvements. B. A. Holderness, "Landlord's Capital Formation in East Anglia, 1750–1870", *Econ. Hist. Rev.*, 2nd ser., xxv (1972), pp. 435–40, 442, esp. table 2, p. 439.

[45] A. L. Lavoisier, "Sur l'agriculture et le commerce de l'Orléanais", in *Oeuvres de Lavoisier*, 6 vols. (Paris, 1862–93), vi, pp. 258–9: "the maintenance and rebuilding of such a large number of buildings amounted to an expense which, added to taxation, took the greater part of the owner's revenue". Adam Smith thought that there was little investment in improvement, except by farmers: "After small proprietors . . . rich and great farmers are, in every country, the principal improvers. There are more such perhaps in England than in any other European monarchy": Smith, *Wealth of Nations*, bk iii, ch. 2 (20), ed. E. Cannan, 2 vols. in 1 (Chicago, 1976), i, p. 418.

[46] Forster, "Obstacles to Agricultural Growth in Eighteenth-Century France", p. 1613.

the average was about a third.[47] Estimates or guesses based on Gregory King suggest that freeholders held about 30 per cent of England and Wales with an average of some 50 acres of arable each.[48] According to Brenner, the failure of peasant revolts in sixteenth-century England meant that by 1700 "English landlords controlled an overwhelming proportion of the cultivable land – perhaps 70–75 per cent".[49] But this is much the same proportion as that held by non-peasant proprietors in northern France. More important, King's average arable acreage of the larger farms was apparently 75 acres, well within the range of Jacquart's middling peasant farm south of Paris with one plough-team and 10–40 hectares.[50] This hardly seems to fit well with Brenner's "larger-scale capitalist farming . . . necessary for real agricultural breakthrough leading to economic development in this period" or, if this is what was meant, the size of farm was common in northern France and growing in numbers. Brenner sees "the only real alternative to the 'classic English' landlord / large tenant / wage-labourer form of capitalist agriculture" as "an equally capitalist system based on large-scale owner-cultivators", as in Catalonia.[51] Large farms of this kind were important there, but a large if unquantifiable part was played by share-cropping in the progressive agriculture of Catalonia.[52] This is of interest since share-cropping was regarded by

[47] M. Vovelle, *La chute de la monarchie* (Paris, 1972), pp. 14–15.

[48] R. Floud (ed.), *Essays in Quantitative Economic History* (Oxford, 1974), pp. 114, 118, 126; *Seventeenth-Century Economic Documents*, ed. J. Thirsk and J. P. Cooper (Oxford, 1972), p. 811. King's estimates of income imply that the 40,000 greater freeholders had 100–130 acres of land each, and the 140,000 lesser freeholders 50–60 acres each, giving an overall acreage of 60–75 acres. There is a problem of definition, as French historians include customary tenants as proprietors; also King may have included some copyholders in his freeholders, but some lesser ones must be in his category of "cottagers and paupers". It is also relevant to note that F. M. L. Thompson has argued that the amount held by freeholders did not fall in the eighteenth century: F. M. L. Thompson, "Landownership and Economic Growth in England in the Eighteenth Century", in E. L. Jones and S. J. Woolf (eds.), *Agrarian Change and Economic Development* (London, 1969), pp. 42–3.

[49] Above, p. 48.

[50] J. Jacquart, *La crise rurale en Ile-de-France, 1550–1670* (Paris, 1974), p. 349.

[51] Above, p. 49, n. 81.

[52] P. Vilar, *La Catalogne dans l'Espagne moderne*, 3 vols. (Paris, 1962), i, p. 578, and ii, pp. 500, 505, 567, 576.

the Physiocrats, Adam Smith[53] and Arthur Young as incompatible with improvements.

It has been suggested that demographic and subsistence crises were much more severe in France than in England in the seventeenth century. If demographic and economic fluctuations were also much greater from the fourteenth century, is this part of the explanation of long-term differences in agrarian and economic structures? In fact little is known with any certainty about English population movements before 1600 but, if we accept Hatcher's hypotheses, the long-term changes were similar to those in France, though the impact of war was greater there.[54] On this view, both countries experienced demographic and economic growth from the late fifteenth century, but in France this was faster down to about 1560, especially in the early sixteenth century. Can changes in landholdings be related to these fluctuations?

Cicely Howell argues that, in midland England, population pressure by 1300 tended to reduce customary holdings to half yardlands (about 12 acres, or 4.8 hectares); by 1500 such holdings were becoming rare; by 1700 they "had all but disappeared in Leicestershire". The numbers of "commercial family farms" of 50–60 acres grew.[55] In Chippenham, Cambridgeshire, in 1279 the dominant holding was the half virgate; in 1544 there were only six such holdings and 60 per cent of the land was in holdings of over 50 acres; by 1636 there were no half virgates and 69 per cent of the land was in holdings of over 90 acres. A similar pattern of growth of large farms prevailed in the Chalk Country of Wiltshire; in the Cheese Country the smallholding and family farm continued into the eighteenth century. In the fenlands of Lincolnshire and Cambridgeshire small-

[53] Smith, *Wealth of Nations*, bk iii, ch. 2 (20), ed. Cannan, i, p. 414; tithe was a "very great hindrance to improvement" and *métayage* "an effectual bar to it".

[54] J. Hatcher, *Plague, Population and the English Economy, 1348–1530* (London, 1977), pp. 68–9, figs. 1–2, suggests that population in 1450 was 60 per cent less than in 1348. Hugues Neveux suggests a general fall in rural population of around 50 per cent, which in war-devastated areas reached 70 per cent: H. Neveux, "Déclin et reprise: la fluctuation biséculaire, 1330–1560", in Duby and Wallon (eds.), *Histoire de la France rurale*, ii, pp. 74, 101. Ian Blanchard has argued that population and rent did not show sustained rises until the 1520s: I. Blanchard, "Population Change, Enclosure and the Early Tudor Economy", *Econ. Hist. Rev.*, 2nd ser., xxiii (1970), pp. 433–5.

[55] C. Howell, "Stability and Change, 1300–1700", *Jl Peasant Studies*, ii (1974–5), p. 474. Such a farm would need some wage labour.

holdings survived or multiplied.[56] Freeholders were numerous in Leicestershire and Warwickshire; in Leicestershire in the fifteenth century some of them built up larger holdings than the customary tenants. By 1500 "a small class of rich peasants had consolidated itself . . . men able to cultivate an arable area of 60 to 80 acres, whereas in 1341 the largest peasant holdings were not greater than 30 arable acres in extent". Instead of producing a more homogeneous distribution of land among the peasants, the falling-in of customary tenements and the leasing of demesnes since 1349 had produced larger holdings using some wage labour in arable farming. Wholesale conversion to pasture produced even larger farms, often let to rising yeomen.[57]

In order to compare the course of agrarian change in France, we need first to relate it to Le Roy Ladurie's cycle derived from lower Languedoc. This also starts from a situation of over-population and even more drastic fragmentation of peasant holdings around 1300. The fall of population in the fourteenth century and the beginnings of recovery in the fifteenth accompany a building up of middling "yeoman" holdings of about a dozen hectares (about 30 acres,

[56] M. Spufford, *Contrasting Communities* (Cambridge, 1974), pp. 65–84, tables 1, 3, pp. 90–2, 101–4; E. Kerridge, "Agriculture, *c.*1500–*c.*1793", in *V.C.H. Wiltshire*, iv, pp. 57–9: "In the sheep-and-corn countries . . . in the early 16th century most of the land was in the hands of capitalist farmers . . . Family and part-time farmers . . . occupied more than half the farmland . . . [but in the mid-seventeenth century] no more than one-third"; Spufford, *Contrasting Communities*, pp. 160–1, 165–7; J. Thirsk, *Fenland Farming in the Sixteenth Century* (Leicester, 1953); J. Thirsk, *English Peasant Farming* (London, 1957), p. 98, table 19 (early seventeenth-century surveys of some 6,000 acres of Lincolnshire clays), implies that some 59 per cent of the land was in holdings over 60 acres, 43 per cent in holdings over 90 acres, and 12 per cent in holdings under 30 acres. The tenants of holdings of 10 acres and under were nearly 30 per cent of the total number of tenants, but had about 4 per cent of the land. The table only gives the numbers holding land in each category (1–5 acres, etc.). The percentages were calculated by assuming that all holdings in each category averaged the middle acreage of that category (that is, 15 acres in the category 10–20 acres, etc.). The four farms with over 200 acres were assumed to have 250 acres each.

[57] R. H. Hilton, *The Economic Development of Some Leicestershire Estates in the Fourteenth and Fifteenth Centuries* (Oxford, 1947), p. 105; R. H. Hilton, "Medieval Agrarian History", in *V.C.H. Leicestershire*, ii, pp. 183–96; W. G. Hoskins, "The Leicestershire Farmer in the Sixteenth Century", in his *Essays in Leicestershire History* (Liverpool, 1950). Hilton writes more generally of some forty villages on large estates in the west midlands: "The trend at this period toward the diminution of the small-holding group and the increase in the number of large holdings [30–100 acres of arable] seems fairly certain": R. H. Hilton, *The English Peasantry in the Later Middle Ages* (Oxford, 1975), pp. 39–40.

roughly comparable to an English yardland), though much larger holdings also existed. These middling properties were eroded again, as population and rent rose in the sixteenth and seventeenth centuries, by the increasing numbers both of very large and, to a lesser extent, of large properties. With the depression of rents and population in the later seventeenth century, there was another rebuilding of larger properties, but this time by urban élites, not by rural "yeomen".[58]

Bois, whose *Crise du féodalisme* did not appear until after Brenner's article, has seen a similar pattern in eastern Normandy for the period 1300–1520. This is of interest both because of the region's resemblances to open-field England and because Bois has constructed a Marxist model of feudalism in crisis around his findings. At the beginning he finds extreme fragmentation of peasant tenures with most holdings of 2 hectares or less, though a few very much bigger holdings existed. He argues for a very rapid increase of rural population in the second half of the fifteenth century, and also that the number of middling peasant proprietors (*censitaires*) increased between 1397 and 1477 while the number of very small ones decreased. By 1527 continuing population growth had produced a proliferation of small properties and a decline of middling ones. However, this fifteenth-century expansion of middling properties is much less marked than in Languedoc, or in that of larger holdings in midland England, and it disappears altogether if another definition of "middling" is used.[59]

[58] E. Le Roy Ladurie, *Les paysans de Languedoc*, 2 vols. (S.E.V.P.E.N. edn, Paris, 1966), i, pp. 151–60, 580–1. "Yeomen" is his word. A middling holding is put within the range of 20 to 100 *setérées* (3.6 to 18 hectares). In his "Masses profondes: la paysannerie", p. 518, Le Roy Ladurie suggests a dozen hectares as the typical figure. As there was a two-field system in Languedoc, 30 acres of arable would produce less than in an English three-field system.

[59] Bois, *Crise du féodalisme*, pp. 49–72, 148–50, 138–46. These findings come from the analysis of the numbers of *censitaires* in St Nicholas d'Aliermont (p. 140). In 1397 those with holdings of 6–15 hectares were 34 per cent of the total number; in 1477 they were 43 per cent; in 1527, 32 per cent. However, if we take Bois's definition of the middling holding as 10–20 hectares (p. 146), the percentages are 25 in 1397, 26 in 1477, 19 in 1527; if 8–20 hectares is taken, the percentages are 34, 40 and 27. In 1527 some 47 per cent of all the property was held by 17 owners (11 per cent of the total) with over 20 hectares, 25 per cent by the 32 per cent of owners with 10–20 hectares, a pattern somewhat like Chippenham (Cambridgeshire) in 1544, where 11 tenants (18 per cent of the total) with holdings over 50 acres had 60 per cent of the land. Bois believes that in Normandy population pressure did not produce so much erosion of larger holdings as in Languedoc (pp. 157–8).

For Bois, the middling peasant holding of one plough-team is the basic form of production, the foundation of feudalism. Multiplication of these units means the expansion of production; its decline means the reverse. Prices fall when this peasant production rises and vice versa. The repetition of the cycles and mechanisms of growth, blockage and regression demonstrates the existence of a system.[60] This system would through its own contradictions generate the cycles of growth and regression to which epidemics, war, climatic changes and stagnation of techniques contribute without actually being determining causes. Such causes arise from social relationships, the domination of lords over peasants and their levying of tribute, and the appropriation of surplus.

A falling rate of appropriation[61] encourages peasants to expand production and consumption. Given static agricultural techniques, growth in production means expansion of the cultivated area and the eventual use of marginal land. This is accompanied by rising agricultural prices (relative to industrial ones) and by population growth. This leads eventually to fragmentation of holdings and fall-

Le Roy Ladurie has also seen confirmation of the long-term trends in Languedoc at Neubourg in Normandy: Le Roy Ladurie, "Masses profondes: la paysannerie", pp. 518–19. Although the fluctuations in the numbers of very small proprietors do follow the southern pattern from 1397 to 1775, those with middling holdings around a dozen hectares do not. Those with 10–30 Norman acres (7.4 to 22.2 hectares) occupied 34.1 per cent of the total area of the *mouvances* in 1397, 35 per cent in 1497, and 32.2 per cent in 1775, while those with over 30 acres occupied 11 per cent, 12.6 per cent, and 17.1 per cent at the same dates. The area for which information exists in 1775 is less than a third of that for the earlier dates. The number of owners of 10–30 acres, adjusted for 1775 on the assumption that the area known is representative of the other two-thirds, is 32 for 1496, 38 for 1397, and 31 for 1775. Calculated from A. Plaisse, *La baronnie du Neubourg* (Paris, 1961), table 9 at p. 44, table 52 at p. 348, and table 55 at p. 357.

60 Bois, *Crise du féodalisme*, pp. 350–61.

61 This is a basic long-term phenomenon, arising from perpetual tenures, where the peasant as an independent producer is able to reduce his dues. The falling rate of appropriation does not fit very well with Hilton's emphasis on "the high level of rent and other demands made by landowners of tenants": Hilton, *English Peasantry in the Later Middle Ages*, p. 213, cf. pp. 235–6. Is there a basic difference between French and English developments before 1340, or is it a matter of terminology? French historians do not seem to distinguish so sharply between free and customary tenants as do English ones, so that once villeinage largely disappears as a personal condition the typical *censitaire* is taken to be nearer to the English freehold tenant than to the English customary tenant or tenant at will. If dues in kind were more important in France than in England, as Duby has suggested, their commutation would produce a long-term shift in favour of the tenants. Freehold tenants with fixed rents were more numerous than bond tenants in some parts of England.

ing productivity, as does the use of marginal land. Hitherto, growth has meant that the falling rate of appropriation can still give the appropriators greater returns, because the volume of production is rising. Now falling productivity reduces the volume, while the peasants are cutting their consumption and inputs to precarious levels. The appropriators try to maintain their takings and so increase the rate of appropriation and thus turn growth into regression by ruining the basis of peasant production. Bois allows that it was probably royal taxation which performed this regressive function in the fourteenth century and prevented expansion back to former levels of rural population in the sixteenth century.[62] The phase of regression reverses the former cycle. The cultivated area contracts to better land; the size of peasant holdings rises, as does productivity. The rate of appropriation rises, but the volume falls along with total production; population and agricultural prices fall; and wages and industrial prices rise. The process of decline is limited by the growth of productivity on the larger peasant holdings, enabling these peasants to increase their own consumption and inputs and pay taxes. The process of growth will start again.

Given unchanging technology, the cycles could apparently repeat for ever. But in fact each cycle of growth produces accumulation of resources with merchants and large peasants, weakens the original feudal structures and pushes more small peasants towards proletarianization. In Normandy the years 1495–1500 saw the beginnings of a rural textile industry as well as an expansion of maritime trade; this was accompanied by the buying up of customary tenements by bourgeois. By 1510 the attitude of seigneurs had changed: they became "more concerned to expel tenants than to maintain them in their tenures", so as to add more land to their demesnes. Despite increasing their revenues from demesnes, forests and *banalités*, great lords failed to restore the purchasing power which their revenues had had in 1300; they were dependent on office and favours from the crown to support their increasingly costly way of life.[63]

This contradicts Brenner's view that French lords, unlike English

[62] Bois, *Crise du féodalisme*, pp. 193, 336.

[63] *Ibid.*, pp. 342, 246–7, 230–4. Unfortunately, little detailed information or evidence about the expulsion of customary tenants is given, other than that on p. 204.

ones, could not expel customary tenants.[64] Bois also accepts Le Roy Ladurie's neo-Malthusian model to a greater extent than Brenner and writes of "the relative autonomy of the demographic regime in relation to the economic system".[65] Bois's argument centres on middling peasant farms, whose numbers, investment and productivity determine agricultural prices and the cycles of growth and depression. Providing it was large enough for a plough-team – that is, between 10 and 20 hectares (1–2 English yardlands) – "the family farm was the most efficient unit". Large farms could only overcome their handicap of relative inefficiency if they had ready access to urban markets, or when prices were high and wages were low. They were marginal to an economy whose dynamics were controlled by the family farm.[66]

There is some evidence that peasant farms produced higher yields than demesne farms using serf labour in the early modern period in eastern Europe,[67] but there is evidence to the contrary for farms using wage labour in the late medieval west.[68] Yields in open-field sheep-and-corn husbandry would be influenced by the number of sheep kept, which could be relatively higher on demesne farms. We have already seen that the increase in the number of middling farms in Aliermont was not as clear and decisive as the model requires for the fifteenth century, though the number and area of larger properties did decline.[69] By 1527, 47 per cent of the area was in properties over 20 hectares, and 59 per cent in properties over 16 hectares, all of which would have needed considerable amounts of

64 Above, pp. 56–7. 65 Bois, *Crise du féodalisme*, p. 336.

66 *Ibid.*, pp. 224–5, 352–3, 146. Yet on p. 226 Bois shows that the demesne farm of La Bergerie with 50 hectares of arable and 500 sheep (p. 220) had greater grain yields than the average peasant farm.

67 Z. Kirilly and I. N. Kiss, "Les exploitations paysannes en Hongrie", *Annales E.S.C.*, xxiii (1968), p. 1236. This view has also been expressed decisively by many Polish historians: for example, W. Kula, *Théorie économique du système féodale* (Paris, 1970), p. 87.

68 Bois, *Crise du féodalisme*, p. 336; P. F. Brandon, "Cereal Yields on the Sussex Estates of Battle Abbey during the Later Middle Ages", *Econ. Hist. Rev.*, 2nd ser., xxv (1972). The size of farm specified by Bois relates to open-field arable; he is not thinking of the intensive Flemish farming: see above, pp. 149–50, n. 39.

69 See above, pp. 155–6, n. 59. Bois points out that in 1477 many tenures (30 per cent of the total area) were vacant and were let on temporary leases, increasing the size of many proprietors' holdings, so that 42 (58 per cent) of the 72 proprietors were *laboureurs*; but in 1397, 44 proprietors had over 10 hectares: Bois, *Crise du féodalisme*, pp. 140–6.

wage labour.[70] According to Bois, the tendencies to weaken "the feudal mode of production" were stronger in the sixteenth century than in the thirteenth, but the system did not fundamentally change and accumulation was checked again in the mid-sixteenth century. Unfortunately, Bois does not pursue his analysis. The logic of his model would require the check to be due to rising rates of appropriation through rents and taxes, which would be plausible for the period 1550–1660. This ought then to produce a rebuilding of family farms to inaugurate a new phase of growth. What our admittedly imperfect knowledge of northern France appears to show is that there was considerable loss of peasant property from 1550 to 1700 and a relative increase in the importance of larger holdings of over 20 hectares.[71]

Bois claims general applicability for his model, but were there peculiarities about the Norman situation on which it was built? Bois shows that demesne lands (outside the Vexin where large farms of 100 or 150 hectares prevailed) were usually let in farms of 20–30 hectares and demesnes were only 5–10 per cent of the total arable area, a proportion which already existed in the thirteenth century or earlier.[72] But, in the sixteenth century, demesnes around Paris were 25–30 per cent of the total area and about 18 per cent of the arable.[73] In midland England in 1279 demesne was a quarter of great estates and 41 per cent of smaller ones.[74] In France from the fifteenth century very different patterns can be found: the creation of large *métairies* at the expense of customary tenants by seigneurs in the Gâtine of Poitou; the restoration of heavy dues and the increase of rents on emphyteutic tenures by seigneurs in the Lyonnais, whose

[70] Bois acknowledges that his family farm needed some wage labour and that *laboureurs* depended on the availability of *manouvriers* (cottagers). He also claims that large numbers of semi-proletarianized *manouvriers*, as at Aliermont in 1527, would mean a fall in the average productivity of labour, but as he has already shown that many of them were artisans, it is difficult to see how this would affect agricultural productivity. *Ibid.*, pp. 141, 168–9, 311 n. 2.

[71] Le Roy Ladurie, "Masses profondes: la paysannerie", pp. 792, 795.

[72] Bois, *Crise du féodalisme*, pp. 216–20.

[73] Jacquart, *Crise rurale en Ile-de-France*, pp. 65–6, 75 n. 27. In Normandy the great seigneuries had extensive forests; some 40 per cent of the barony of Neubourg was forest. These were the most valuable part of the demesne. While church, crown and nobility also owned most of the forest around Paris, seigneurial demesnes occupied a much greater amount of the cultivated area than in Normandy.

[74] G. Duby, *Rural Economy and Country Life in the Medieval West* (London, 1968), p. 263, citing Kosminsky.

demesnes continued to consist of a few scattered parcels; the building up of concentrated share-cropping farms of 20–40 hectares around Toulouse.[75]

On some Flemish estates after 1400 large farms over 15 hectares, which had been 11.4 per cent of the total, disappear, although population was stagnating or falling. In the sixteenth century, farms over 7.5 hectares virtually disappear, and those of 0.75–1.5 hectares and under increased their preponderance, while population had increased sharply in the first decades and fallen even more in the last ones. This atomization was accompanied by intensification, improvement of techniques and productivity, which once again raised production to higher levels than ever before in the sixteenth century, along with rising levels of population.[76] These developments fit none of the models discussed, least of all Bois's assumptions about technical stagnation or that microfundia lead to lower productivity. Le Roy Ladurie sees it as "a green revolution, which is aberrant from developments elsewhere in the period 1400–1600, except for parts of Lombardy".[77]

Everywhere as a result of depression landlords had to make concessions to get or keep tenants. Customary tenants often benefited by getting better terms.[78] Where customary dues and rents were high, tenants might prefer to convert hereditary customary tenures

[75] L. Merle, *La métairie et l'évolution agraire de la Gâtine poitevine* (Paris, 1974), pp. 57–74; M.-T. Lorcin, *Les campagnes de la région lyonnaise aux XIVᵉ et XVᵉ siècles* (Paris, 1974), pp. 441–3, 462–3; G. Sicard, *Le métayage dans le Midi toulousain à la fin du moyen âge* (Toulouse, 1956), pp. 25–31.

[76] E. van Cauwenberghe, "Les changements de la productivité, du revenu et des formes des exploitations paysannes aux Pays Bas XIVᵉ–XVIᵉ ss.", *Studia historiae oeconomicae*, x (1975); this covers three groups of estates in Flanders and two in Brabant. See also H. van der Wee and E. van Cauwenberghe, "Histoire agraire et finances publiques en Flandre du XIVᵉ au XVIIᵉ siècle", *Annales E.S.C.*, xxviii (1973); P. Deprez, "De boeren in de 16ᵈᵉ, 17ᵈᵉ en 18ᵈᵉ eeuw", in J. L. Broeckx (ed.), *Flandria nostra*, 5 vols. (Antwerp, 1957–60), i.

[77] Le Roy Ladurie, "Masses profondes: la paysannerie", pp. 512–13, 520–1. He attributes this to density of population and large urban markets, and to relatively small demographic changes. But the fact that the percentage of farms under 1.5 hectares remained constant when population was rising, and rose when the population fell in the late sixteenth century, is in striking contrast to his findings for Languedoc.

[78] Buildings were often repaired at the landlord's expense, vacant holdings which had reverted to waste might be restored, or no rent or a reduced rent might be taken for an initial period.

into terminable leases at lower rents.[79] The fifteenth century undoubtedly saw an increase in "customary leases" for years and lives on several English monastic estates.[80] Whether or not they came about for similar reasons, this process meant that the amount of leasehold land could increase during depression to the eventual profit of lords when prices and rents rose again. At Neubourg and Aliermont, although vacant customary holdings were leased in the fifteenth century, they had reverted to customary tenures by 1500. In England demesne parcels leased to customary tenants could become assimilated to customary land, while in France in some cases demesne or leasehold was converted into hereditary, long-term or perpetual tenures. The relative amounts of such changes and the extent to which they were legally or economically lasting needs investigation. If there was a difference in these sorts of developments between France and England and the Netherlands, the fifteenth century would seem to be the decisive period. However, we are chiefly concerned with the leasing of demesnes, where advances, greater capital investments and longer leases were the main inducements offered by landlords in France and England. The most important difference seems to have been that in England the terms of leases remained more favourable to tenants when the price rise was under way. In both England and France the evidence of how and to whom demesnes were leased comes overwhelmingly from ecclesiastical estates.

Initially, leases of demesne were usually stock and land leases. From the tenant's point of view, the stock was an advance of working capital; from the landlord's, it kept open the option of resuming direct farming.[81] What seems the logical development happened on

79 Van der Wee and Van Cauwenberghe, "Histoire agraire et finances publiques en Flandre", pp. 1057–8; G. Sivery, *Structures agraires et vie rurale dans le Hainaut de la fin du XIIIe au début du XVIe siècle*, 3 vols. (Lille, 1973), ii, pp. 842–3.

80 The most striking example is at Durham, where the customary tenants became leaseholders for terms of between five and fifteen years: R. B. Dobson, *Durham Priory, 1400–1450* (Cambridge, 1973), pp. 282–3. The same process can be seen in several religious houses in the west country, but there the lease usually developed into one for years and lives: for example, H. P. R. Finberg, *Tavistock Abbey* (Cambridge, 1951), pp. 250–1, 256–7.

81 A variant, which made the stock a returnable advance, is found in some late fifteenth- and early sixteenth-century leases of East Anglian lands, where the tenant received cattle and corn worth £20, and repaid at 20s. a year over a twenty-year term; for example, the manor of Calcott Hall, Suffolk: Magdalen College, Oxford, muniments, Ledger B, pp. 93–5, 120–1.

Westminster Abbey's estates; as the terms lengthened from twelve years around 1400 to thirty or forty years around 1450, they ceased to include stock, while tenants continued to do repairs. However, one demesne out of twenty remained on a stock lease until 1525[82] and such leases still existed on the estates of many of the larger monasteries, while options to take grain instead of money rents became more frequent.[83] On some estates, leases only became longer in the early sixteenth century; this was particularly marked on the estates of the archbishop of Canterbury, where terms of five to ten years before 1500 lengthened to fifteen and then in the 1520s to thirty or forty years.[84] But the bishops of Worcester were leasing their demesnes for forty years or more by the mid-fifteenth century; by then, or at latest by 1500, terms of forty years or longer were common on monastic estates.[85] In the west country, leases for lives were common and by the early sixteenth century the lease for three lives determinable on years was making its appearance. During the sixteenth century this became the predominant form of tenure in Wiltshire and the west country. These leases remained at low old rents, but high entry fines were taken when a new lease was granted or when new lives were put into a lease.

The leasing of demesnes did not necessarily perpetuate large holdings; in some cases demesnes were fragmented, or let to a group of customary tenants, or even eventually turned into perpetual fee-farm holdings. Nevertheless, the majority of ecclesiastical demesnes which have been studied were let as large, often very large, holdings and the majority of those who leased them, from Kent or Devon to Yorkshire, were either substantial peasants, or aspiring or actual yeomen, though there was also a minority of gentry. In Leicestershire these yeomen farmers often leased mon-

[82] B. Harvey, "The Leasing of the Abbot of Westminster's Demesnes in the Later Middle Ages", *Econ. Hist. Rev.*, 2nd ser., xxii (1969).

[83] J. Youings, "Landlords in England: C, The Church", in J. Thirsk (ed.), *The Agrarian History of England and Wales*, iv, *1500–1640* (Cambridge, 1967), pp. 321–2.

[84] F. R. H. Du Boulay, *The Lordship of Canterbury* (London, 1966), pp. 220–31; C. Dyer, "A Redistribution of Incomes in Fifteenth-Century England?", *Past and Present*, no. 39 (April 1968), pp. 14, 28–9.

[85] Forty-year terms had replaced shorter ones in Leicestershire and on the Ramsey estates in Huntingdonshire, but much longer terms were granted by Buckland in Devon: Youings, "Landlords in England: C, The Church", pp. 319–21. Of the 18 monastic leases granted before 1533 on the Seymour estates in and near Wiltshire, 15 were from thirty to seventy years; 3 were for lives.

astic tithe as well, but ecclesiastical landlords did not usually farm out whole manors. Nevertheless, in Leicestershire leases to the gentry had become more numerous in the decades before the dissolution. In Leicestershire they were replacing yeomen, who seem to have monopolized the leases of demesne and tithe in the late fifteenth century.[86] This raises the question as to how far these gentry lessees sublet to peasant farmers. In many cases the presumption is that they did not. Yeomen lessees who prospered further would rise to gentry status.

Evidence about the results of leasing English lay estates, and even about the prevailing length of leases, is much scantier. However, it seems likely that most were twenty-one years or longer in the early sixteenth century[87] and that twenty-one years and three lives were the dominant terms for the sixteenth and seventeenth centuries. Further consideration of this later phase can be postponed; the immediate point is the one made by Thorold Rogers that English leases in the early modern period were long ones. He saw this in the context of eighteenth- and nineteenth-century advocacy of long leases as essential to encourage tenants to invest in improvements. We must look at it in relation to the position in France.

There landlords offered even more lavish inducements, though of the type already discussed, in order to encourage tenants to take

[86] S. Jack, "Monastic Lands in Leicestershire and their Administration on the Eve of the Dissolution", *Leics. Archaeol. and Hist. Soc. Trans.*, xli (1965–6), pp. 14–17; the leases of one house, Croxton Kerriall, "besides the usual clause concerning sub-letting without the convent's permission . . . also contained a strongly-worded proviso that the lease would be void if a gentleman or even a gentleman's servant were permitted to inherit the interest" (p. 16).

[87] Twenty-one-year leases prevailed on the Percy estates in Yorkshire, Sussex, Kent, Dorset, Somerset and Northumberland, though entry fines were also taken: J. M. W. Bean, *The Estates of the Percy Family, 1416–1537* (Oxford, 1958), pp. 54–6; the earls of Shrewsbury were granting twenty-one-year leases in Shropshire from the later fifteenth century: A. J. Pollard, "Estate Management in the Later Middle Ages", *Econ. Hist. Rev.*, 2nd ser., xxv (1972); of 13 leases granted on the Seymour estates in 1514–35, 8 were from twenty-one to thirty-six years, 5 for three to four lives: survey of Seymour lands, *c.* 1540, Longleat, Seymour papers, vol. xii; the earls of Rutland generally granted twenty-one-year leases from 1540, and the earls of Oxford were granting terms of twenty years, twenty-one years and three lives in the 1550s, though the receiver general's accounts frequently only mention unspecified terms of years when recording fines paid: Essex County Record Office, DDpr/ 140–2. That a norm or minimum was taken to be twenty-one years or three lives (the two terms were treated as equivalent until the later seventeenth century) is suggested by the fact that tenants in tail were empowered to grant such terms by 32 Henry VIII, *cap.* 28.

up holdings on war-devastated or run-down land. In general, great landlords had to advance capital for rebuilding and stocking both demesne leases and customary holdings.[88] Another form of advancing working capital (rarely found in England) was *métayage*. This did occur both in upper Normandy and in the Paris region but, except in the form of leasing livestock (*bail à cheptel*), it did not survive beyond 1500; whereas in the south and west of France *métayage* probably increased in the fifteenth century and certainly did so in the sixteenth.[89] Some farmers in the Paris region and elsewhere had enjoyed leases for three lives, or for long terms of years (up to ninety-nine). But in the later fifteenth century the great majority of leases were for six to nine years, and these were the normal terms in the sixteenth century. In Picardy and Normandy nine years was the common term, though longer ones are found in the Soissonnais and Beauvaisis.[90] Six to nine years was normal in Languedoc and probably much of the south. In the Paris region and Normandy the relative areas of demesne and customary tenures had changed little between 1350 and 1500, but from the late fifteenth century there was increasing acquisition of customary tenures by merchants and officers from Paris and other towns. In the Paris region after 1500 seigneurial dues and demesne lands (sometimes including tithe) were increasingly leased together; the takers were mostly rich peasants, but also included officers and bourgeois.[91]

Comparing France and England in the early sixteenth century and recalling that most of the evidence comes from ecclesiastical estates, the contrast in length of leases is striking. The trend in France was towards shorter leases after reconstruction; in England, if it was not everywhere towards longer leases, there was certainly

[88] G. Fourquin, *Les campagnes de la région parisienne à la fin du moyen âge* (Paris, 1964), pp. 421–2, 430–55, 474–83; I. Guérin, *La vie rurale en Sologne aux XIVe et XVe siècles* (Paris, 1960), pp. 254–62; R. Boutruche, *Bordeaux de 1453 à 1715* (Bordeaux, 1966), pp. 31–59; Neveux, "Déclin et reprise", pp. 10–20.

[89] Bois, *Crise du féodalisme*, p. 221; Fourquin, *Campagnes de la région parisienne*, p. 355; Guérin, *Vie rurale en Sologne*, pp. 262–6; Jacquart, *Crise rurale en Ile-de-France*, p. 130.

[90] Jacquart, *Crise rurale en Ile-de-France*, pp. 47, 102 n. 3, 130; Fourquin, *Campagnes de la région parisienne*, p. 355; P. Deyon, *Contribution à l'étude des revenus fonciers en Picardie* (Lille, 1968), pp. 67–8; Postel-Vinay, *Rente foncière dans le capitalisme agricole*, pp. 18, 24; P. Goubert, *Beauvais et le Beauvaisis de 1600 à 1730* (Paris, 1960), p. 517.

[91] Fourquin, *Campagnes de la région parisienne*, pp. 479–80; Jacquart, *Crise rurale en Ile-de-France*, pp. 83–5.

no general trend to shorten them down to 1530. The other difference seems to be that in northern France rents rose faster in the first half of the sixteenth century, though they had probably fallen to much lower levels in the mid-fifteenth century. In some places, such as Hurepoix, the levels of rents of large farms around 1550 were not surpassed in real terms for some two hundred years. The evidence for England is poor for the first half of the sixteenth century, but there is no doubt that the fastest increases of rent were from the later sixteenth century, reaching a peak around 1640. This resembles the pattern in lower Languedoc, where there were few great increases of rent until after 1600.[92] Another difference in France is the greater predominance of corn rents.

Fourquin has argued that along with the reconstruction and repeopling of the countryside there was a rebuilding and reinvigorating of the rural seigneurie so that he sees a basic continuity of rural structures from the thirteenth century through the *ancien régime*.[93] This would, of course, fit in with the views of Bois and Brenner and would make another contrast with England, where it has usually been assumed that manorial courts suffered uninterrupted decline from the later middle ages. However, Le Roy Ladurie has claimed that in the sixteenth century rural society at least begins to take on a new complexion, precisely because of the relative weakness of the seigneurie. Except in a few exceptional areas, notably Burgundy and Brittany, what is happening is "a process of de-seigneurialization and de-feudalization of society".

[92] J. Jacquart, "La rente foncière, indice conjoncturel?", *Revue historique*, ccliii (1975), pp. 363–4; Jacquart, "Immobilisme et catastrophes", pp. 250–1; E. Kerridge, "The Movement of Rent, 1540–1640", *Econ. Hist. Rev.*, 2nd ser., vi (1953–4), p. 28, table IV; the percentage rise in Kerridge's index of new takings on the Herbert estates deflated by the price of wheat is about the same (?2 per cent) as that of the corn rent per acre on Desaives's eight farms of Notre-Dame in 1500–60, but Jacquart gives two other examples of rises of 50 and 40 per cent. With regard to Languedoc, it should be noted that the tenants in *métayage* paid half shares after 1540, instead of a third or less earlier: Le Roy Ladurie, *Paysans de Languedoc*, ii, p. 865. Of Le Roy Ladurie's sixteen corn-rent series, only two start before 1525; of the six which start in or near 1525, three show appreciable rises of 25 per cent or more by 1550 (pp. 1022–3). Nonetheless, the proportion of rent per hectare was very much higher in the seventeenth century than before 1560.

[93] Fourquin, *Campagnes de la région parisienne*, p. 530; G. Fourquin, *Seigneurie et féodalité au moyen âge* (Paris, 1970), pp. 222–4, 243; here he writes of a "seigneurial reaction" and denies that seigneurs had become *rentiers* to any greater extent than in 1300.

Feudal dues (in the eighteenth-century sense), except tithe, make up a very small percentage of proprietors' revenues in most areas. In rightly stressing this, he underemphasizes the considerable part played by seigneurial justice in the lives of many peasants. The dominant class is a class of proprietors in the Physiocratic sense, in which urban élites and markets play an increasingly important part. He sees in the predominant share of bourgeois and officers as purchasers of church lands in the open-field areas after 1560 signs of an aborted revolution in landed property (*révolution foncière*), apparently analogous to the effects of the dissolution of the monasteries in England.[94]

Although landowners and townsmen certainly did acquire monastic property, they had nothing like the preponderance implied by Le Roy Ladurie's analogy. The comparison might even suggest that urban élites were less active in the English land market. But his picture of a mid-sixteenth-century France, in which large farmers and peasants were not overburdened by high rents and taxes and profited from the fall in real wages after 1500, is even truer of England where longer leases, lower taxes and possibly a slower increase in rents favoured yeomen and larger husbandmen still more. However, as we have already seen, Le Roy Ladurie believes that his "yeoman" proprietors of fifteenth-century Languedoc were destroyed by parcellation and population pressure in the sixteenth century. He is unwilling to see the *laboureurs* of open-field France as forming a numerous yeomanry, or as the standard-bearers of a "rural capitalism" which was to develop in later seventeenth-century England and not until the eighteenth, or even nineteenth, century in France. He argues from Jacquart's analysis of Hurepoix that the class of rich *laboureurs*, farmers of demesnes, tithes and seigneurial dues, was tiny – under 5 per cent of the active peasant population. Even most of those styled as *laboureurs* were not entrepreneurs but simply peasants, "often very small peasants".

However, this conclusion seems to be based on analysing peasant ownership of land, rather than the actual *size* of the units farmed. Thus of those styled *laboureurs* in Jacquart's surveys, 68.5 per cent

[94] Le Roy Ladurie, "Paysans français du XVIe siècle", p. 346; Le Roy Ladurie, "Masses profondes: la paysannerie", pp. 633–6, 704–9. He contrasts France with western Germany where until the eighteenth century rural structures were dominated by a "feudal" system based on seigneurial dues and *banalités*.

(270) had less than one hectare, only 11 out of 394 (2.8 per cent) had over 10 hectares, and only 5 had over 15 hectares.[95] But in 1550 one-third of the customary tenures in Jacquart's sample belonged to townsmen and he shows that such owners normally let their land (except vineyards) in holdings of 10–40 hectares, farms for one plough-team. Thus some of Le Roy Ladurie's *mini-laboureurs* were farming far more than 1–2 hectares. They would still be a minority, but a bigger one than he suggests.[96] More important is the proportion of land in such farms over 10 hectares. From Jacquart's samples, it would seem that in a typical mixed-farming village, like Avrainville, nearly two-thirds of the land was in farms over 10 hectares and that much more than half of this was in farms which would have needed to employ wage labour. As Parisians and others acquired more peasant lands in the hundred and fifty years after 1550, the number of holdings in this category would increase.[97]

While this does not demonstrate the existence of potential rural capitalists, it is very much more like the situation and trend in open-field England which we have already seen at Chippenham (Cambridgeshire) and in Leicestershire and which, according to Le Roy Ladurie, did lead in the later seventeenth century to rural capitalism.

If we consider the proportion of those mainly dependent on wage labour in Jacquart's typical Avrainville, it was about 25 per cent around 1550; in Leicestershire and Lincolnshire in the 1524 subsidy,

---

95 Le Roy Ladurie, "Masses profondes: la paysannerie", pp. 651–8; Le Roy Ladurie, "Paysans français du XVIe siècle", pp. 345, 348–50.

96 Le Roy Ladurie, "Masses profondes: la paysannerie", pp. 625–6; Le Roy Ladurie suggests that a general proportion for bourgeois land was likely to be nearer 40 per cent. In Jacquart's sample, peasants owned 69 per cent of the vineyards.

97 Jacquart, *Crise rurale en Ile-de-France*, pp. 129–32, 349. In the case of Avrainville, around 1650 the 5 principal farms covered 37 per cent of the parish (p. 348 n. 59); the demesne was 116.5 hectares (p. 106); the table (p. 133) shows also *c.* 1560 one farm over 50 hectares, which is assumed to be 60 hectares, 4 of 25–50 hectares which, averaged at 37 hectares, give 108 hectares, so the total over 25 hectares would be 284.5 hectares, or 43.6 per cent of the total area of the seigneurie. If the 7 holdings between 10 and 25 hectares, averaged at 17 hectares each, are added, the percentage would be 61.8 of the total area. At Trappes, "terroir de concentration précoce" (p. 134), the demesne farm and 11 properties over 25 hectares occupied 71 per cent of the cultivated area in *c.* 1560, and 69 per cent in 1507 (p. 122). At Wissous the demesne farm was 92 hectares (p. 84); in *c.* 1650 the 6 largest farms covered 47 per cent of the area (p. 348 n. 59).

it was 20 and 33 per cent respectively.[98] What does seem different from England is the extent to which urban élites owned land and were involved in making advances to their tenants, particularly of livestock by *baux à cheptel*. Potentially, this could be either productive investment of urban capital or usurious exploitation of peasants by townsmen. However many and minuscule its peasant proprietors, the fact that they were the majority of country-dwellers does not prove it to be a peasant-dominated economy in Chayanov's or Thorner's sense, any more than the presence of bourgeois landowners or large farmers makes it a capitalist-dominated one; but it was a market-dominated one, with trends and potentials not obviously and qualitatively different from those in England in the sixteenth century.[99]

Brenner rightly points out that the French crown was concerned to acknowledge the legal identity and collective responsibility of village communities by using their assemblies and elected officers in levying taxes. In so far as he implies that the village community was in consequence stronger and better organized to resist landlords than in England, this seems doubtful.[100] In England, if some villages were to end as closed villages dominated by one landlord, or with

[98] Both Chayanov and Thorner see a peasant economy as one dominated by family farms. Chayanov's general model is not applicable, since its dynamics depend on relative abundance and availability of land. Thorner's most fundamental criterion of a peasant economy is that half or more of crops are produced by peasant households, in which the contribution of non-family labour to production is much less than that of the family: D. Thorner, "Peasant Economy as a Category in Economic History", in T. Shanin (ed.), *Peasants and Peasant Societies: Selected Readings* (Harmondsworth, 1971), p. 205. I would guess that, in open-field arable farming, farms upward of 60 acres with one or two plough-teams were using more wage than family labour. On this showing, in Jacquart's sample certainly Trappes and probably Wissous were not dominated by peasant production in this sense; the more typical Avrainville was more or less evenly divided between family units and larger ones. See above, p. 167, n. 97.

[99] Jacquart, *Crise rurale en Ile-de-France*, pp. 138–9; there were 88 tenants, 14 *vignerons*, 13 *manouvriers*; I have excluded the 7 *vignerons* who had over a hectare of land (p. 153) and included 2 craftsmen. These terriers, though they include all householders (p. 137), do not include servants living in, as the 1524 subsidy did; it also included village craftsmen: A. Everitt, "Farm Labourers", in Thirsk (ed.), *Agrarian History of England and Wales*, iv, p. 397. At Wigston, Leicestershire, of 67 taxpayers, 25 (37 per cent) were assessed on wages, of whom Hoskins thinks 10 were sons of yeomen or substantial peasants, which would make ordinary labourers 22 per cent: W. G. Hoskins, *The Midland Peasant* (London, 1957), pp. 143, 147.

[100] Above, pp. 55, 56–7.

select vestries, still parish and village meetings, leet and manorial juries actively sustained communal consciousness and interests in many villages well into or beyond the seventeenth century.[101]

Again, if tithe was a much heavier burden than seigneurial dues over much of France, in England it was levied at a higher rate than was general in France and 18 per cent was still collected in kind in 1813.[102] Although friction over collecting tithe was perpetual, the sixteenth century does not seem to have seen the widespread resistance and wholesale withholding of tithe which occurred in many parts of France from the 1520s.[103] It is difficult to believe that the transfer of much of the monastic tithe to lay ownership made it any more popular with the tithe-payers. Although the burden of direct taxation was more constant and heavier in France, in England in the 1520s it reached more people than ever before and the amounts raised then and in the 1540s were greater than ever before and seemed to be becoming a regular annual event. There had been more widespread rebellions triggered by resistance to taxation in England than in France down to 1548. Rural revolt in England in 1549 was concerned with religion, rents, the sheep tax, enclosures and stocking of commons, and there was a general animus against the gentry in both the western rising to defend the old religion and in Kett's Protestant-orientated rebellion in Norfolk. In France in the 1560s tithe was the general target of Huguenots and Catholic peasants, though in parts of the south-west seigneurial rights and dues were also attacked. The discrepancies in fiscal burdens, in political developments and in the effects of rising rents and prices became much greater after the mid-sixteenth century; the agrarian divergencies culminate in the later seventeenth century.

The first divergence came after 1560 when rents and agricultural production in France fell as a result of civil war, and rural population and rents ceased to grow and then fell. Bad harvests and high prices affected both countries severely in the 1590s, but whereas in France it was a culmination of depression and disasters, in England

[101] C. Bridenbaugh, *Vexed and Troubled Englishmen, 1590–1642* (Oxford, 1967), pp. 240–9, may exaggerate the elements of democratic participation, but remains generally valid. Jacquart holds that the French village community was at its strongest *c.* 1560 and that thereafter it became steadily weaker in relation to both state and seigneurs: Jacquart, "Immobilisme et catastrophes", p. 284.

[102] E. J. Evans, *The Contentious Tithe* (London, 1976), p. 22 and n. 35.

[103] Le Roy Ladurie, "Masses profondes: la paysannerie", pp. 712–13.

it was a disturbance in a phase of rising population and rents, without any serious popular or political rebellions, compared with those before 1550. Though in England the costs of foreign war were high in the 1590s with significant political repercussions, they were lower than those of the 1540s and much lower than the cost of civil war in France. There a new phase of reconstruction had to be undertaken. Round Paris and elsewhere landlords had to encourage tenants to take up farms by offering better terms, as they had done in the fifteenth century. These mainly took the form of lower rents, advances either of money or of seed and stock, and rebuilding by the landlord. In some cases longer leases were given, but this seems to have been exceptional. Most of Jacquart's dynasties of large farmers, who also dealt in grain, cattle or timber, survived the devastations and some even increased their own wealth.[104]

However, although recovery and population growth in France north of the Loire continued down to about 1640, Jacquart believes that neither production nor population had returned to the levels of 1560 in most areas when they were again reduced by the crisis of the Fronde.[105] In the south, growth continued through the years of the Fronde to 1670 and rents continued to rise, reaching levels in grain equivalents around 1650 which were double those of the sixteenth century. In the Paris region most big farmers again survived the crisis years, though much less securely than before, and rents recovered until the 1680s. There seem to have been differences to the south of Paris where in real terms rents did not exceed the level of around 1560, whereas north of Paris they did (by 14 per cent in 1680 for grain rents per acre). Record levels were also reached in Picardy after 1662.[106] Moreover, the rents of small pieces of land around Paris rose much more, by about 70 per cent measured in grain equivalents, comparing 1560 and 1675 for arable, and even more for meadow.[107] The demand for small parcels of land was

[104] Jacquart, *Crise rurale en Ile-de-France*, pp. 186–7, 239–40, 265, 335, 341; Jacquart, "Immobilisme et catastrophes", pp. 200–2.

[105] Jacquart, "Immobilisme et catastrophes", pp. 251–2.

[106] Jacquart, "Rente foncière, indice conjoncturel?", pp. 364–6, 370; J.-P. Desaive, "A la recherche d'un indicateur de la conjoncture", in Goy and Le Roy Ladurie (eds.), *Fluctuations du produit de la dîme*, pp. 50–7; Deyon, *Contributions à l'étude des revenus fonciers en Picardie*, pp. 75–6; Le Roy Ladurie, "Masses profondes: la paysannerie", pp. 637–8, 807–8.

[107] B. Veyrassat-Herren and E. Le Roy Ladurie, "La rente foncière autour de Paris au XVIIe siècle", *Annales E.S.C.*, xxiii (1968), pp. 549–55.

always high enough to make their rents per acre higher than for larger holdings. But more significant for comparison with England is that for both large and small holdings the rents did not fall with prices after 1663 until after 1690, or even 1700 in the case of small parcels. Even more important is the decline in the amount of land owned by peasants and the increase both of demesnes and of urban ownership.

At Avrainville peasant property had fallen from 47 per cent to 20 per cent from 1560 to 1670; in villages further from Paris and other towns the fall was less. In Jacquart's entire sample, the number of villagers without any real property, even a cottage, had grown from almost none to a quarter or even a third of the whole.[108] Over half the land was now in farms of over 50 hectares at Avrainville and in other villages.[109] From the later sixteenth century there was indebtedness of village communities leading to the sale of communal lands, aggravating still further the plight of poorer peasants who in turn were forced to sell land. Engrossing by seigneurs and townsmen was certainly not confined to the Paris region; in Burgundy it led to the building up of share-cropping farms, and also in the poor regions of the Sologne and of the pastoral Haut Auvergne. In Burgundy this was accompanied throughout the seventeenth century by reassertion and extension of seigneurial rights and a progressive weakening of the village communities.[110] In Beauce in the sixteenth century the farms engrossed from customary tenures had averaged 40 hectares, and in 1696 they averaged 73 hectares; here, as around Paris, local merchants had been active in the sixteenth century and were replaced by officers in the seventeenth.[111] In open-field France there was a trend to larger farms and the pauperization and proletarianization of small peasants as marked as anything claimed for England.

108 Jacquart, *Crise rurale en Ile-de-France*, pp. 724–5.

109 *Ibid.*, p. 740; 52, 53 and 61 per cent at Avrainville, Wissous and Trappes respectively.

110 Saint-Jacob, "Mutations économiques et sociales dans les campagnes bourguignonnes à la fin du XVIe siècle"; M. Simonot-Bouillot, "La métairie et le métayer dans le sud du Châtillonnais du XVIe au XVIIIe siècle", *Annales de Bourgogne*, xxxiv (1962); S. Dontenwill, *Une seigneurie sous l'ancien régime* (Roanne, 1973), pp. 141–65, 186–9; J. L. Goldsmith, "Agricultural Specialization and Stagnation in Early Modern Auvergne", *Agric. Hist.*, xlvii (1973), pp. 221–3, 226–9.

111 Constant, "Propriété et le problème de la constitution des fermes", pp. 374–5.

In England rents rose faster than prices from 1560 to 1641, though there were interruptions, notably in the depression of the 1620s. The rate of increase was probably faster after 1590 than before, and with arable rising more than pasture.[112] The civil war caused a drop in the rents reaching landlords, with irrecoverable arrears piling up, but rents recovered again quickly after the war and were back to pre-war levels by 1650.[113] There may have been some increases down to the early 1660s, but by 1668 there were universal complaints about the decay of rents. In most areas they stagnated or fell, in some areas by as much as a quarter by 1682, with some recovery after the late 1690s.[114] An exception to this trend is Northumberland and Durham, where rents increased substantially from the 1650s to 1700 and again to 1750.[115]

From 1550 to 1700 and beyond, the prevalent terms of leases by great landowners were twenty-one years and three lives, usually determinable on ninety-nine years. Certainly, shorter leases and longer ones can be found, but they were usually the result of special circumstances.[116] While generalizations about covenants in leases

112 P. Bowden, "Agricultural Prices, Farm Profits, and Rents", in Thirsk (ed.), *Agrarian History of England and Wales*, iv, pp. 689–94; L. Stone, *The Crisis of the Aristocracy, 1540–1640* (Oxford, 1965), p. 772; A. Simpson, *The Wealth of the Gentry, 1540–1660* (Cambridge, 1961), pp. 196–211; M. E. Finch, *Five Northamptonshire Families* (Northants. Rec. Soc., xix, Northampton, 1955), pp. 200–1, 163.

113 C. Clay, "The Landowners and the English Civil War" (unpublished seminar paper, Oxford, 1977) [since published as part of his "Landlords and Estate Management in England", ch. 14 of J. Thirsk (ed.), *The Agrarian History of England and Wales*, v, *1640–1750*, pt 2 (Cambridge, 1985)].

114 *Seventeenth-Century Economic Documents*, ed. Thirsk and Cooper, pp. 68–88, 179, 304; C. Clay, "The Price of Freehold Land in the Later Seventeenth and Eighteenth Centuries", *Econ. Hist. Rev.*, 2nd ser., xxvii (1974), pp. 181–2; H. D. Turner, "George, Fourth Earl of Northampton: Estates and Stewards, 1686–1714", *Northamptonshire Past and Present*, iv, no. 2 (1967–8), pp. 100–5; J. D. Chambers, *The Vale of Trent, 1670–1800* (*Econ. Hist. Rev.* Supplement no. 3, London, 1957), p. 42; R. A. C. Parker, *Coke of Norfolk* (Oxford, 1975), p. 4; rents on six manors on the Belvoir estate of the earl of Rutland declined by 12 per cent over the period 1671–92.

115 P. W. Brassley, "The Agricultural Economy of Northumberland and Durham, 1640–1750" (Oxford Univ. B.Litt. thesis, 1974), pp. 70–85. Some of these estates may have been under-rented in the seventeenth century.

116 Very short, or annual, agreements were often an alternative to the landlord taking the farm in hand, when he could not find a tenant willing to take on a longer term at a higher rent. Longer terms might be a means of raising money. Entry fines were very often taken on a twenty-one-year lease in the seventeenth century (for example, by the earls of Warwick in Essex, the earls of Rutland in

are even more uncertain, it seems likely that by the later sixteenth century repairs to buildings were done at the expense of the tenant,[117] though the landlord provided timber and stone which was carted by the tenant. Hedging and ditching were done by the tenant and he was often required to plant a specified number of trees a year. When new buildings or rebuilding were needed, the tenant often provided them and was given an allowance in his entry fine, or rent. The tenant was bound to leave the farm in good repair. Obviously, landlords did invest in costs of enclosure and reclamation and in some new building, but this type of estate management seems to have aimed at making tenants provide advances which the landowner himself would have borne in the eighteenth century.

Although leases were concerned to ensure good husbandry, covenants well into the eighteenth century often included seigneurial obligations: to grind at the lord's mill, do boon works, especially carting, to do suit of court, give rent capons or geese, or not to destroy game.[118] The inclusion of such covenants, especially

Leicestershire, Lincolnshire and Yorkshire, on the Leveson-Gower estates in Shropshire and Staffordshire, by the earls of Southampton in Hampshire, and by the earls of Salisbury in Northamptonshire, Hertfordshire and Surrey), but they were usually much smaller in relation to the rent than in the leases for lives of the west country, south Wales and Lancashire.

117 Earlier the tenant was often required to do minor repairs, such as thatching and daubing, while the landlord paid for major repairs requiring timber, tiles, slate or stone. This distinction continued in some leases, but not in most of those known to me. It seems to be implied as having existed more recently in the specimen covenant providing that as the lord "has been at an extraordinary Charge in covering the Farm-house and Out-houses with Slate and Tile, instead of thatching them with Straw" the tenants are obliged to maintain them in the future: E. Laurence, *The Duty of a Steward to his Lord* (London, 1727), p. 130. The shorter the lease the more repairs a landlord undertook: see the specimen seven-year lease in G. Jacob, *The Compleat Court-Keeper* (London, 1713), p. 485.

118 Laurence, *Duty of a Steward to his Lord*, pp. 129–32; Covenant XVII, not to keep "any Greyhounds, Guns, etc. nor to set any Snares, Ginns, etc. so as to destroy the Lord's Game"; Covenant XIX, to send teams "to lead home the Hay and Corn" from demesne kept in hand, and stone and timber for building or repairs; Covenant XXII, to present capons, turkeys, or geese or other fowl to the lord. Some Sidney leases under James I and Charles I required harvest work with a team for one or two days and some required marling of grounds throughout the century. The Rutland leases on the Belvoir estate in the seventeenth century provided that the tenant "shall . . . Bowne yearely . . . with his carts and carriage and other usual bownes", grind at the lord's mill, plant trees, and from about 1648 was also to pay towards the new building or enlarging of the earl's houses in Leicestershire. The accounts show that the boon carting services were used for timber, coal

for carting services, was common in France. However, the position about repairs there is less clear, but on large farms in the Paris region major repairs were normally done by the lord; some lay lords spent more on repairs than English magnates.[119] In share-cropping leases, labour for roofing and repairs was provided by the tenant, and materials, though not their carriage, by the owner.[120] The process of engrossment of customary tenures and the building up of larger farms necessarily involved a good deal of investment in farm buildings. Apart from the rebuilding after the devastations of the League and the Fronde, the seventeenth century saw investment of urban wealth in the great stone-built courtyard farms of open-field France, as well as in the country residences and châteaux of *officiers* and financiers. This remodelling of landed property did not happen in the *bocage*, areas of dispersed settlement and stronger peasant proprietorship. It was the changes in open-field France in the seventeenth century which Le Roy Ladurie sees as the foundation for the growth in production of the eighteenth century and for development along the lines conceived by Quesnay. In this French, as against English, road to agrarian capitalism, "engrossing [*rassembler la terre*] prepared the way for agrarian capitalism and the ground for the still distant modern type of rural growth".[121]

and tiles (156 loads in 1614) and were still used in 1712. A draft lease of 1814 for a newly built farm by Sir Thomas Hesketh required suit of court and the keeping of a greyhound or cock for the lord when required: Fletcher, "Agrarian Revolution in Arable Lancashire", p. 103; heriots, suit to court and mill appear in the Thynne leases of the seventeenth century, and in the specimen lease for three lives in Jacob, *Compleat Court-Keeper*, pp. 305–8.

119 Jacquart, *Crise rurale en Ile-de-France*, p. 343, says, without specifying further, that "grosses reparations" were done by the lord, "menues" by the farmer, who also carted materials. Deyon, *Contribution à l'étude des revenus fonciers en Picardie*, pp. 67–8 and n. 11, cites Picardy leases where the maintenance of buildings and hedging and ditching were at the farmer's expense. On the other hand, Mireaux, *Province française au temps du Grand Roi*, p. 113, in summarizing the content of leases does not include any repairs by the tenant, while M. Fontenay, "Paysans et marchands ruraux de la Vallée de l'Essonnes dans la seconde moitié du XVIIe siècle", *Paris et Ile-de-France*, ix (1958), p. 176, would seem to indicate major repairs by the lord. Even before the Fronde, Baron d'Auneau was spending 5 per cent of his gross revenue on repairs, far more than the earls of Rutland and Salisbury: J.-M. Constant, "Gestion et revenus d'un grand domaine aux XVIe et XVIIe siècles d'après les comptes de la baronnie d'Auneau", *Revue d'histoire économique et sociale*, l (1972), p. 199.

120 Merle, *Métairie et l'évolution agraire de la Gâtine poitevine*, pp. 212, 217, 220, 228, 233.

121 Le Roy Ladurie, "Masses profondes: la paysannerie", pp. 796–9. It is perhaps worth noting how little is known about the "middle" France of *bocage* and

Before assessing this conclusion, we need to compare the behaviour of greater landowners in the critical years of the mid-seventeenth century, when they were confronted by the effects of civil war and the transition from a phase of rising prices to one of falling or stagnating agricultural prices. English landlords faced by huge arrears resulting from the civil war had to write them off. Faced with unprecedentedly heavy and continuous direct taxation, some of the greatest landowners tried to make their tenants pay, despite ordinances to the contrary.[122] The differences between France and England seem most marked after 1670, though so far there is little information about the behaviour of great lay landowners in France. An exception is the estate of Baron d'Auneau in Beauce. This shows stability among the farmers, with the baron remitting rent in difficult years and no great build-up of arrears even during the Fronde. Whereas many large farms were subdivided in the twenty years before 1650, afterwards they were let undivided. In the 1640s there had been a change from corn to money rents, but by 1653 farms were being let at 31 per cent below their previous rents and the cost of repairs had risen. The baron kept up his revenue by increasing the yield of seigneurial dues and of wood sales and by buying farms which gave a return of 7 per cent.[123]

The baron's success in finding farmers capable of leasing big farms is a reminder that the crisis bankrupted many middling ones. The turn of the big farmers was to come. By 1663 the lords had managed to raise rents to or beyond the levels prevailing before the Fronde. As we saw, this was also true of English rents in relation to the civil war. The difference seems to be that French lords tried to maintain rents at these levels until the 1680s or later. The result, both in the north and the south, where the rise in rents had not been

métayage in the seventeenth century. Brenner's contention that "strong peasant property and the absolutist state developed in mutual dependence upon one another" (above, p. 58) might apply better to Le Roy Ladurie's assumptions about the *bocage* regions.

122 L. Stone, *Family and Fortune* (Oxford, 1973), pp. 146–52; the earl of Southampton managed to make some tenants pay part of the assessment (pp. 235–6). John, earl of Rutland, included clauses in his leases in the 1640s and 1650s for the tenant to pay all taxes and free quarter "any act or Ordinance to the contrary notwithstanding": for example, Bottesford, deed no. 5371, 10th Mar. 1649/50: Belvoir Castle muniments. The same principle was later applied to the land tax on some Rutland estates. For these and other references to the Belvoir Castle muniments, I am grateful to His Grace the Duke of Rutland.

123 Constant, "Gestion et revenus d'un grand domaine".

interrupted during the years of the Fronde, was the bankruptcy of farmers, caught between low grain prices and high rents, followed by falls in rent until various dates in the second quarter of the eighteenth century in different regions. The farmers' bankruptcies meant not just uncollectable arrears and the throwing-in of leases, but the distraint and sale of the farmers' stock, plough-teams, sheep and cattle – a destruction of working capital.[124] The result was that many farms had to be kept in hand for lack of tenants; some were divided into smaller units, while others were concentrated in the hands of the biggest farmers, who were also farmers of seigneurial dues and tithe, money-lenders and merchants.

Why did landlords who had advanced large sums to restore farms and farmers under Henry IV and after the Fronde thus sell up their farmers? Leases had tended to shorten from nine to six years, while the number of owners increased.[125] When the lease was renewed, the farmer had to give land to pay the arrears, and as his debts continued to rise his profits fell because of low prices and rising taxation[126] and arrears continued. The lord's only way to restore some current income seemed to be to seize the farmer's stock before his arrears far exceeded its value. Where corn rents survived, the lord's revenue fell immediately with low prices. It has been argued that in the Soissonnais even before the Fronde there was considerable indebtedness and lack of continuity in renewing leases among big farmers.[127] In Marxist terms, the whole process can be seen as the triumph of "feudal" rent and social order over incipient rural capitalism, and is so interpreted by Postel-Vinay, whereas Brenner

[124] Jacquart, *Crise rurale en Ile-de-France*, pp. 714–15; Jacquart, "Immobilisme et catastrophes", pp. 254–5; M. Venard, *Bourgeois et paysans au XVIIe siècle* (Paris, 1957), pp. 99–102; Postel-Vinay, *Rente foncière dans le capitalisme agricole*, pp. 23–5, 29; Mireaux, *Province française au temps du Grand Roi*, pp. 138, 149; Goubert, *Beauvais et le Beauvaisis de 1600 à 1700*, pp. 526, 529–30; Fontenay, "Paysans et marchands ruraux de la Vallée de l'Essonnes", pp. 254–5, 208 n. 2.

[125] Unfortunately, the only systematic account of the incidence of arrears is that given in Goubert, *Beauvais et le Beauvaisis de 1600 à 1700*, pp. 526, 529–30.

[126] The *taille* increased with the Dutch war, but Colbert's reforms in its administration after 1663 probably augmented the burden on larger farms. Although arrears were written off and the total levied was reduced, the assessment no longer favoured the farmers of magnates and local notables to the same extent as before. Postel-Vinay gives examples of farmers mortgaging their cattle to bourgeois to pay their *taille* from 1669: Postel-Vinay, *Rente foncière dans le capitalisme agricole*, p. 25.

[127] *Ibid.*, pp. 16, 20, 24, 26.

overestimates the extent to which peasant property especially in northern France was able to survive the pressures of debt and engrossers.

Such interpretations implicitly or explicitly demand comparison with England. Brenner sounds like a Tory defender of the Corn Laws in his account of the fruitfulness of the partnership between capitalist farmers and beneficently far-sighted landlords.[128] Preachers had long denounced "covetous Land-Lords, that stretch their Rents on the Tenter-hookes of an evill conscience, and swell their Coffers by undoing their poore Tenants".[129] Landlords aspired to live "without Injury to any Man, or Pressure of my Tenants . . . [so] I know I have their Affections".[130] Thomas Fuller arrived at a position which was to be repeated for centuries in describing the good landlord: "that lets his land on a reasonable rate, so that the Tenant by employing his stock, and using his industry, may make an honest livelihood thereby . . . where Landlords are very easy, the Tenants (. . . out of their own lazinesse) seldome thrive . . . our Landlord puts some metall into his Tenants industry, yet not grating him too much, lest the Tenant revenge the Landlords cruelty to him upon his land . . . he raiseth his rents (or fines equivalent) in some proportion to the present price of other commodities". Fuller denounced depopulating enclosure, but found enclosure without depopulation profitable both to individuals and the commonwealth.[131] He wrote at a time of rising prices, but his principle was invoked by Dudley, Lord North, for the abatement of rents in 1669.[132] More immediately, Fuller's precepts were cited and repeated by the agricultural improvers around Hartlib under the

[128] Above, pp. 48–50.

[129] *The Workes of Thomas Adams, being the Summe of his Sermons, Meditations Divine and Discourses* (London, 1630 edn), p. 53, Paul's Cross sermon, 7th March 1612.

[130] Sir C. Wandesforde, *A Book of Instructions* [1636], ed. T. Comber, 2 vols. (Cambridge, 1777–8), i, pp. 90–1.

[131] Fuller, *Holy State*, pp. 99–102.

[132] [Dudley, Lord North], *Observations and Advices Oeconomical* (London, 1669), pp. 105–6. Rather than take in hand a distant farm, "He shall . . . do much better, to abate Rent in a moderate proportion . . . I have alwayes found most comfort, where I have let good pennyworths, otherwise our Farmes are now and then thrown up into our hands . . . by which means more losse is contracted in one year, then abatement of Rent would arise to in many. And Divines will also have it, that Gods Blessing doth not accompany such persons as are too hard to their Tenants".

Commonwealth; Blith and Hartlib also called for legislation to compensate tenants for improvements.[133]

This was not forthcoming; instead the duty of landlords to make their tenants industrious improvers continued to be stressed and the convention grew up that corn land should produce treble the rent exclusive of the seed corn. But in fact opinion seems to have differed as to whether or not average land produced two rents or nearer four around 1700.[134] Actual behaviour and injunctions by great landowners show that they did tolerate large accumulations of arrears in times of difficulty; some like Sir Richard Newdigate were prepared to invest in improvements, but were intolerant of arrears.[135] Others

[133] W. Blith, *The English Improver Improved*, 3rd impression (London, 1652), sig. [C 4ʳ] -d, sig. [A 3ʳ–4ʳ]; *Samuel Hartlib his Legacie*, 2nd edn (London, 1652), sig. B 2ᵛ: "That according to the usual custome of Flaunders, a Law may be made of letting and hiring Leases upon improvement . . . That the Farmer covenanteth on his part, to improve the land to such or such a greater Rent, by an orderly and excellent management of Husbandry . . . The Landlord . . . covenanteth . . . at the expiration of the said Lease, to give so many years purchase of the Improvement . . . which is 3 or 4 years, or somtimes more".

[134] Gregory King in 1697 thought "the common way of reckoning" the produce of corn land as treble the rent, exclusive of seed, was true for highly rated land, but for poor land it might be four rents. Harley had a computation for average arable of four rents: *Seventeenth-Century Economic Documents*, ed. Thirsk and Cooper, pp. 796–7. J. Mortimer, *The Whole Art of Husbandry*, 4th edn, 2 vols. (London, 1716), i, p. 391 (first published 1707): "They commonly allow a Farm to make three Rents, one for the Landlord, one for Charges, and one for the Tenant to live on . . . but few Farms . . . will constantly afford that Increase, or be maintained for that Charge"; taking a farm of £100 per annum, if the land is worth 20s. an acre, £100 may defray the charges, but if it is worth only 10s. an acre, £120–30 per annum is needed and you must reckon 250 acres of such land at £100 per annum, "or you will lose by it, unless 'tis very improveable Land". Laurence, *Duty of a Steward to his Lord*, p. 53, reckoned (1727) that a "careful provident Farmer" needed to sell two rents at least off the premises, while keeping his family with home-produced provisions. The farmers in Kent, Essex and other southern counties around London "us'd to make it a Maxim, that three rents should be sold". If they rented £200 or £300 a year, they soon purchased estates and let them to tenants who were forced to be content with two rents.

[135] In 1680 he wrote: "Never stay with any tenant above six months whatever pretence hee hath to persuade forbearance, for he who cant pay one Rent cant pay two together, but if (as sometimes happens) there should bee an extraordinary occation rather lend a tenant so much without interest to be paid three months after on a penall bond", and went on to advise distraining on the cattle of "whoever has a good stock" to enforce payment of rent. In 1696 he was considering improvements at Chilvers Coton by floating 400 acres and buying in farms: "Settle the Linnen Manufacture at Coton to prevent increase of Poor . . . Establish a market at Chilvers Coton, if it may be". He had just spent £7,000 at Long Itchendon on improvements, mostly on building fourteen farms from which he

like Lord Delamer still wanted to put the cost of improvements on to their tenants,[136] as did the dukes of Rutland, who were also prepared to carry large amounts of arrears.[137] The duke of Kingston, on the other hand, beset by low corn prices in the 1730s, carried large arrears, spent rather more on repairs, reduced rents, distrained any tenants from whom something might be recovered, and let some farms in smaller parcels.[138] The reaction of many great landlords to depressed rents in the late seventeenth and early eighteenth centuries was to invest more in repairs and improvements in order to attract substantial tenants.[139]

In so far as all this shows different reactions and behaviour by great English landowners to low grain prices from the later seventeenth century, it is difficult to believe that it was just that English landowners were more heedful of the precepts of conventional Christian teaching and of enlightened self-interest than the French.

got 5 per cent return, probably no more than the current yield on buying freehold land. Sir Richard also noted that "men of great estates must set their land cheaper than others". Warwickshire County Record Office, Newdigate MSS., vol. 183, pp. 26, 147–8, 43, 56, 84.

136 *The Works of the Right Honourable Henry Late L. Delamer and Earl of Warrington* (London, 1694), pp. 28–9, (written 1688) advocates leases for twenty-one years with an entry fine of about a year's value; "if your Tenant be behind with his Rent, if it be not above a Year, this Fine will set you right". The raising of the fine demonstrates the farmer's wealth, and the lower rent will encourage him to make improvements, which will secure the rent and leave the farm better; "tye your Farmers to Repairs, for they will do that for Six pence, which they will set down to you at Eighteen Pence". As Habakkuk remarks, the ideal estate was still regarded as one where tenants did the repairs: H. J. Habakkuk, "English Landownership, 1680–1740", *Econ. Hist. Rev.*, 1st ser., x (1939–40), p. 14.

137 Arrears in 1693 were about 12 per cent of total rent receipts. On the Belvoir estate only arrears and repairs were low in the early eighteenth century. Arrears became very high from the late 1720s, reaching £9,339 in 1735 when, on a rental of £6,800, only £2,089 was actually received. Repairs from 1729 to 1742 averaged 2 per cent of the rental, and were no more in the early eighteenth century. Arrears were mostly paid off in the 1740s at Belvoir, but later than this at Haddon.

138 G. E. Mingay, "The Agricultural Depression, 1730–1750", *Econ. Hist. Rev.*, 2nd ser., viii (1955–6), pp. 327–33.

139 Holderness, "Landlord's Capital Formation in East Anglia, 1750–1870", pp. 442–3; E. L. Jones, "Eighteenth-Century Changes in Hampshire Chalkland Farming", *Agric. Hist. Rev.*, viii (1960), pp. 8–9. For the Naworth estate of the earls of Carlisle, see Brassley, "Agricultural Economy of Northumberland and Durham, 1640–1750", pp. 81–4, 88; in some years around 1740, 15 per cent of rents were spent on repairs and new building: Habakkuk, "English Landownership, 1680–1740", pp. 14–15.

Doubtless contrasting Protestant and Counter-Reformation *mentalités* could be constructed by way of explanation. The fate of smaller tenant farmers in the English arable areas was shown to be desperate by Richard Baxter in 1691. He urged landlords to reduce their rents by a third so that the tenants could live decently and bring up their children; instead, "This impoverishing of them is the impoverishing of all the rest of the land . . . Their poverty will debase the spirit of the Nation, as it hath done the Moscovites, the Polanders and much the French". The poor husbandmen lived worse than handicraftsmen, or smallholders with a by-employment. They were worse off than their own unmarried servants and labourers. This reminds us that Baxter is not writing about those with dwarf holdings, but men paying £20 rent. At Gregory King's average arable rent of nearly 6s. an acre, their holdings would be about 66 acres.[140] Baxter is thinking of tenants of from about 30 to 60 acres, the *moyen laboureurs* of the French countryside with at least one plough-team. To take a specific example, of nearly 26,000 acres of the Belvoir estate surveyed around 1692, 300 holdings were under 21 acres, and 297 over 21 acres; of the latter, 191 were between 21 and 80 acres, and occupied 45 per cent of the total acreage, another 40 per cent of which was in farms over 100 acres, and 53 per cent was in farms of 81 acres and above.[141]

Baxter argued that competition for smaller holdings pushed up their rents; by implication it was landlords who competed for the big farmers. Joan Thirsk has argued that in the pastoral regions peasant farmers were relatively prosperous and increased in numbers during the seventeenth century, while the tendency in most of the corn-

[140] R. Baxter, "The Poor Husbandman's Advocate to Rich Racking Landlords", in "The Reverend Richard Baxter's Last Treatise", ed. F. J. Powicke, *Bull. John Rylands Lib.*, x (1926), pp. 180, 184, 188, 197, 183 (5). Baxter excludes from his picture tenants near London and those with pasture farms forty miles or further away (pp. 184–5). At King's final revision to 5s. 6d. an acre in 1697 the holdings would be 36–73 acres.

[141] Belvoir Castle muniments, Barker's survey, 1691–2. The lands were mostly in Leicestershire; one Warwickshire manor, Pillarton, is included. Although they include some seventeenth-century enclosures, they were mostly open-field arable. The duke's leases forbad subletting, except for the custom on some manors of allowing this for less than a year. The total surveyed was 26,563 acres, but 786 acres in hand at Croxton have been excluded from the computations. There were also 300 holdings, mostly cottagers, with 20 acres or under, of which those with 10–20 acres occupied 10 per cent of the total area. Holdings of 81–100 acres occupied 12.5 per cent.

growing regions favoured larger farms.[142] This is the same sort of contrast between corn-growing regions (still much of them open-field) and pastoral regions which Le Roy Ladurie makes between the corn-growing open-field regions of northern France and the backward, peasant-dominated *bocage* regions.[143] One difference lies in the amount of investment in improvements in the English arable areas, such as the floating of water-meadows and the increased numbers of livestock; another difference is the development of rural textile industries in the French arable areas in the later seventeenth century, in contrast to England where rural industries were more associated with pastoral regions. Postel-Vinay and Le Roy Ladurie argue that the level of rent in France inhibited investment and growth, which is also Baxter's argument about farmers who by Flemish standards were large ones. Le Roy Ladurie argues that rent of arable around Paris in 1650–70 was equivalent to nearly half the grain produced per hectare.[144] But we have seen that there was doubt as to whether English farms produced much more than two rents, while Gregory King's global figures of rent and agricultural production suggest that rent was about half the product.[145] Thus it is not clear that excessive rent alone was a crucial difference.

An area where there was an apparently important difference was in the amount and nature of rural credit. Unfortunately, the information available is not strictly comparable. French studies have concentrated on peasant indebtedness, using sources which show borrowing by creating rent charges, or pledging stock leading to sale of land, or distraint and forced sales of goods. So far, English studies

[142] J. Thirsk, "Seventeenth-Century Agriculture and Social Change", in J. Thirsk (ed.), *Land, Church and People: Essays Presented to Professor H. P. R. Finberg* [Supplement to *Agric. Hist. Rev.*, xviii (1970)].

[143] Le Roy Ladurie, "Masses profondes: la paysannerie", pp. 637, 573.

[144] *Ibid.*, p. 637; given his other assumptions about average yields, the proportion of rent to grain produced (net of seed) would appear to be a little over 40 per cent.

[145] King put rents at £10 million and the value of agricultural produce at £21,275,000; Deane and Cole, *British Economic Growth, 1688–1959*, p. 156, table 35, revised the figure for produce to £19.3 million. However, later he also argued that the product of arable grain land was nearer four rents than three. Thus King's estimates vary between 25, 36 and 47 per cent, of which the first two are directly comparable to Le Roy Ladurie's figures: *Seventeenth-Century Economic Documents*, ed. Thirsk and Cooper, pp. 782–3, 796–7. Lavoisier estimated that landowners in general took 31 per cent of grain produced, or 38 per cent after deducting seed, 22 per cent of total agricultural production and 50 per cent of net (or taxable) product: Lavoisier, *Oeuvres*, vi, pp. 426, 428.

have concentrated on evidence from probate inventories, which are much richer in information about credits owned than about debts. All the French studies so far show a growing burden of indebtedness among small peasants and a transfer of lands from them to urban élites and to seigneurs during the whole period 1560–1720 and particularly after 1640. The analogous process in England was the buying up of freeholds around great estates. Jacquart's inventories for 1580–1664 show numbers of poor peasants, *vignerons* and a few large farmers heavily in debt; the real troubles for the large farmers came after 1670.[146] More generally, they show lack of livestock owned by the villagers. Holderness's findings in south-east Lindsey show farmers increasing their wealth, livestock and lending in the 1690s after the depression of the 1670s and 1680s, at the very time when many farmers in Ile-de-France and the Soissonnais were going under. On the other hand, periods of low prices did see a contraction of lending by farmers and a number did go bankrupt in the years 1723 to 1745. A large part in providing credit was played by widows (who seem to have been excluded from Jacquart's sample), single persons and clergy. Most borrowing in England was for consumption, even that on mortgages, rather than for productive investment; in this there seems a resemblance to France. The differences seem to be in the lesser dependence on urban élites, or on a few great farmers, and in the relative abundance of credit on simple bonds at the village level, though of course much did come from towns, especially through attorneys who used mortgages to acquire land.[147] The "diffusion of money-lending in English village society was significant in preventing the growth of usurious monopolies"; the arrangements were short-term, unlike the constitution of *rentes*. "The eighteenth century had no need to create a money market in order to provide low-risk capital. It already existed". Credit facilities "were used to enlarge capital in the pre-industrial village community but . . . the distinction which modern economists make

[146] Jacquart, *Crise rurale en Ile-de-France*, pp. 459–84, 715. One of the best accounts of the working of the French credit system is P. Deyon, *Amiens* (Paris, 1967), pp. 309–38.

[147] B. A. Holderness, "Credit in a Rural Community, 1660–1800", *Midland Hist.*, iii (1975–6). For further examples from Dorset of an average investment of 12 per cent of personal wealth in credits, see *Probate Inventories and Manorial Excepts of Chetnole, Leigh and Yetminster*, ed. R. Machin (Bristol, 1976), pp. 21–2.

effortlessly [between capital and consumption] was at best obscure in the seventeenth and eighteenth centuries".[148]

If there was less economic domination of town over country in England, partly because urban élites were less powerful and privileged, there was, paradoxically, less urbanization in France as a whole than in England. Here again, northern France was probably much nearer to England than the other regions.[149] Patten has shown that there was an appreciable increase of urban population of around 49 per cent in Norfolk and Suffolk in the first three quarters of the seventeenth century.[150] Chartres has shown that there was considerable increase in the capital used in the overland carrying industry and the services it provided in the later seventeenth century,[151] quite apart from improvements in water transport. Again, this is partly due to the exceptional preponderance of London and the locational advantages of a long island coastline. As we also saw, the English economy was assisted by continuing, but not excessive, demographic growth, particularly down to the 1720s, while the problems of low agricultural prices were compounded in France by the direct effects of war and subsistence crises. By 1760 the differences between English and French agriculture were certainly much greater than in 1560, even if the comparison is restricted to the predominantly arable regions of open-field France. The divergence came in the seventeenth century and perhaps especially between about 1670 and 1720, when in England agricultural stocks and output were maintained and in some cases increased, while in France they may well have diminished.

If markets, communications, demand and agricultural production were growing in late seventeenth-century England to a greater extent than in France, is this no more than reiterating the old

[148] B. A. Holderness, "Credit in English Rural Society before the Nineteenth Century, with Special Reference to the Period 1650–1720", *Agric. Hist. Rev.*, xxiv (1976), pp. 105, 106, 108.

[149] G. Rozman, *Urban Networks in Russia and Pre-Modern Periodization* (Princeton, 1976), pp. 222–36. In the 1680s England's percentage of population in towns and cities was 20–21 per cent; in France in the 1760s it was 16 per cent, but in northern France (Ile-de-France, Champagne, Picardy, Flanders, Artois and Boulonois) it was 25 per cent.

[150] J. Patten, "Population Distribution in Norfolk and Suffolk during the Sixteenth and Seventeenth Centuries", *Trans. Inst. Brit. Geographers*, lxv (1975), pp. 48–9.

[151] J. A. Chartres, "Road Carrying in England in the Seventeenth Century", *Econ. Hist. Rev.*, 2nd ser., xxx (1977), pp. 84–8.

cliché that rural Englishmen, especially farmers, were better off than rural Frenchmen? Despite Baxter this still seems plausible. The will of French landlords to invest in recovery had been apparent, just as new crops had been used in the Paris region in the early seventeenth century. But the French had to provide for two phases of recovery and reconstruction, while the English had only one; for them continuous direct taxation only existed from 1641 to 1661 and was to be resumed in the 1690s. In France there was continuous fiscal pressure; the respite of the 1660s may not have helped large farmers, and the renewal of fiscal pressure after 1670 and still more after 1688 came when agricultural incomes, especially in the grain-producing areas, were falling. Recovery and some growth came when fiscal pressure and the incidence of direct taxation were less after 1720, at any rate until the 1770s. In England the burden of taxation in the eighteenth century was greater than in France. Mathias and O'Brien have shown that the per capita tax revenue in wheat equivalents was always much higher than in France and frequently twice as high, and that the share of commodity output at current prices taken as taxes was higher in Britain and became relatively higher still after 1750. The proportion raised by indirect taxation on consumption was always much higher in England, while that raised by direct taxation was always much higher in France. Most French urban populations were more lightly taxed than English ones; agricultural producers were much more heavily taxed.[152]

The burden of taxation can be seen in the estimates of Morineau, Spooner and Briggs, which suggest that in the last quarter of the seventeenth century nearly a fifth of France's total agricultural production, or over a third of the total value of grain production, and in the last years of Louis XIV about a quarter of agricultural production, went in taxation.[153] In France foreign and civil wars had a greater disinvestive effect on agriculture throughout the century,

[152] P. Mathias and P. O'Brien, "Taxation in Britain and France, 1715–1810", *Jl European Econ. Hist.*, v (1976). I am grateful to the authors for allowing me to see their calculations in advance of publication.

[153] M. Morineau, "La conjoncture ou les cernes de la croissance", in Braudel and Labrousse (eds.), *Histoire économique et sociale de la France*, i, pt 2, pp. 978–80; F. C. Spooner, *The International Economy and Monetary Movements in France, 1493–1725* (Cambridge, Mass., 1972), pp. 305–15; R. Briggs, *Early Modern France, 1560–1715* (Oxford, 1977), graph 5. I am indebted to Robin Briggs for giving me copies of his graphs before their publication.

and especially after 1635. After 1693 Boisguilbert, the precursor of Quesnay, and Vauban attacked the French fiscal system for inhibiting mass consumption and the growth of agricultural output and investment for most producers, except farmers of magnates.[154] The fiscal burdens of the wars of William and Anne produced prophecies of woe for the landed interest and certainly worsened the lot of lesser landowners, but tenants were supposed not to pay the land tax. Taxes were about a fifth of agricultural production in England in 1694–7 and perhaps nearer a quarter under Anne, but even then they constituted about 11 per cent of the national income, to which agriculture contributed about 40 per cent and commerce 12 per cent. There was even a modest redistribution in favour of mass consumption: the poor rates were about 22 per cent of the land and assessed taxes in 1694–5, and about a third in 1748–50.[155]

In Marxist terms, the tax burden can be taken as part of the "feudal" levy, as Bois does for the earlier period. For this period Perry Anderson sees absolute monarchies as the allies of the nobilities: "The rule of the Absolutist State was that of the feudal nobility in the epoch of transition to capitalism".[156] Here "seigneurial reaction" is part of a tacit bargain between the state and the nobility at the expense of the peasantry. In fact nobilities were not homogeneous; the French monarchy favoured *les Grands*, some of the high robe and the financiers at the expense of the interests of the lesser nobility and local élites. The triumph of the interests of magnates over those of lesser nobles could be achieved without an absolutist state, though at the expense of military power, as in Poland.

Whereas in France local seigneurs and notables had been able in

[154] "Le détail de la France", in *Pierre de Boisguilbert, ou la naissance de l'économie politique*, 2 vols. (Paris, 1966), ii, pp. 622–8; S. le Prestre de Vauban, *Projet d'une dixme royale*, ed. E. Coornaert (Paris, 1933), pp. 26–8.

[155] B. R. Mitchell and P. Deane, *Abstract of British Historical Statistics* (Cambridge, 1962), p. 386; Deane and Cole, *British Economic Growth, 1688–1959*, p. 156; S. and B. Webb, *English Poor Law History*, pt 1, *The Old Poor Law* (London, 1927), p. 153 and n. 1.

[156] P. Anderson, *Lineages of the Absolutist State* (London, 1974), p. 42: "It was a State founded on the social supremacy of the aristocracy and confined by the imperatives of landed property" (p. 41). Whatever the shortcomings of these generalizations, they seem nearer to reality than Brenner's account of the French state as "a class-like phenomenon . . . an *independent* extractor of the surplus", protecting peasants against lords (above, p. 55) though French administrators may have developed aspirations to do so.

varying degrees to act as the protectors of their farmers and peasants against royal taxation, this became increasingly difficult in the later seventeenth century for the ordinary provincial noble or officer. Such favours were now the perquisite of the magnates or those who were connected with the controller-general and ministers as kin or clients. This meant that, despite the survival of seigneurial justice, the role of the lesser noble as protector and mediator between peasants and outside authorities was eroded. In England, by contrast, the administration of the land tax provided opportunities for local notables and let the leaders of local communities participate in national administration with surprisingly little friction from political partisanship or social dislocation.[157]

One unexpected outcome of falling rents and prices after 1670 and the bankruptcy of so many farmers was the emergence or spread in parts of northern France of customs which enabled large farmers to dominate both landlords and village communities. This was the custom of *mauvais gré* (ill will) by which a lord could not relet a farm at the end of a term without the consent of the sitting tenant. If he did so and put in another tenant, that tenant would be boycotted by the villagers; threats to burn down the farm buildings would be made and were very often carried out. As a result, and in defiance of repeated royal edicts against these customs from 1707 onwards, dynasties of farmers intermarrying with each other flourished. They treated the farms as their private property, arranging exchanges of land with each other, using them to raise portions, even partitioning them among their heirs, sometimes without even troubling to get their leases formally renewed by the owners. The most striking change in this direction was in the Soissonnais, where the turnover of farmers had been considerable even before the crisis years after 1670; there, in the eighteenth century, lords were at the mercy of their farmers until the decade before 1789 when, for reasons which Postel-Vinay leaves unexplained, they were able to raise their rents substantially. Postel-Vinay also sees a mechanism for promoting the domination of capitalist farmers, whereby middling and small peasants were subjected to heavier unit rents than the farmers in order to create a semi-proletarianized labour force for their farms. However, given demand, relatively higher rents for smallholdings frequently occur without necessarily producing such

[157] C. Brooks, "Public Finance and Political Stability", *Hist. Jl*, xvii (1974).

a result. Jacquart believes that in Ile-de-France great farmers enjoyed a similar oligopoly, because there was no real competition for leases as only a handful of families had the necessary wealth.[158] The custom of *mauvais gré* may go back to the late sixteenth century in Cambrésis and parts of eastern Picardy. There and in the neighbouring parts of the Walloon provinces of the southern Netherlands the *censiers* (farmers of lands, dues and tithe) already dominated the villages.[159] In northern France the economic domination of both landlords and villagers by the great farmers was reinforced by the revolution, and in the first half of the nineteenth century.[160]

Thus the economic and social preponderance of capitalist farmers became greater in much of northern France than in England. According to the principles of Fuller and classical political economy, one of the reasons for the relative inefficiency of French arable farming could have been not peasant conservatism, but lack of competition for farms and lack of power by landlords to put up rents before 1780 and after 1810. Laurence regarded it as one of the most important duties of the steward of a great lord to prevent combinations by farmers, sometimes encouraged by local gentry, to prevent rents being raised.[161] Perhaps Postel-Vinay would interpret this as subjecting the farmers to a "feudal" rent. It can be argued that the greater English gentry became increasingly absentee landlords in the eighteenth century, spending more of their time and money on urban society in county towns and London. Certainly, they left more and more of county and local government to clerical magistrates.

In defining capitalism, agriculture presents acute terminological problems. It has often been remarked that capital existed before capitalism and this is above all true of settled agriculture, where

[158] P. Deyon, "Quelques remarques sur l'évolution du régime seigneurial en Picardie, XVIe–XVIIIe siècles", *Revue d'histoire moderne et contemporaine*, viii (1961), pp. 277–8; Postel-Vinay, *Rente foncière dans le capitalisme agricole*, pp. 31–3, 90–2, 255–62, 43–53, 36–40, 64–70; Jacquart, "Rente foncière, indice conjoncturel?", pp. 374–5.

[159] Neveux, "Déclin et reprise", pp. 149–51; H. Neveux, *Les grains du Cambrésis* (Lille, 1974), pp. 661–7; S. Gruzinski, "Recherches sur le monde rural dans les Pays-Bas méridionaux, 1480–1630", *Ecole Nationale des Chartes: Position des thèses* (1973).

[160] Postel-Vinay, *Rente foncière dans le capitalisme agricole*, pp. 110–12, 128–38.

[161] Laurence, *Duty of a Steward to his Lord*, pp. 12–15.

some form of advances and stock are necessary. As we saw, Turgot's analysis of industrial and commercial capitalism is an extension of his analysis of agriculture. As in any pre-mechanized European agriculture, the most important and essential stock was livestock; any wealthy farmer is a capitalist and we find Hoskins speaking of "capitalist peasants" in the fifteenth century, the yeoman or peasant aristocracy of Wigston.[162] A critical difference between French and English agriculture in the seventeenth century is probably the fact that England had a higher and increasingly higher proportion of livestock to land, above all in the arable areas. But Brenner and others wish to say something more significant than that England was more prosperous than France. For them it is part of a teleological process of investment in productivity and the expropriation of labour from the means of production, as the necessary basis for industrial capitalism which can only be achieved by agricultural capitalism creating a proletariat. What hinders comparative analysis is the built-in assumption that small-scale peasant farming cannot achieve the increase in productivity necessary to support industrialization, although the example of Flanders shows that this was in fact possible.[163]

When English historians such as Hoskins and Thirsk write about peasant farming, are they dealing with something conceptually different from French writers? According to Mendras they must be, since he writes: "England compared with the Continent had never been a land of peasants".[164] This assertion is made more plausible by his model of the peasant economy in which capital has no meaning. Money is part of the external economy surrounding the peasant economy, which is founded on self-subsistence and barter. The peasants' earnings from external monetary transactions are neither a capital nor an income, but simply savings in his stocking, to be used to pay taxes, buy stock or land, or pay portions. The savings become part of the family patrimony and give money a marginal character, part of the movables of the patrimony, not part of its

[162] Hoskins, *Midland Peasant*.

[163] Lavelaye, *Essai sur l'économie rurale de la Belgique*, pp. 55–6; productivity of land was greater in Flanders than in England or elsewhere in Europe, except parts of Lombardy; also "working capital, more considerable in Flanders than anywhere else, has not been provided by rich landowners or large farmers" (p. 95).

[164] H. Mendras, *Sociétés paysannes* (Paris, 1976), p. 194.

daily economic functioning.[165] Yet as peasant communities were subjected to levies and taxes in money, it would seem that money, even though external to the autonomous aspirations of the peasant economy, was still fundamental to the system within which peasant households functioned. In both France and England peasant economies were strongest in pastoral regions. However much French peasants gave priority to self-sufficiency in grain or its substitutes, there must have been sales of livestock and their products to local and more distant markets. It may be that rural industries dependent on distant markets were more important in the English pastoral regions, while the French ones produced more migrant labour. Not surprisingly (except to some rural sociologists or connoisseurs of proletarian consciousness) the English farm labourer in the nineteenth century, given access to land, gave the same priority to self-subsistence as the French peasant.[166] As the marketing network in England was by 1700 already more developed and less localized than in France, the English peasant family farm was more market-orientated, while the French one may have needed money primarily to pay taxes.

Agrarian capitalism has sometimes been taken to exist when land is regarded as a factor of production, as a capital having a return like any other factor of production, or form of capital. Such a commercialized agriculture dominated by large capitalist farms would not necessarily have the magical powers of increasing productivity which Brenner attributes to agrarian capitalism, as the example of nineteenth-century Andalusia suggests;[167] on the other hand, Flemish agriculture in the period 1750–1860, though dominated by peasant capitalist farming, did show such powers. An extreme variant of this market-dominated approach is provided by Wallerstein, who describes any agricultural producers for markets related to international trade as capitalist entrepreneurs, whether Polish nobles farming demesnes with serf labour, Spanish American

165 *Ibid.*, pp. 44–5.

166 J. Obelkevich, *Religion and Rural Society* (Oxford, 1976), pp. 62–3.

167 T. Kaplan, *Anarchists of Andalusia, 1868–1903* (Princeton, 1977), p. 39, takes agrarian capitalism as indicating "that land itself was a commodity that could be bought and sold; that laborers increasingly lost access to land; and that production for a cash economy shaped social and political relationships".

encomenderos using Indian labour, or religious corporations in Italy.[168]

Mendras argues that to identify land with capital is to obstruct analysis. It fails to explain the pricing of land "which varies more as a result of demographic densities than of its agronomic value . . . neither owners of ground rents nor peasant proprietors are capitalists".[169] Yet historically men have always accepted lower returns from land than from other forms of investment, not simply because land is usually a safer investment, but also because they are investing in non-monetary returns. In the case of large landowners, whether bourgeois, seigneurs, gentry or magnates, they were and still are buying prestige and authority. At the other end of the scale, peasants were buying or seeking independence by procuring the means to self-subsistence. While this shows that the return on land cannot be measured exclusively in money, it does not necessarily indicate either that landowners or peasants were non-capitalist, or pre-capitalist, or that they were excluded from developing a commercialized agriculture by such behaviour. If peasants allowed their desire for self-subsistence to impede the pursuit of commercial rationalization and maximization of profit, so did nineteenth-century English landowners in preserving game and the amenities of fox-hunting.

Other problems are created by the concept of capitalism as the pursuit of profit and economic rationality. De Vries has remarked that the constant fall in interest rates in the seventeenth and eighteenth centuries might suggest that shortage of capital was not a major constraint.[170] If Sir Richard Newdigate is at all typical of late seventeenth-century improvers in being content with a rate of return as low as 5 per cent, how far was he investing in non-monetary returns? Were French urban notables who often got higher returns from investing in share-cropping farms being economically irrational? In England it was not until F. M. L.

[168] I. Wallerstein, *The Modern World-System* [2 vols. (New York, 1974–80)], i, pp. 90–102, 159–62; "it is *not* the case that two forms of social organization, capitalist and feudal, existed side by side, or could ever so exist. The world-economy has one form or the other. Once it is capitalist, relationships that bear certain formal resemblances to feudal relationships are necessarily redefined in terms of the governing principles of a capitalist system" (p. 92).

[169] Mendras, *Sociétés paysannes*, p. 96.

[170] J. de Vries, *The Economy of Europe in an Age of Crisis, 1600–1750* (Cambridge, 1976), p. 211.

Thompson's second agricultural revolution that "something like half the farmland and half the farm output – though undoubtedly a good deal less than half the individual farmers – came under the sway of a system of commercialized farming, in which farmers regarded their activities as a business; a business that required them to purchase raw materials in the cheapest market, process them in their factories, and sell the final products in the dearest market, just like any cotton lord".[171] We know that landlords' returns on capital invested in all this productivity were extremely low; we do not know what tenants got on their growing investment. If we did, it "might then turn out that the enterprise shown by tenants was quite often equally unprofitable or misdirected".[172] Like the notables of mid-nineteenth-century Lyons whose share-croppers performed more personal services than most seigneurs had ever exacted under the *ancien régime*,[173] English landlords were still investing in authority and a social system in the nineteenth as they had done in earlier centuries, and had if anything become more interested in maximizing their returns in that direction than in the pursuit of profit.

[171] F. M. L. Thompson, "The Second Agricultural Revolution, 1815–1880", *Econ. Hist. Rev.*, 2nd ser., xxi (1968), p. 71.
[172] *Ibid.*, p. 73.
[173] G. Garrier, *Paysans du Beaujolais et du Lyonnais, 1800–1970* (Grenoble, 1973), pp. 148–9. The notables invested in parks and buildings rather than in agricultural production (p. 686).

9. *Agrarian Class Structure and Economic Development in Pre-Industrial Bohemia**

ARNOST KLIMA

With one exception, all the other contributors to this Symposium on Robert Brenner's article have concentrated on developments in England and France. If they have mentioned the situation in central and eastern Europe at all, it has been merely to make general assertions. The single exception is Heide Wunder, who drew the conclusion that "central European historians have not been particularly successful in presenting their findings to their British and French colleagues".[1]

In the context of the Brenner debate, the development of Bohemia is of particular significance: first, because of its central geographical location and its consequent economic importance to pre-industrial Europe as a whole; second, because it provides the example of a variant case of development, in marked contrast with the economic and social evolution of England and France. From the mid-seventeenth century onwards Bohemia developed along very different lines from the countries of western Europe. It is thus a useful corrective to any stereotype of the transition from feudalism to capitalism, and offers fresh perspectives on the various issues and problems involved.

In their contribution to this Symposium, M. M. Postan and John Hatcher cite the observation of Z. P. Pach that in Hungary until the end of the fifteenth century "labour dues played a merely subsidiary role" and that the "rural economy was fundamentally concordant with that of the west European countries".[2] They further expressed the view that "Similar conclusions have emerged from Bohemian and Polish sources, and are contained in the works of Kula, Graus,

* I am indebted to Josef Macek for reading and commenting on an earlier version of this contribution.

[1] Above, p. 97.

[2] Above, p. 67, citing Z. P. Pach, "The Development of Feudal Rent in Hungary in the Fifteenth Century", *Econ. Hist. Rev.*, 2nd ser., xix (1966), p. 13.

Malowist and others".[3] This is certainly correct. But it is important to emphasize that the Thirty Years War played an absolutely crucial part in the social and economic development of Bohemia and that, as a direct consequence of the war, the mid-seventeenth century marked a major turning-point in the country's history. Largely for this reason, any attempt at a general assessment of the transition from feudalism to capitalism in Bohemia cannot be confined solely to the events of the middle ages. Instead, the emphasis must be shifted to much later developments – it is indeed the seventeenth and eighteenth centuries which constitute the real pre-capitalist phase of Bohemia's history.

In his own contribution to this Symposium, Guy Bois writes that in western Europe in the first half of the sixteenth century the séigneurial class "decided to increase the demesne at the expense of holdings and to recruit hired labour", because of "the very low level of the various rents levied on those holdings". This, he asserts, led to "a sudden upsurge of agrarian capitalism in western Europe".[4] In Bohemia, however, from the mid-seventeenth century onwards, the very opposite happened. True, Bohemian lords also enlarged their demesnes, but not at the expense of peasant holdings, as in western Europe, because at the conclusion of the Thirty Years War so much of the country's land already lay fallow. A further legacy of the war was a serious shortage of labour, with the inevitable consequence that whatever labour was available was also exceptionally costly. Instead of *hiring* labour to work their demesnes, therefore, lords opted instead to burden their serfs with additional labour services. Thus, whereas in western Europe the extension of the demesnes served, through the employment of *hired* labour, to strengthen the impetus towards capitalism, in Bohemia on the other hand, because of the chronic shortage of manpower, the extension of the demesnes led instead to the consolidation of serfdom. The economic and class structure of Bohemia during this period rested of course, on the fundamental economic relationship of feudal lords and their serfs. The various features stressed by Kula in his works on Poland from the sixteenth to the eighteenth centuries hold true for Bohemia also.[5] And this fundamental economic relationship was reinforced and strengthened by the fact that, in Bohemia as

[3] Above, p. 67. [4] Above, p. 112.
[5] W. Kula, *An Economic Theory of the Feudal System* (London, 1976), p. 25.

elsewhere, the serf was also subject in political and legal matters to the jurisdiction of his lord, who was thus empowered to coerce and constrain the serf as and when circumstances required.[6]

The greater part of the population of Bohemia in the seventeenth and eighteenth centuries – that is, approximately 80 per cent – lived in the countryside and was engaged in agriculture; the remainder lived in the towns. These figures correspond to those given by Paul Bairoch as being generally valid for the period.[7] But many town-dwellers too were involved in agriculture. According to the cadastre (land survey) of 1748, those who lived in towns in Bohemia owned approximately 123,825 hectares, or 10.3 per cent of all the arable land in the country.[8] And in some regions, towns had a completely agrarian character.[9] In numbers, therefore, the agricultural sector significantly exceeded 80 per cent of the population. According to the Renewed Land Ordinance (*Verneuerte Landesordnung*) of 1627, the vast majority of the population of rural areas and tributary towns were tied to the soil and unable to move without the agreement and sanction of the lord. This characteristically feudal restriction on mobility was frequently lifted at harvest and hay-making time, when those from less fertile areas might, for instance, move to estates where there was a shortage of manpower, but they were always required to return home again when the harvest was over. Labour mobility on such a partial and purely temporary basis cannot therefore be regarded as symptomatic of a "weakening" of the feudal system. It did not in any realistic sense represent a relaxation of feudal constraints or obligations, and thus in no way signified a trend towards emancipation.[10]

[6] Above, pp. 26–7, 33–5, 127.

[7] P. Bairoch, "Agriculture and the Industrial Revolution, 1700–1914", in C. M. Cipolla (ed.), *The Industrial Revolution* (Fontana Economic History of Europe, iii, London, 1976), pp. 452, 467.

[8] J. Křivka, *Výrobní a peněžní výsledky měšťanského zemědělství v 18. století v severních Čechách* [Production and Financial Results of Burgher Agriculture in Northern Bohemia in the Eighteenth Century] (Prague, 1975), p. 3. See also A. Míka, "On the Economic Status of Czech Towns in the Period of Late Feudalism", *Hospodářské dějiny*, ii (1978), pp. 239, 247.

[9] Křivka, *Výrobní a peněžní výsledky měšťanského zemědělství*, p. 12.

[10] Similarly, as Brenner states, in England as early as the twelfth century "commutation was an extremely widespread development . . . but this trend did not signify the emancipation of the peasants": above, p. 26, citing M. M. Postan, "Medieval Agrarian Society in its Prime: England", in *Cambridge Economic History of Europe*, i, 2nd edn, pp. 604–8, 611.

Of crucial importance to the subsequent history of the country is the fact that in the course of the Thirty Years War the population of Bohemia declined by more than 40 per cent, from a pre-war total of over 1,700,000[11] to a post-war figure of only 950,000.[12] The impact on the economic sphere was dramatic. Large numbers of agricultural holdings were abandoned and much of the land became fallow. One result was that landless peasants were enabled, with their lord's approval, to occupy and cultivate the countless vacant holdings, and the numbers of those who were truly landless virtually disappeared. Also the lords themselves were encouraged to take over fallow land, either adding it to their existing demesnes or establishing new ones, and from the mid-seventeenth century onwards the number of demesnes in Bohemia greatly increased. For instance, in the years 1650–80 the Trautmannsdorffs on their vast estate in the Litomyšl district of eastern Bohemia established a total of eleven new demesnes in addition to the two previously existing there.[13] And the trend was general throughout Bohemia. In the north, for example, on the Frýdlant estate, which amounted to 69,000 hectares, the lord had eighteen demesnes,[14] whereas in 1631 there had only been three.[15] These eighteen demesnes consisted of 1,700 hectares of arable land, or an average of about 100 hectares for each demesne.[16] However, in addition to the arable land, an estate would often also include forests, fishing lakes, and such industrial enterprises as breweries and brickworks. In southern Bohemia the estate of Jindřichův Hradec (Neuhaus), comprising forty-eight villages and one town, had ten demesnes with a total of 700 hectares of arable land, and in addition a further 6,000 hectares of forests and 2,000 hectares of fishing lakes.

The establishment of new demesnes during the second half of the

[11] O. Placht, *Lidnatost a společenská skladba českých zemí 16.–18. století* [Population and Social Structure in the Czech Lands from the Sixteenth to the Eighteenth Centuries] (Prague, 1957), p. 39.

[12] J. Pekař, *České katastry, 1654–1789* [Czech Cadastres, 1654–1789] (Prague, 1912), pp. 21–2, gives a figure of 934,000 people.

[13] A. Tomíček, *Nás sedláky každý šidí* [We Peasants are Cheated by Everybody] (Litomyšl, 1927), p. 6.

[14] E. Janoušek, *Historický vývoj produktivity práce v zemědělství v období pobělohorském* [The Historical Development of Labour Productivity in Agriculture in the Period after the Battle of the White Mountain] (Prague, 1967), p. 83.

[15] J. Kočí, *Odboj nevolníků na Frýdlantsku, 1679–1687* [The Uprising of the Serfs in the Frýdlant Region, 1679–1687] (Liberec, 1965), p. 43.

[16] Janoušek, *Historický vývoj produktivity práce v zemědělství*, p. 104.

seventeenth century, combined with the decline in population as a result of the Thirty Years War and the resultant manpower shortage, had a number of predictable social and economic consequences. The landless peasants who settled on fallow land after the war were no longer obliged to rely on wage labour to make a living, and this both further aggravated the already acute manpower shortage and also contributed to the general rise in wage levels for such labour as continued to be available. On the other hand, the demand for agricultural produce fell markedly, reflecting the decline in the size of the urban population, one of its principal markets throughout the sixteenth century. Under these twin pressures, lords looked for the means to cut production costs on their estates, and this was made possible by the increased exploitation of the various labour services (*corvée* or *Robot*) of the serfs, for which of course the lords paid nothing at all. The extension of labour services on their demesnes enabled the lords to sell their produce cheaply both at home and on the international market, and accordingly labour services were increased considerably from the mid-seventeenth century onwards, facilitated by the lord's political and legal jurisdiction over the serf and the considerable powers of non-economic coercion at his disposal.

The increase in the incidence of labour services in Bohemia was great. According to the Feudal Labour Services Decree (*Robotpatent*) of 1680, a serf was obliged to perform labour services on the demesne of his lord for three days a week, but at hay-making and harvest time, and also at the fish harvest, the number of days could be increased by the lord "at will".[17] There are numerous examples during the eighteenth century of lords requiring as many as six days of labour service a week.[18]

In Bohemia in the mid-seventeenth century, land was owned mainly by the nobility (in turn subdividing into upper and lower nobility); these, together with the church, the towns and the crown, owned practically all the available land. Even in 1757 the freeholders owned a mere 0.5 per cent of the total. Those who actually worked the land were of course the serfs, who can be divided into

[17] The Feudal Labour Services Decree of 1680, paragraph 2. The text of this decree is printed in German and Czech in *Archiv český*, xxiii (1906), pp. 485–90.

[18] A. Chalupa, "Venkovské obyvatelstvo v Cechách v tereziánských katastrech, 1700–1750" [The Rural Population of Bohemia in the Teresian Cadastres, 1700–1750], *Sborník Národního Muzea*, xxiii (1969), pp. 320–1.

three groups according to the size of their holdings. Those whose holdings were up to 4.5 hectares in size and who paid taxes of 14 guilders 15 kreuzers or more per annum were classed as serfs who performed labour services with draught animals (*Zugrobot*). Those with smallholdings who paid no more than 9 guilders 30 kreuzers in taxes per annum performed manual labour services (*Handrobot*). The third group comprised the landless. In 1656 the figures for feudal landownership in Bohemia were as follows: upper nobility, 59.5 per cent; lower nobility, 9.6 per cent; towns, 13.1 per cent; the church, 12.3 per cent; the crown, 5.0 per cent.[19] Almost exactly a century later, in 1757, the corresponding figures for feudal landownership were: upper nobility, 62.4 per cent; lower nobility, 6.1 per cent; towns, 12.2 per cent; the church, 13.6 per cent; the crown, 5.0 per cent; with freeholders holding a mere 0.5 per cent.[20] Furthermore, contemporary reports show that in 1654 Prince Eggenberg had on his estates a total of 5,540 serfs holding land, Count Trautmannsdorff 4,094, Count Buquoy 3,100 and Count Gallas 3,066. No figures are available for the numbers of landless serfs.[21]

According to the Teresian Cadastre, there were 215,270 holdings in Bohemia in the first quarter of the eighteenth century. Of these, 5.5 per cent were holdings of over 17.5 hectares in size, 17.4 per cent of between 8.5 and 17.5 hectares, and 20.4 per cent between 4.5 and 8.5 hectares; 21 per cent were smallholdings of between 1.5 and 4.5 hectares, while 35.7 per cent were held by cottagers with less than 1.5 hectares.[22] These figures show that, even in the first quarter of the eighteenth century, smallholders and cottagers together constituted the largest section of the agricultural population of Bohemia.

In the hundred years from the mid-seventeenth to the mid-eighteenth century, rural conditions again changed dramatically. During that period Bohemia's population doubled, from a figure of 950,000 at the close of the Thirty Years War to 1,970,000 in 1754. Between 1754 and 1776 it increased by a further 20 per cent to 2,400,000.[23] This unusually rapid rise in population converted the earlier shortage of manpower in the countryside into a substantial

[19] Pekař, *Ceské katastry*, p. 456. [20] *Ibid.*

[21] Placht, *Lidnatost a společenská skladba českých zemí*, p. 222.

[22] Chalupa, "Venkovské obyvatelstvo v Cechách v tereziánských katastrech", pp. 250–1.

[23] L. Kárníková, *Vývoj obyvatelstva v českých zemích, 1754–1914* [The Growth of Population in the Czech Lands, 1754–1914] (Prague, 1965), p. 327.

surplus. In consequence, there was a significant increase in the numbers of the landless; by the last quarter of the eighteenth century they accounted for between 40 and 60 per cent of the entire rural population, depending on region. According to the Feudal Labour Services Decree of 1738, all serfs were required to perform labour services for their lord, whether they had land or not, and the lord now found himself with far more labour at his disposal than he could fully utilize. The following course was therefore adopted. Serfs who lived locally continued to work on the lord's demesne, in much the same way as before, but in the case of those living at a distance from the demesne the labour services were commuted to a money rent.[24]

This phenomenon also occurred in England although, of course, at a much earlier date. As Brenner says, where "the lord did not decide to take labour services, the peasant was still required to pay money fees to buy off his labour dues and moreover remained subject to those arbitrary exactions (tallages, entry fines and so on) which were bound up with his status as a bondsman".[25]

According to the provisions of the 1775 Labour Services Decree,[26] the working day throughout the six-month period from 1st October to 31st March was to be eight hours in duration and from 1st April to 30th September twelve hours. During the former period the serf and his draught animals were entitled to a one-hour break, and in the latter to a break of two hours. The decree, however, permitted the working day to be prolonged during harvesting for another one or two hours as required.

According to the decree, serfs who performed labour services were divided into eleven categories. The lowest category comprised those who had no land but were nevertheless required to perform labour services. These landless serfs (*Inleute*), who either worked for better-off peasants or earned their living in various other ways, were only required to work for their lord for thirteen days every year. In the second category were those serfs who had a cottage but no land, and they were required to perform labour services for twenty-six days a year. Then there came serfs who had smallholdings, and these performed what was known as manual labour ser-

[24] Janoušek, *Historický vývoj produktivity práce zemědělství*, pp. 30–1.

[25] Above, p. 26; and see Postan, "Medieval Agrarian Society in its Prime: England", pp. 604–10.

[26] The text of the Feudal Labour Services Decree of 1775 is printed in *Archiv český*, xxiv (1908), pp. 488–508.

vice. This category was subdivided into five different sub-groups depending on the size of holding, according to which the requirement for manual labour services ranged from one to three days a week. Serfs with larger holdings were required to perform labour services with their own draught animals for three days a week. Those with 4.5 hectares of land had to perform labour services with one draught animal; those with between 4.5 and 8.5 hectares with two. But in addition, during the period from 15th May to 28th September, they had to provide an additional person for manual labour services for one day a week. Serfs who had between 8.5 and 13 hectares of land were required to perform labour services for three days a week with three draught animals and in addition, from 15th May to 28th September, provide another person for manual labour services for two days a week. In the final group were those peasants who had over 13 hectares of land, being required to perform labour services for three days a week with four draught animals and, from 15th May to 28th September, to provide an extra person for manual labour services for three days a week. The Labour Services Decree of 1775 thus placed by far the heaviest burden of labour service upon the better-off peasants and their obligations were indeed considerable. On the other hand, it greatly reduced the obligations of smallholders, cottagers and landless serfs, their requirement for labour service being relatively moderate. There were several reasons for weighting the incidence of labour services in this way, but in particular the state was anxious to free some of the labour in rural areas for work in domestic industry and the manufactories. The decree in no way endangered the economic viability of the demesnes, because of the general manpower surplus.

The heavy burden of labour services with draught animals arose largely from the fact that lords had few draught animals of their own on their demesnes and the greater part of all field, forest and other carting had thus to be apportioned elsewhere. For many, labour service obligations were in practice not as burdensome as might at first appear. Peasants with large or medium-sized holdings were often comparatively well-off, with labourers of their own. In consequence, they themselves did not personally perform the labour services required of them, rather devoting themselves to their own holdings and sending a labourer in their place.

Article 1, paragraph 15 of the Labour Services Decree of 1775 stipulated that "serfs had no entitlement to any reward either for labour services with draught animals or for manual labour services". Only those peasants who were required not only to perform three days service a week with draught animals, but also to provide another person for manual labour services from 15th May to 28th September, had the right to some recompense – this being in the form of three-quarters of a kilo of bread a day. The decree further stipulated that, as and when the lord required, serfs who did less than three days a week labour services were required to work for pay (*Lohntag*) to make their time up to three days a week. The decree laid down pay-scales for this work: 7 kreuzers a day if the work was done in the period from 1st October to 28th February, 10 kreuzers a day from 1st March to 30th June, and 15 kreuzers a day from 1st July to 30th September – the working day varying in length from eight to twelve hours.

The various labour service obligations which prevailed in the mid-seventeenth century were without doubt very considerable. At first, lords demanded unlimited labour services – "whenever the lord so orders". After the promulgation of the first Labour Services Decree in 1680, labour services of three days a week were required, but at hay-making or harvest time this increased to as many as five or even six days a week. This requirement remained in force until the new Labour Services Decree of 1775.

The unprecedented exploitation of the serfs in the period prior to 1680 had in many places caused them to withhold labour services, to run away, and even to participate in organized uprisings. The vast majority of these revolts were small-scale, confined to particular estates, but in both 1680 and 1775 a wave of revolt spread throughout the country. In the 1680 uprising 129 estates in Bohemia were affected. The rebels demanded the abolition or reduction of labour services, attacked the castles and demesnes of the nobility, and withheld their labour services. The troops garrisoned in Bohemia itself proved unequal to the task of putting down the risings and two more regiments, one infantry and one cavalry, were brought in from Silesia. Gradually, the troops succeeded in suppressing one uprising after another. Revolts had broken out not only on estates where the serfs were Czech, but also on estates where they were German.[27] On

[27] E. Strauss, *Bauernelend und Bauernaufstände in den Sudetenländern* (Prague, 1929), p. 63.

the latter, ninety-nine leaders of the uprising were sentenced to death, with fifty-five of them actually being executed.[28] The 1680 uprising led directly to the issuing of Bohemia's first Labour Services Decree by the Emperor Leopold I on 28th June. With this decree the state intervened for the first time in relations between serfs and their lords (previously these had been determined solely by the latter), and it intervened decisively on the side of the lords. The decree virtually sanctioned the situation as it then existed. Its many vaguely worded clauses enabled the lords to interpret it in whatever way best served their own interests.

From 1680 onwards there were further uprisings of serfs against their lords, but the risings were isolated and all of them suppressed without the serfs securing any improvement in their situation. In 1775, almost a hundred years after the great revolt of 1680, another general uprising broke out in Bohemia. And this time a change in the social balance was effected. The main centre of the uprising was in north-eastern Bohemia at the estate of Náchod, and here a peasant *gubernium* was established for the general direction of operations. Contact was established between Náchod and a wide surrounding area and a march on the capital was planned for the middle of May. But the uprising broke out prematurely on 19th March 1775, quickly spreading from estate to estate. Armies of serfs, often numbering several thousand, advanced on the capital, attacking the castles of their lords and exacting formal agreement to the abolition or reduction of their labour services. But the peasant *gubernium* at Náchod had lost overall control of the rising, and it lacked proper cohesion. After numerous minor engagements, an army forty thousand strong was sent against them and finally, at the very outskirts of Prague, the defeat of the rebel armies was achieved.

Nevertheless, the lessons of the rising were not lost on the government. The issuing of the Labour Services Decree of 13th August 1775 was its direct result. The rising of 1775 marked the culmination of the class struggle in the Bohemian countryside, the climax of long and bitter strife between the serfs and their lords, and it caused the government to take a hard look at the rural situation In addition to the decree itself, there was a radical plan for land

[28] K. Krofta, *Dějiny selského stavu* [The History of the Peasants], 2nd edn (Prague, 1949), p. 269.

reform, taking the form of a partition of the demesnes among the serfs. Serfdom was putting a brake on the further development of the economy, some asserted, particularly industrial production, and the future economic progress of the country required its abolition.

* * *

As well as the relative positions of lord and serf in the feudal economy, the various contributors to this Symposium have devoted much attention to the extent to which the peasant was able to sell his surplus produce on the open market.[29] In eighteenth-century Bohemia, as in Poland, the organization of labour in the agricultural sector had not changed in its essentials for hundreds of years – even the implements used in the countryside were virtually the same.

Demesnes in Bohemia concentrated primarily on cereal production. In the main, a three-year system of crop rotation was used, although on some estates, for example that of Frýdlant, a five-year cycle was in operation, with only 20 per cent of the land therefore lying fallow each year. Harvest yields did not differ greatly between lowland demesnes and those in the mountain foothills. For example, on the Frýdlant estate, which was in a mountain foothill area, harvest yields per hectare were as follows: wheat 10.7 centners, rye 9.5 centners, barley between 9.5 and 10 centners, and oats between 7.5 and 8.5 centners;[30] while on the Roudnice estate, lying in the fertile lowlands of the Labe (Elbe) valley, harvest yields per hectare were roughly the same: wheat 10.2 centners, rye 8 centners, barley 10.7 centners, but oats, however, only 5 centners. On the Jindřichův Hradec estate in southern Bohemia in 1722, the corresponding figures were: wheat 9.4, rye 7.7, barley 5.6 and oats 4.6 centners per hectare – yields being lower here because of the poorer quality of the soil. Calculations show that on the Frýdlant estate the raising of cereal crops on one hectare of land required approximately 80 working days in terms of labour services, but in the lowland Mělník estate only 60 days. On the Frýdlant estate the production of one centner of cereals required approximately 15 days of labour services, whereas in southern Bohemia the figure was only 10.8 days and in the lowlands of central Bohemia only 10 days.

Regarding the general effectiveness of serf labour services in

[29] Above, pp. 37–8, 97–9, 127–8, 129.

[30] Janoušek, *Historický vývoj produktivity práce v zemědělství*, pp. 65–70. A centner is a German measure of weight, equivalent to approximately one hundredweight.

Bohemia during the eighteenth century it appears that, on demesnes where labour services with draught animals were used in addition to the lord's *own* draught animals, the performance of the former was only half that of the latter.[31] Indeed Article 11 of the Decree for the Abolition of Labour Services for Payment of 4th March 1849 went so far as to rate serf labour service at only one-third the value of "free" manpower.[32] Czech agrarian historians have no doubt, however, that harvest yields on peasant holdings during the seventeenth and eighteenth centuries were higher than those of the demesnes, largely because farming was far more labour-intensive on the former than on the latter.[33]

* * *

Most of the cereals produced were sold on the local market, but the lords also used a large proportion of their grain, particularly wheat and barley, for the production of beer and spirits. The breweries belonged to the lords, and they had an assured market for their beer as their serfs were only allowed to purchase beer brewed on the estate. Also, every brewery could count on all the inns in its area taking large amounts of beer depending on the size of the local villages and townships. Revenue from the breweries formed a substantial proportion of the lord's income from the estate. At the beginning of the eighteenth century 26 per cent of the total income of lords in Bohemia came from fees and payments from serfs. Receipts from the demesnes constituted 69 per cent. Of this, one-third came from the sale of cereals, one-third from the sale of beer, and a sixth from livestock-rearing.[34] In the mid-eighteenth century, according to the Dominical Cadastre (Land Survey of the Nobility) of 1757, receipts from breweries represented no less than 43.1 per cent of the entire income of lords.[35] In some places the demesne's

[31] *Ibid.*, p. 150.

[32] A. Klíma, *Revoluce 1848 v českých zemích* [The Revolution of 1848 in the Czech Lands] (Prague, 1974), p. 109.

[33] E. Maur, "Genese a specifické rysy českého pozdněfeudálního velkostatku" [The Origins and Principal Characteristics of Czech Demesnes in the Late Feudal Period], *Acta Universitatis Carolinae: philosophica et historica* (1976), p. 247.

[34] J. Purš, "Struktur und Dynamik der industriellen Entwicklung in Böhmen im letzten Viertel des 18. Jahrhunderts", *Jahrbuch für Wirtschaftsgeschichte* (1965), p. 174.

[35] J. Křivka, "Príspěvek k dějinám poddanského hospodářství v první polovici 18. století" [A Contribution to the History of Serf Holdings in the First Half of the Eighteenth Century], *Historie a Muzejnictví*, ii (1957), p. 94.

own cereal production proved insufficient to keep the breweries supplied and in such circumstances the lord either obtained the necessary wheat and barley from the serfs as a rent in kind or purchased supplies on the open market.

This brings us to the question of Bohemia's export of cereals abroad. A number of historians have asserted that in countries to the east of the Elbe serfdom was actually *caused* by the export of cereals, especially to western Europe.[36] Brenner does not share this view, pointing out that the export of cereals was caused simply by insufficient outlets on the home market. This was because of the low purchasing power of the population, which was in turn due to a general economic decline.[37]

It is certainly the case that some of the grain produced in Bohemia was sold on foreign markets, particularly to those neighbouring countries whose own cereal production was insufficient to meet internal demand – for example, Austria, the Tyrol and Salzburg, the Upper Palatinate, Nuremberg,[38] Meissen and Upper Lusatia.[39] And there is evidence that cereals from Bohemia were exported as far afield as Hamburg.[40] As one would expect, it was the lords who were primarily involved in the export of grain. However, serfs too, on occasion, sold their surplus produce on the open market, where it was sometimes purchased by merchants and exported from the country, but any surplus the serfs might have at their disposal was, of course, primarily destined for local consumption.

It is moreover highly probable that in Bohemia, as in Poland, the export of agricultural produce represented only a very small proportion of total production and that only a tiny section of the population played any part in it, just as only a similarly small section of the population was in any way involved in the importing of produce from abroad.[41] It should perhaps be remembered that even in the

[36] Above, pp. 37–8.

[37] Above, pp. 38–9, 45–6. "Most spectacular, as Postan pointed out, was the case of eastern Europe, where during the late medieval and early modern period the powerful impact of the world market for grain gave a major impetus to the tightening of peasant bondage" (above, p. 25).

[38] J. Janáček, "Export of Agricultural Products from the Czech Lands and Transportation Expenses in the Sixteenth Century", *Hospodářské dějiny*, ii (1978).

[39] Maur, "Genese a specifické rysy českého", p. 247.

[40] A. Klíma, *Manufakturní období v Cechách* [The Manufactory Period in Bohemia] (Prague, 1955), pp. 73–7.

[41] See Kula, *Economic Theory of the Feudal System*, p. 132.

Low Countries, which imported relatively large quantities of cereals, imports still amounted to only 13 or 14 per cent of total consumption, while the inhabitants there constituted a mere 3 per cent of the total population of Europe. Imports of wheat into England at the beginning of the nineteenth century represented only 3 per cent of total consumption.[42] Paul Bairoch drew the conclusion that "before the eighteenth century less than 1% of total cereal production went into international trade".[43] The enserfment of the rural population of Bohemia was a long and involved process for which there were many causes.[44] To speak of the export of grain to foreign markets as the *sole* cause would be drastically to oversimplify an important problem.

In the livestock sector the lord relied on sales at the local market. Stock-rearing was not practised to any great extent on demesnes in Bohemia in the seventeenth and eighteenth centuries, but whatever *was* produced for sale was sent to butchers in towns and townships on the lord's own estate, not further afield. The shortage of home-reared meat in Bohemia was met by the import of bullocks from Hungary and Poland. A significant proportion of the country's total livestock came from the peasants, who reared both beef cattle and pigs on their holdings and sold them at the local market.

On some estates there were large flocks of sheep. On the Frýdlant estate, which had eighteen demesnes, for instance, there were three large flocks with a combined total of some 3,000 sheep; on the Jindřichův Hradec estate, where there were ten demesnes, there were four flocks with 6,364 sheep. Sheep, of course, were kept both for their meat and for their wool. On the eighteen demesnes of the Frýdlant estate there were 770 milch cows, 136 oxen, 26 bulls and 346 calves and bullocks. The relatively large number of oxen on the Frýdlant estate was, however, exceptional and demesnes in the more fertile areas of central Bohemia had far fewer draught animals. Thus, for example, on the Roudnice estate, with fourteen demesnes and 2,200 hectares of arable land, there were only 42 oxen. It follows, of course, that lords on estates such as these had a far greater need for labour services with draught animals.

[42] Bairoch, "Agriculture and the Industrial Revolution", p. 477.
[43] *Ibid.*, p. 476.
[44] A. Klíma, "Probleme der Leibeigenschaft in Böhmen", *Vierteljahrschrift für Sozial- und Wirtschaftsgeschichte*, lxii (1975).

On the Frýdlant estate, with its 770 milch cows, or about 38 per demesne, most of the milk, butter and cheese that was produced was consumed locally on the estate, only a small proportion of the butter and cheese being available for sale as surplus. At Frýdlant each cow was expected to give an annual yield of 1,000 to 1,200 litres of milk, 20 to 30 kilos of butter and 35 to 50 kilos of cheese.[45]

Most of the work on the demesnes, especially in the fields, was undertaken by serfs in the form of labour services. For the smooth running of a demesne, particularly in cattle and poultry-farming, there were ten labourers under the direction of a steward. These labourers lived in their own quarters on the demesne and as well as their food received a small wage. In addition to these teams of labourers, there were also paid threshers, who threshed grain from the beginning of October to the end of April. On the estate of Jindřichův Hradec, where 560 hectares were under cereal crops, there were 91 threshers, working throughout the season and receiving wages in kind amounting to one-sixteenth of the total cereals they threshed. All other work on the demesnes was in the form of labour service. At harvest time the working day totalled some fifteen hours, from about 4 a.m. to 9 p.m. – even longer than was laid down in the Labour Services Decree of 1775.

Virtually all serfs on an estate were under some obligation to perform labour services for their lord, and owners of individual estates of course knew exactly how many days of labour service they were entitled to. For example, after the promulgation of the Labour Services Decree of 1775 the estate of Jindřichův Hradec had at its disposal nearly 110,000 days of labour service with draught animals and more than 51,500 days of manual labour service; the Frýdlant estate could draw on more than 24,000 days of labour service with draught animals and over 83,000 manual labour service days. These amounts were far more than either estate actually required, and the situation was similar on other estates. On the Jindřichův Hradec estate, though nearly 110,000 days of labour service with draught animals were theoretically available, only 67,200 of these were actually required; and of the more than 51,500 days of manual labour service available, only 47,500 were needed. Thus, in each sector of the estate economy, including grain cultivation, only a proportion of the total number of days of labour service technically

[45] Janoušek, *Historický vývoj produktivity práce v zemědělství*, pp. 93–4.

available was actually utilized in practice. On the Jindřichův Hradec estate, for example, only 57 per cent of the total number of available working days were used in cereal production; for work in the forests, the felling and carting of timber, the figure was 17.6 per cent; for building work, 14.3 per cent.

The considerable amounts of labour services at the disposal of the lord enabled him to supply all manpower requirements on his estate without difficulty. But any sort of surplus naturally constituted a wasted resource. One way of utilizing this resource was to commute various surplus labour services to a money rent, and development in this direction is much in evidence on many estates in Bohemia during the eighteenth century. The extent of this trend is well illustrated by the example of the Litomyšl estate where in 1732, in place of their labour services, serfs paid money rent totalling 5,069 guilders 15 kreuzers; in 1773 the amount had increased to 12,329 guilders 2 kreuzers.[46] By the middle of the eighteenth century a proportion of the labour service requirements of serfs in Bohemia had been commuted to a money rent on about 20 per cent of all estates.

This replacement of feudal labour services by a feudal money rent was of the greatest significance for the development of agriculture in Bohemia. According to Marx, "With money-rent prevailing, the traditional and customary legal relationship between landlord and subjects who possess and cultivate a part of the land, is necessarily turned into a pure money relationship fixed contractually in accordance with the rules of a positive law. The possessor engaged in cultivation thus becomes virtually a mere tenant".[47]

* * *

If a serf was to pay his lord a money rent in place of his labour service requirement, he naturally had to be able to acquire this money from somewhere, and this raises the important question of the relationship of the peasant to the market. What Witold Kula said of this relationship with regard to Poland – namely, that "The peasant maintained regular contact with the town market as a general rule, even when the system of serfdom was completely dominant"[48] – is

[46] Klíma, *Manufakturní období v Čechách*, p. 287.
[47] Marx, *Capital*, iii (Moscow, 1972 edn), p. 798.
[48] Kula, *Economic Theory of the Feudal System*, p. 68.

true of Bohemia also. In Bohemia, too, the peasant had to sell a part of his produce on the market in order to acquire the money both to purchase those products he himself was unable to produce and also to pay fees to the lord and taxes to the state. Naturally, the more substantial peasant was able to sell more produce than the smallholder. In the most fertile parts of Bohemia, in the Labe (Elbe) and Ohře (Eger) valleys, a peasant with a holding of 11.5 hectares of arable land was able to sell about a third of his produce on the market, and in the first half of the eighteenth century, whenever there was a good harvest, the figure was as much as 45 per cent. In 1732 one such peasant employed on his farm two farm labourers, a maid, and a nurse for his children, paying them the following wages per annum: the first farm labourer (*nádvornik*) 15 guilders; the second farm labourer, or stableman (*volák*), 8 guilders; the maid 8 guilders; and the nurse 2 guilders. These wages corresponded more or less to those paid to other workers on neighbouring demesnes. This peasant obtained from his land an average cereal harvest of 10.97 centners per hectare, which was a level of yield only rarely achieved on demesnes at that time.[49] His holding was, indeed, very profitable. Evidence from other areas shows that in the fertile parts of the Ohře (Eger) valley in 1730–42 a peasant was able to sell on the open market as much as 46 per cent of his cereal crop.[50] A peasant with a holding of 8.5 hectares near the town of Podbořany in a fertile part of the Zatec (Saaz) region of north-western Bohemia sold nearly 44 per cent of the cereals from his 1782 harvest, mainly barley and rye. In addition he sold fruit from his two orchards, and also cattle and wool. In the fourteen years from 1777/8 to 1791/2 the total income from the sale of produce from his farm was made up as follows: grain and straw 41.2 per cent; fruit 41.4 per cent; cattle 14.4 per cent; wool 2.4 per cent. It is perhaps surprising to note that the biggest proportion of all (by however narrow a margin) came from the sale of fruit.[51]

In marked contrast to such examples of relative prosperity were the vast majority of smaller peasants whose holdings yielded barely enough to supply the essential needs of their families – and also the overwhelming majority of the landless who, to supplement their earnings from the agricultural sector (usually not sufficient to

[49] Křivka, "Příspěvek k dějinám poddanského hospodářství", p. 304.
[50] Křivka, *Výrobní a peněžní výsledky měšťanského zemědělství*, p. 43. [51] *Ibid.*

support their families), sought seasonal work in such domestic industries as spinning and weaving, glass-making and the like. For a large section of the rural population, domestic industries such as these continued to provide supplementary part-time employment well into the capitalist period.

* * *

Although there had been some division of the demesnes and renting of land to the peasants in Bohemia as early as the fourteenth century,[52] as in western Europe, it was the impetus to this movement that was given in the late eighteenth century that was of really crucial significance to the further development of agriculture in the country during the pre-industrial period. Count Josef Kinský, who owned the estate of Sloup (Bürgstein) in northern Bohemia, was also actively engaged in the production of textiles and glass and had been responsible for the building of several manufactories. Partly as a result of his entrepreneurial activities, Kinský proceeded in the mid-eighteenth century to partition the land of his demesnes among his serfs, holdings being allocated in return for a stipulated money rent.[53] Similarly, in 1768 the abbot of Teplá monastery also proposed the partitioning of demesnes among his serfs. He pointed out the considerable advantages of such a course: lords would have a guaranteed income from money rent; moreover, serfs released from labour services would assuredly prosper and thus have more money to spend on beer, spirits and timber, which would mean additional income for the lord.[54]

Such views as these, reinforced by the experience of other countries and the fear of future revolt within Bohemia itself, induced court counsellors Koch, Blanc and Gainer to submit a proposal to the government for the partition of the demesnes and, accordingly, the complete abolition of labour services in Bohemia. The partial implementation of this project was entrusted in 1775 to court counsellor Francis Anton Raab, who maintained that the reform should be carried out in such a way as to benefit the landless and the smallholders. According to Raab's system, those who received land had to pay rent, and the rent was to be in the form of

[52] Maur, "Genese a specifické rysy českého", p. 238.
[53] A. Paudler, *Graf Josef Kinsky, Herr auf Bürgstein und Schwoyka* (Leipa, 1885).
[54] Strauss, *Bauernelend und Bauernaufstände in den Sudetenländern*, pp. 82–3.

money rather than labour services. Those who hitherto had performed manual labour services were liable for 3 guilders; those who had performed labour services with draught animals for 6 guilders.[55] On those estates where the reform was carried out, a new class of peasants came into being, who built their own farm buildings and houses on land that had formerly been part of the demesnes. Raab proposed that the land should be rented to the serfs under the terms of hereditary leasehold. According to his calculations, this new arrangement would benefit not only the serfs themselves but also the lords. Taking the specific example of the estate at Brandýs nad Labem (Brandys on Elbe), he calculated that in the previous ten years the estate had brought in a total of 286,262 guilders, or an average of 28,626 guilders per annum. After the partition of the demesnes and the distribution of the land to the peasants, receipts from leases would amount to 18,763 guilders; money rent from commuted labour services, and *laudemium* payments, would together amount to a further 17,507 guilders, giving a total annual income of 36,270 guilders[56] – that is, 7,644 guilders (26 per cent) more than previously. Moreover, the arrangement would also benefit the lord in that he would no longer have to maintain either farm buildings or equipment. Indeed, by selling these off to the new tenants, he stood to gain another 20,000 guilders. In 1781 Raab submitted a report on the implementation of the partition as it had so far affected thirty-nine estates. The total population of these estates had risen by nearly 20 per cent from 111,638 to 131,801, the number of cattle by more than 27,500 head, while the annual receipts of the lords had increased by no less than 60,000 guilders. All this, he declared, clearly demonstrated the transition to be to the advantage of both parties.

Nevertheless, the majority of the nobility in Bohemia proved hostile to land reform along the lines proposed by Raab – or Raabization, as it was termed. They particularly objected to the fact that serfs were to receive their holdings by hereditary leasehold, fearing that any future inflation would involve them in severe losses. They

[55] V. Cerný, "Pozemková reforma v 18. století" [Land Reform in the Eighteenth Century], *Casopis pro dějiny venkova*, xiv (1927), p. 45.

[56] *Ibid.*, p. 48. *Laudemium* was a fee paid to the lord when the holding of a serf changed hands. For the transfer of a holding within the immediate family, it was 2.5 per cent of its value – in other cases 5 per cent.

preferred instead the proposal of Johann Paul von Hoyer for short-term leases of from three to six years only.[57]

The partition of the demesnes into smaller holdings had been effected at a much earlier date in England[58] and France. In England it had been primarily the church lands that had been partitioned, in the course of the Reformation, and here too the tendency had been to opt initially for short-term leases of up to five years only. But these had gradually been replaced by longer and longer leases so that during the seventeenth century a term of three lives was common. Long leases such as these continued to be common in England during the eighteenth and nineteenth centuries and, according to Cooper, "encourage[d] tenants to invest in improvements".[59] In France land was generally let on short-term leases for periods of from six to nine years, though in the Paris region and a few other parts of the country leases could be for as long as ninety-nine years or three lives. It would be unwise to draw too close a parallel between conditions in England and France and those in Bohemia, because the position of tenants in the latter was substantially different. In Bohemia the vast majority of tenants still retained the status of serfs, subject in all political and legal matters to the jurisdiction of their lords. Nevertheless, there were similarities, for in Bohemia as in England and France, and notwithstanding the continuing burden of his feudal obligations, the tenant now produced both for himself and for the market.

The transition from feudal rent in the form of labour services to a money rent undoubtedly provided new incentives for the peasants, rewarding initiative and encouraging hard work. The "freeing" of the landless rural population from the agricultural sector as a result of the Labour Services Decree of 1775 met the growing demand for manpower in the various industrial enterprises that were coming into existence, and gave a much-needed boost to their development. Coercion of the serf by his lord was, in the course of time, replaced by a contractual relationship between worker and entrepreneur, based on agreement rather than non-economic coercion. Symptomatic of this important change was the attitude of

[57] E. Wright, *Serf, Seigneur and Sovereign* (Minneapolis, 1966), p. 97.

[58] "in some cases demesnes were fragmented, or let to a group of customary tenants" (above, p. 162).

[59] Above, p. 163.

the government as expressed in a pronouncement of 17th July 1779, when it declared that in order to ensure a sufficient labour force for the textile manufactories "it was necessary to have voluntary agreements concluded on the basis of bilateral agreements binding both parties . . . for no unilateral agreement could be imposed on the serfs. In industry there must always be the least possible coercion . . . To subordinate many thousands of serfs to a single entrepreneur (*Fabriksunternehmer*) would not be consistent either with the natural freedom of the individual or with the interests of the state".[60]

Although in theory retaining their status as serfs, workers in the developing industries tended in practice to secure an economic relationship with the entrepreneur which was contractual in nature and based on bilateral agreement. Industrial development was conducive to the removal of the remaining feudal restraints, and the transformation of hitherto tied manpower into a free labour force. After the government's pronouncement of 17th July 1779, it could not be long before serfdom was completely abolished in Bohemia and serfs permitted to move freely about the country, seeking work wherever they liked. And the step was actually taken with the enactment of the Decree for the Abolition of Serfdom on 1st November 1781.[61] This decree was of immense and lasting significance for the future development of Bohemia, with wide social and economic implications – a major milestone on the road from feudalism to capitalism.

[60] Státní Ustřední Archiv [State Central Archives, Prague], CG. com. 1773–83, A 19/28.

[61] The text of the Decree for the Abolition of Serfdom of 1st November 1781 is printed in German and Czech in *Archiv český*, xxv (1910), pp. 25–8.

10. *The Agrarian Roots of European Capitalism**

ROBERT BRENNER

INTRODUCTION

In my original article I began from the idea that social-property systems, once established, tend to set strict limits and impose certain overall patterns upon the course of economic evolution. They do so because they tend to restrict the economic actors to certain limited options, indeed quite specific strategies, in order best to reproduce themselves – that is, to maintain themselves in their established socio-economic positions. On this basis I argued that those long-term demographic and commercial trends, which hitherto have formed the foci of the standard interpretations of long-term economic development in pre-industrial Europe, acquired their economic significance for the distribution of income and the development of the productive forces only in connection with specific, historically developed systems of social-property relations and given balances of class forces. Under different property structures and different balances of power, similar demographic or commercial trends, with their associated patterns of factor prices, presented very different opportunities and dangers and thus evoked disparate responses, with diverse consequences for the economy as a whole. Indeed, as I tried to show, under different property structures and balances of class forces in various European regions, precisely the same demographic and commercial trends yielded widely divergent economic results, not only with respect to long-term trends in the distribution of income, but to overall patterns of the development or non-development of the productive forces. For this

* I am deeply indebted to Perry Anderson, Lawrence Stone and Geoffrey Symcox for the substantial time and effort they gave in criticizing and suggesting improvements to this article. I wish also to thank Josh Cohen, Jon Elster, Franklin Mendels, Jon Wiener and Ellen Wood for their helpful comments.

reason the relatively autonomous processes by which class structures were established, developed and transformed have to be placed at the centre of any interpretation of the long-term evolution of the pre-industrial European economy.

My argument thus started with the assertion that the feudal social-property system established certain distinctive mechanisms for distributing income and, in particular, set certain limits on the development of production, which led to economic stagnation and involution. It did so, most crudely, because it imposed upon the members of the major social classes – feudal lords and possessing peasants – strategies for reproducing themselves which, when applied on an economy-wide basis, were incompatible with the requirements of growth. In particular, reproduction by the lords through surplus extraction by means of extra-economic compulsion and by peasants through production for subsistence precluded any widespread tendencies to thorough specialization of productive units, systematic reinvestment of surpluses, or to regular technical innovation. The system-wide consequence of this structure of reproduction – especially given the tendency to long-term demographic increase – was a built-in secular trend towards declining productivity of labour and ultimately to large-scale socio-economic crisis.

I argued, correlatively, that the original breakthrough in Europe to a system of more or less self-sustaining growth was dependent upon a two-sided development of class relations: first, the breakdown of systems of lordly surplus extraction by means of extra-economic compulsion; second, the undermining of peasant possession or the aborting of any trend towards full peasant ownership of land. The consequence of this two-sided development was the rise of a novel social-property system, above all on the land, in which, for the first time, the organizers of production and the direct producers (sometimes the same persons) found it both *necessary* and *possible* to reproduce themselves through a course of economic action which was, on a system-wide scale, favourable to the continuing development of the productive forces. Because in this system the organizers of production and the direct producers were separated from direct, non-market access to their means of reproduction or subsistence (especially from possession of the land), they had no choice, in order to maintain themselves, but to buy and sell on the market. This meant that they were compelled to produce competitively by way of cost-cutting and, therefore, that they had as a rule to attempt to specialize, accumulate and innovate to the greatest extent possible. They were, on the whole, able to succeed in this because the collapse of the system of surplus extraction by extra-economic compulsion, in connection with the separation of the direct producers from their means of subsistence, freed labour power, land and the means of production to be combined in the most profitable manner. In particular, the rise of the landlord / capitalist tenant / wage-labourer system provided the basis for the transformation of agriculture and, in turn, the breakthrough to the ongoing economic development which took place in early modern England. On the other hand, throughout most of the Continent in the same period, the perpetuation, in various forms, of social-property systems characterized by peasant possession and surplus extraction by extra-economic compulsion (the tax/office structure in France, serfdom in eastern Europe) was at the root of continuing agricultural stagnation, involution and ultimately general socio-economic crisis.

In light of the foregoing I argued finally that it is of critical importance to recognize and analyse systematically the differing *long-term processes of class formation* which characterized the various regions within feudal Europe. For, in my view, these divergent processes critically conditioned the different forms and outcomes of the lord/peasant class conflicts which were endemic to later medieval Europe in the wake of the generalized crises of feudal production and seigneurial revenues. It was the various property settlements which emerged, in different places, from the later medieval seigneurial reaction and the class conflicts which accompanied that reaction which laid the basis for the dramatic regional divergences that were to characterize European economic evolution in the subsequent epoch.

The central elements of this interpretation have been called into question. First, my view of what might be called the internal dynamics of the European feudal economy has been challenged. M. M. Postan and John Hatcher, along with Emmanuel Le Roy Ladurie, have reaffirmed their population-centred interpretation of long-term economic development in pre-industrial Europe. Guy Bois, while critical of the demographic interpretation, has found my accounts of feudal economic development and class formation to be essentially arbitrary, especially in the absence of a fuller presentation of what he would term the "economic laws of motion" of feudalism – in particular, his own organizing conception, "the falling rate of feudal levy".

Second, doubts have been registered as to my account of the divergent developments, out of the later medieval crisis of seigneurial revenues and associated class conflicts, of different systems of property relations in various European regions. Heide Wunder, as well as Postan and Hatcher, has challenged my explanation of why serfdom arose in eastern Europe while it declined in the west. In parallel fashion, Bois and Patricia Croot and David Parker have questioned my explanation of the divergent evolutions of property relations in England and France – the rise of agrarian capitalism versus the consolidation of peasant property in connection with absolutism.

Finally, my view of the way in which diverse property systems, once installed, structured qualitatively different long-term patterns of economic evolution in various European regions during the early modern period has been sharply debated. My view that the imposition of serfdom had deleterious consequences for the long-term evolution of the east European economy is, I believe, widely accepted. My argument, however, that the strengthening of peasant proprietorship in connection with absolutism in France was significantly less favourable for the development of agricultural production than was the rise of capitalist social-property forms in England has been questioned, from different angles, by Croot and Parker, by Le Roy Ladurie, and by J. P. Cooper.

In what follows, I will take up each of the foregoing objections in the course of presenting a more fully developed interpretation of the problems of European feudal evolution and of the transition to capitalism. In Section I, I will attempt, once again, to lay bare what I believe to be the faulty foundations upon which the demographic interpretation has been constructed. In Section II, I will try to sketch a general approach to long-term feudal socio-economic evolution, and then to demonstrate that this approach can better grasp the actual course of medieval economic development, income distribution and feudal crisis in the different European regions than can either the demographic interpretation or Bois's "falling rate of feudal levy" approach. Finally, in Section III, I will, in direct response to the criticisms that have been raised, lay out what I take to be the origins of the different property systems which emerged in different regions of Europe during the early modern period, and explain why these property systems were in fact central in determining the subsequent paths of economic development.

I THE DEMOGRAPHIC MODEL AND CLASS RELATIONS

To lay the basis for my own argument, I offered a criticism of the dominant approaches to long-term economic trends in medieval and early modern Europe: the "demographic model", overwhelmingly predominant these days, as well as the "commercialization model", out of favour in recent years. To this end, *pace* Postan and Hatcher, I made no attempt to "minimize the role of population", nor for that matter the growth of trade, "in the promotion of economic . . . change".[1] My argument began from the *acceptance*, at least in broad outline, of the main long-term economic trends described by the demographic interpreters. Nor, of course, did I challenge the internal coherence, the logic, of the neo-Malthusian cum Ricardian models, *given* their highly restrictive premises. This, I should have thought, was obvious, since my explicit point of departure was precisely the two-phase grand agrarian cycles of non-development, bound up with demographic change. Population growth, in the face of stagnant technique, led in the up-phase of the cycle to increased returns to land relative to labour, increased food prices relative to manufactures, and declining output per person (sometimes interpreted as the declining productivity of labour). Ultimately, over-population was self-correcting, eventuating in a reversal of the demographic trend and, in turn, a down-phase characterized by the opposite trends in the land/labour ratio and in relative factor prices. This two-phase cyclical pattern prevailed in the economy of most of Europe in the later medieval period (1100–1450), and continued to predominate over large parts of it into the early modern period (1450–1700). My intention was not to deny the existence of these two-phase cycles; it was to expose the limitations of the neo-Malthusian cum Ricardian models advanced by the demographic interpreters in actually *explaining* the long-term patterns of income distribution, of cyclical fluctuations, and of economic non-development associated with them.[2]

[1] Above, p. 70. [2] Above, pp. 10–24, esp. pp. 13–14, 18–19.

(I.1) DEMOGRAPHIC CHANGE AND INCOME DISTRIBUTION

No one would deny, concerning income distribution, that in an economy where the potential for increases in the productive forces is limited, population growth will tend to bring about rising returns to land relative to labour, and rising prices of food relative to manufactures (and vice versa). Postan and Hatcher pile fact upon fact to "prove" that these relationships held in medieval Europe, as if I had argued the contrary, which of course I did not. My point was that the demographic interpreters have erred in attempting to use this model of demographically determined returns to factors to explain the distribution of income between classes. In order to do so they have been compelled to assimilate – illegitimately in my view – the evolution of class relations to the demographic model. On the other hand, where they have avoided this pitfall, they have been obliged to introduce class relations in an *ad hoc* manner to cover trends in income distribution which their model cannot explain; but to do this is, of course, to beg the question.

It was my argument that changes in relative factor scarcities consequent upon demographic changes exerted an effect on the distribution of income in medieval Europe only as they were, so to speak, refracted through the prism of changing social-property relations and fluctuating balances of class forces. Thus, any effect of demographically induced changes in relative factor scarcities or prices on the distribution of income was obviously strictly dependent upon the relative amounts of land held outright by lords and by peasants. It was this *prior* allocation which determined the degree to which lords or peasants could potentially benefit from changes in the land/labour ratio. Of course, for most of the medieval epoch, much of the land was owned outright by neither lords nor peasants; it was "possessed" by peasants, subject to exactions by the lords which were in theory fixed, but in practice often fluctuating (this was land held by peasants from lords in customary tenure). The effect, if any, of demographic changes on the distribution of income between lords and peasants holding this customary land depended entirely upon whether the peasants succeeded in getting the dues fixed, or on whether the lords retained the power to alter them. In the former case, the peasants could assume something akin to full property in the land, appropriating most of its fruits. In the latter case, the lords could levy a rent which might be less than, equal to, or even greater than, the market-determined rent for the same amount of land, depending on their powers over their customary peasants and their desire to exercise these powers. Once again, a *prior* distribution – this time of the capacity to coerce – structured the significance of demographically determined market forces.

To cope with the foregoing considerations, the demographic interpreters have been more or less compelled to make surplus extraction or class relations a dependent variable in their population-centred models. In order to explain trends in income distribution in medieval Europe in terms of trends in population, they have been obliged to argue, explicitly or implicitly, that demographic developments determined not only relative factor scarcities or prices, but also the distribution of power and property. They have asserted, as do Postan and Hatcher once again in their contribution, that the demographic rise of the thirteenth century not only brought about high land prices relative to those for labour, but made for the lords' increased capacity to impose levies on their customary tenants (an intensification of serfdom) and, more generally, for lordly prosperity in England.[3] They have argued in turn that the medieval demographic decline determined not only the opposite constellation of relative factor scarcities and prices, but also the decline of serfdom in western Europe.[4]

I would simply reassert that this line of argument can be refuted by demonstrating, as in my original essay, that the same demographic trends in roughly the same periods were accompanied by the opposite trends in income distribution in different European regions. During the population upturn of the later twelfth and thirteenth centuries, there was in England a shift, *grosso modo*, favourable to the lords over and against the peasants; this was made poss-

[3] "The reason why landlords were now not only desirous to increase the weight of labour dues but also 'got away with it' are not difficult to guess. With the growing scarcity of land and with the lengthening queues of men waiting for it, the economic powers of a landowner over his tenants were more difficult to resist": M. M. Postan, "Medieval Agrarian Society in its Prime: England", in *Cambridge Economic History of Europe*, i, 2nd edn, p. 608. Above, p. 72. See also below, p. 248, n. 50.

[4] "In the end economic forces asserted themselves, and the lords and employers found that the most effective way of retaining labour was to pay higher wages, just as the most effective way of retaining tenants was to lower rents and release servile obligations": Postan, "Medieval Agrarian Society in its Prime: England", p. 609.

ible by an interrelated strengthening of lordly property (stable or growing demesnes) and the strengthening of lordship (the lords' increased capacity to make arbitrary levies on customary tenures). But in France, under the same conditions, there was just the opposite shift in the distribution of income, favourable to the peasants over and against the lords; this was made possible by the interrelated weakening of lordship (fixing of peasant dues) and of the lords' control over property (shrinking demesnes). During the population downturn of the later medieval period, there was in western Europe a shift in the long run favourable to the peasants over and against the lords, manifested in the decline of serfdom. But from the fifteenth century onwards in eastern Europe, especially eastern Germany, there was just the opposite trend.[5]

Postan and Hatcher apparently would reject not only the content of this argument, but its entire method, its "logic". They ask, rhetorically, "Does Brenner mean that no causal factor can be proved true unless it can be shown to produce identical results in totally different circumstances?".[6] But they can easily be answered in kind. Do Postan and Hatcher really wish to argue that a historical explanation can be counted adequate when the factor imputed to be cause (demographic increase/decline) can be shown to produce the opposite effects (in terms of income distribution) in very similar conditions? Can Postan and Hatcher deny, in particular, that the French and English countrysides of the later twelfth and thirteenth centuries are inappropriate objects for the comparative analysis which I suggested, when their rural structures were so very similar and when their evolutions were so closely intertwined? Apparently not, for in their contribution Postan and Hatcher (somewhat curiously, it is true) seek to refer me to precisely the contrast between the decline of lordship in thirteenth-century northern France and its consolidation in England in the same period, in the face of similar population trends, as one of the "better examples of 'contradictory' processes" – better, that is, than those I invoked.[7]

[5] In view of doubts concerning the foregoing propositions, for example I. Blanchard, "Review of Periodical Literature, 1977", *Econ. Hist. Rev.*, 2nd ser., xxxii (1979), p. 137, further evidence is given below of divergent trends in income distribution, in the face of similar demographic trends, under the impact of divergent evolutions of social-property relations and balances of class forces (England versus France, thirteenth century; eastern versus western Europe, fifteenth century). See pp. 242–53 below.

[6] Above, p. 66.

But, of course, this was one of the two main comparative examples I used![8] Similarly, can Postan and Hatcher consistently assert that the late medieval west German society where serfdom declined and the east German society where serfdom began its ascent in the fifteenth century are too different to be fruitfully compared? I think not. The latter had only recently developed as a colonial extension of the former, on very similar principles of socio-economic organization. As Postan himself asserts elsewhere, "In the early stages of German conquest and settlement the societies of West and East differed in detail and degree rather than in substance".[9]

The point of these comparative analyses was not, of course, to challenge the fact that population growth/decline, by determining changes in relative factor scarcities and prices, created problems and opened up opportunities for lords and peasants throughout the medieval period and beyond. It was to deny that such changes in supply/demand forces could, in themselves, determine the resulting distribution of income. The demographic interpreters are, at times, obliged to grant this, if only implicitly. For they do, on occasion, refer to the (unexplained) development of class relations to account for trends in the distribution of income inexplicable in terms of

[7] Above, p. 68.

[8] Above, pp. 21–2. This oversight on the part of Postan and Hatcher is especially strange since elsewhere in their critique they actually note that "Brenner draws our attention to the disappearance of serfdom in Normandy and the Paris region" (above, p. 71).

[9] M. M. Postan, "Economic Relations between Eastern and Western Europe", in G. Barraclough (ed.), *Eastern and Western Europe in the Middle Ages* (London, 1970), p. 167. Postan and Hatcher seem to want further to argue that it is improper to compare eastern and western Germany from the later medieval period ("totally different circumstances") because the rise of the international grain market stimulated grain production for export in the east, thereby providing the incentive for the rise of serfdom (above, pp. 66–7). Yet their argument is difficult to accept, for the impact of the international grain market was felt as profoundly in western Europe as it was in eastern Europe. It constitutes another point of *similarity, not of difference*, in the experience of the two regions, and for this reason cannot have accounted for their divergence. We shall have to return to this point in greater detail, but for the moment it is enough to quote Postan: "Eastern Europe diverged widely from the West in its economic and social development. *It would have diverged even if it had been unaffected by trade*": Postan, "Economic Relations between Eastern and Western Europe", p. 167 (my italics). For a similar statement, see M. M. Postan, "The Chronology of Labour Services", *Trans. Roy. Hist. Soc.*, 4th ser., xx (1937), pp. 192–3. See also below, pp. 281–2 and n. 128.

trends in population. Indeed in their contribution Postan and Hatcher disarmingly assert that the demographic interpreters "have not maintained that a rising population invariably led to an intensification of serfdom and a falling population to its demise".[10] But, if not, the question naturally arises: *under what conditions* the rise/decline of population did or did not so lead? Merely to ask this question is, in my opinion, to acknowledge that demographic forces in themselves led nowhere as far as the distribution of income is concerned. It is to pose the problem of systematically accounting for the (divergent) evolutions of agrarian class relations in pre-industrial Europe.[11]

(I.2) THE GRAND AGRARIAN CYCLE

The difficulties faced by the demographic interpreters in accounting for their long cycles of economic stagnation are perhaps as intractable as those concerning the distribution of income. No one would

[10] Above, p. 68.

[11] In a recent article Hatcher has attributed to me a position entirely at odds with the one I presented in my original essay. He asserts that, in my view, the feudal lords could essentially determine the distribution of income, by the exercise of virtually unlimited powers over their peasants. But this attribution is obviously unfounded. For the explicit point of the comparative analysis which was at the core of my essay was that under similar "objective" economic conditions (demographic or commercial) *either* lords *or* peasants could benefit at the others' expense, depending especially upon the level of their class organization and power. I concluded that to understand the *divergent* evolutions of income distribution in pre-industrial Europe, it is necessary to analyse the historically specific processes of class formation and class conflict characteristic of the different regions. Cf. pp. 18–24 above, with J. Hatcher, "English Serfdom and Villeinage", *Past and Present*, no. 90 (Feb. 1981), p. 4. Remarkably, in the same article Hatcher adopts several of the central arguments of my original essay, while implicitly attacking, *on the same grounds as I did*, the position of the demographic interpreters which he and Postan defended in their own contribution. Yet he makes no substantive reference to their contribution, let alone to the positions I actually presented. Specifically, Hatcher concludes as I did that "For unfree medieval peasants the strength of custom was ranged against the rights and powers of their lords. Thus although economic and demographic trends and fluctuations invariably generated powerful forces for change, a miscellany of social, political and legal influences acted and reacted upon them, sometimes compounding their impact, sometimes inhibiting, and sometimes reversing. *Changes in the level of population or the supply of land could make labour or land more scarce or more abundant, but for tenants both in the power of their lords and protected by custom these changes alone did not determine the amount and type of rent they paid*" (p. 37; my italics). Moreover, "We can . . . state with assurance that the outcome was rarely, if ever, dictated solely by market forces" (p. 36).

deny that continuing demographic increase in the face of declining labour productivity sooner or later leads to an imbalance between population and resources – ultimately to poverty, famine and death. Over-population leads, therefore, to a compensatory demographic drop-off, resulting in a reversal of the land/labour ratio and a new onset of demographic growth – the two-phase, self-correcting cycle. There is no reason to challenge the logic of this model, in view of its premises. Nor is there much doubt that a two-phase grand agrarian cycle characterized most of western Europe in the medieval period and part of it during the early modern period. In question, however, is the adequacy of the Malthusian model to explain the specific contours of the grand agrarian cycle.

First, the actual appearance of over-population was strictly relative to the distribution of income and wealth (not to mention the availability of uncultivated land). To the extent that the lords owned the land and extracted a surplus from the peasants, the so-called population ceiling was lowered in two ways: directly, as a result of the immediate subtraction from peasant consumption for the lords' unproductive use; and indirectly, as a result of the loss of potential funds for the increase of the peasants' forces of production through investment and innovation. Postan and Hatcher view such references to the class-relative character of the population ceiling as so much obfuscation, since over-population tended to occur *eventually* in any case (under medieval conditions). Nevertheless, as shall be seen, under different balances of power and property between lords and peasants in different regions, demographic growth appears to have led to over-population at very different population densities, at different points in time and with quite different socio-economic effects.[12]

Second, the Malthusian mechanism is supposed to have operated as a process of homoeostatic adjustment, to bring the labouring population into line with the society's potential resources (given existing technology). But, in fact, it could not necessarily accomplish this in pre-industrial Europe, because production and distribution were so profoundly shaped by the surplus-extracting relationships between lords and peasants. Thus the workings of the socio-economic system did not merely tend to match the producing population and its needs with the potential output; at the same time,

[12] Above, pp. 70–1ff. See also pp. 265–6 below.

it tended to match the surplus appropriated from the direct producers with the needs of the non-producing ruling class. All else remaining constant, a decline of the producing population in response to over-population would have tended to bring it into line with potential output. But all else could not remain constant. A decline in the number of direct producers tended simultaneously to reduce the income of the lords; for the level of the lords' income was a function of the number of peasant producers (tenants), *given* a particular rate of surplus extraction. In consequence, in order to maintain or increase their income, in the face of declining population, the lords tended to be obliged to attempt to extract a greater amount from each peasant, as well as to try to take more from one another (via brigandage, warfare and the like). The result, at least in potential, might be the disruption of production leading to *further* demographic decline, rather than a return to equilibrium.

In fact, throughout much of Europe from the middle of the fourteenth century, population drop-off failed to re-establish the conditions for economic revival in accord with Malthusian principles. Hit by declining incomes, the result of fewer rent-paying peasants, the lords resorted to increasing levies (through rents and taxes) and to intra-feudal warfare, in this way undermining the peasants' productive forces and causing additional demographic decline. The outcome was a downward spiral rather than Malthusian adjustment. At least in some places, moreover, population remained at a low point for quite an extended period, long after stable economic conditions had finally been restored. It was this long-term *failure of adjustment* in the later medieval period which gave to Le Roy Ladurie's grand agrarian cycle its dramatic contours – but which seems to place it beyond the power of the Malthusian model to explain.[13]

(I.3) FROM MALTHUSIAN STAGNATION TO ECONOMIC DEVELOPMENT

Finally, because the demographic interpreters do not root their

[13] See especially G. Bois, *Crise du féodalisme* (Paris, 1976); Eng. trans., *The Crisis of Feudalism* (Cambridge, 1984). See also below, pp. 267–73. Le Roy Ladurie is aware of this problem and offers an explanation in terms of disease and war; see pp. 102–3 above, and E. Le Roy Ladurie, "L'histoire immobile", *Annales E.S.C.*, xxix (1974), pp. 680–6.

accounts of the grand agrarian cycle in a theory of economic backwardness and economic development, they cannot provide a satisfactory explanation of either the specific form of stagnation they have isolated, or the forces which made for a break beyond it to regular economic growth – ongoing specialization, capital investment and technical change. They cannot, in other words, tell us why their Malthusian premise of the non-development of the productive forces essentially held true throughout a whole epoch, but then ceased to do so. This weakness is especially manifest with respect to the rising relative food prices which were characteristic of the up-phases of the grand agrarian cycles and which offered the potential of increased profits to those who specialized, invested and improved. Such demographically inspired market incentives failed to call forth a productive response in most of Europe during the thirteenth and early fourteenth centuries or the sixteenth and early seventeenth centuries; yet they do appear to have stimulated the start of an agrarian transformation in early modern England.[14] What accounts for this difference, and how could it possibly be explained in demographic terms?

Le Roy Ladurie maintains in his contribution that his demographic model does hold good for western Europe as a whole.[15] Yet he also acknowledges that England did break from the Malthusian pattern in the early modern period. These would seem to be contradictory assertions. Le Roy Ladurie tries to explain this inconsistency by arguing that his "homoeostatic model also contains a certain unilinear drift in the direction of agrarian capitalism".[16] Yet he never specifies either the sources of this "drift" or the reasons for its ostensibly unilinear direction. At one point he concedes that the action of the seigneurs sometimes played an important part in creating the social conditions for economic development, by expelling the peasants from the land and creating large, unified farms.[17] Yet, if so, this merely poses the problem. For throughout Europe, from the fifteenth century onwards, seigneurs responded to roughly similar demographic conditions in different ways; there was no simple "unilinear drift" towards capitalism. In the east, they ulti-

[14] See P. Bowden, "Agricultural Prices, Farm Profits, and Rents", in J. Thirsk (ed.), *The Agrarian History of England and Wales*, iv, *1500–1640* (Cambridge, 1967).

[15] Above, p. 104. [16] Above, p. 102. [17] Above, pp. 105–6.

mately enserfed the peasants, setting in train a highly restricted process of growth.[18] In France, as Le Roy Ladurie elsewhere tells us, despite the efforts of rural engrossers, peasant property remained largely intact; *morcellement* outran *rassemblement*;[19] and meanwhile there was the development of absolutism. This led to a repetition of the established medieval pattern of declining productivity leading to population and production crisis. Finally, in England, direct seigneurial action to undermine peasant possession did pave the way for the rise of the familiar capitalist agrarian structure, underpinning the growth of agricultural productivity and overall economic development. To observe these divergences is at once to challenge Le Roy Ladurie's assumption of a "unilinear drift" and to raise the question of the *different* responses by the dominant feudal classes to *similar* conditions and problems: how to protect and improve their positions in the face of the later medieval demographic decline and the subsequent development of population, trade and industry in the early modern period. This is, in my view, to pose unavoidably the problem of the divergent paths of class formation within feudal Europe, and the power struggles which lay behind them. Yet for Le Roy Ladurie such a line of investigation is ruled out. "In the final perspective", he writes, "the system contains its own destiny; *the effect of conflict is purely superficial*".[20]

II CLASS STRUCTURE, CLASS ORGANIZATION AND FEUDAL DEVELOPMENT IN MEDIEVAL EUROPE

Countering my emphasis on the way class or property relations shaped economic development, Le Roy Ladurie accuses me of a misleading running together of "the economic" and "the political".

[18] In his contribution Le Roy Ladurie denies that developments in eastern Europe can properly or relevantly be compared to those in the west; yet *elsewhere* he makes precisely this comparison and for the same purpose that I do: in order to help shed light on the decline of serfdom and the strengthening of the peasantry in western Europe in general and France in particular. Cf. p. 104 above, with his "Les masses profondes: la paysannerie", in F. Braudel and E. Labrousse (eds.), *Histoire économique et sociale de la France*, 4 vols. in 7 (Paris, 1970–80), i, pt 2, pp. 526ff.

[19] See E. Le Roy Ladurie, *Les paysans de Languedoc*, 2 vols. (S.E.V.P.E.N. edn, Paris, 1966), i, p. 8, and *passim*.

[20] Le Roy Ladurie, "Histoire immobile", p. 689, quoted by Bois, p. 108, n. 5 above (my italics).

In the words of Le Roy Ladurie, in speaking of the "surplus-extracting, or ruling, class(es)" I have adopted a "simplistic assimilation between power (political) and surplus value (economic)". Paradoxically, Bois, writing from an explicitly Marxian viewpoint, makes a somewhat analogous charge. Mine is a "political" and a "voluntarist" Marxism: a preoccupation with the vagaries of the class struggle prevents me from discerning the *economic* "law of motion" of feudal society – in his view, "the falling rate of feudal levy".[21] Nonetheless, it is, indeed, central to my viewpoint that a "fusion" (to put it imprecisely) between "the economic" and "the political" was a distinguishing and constitutive feature of the *feudal class structure and system of production*. This was manifested in the fact that the "economic" conditions for the reproduction of the ruling class – the income it required to carry out its life activities, including the continuing subjection of the peasantry – depended upon a system of extraction of surplus labour from the direct producers which was characterized by extra-economic ("political") compulsion. In turn, the varying *forms of development* of this system of *surplus extraction by extra-economic compulsion*, in connection and in conflict with the development of the productive forces by peasant *possessors* of the means of subsistence (land, tools and so forth), provide an indispensable key to the evolution of the European feudal economy: to its specific patterns of agricultural and demographic development which resulted in declining labour productivity; to its characteristic types of unproductive industrial production and exchange, dominated by luxury goods to fill the "political" needs of the lordly ruling class; and to its particular forms of crisis, manifested in the exhaustion of the productive forces (including the producing population itself), the decline of lordly revenues, and the seigneurial reaction – as well as the ways in which the system was or was not superseded in different regions by different types of social-productive systems.

[21] Above, pp. 102, 115.

(II.1) FEUDAL DEVELOPMENT AND FEUDAL CRISIS: SOME GENERALIZATIONS

(II.1.1) Peasant Possession and Surplus Extraction by Extra-Economic Compulsion

In the economy which characterized most of medieval Europe, and much of it during the early modern period, production was, as a rule, carried out by peasants in "possession" of the land and tools required to produce their subsistence. "Possession" is here marked off by inverted commas because the question of its changing and conflicted character – manifested in the conditional character of feudal property – lay at the heart of feudal development. Because peasants actually did hold relatively stable and relatively uncontested possession of their means of subsistence, their reproduction required no economic intervention or productive contribution by the lords. As a result, mere ownership of *other* land (demesne) by the lords was not sufficient for them to realize a surplus from the peasants; for the peasants were under no economic compulsion to work for a wage on the lords' land or to pay an economic rent to lease it. In order to secure a rent – that is, to get the peasants to hand over part of their labour or their product – the lords had to be able to exert a degree of control over the peasants' persons. This was made possible by virtue of the lords' capacity to exercise force directly.[22]

Peasant possession tended to be secured, on the one hand, through the growing strength of peasant communities and the peasants' opportunities for mobility (especially to the extent that there was free, unsettled land). It tended to be realized, on the other

[22] This situation should be contrasted with that which characterizes the capitalist economy. Here the working class must sell their labour power to the capitalists for a wage in order to survive. In the process they must alienate a surplus (profit) to the employers, precisely because they do not possess the means of production and cannot therefore provide *directly* for their subsistence or, alternatively, produce a commodity for sale on the market. In turn, the capitalists may appropriate a surplus without, as a rule, any need for *directly* "political" (forceful) domination over the direct producers, for the capitalists' monopoly of the means of production allows them to exert an "economic" compulsion against the workers, who are compelled to depend upon them to make a living. The power of the state is needed only to protect the property of the ruling class and enforce the contractual exchanges between capital and labour.

hand, as a result of the divided sovereignty which characterized lordly rule – that is, the autonomy and the mutual separation of the individual lordships, their political self-sufficiency, which was the obverse side of their direct access to the means of coercion. Divided sovereignty made for competition among lordships and impeded collaboration. It therefore tended to oblige the lords to grant the peasants their plots on a more or less permanent basis, as an incentive to keep them on the land and pay their dues. Even so, by dispersing force among the individual lordships, divided sovereignty also tended to make it difficult for the peasants to secure full property, as it obliged them to put themselves under the "protection" of some lord precisely in order to maintain their land against other lords. Thus peasant possession was ultimately circumscribed by lordly power. Indeed, to the degree that the individual lordships were able to amass force, and especially to the degree that the lords, as a class, were able to lessen the competition among themselves and to increase their collaboration – thereby overcoming the effects of divided sovereignty – they were able to intensify their domination, and even threaten peasant possession. It may therefore be understood why the changing *manner* in which and *degree* to which the lords, as individuals and as a class, were able to apply power in the rent relationship – typically expressed in the changing character and effectiveness of their politico-jurisdictional authority over the peasants – was central to their formation as a ruling class and, in turn, profoundly marked the development of the whole system of production.

It should be emphasized at once that under certain circumstances it did become possible for the feudal ruling classes to extract a surplus from the peasants without recourse to formally feudal arrangements based on extra-economic compulsion – that is, merely on the basis of ownership of land, and even without a monopoly of it. Where the peasant class as a whole had insufficient land to guarantee its subsistence, some peasants would have no choice but to lease additional plots and/or hire themselves out as wage-labourers to make ends meet. They could not avoid, in the process, alienating part of their product to the lord without recompense.

This situation tended to be spontaneously produced as a result of the tendency to demographic growth which was characteristic of the European possessing peasantry, at least from the period *circa* 1050. Within limits (and leaving aside, for the moment, exogenously induced mortalities, diseases and so forth) the rate of demographic expansion appears to have depended on the age of marriage (for fecundity seems to have been, more or less, a constant). Marriage age, in turn, depended upon access to the means to establish a family, and in particular access to a cultivable plot. Given, then, peasant possession and the associated potential for the subdivision of holdings (both of which could be limited to a lesser or greater degree, depending on the strength of lordship and the weight of lordly levies), parents could treat their plots as the basis for the continuance of a family, and children could count upon receiving a holding at a relatively early age. There appears to have been established, in consequence, a west European pattern of *relatively* early marriage, which seems to have underpinned the relatively rapid medieval demographic growth rates – and this pattern may have been slow to change even in the face of the declining economic opportunities which went with the extreme *morcellement* of holdings.[23] The long-term tendency, therefore, appears to have been towards over-population, leading to increasing demand for land, creating the *possibility* of extracting growing rents, *without* direct resort to extra-economic pressures or controls.

Even so, the potential in this way established for what might be termed demographically conditioned surplus extraction was strictly limited, and could provide only an uncertain long-term basis for the lords' continuing hegemony. On the one hand, the manner and the degree to which population growth leading to the appearance of a rural quasi-peasantry/quasi-proletariat would determine a change in the distribution of income between classes depended upon the existing distribution of the land – the extent, relative and absolute, of the lords' lands (the demesnes, where they were free to charge economic rents) versus that of the peasants (customary land). Yet this distribution could not be assumed to favour the lords. On the other hand, to the extent that the lords were dependent for their income upon their landed property alone – that is, lacking *extra-economic* access to the peasants' labour or the peasants' product – their ability to realize a rent (no matter how much demesne land they held) would tend to require over-population. Lordly incomes

[23] For this interpretation of the tendency to population growth in medieval Europe in terms of early marriage age, linked to subdivision of holdings, and, in turn, peasant possession, see Bois, *Crise du féodalisme*, p. 331; C. Howell, "Stability and Change, 1300–1700", *Jl Peasant Studies*, ii (1975).

would thus be subject to drastic threat in the event of population drop-off. Indeed, at successive junctures in the later medieval period, different sections of the European feudal ruling class suffered from (a) an inadequacy of land (demesne) to take advantage of the population increase (the twelfth and thirteenth centuries), and/or (b) a drop-off in population which made it difficult to derive an income from the land they did hold (the fourteenth and fifteenth centuries). These situations revealed the lords' ultimate dependence upon the institutions by which they could extract a surplus by extra-economic compulsion, and forced the lords to attempt, in different ways, to rebuild and/or reshape these institutions.

In sum, *pace* Le Roy Ladurie, it is imperative to "assimilate the economic and the political" precisely in order adequately to characterize the "surplus-extracting or ruling classes" in feudal society, and to understand the basis of their domination. For throughout the medieval and into the early modern period the existence and reproduction of the feudal ruling classes depended upon extra-economic ("political") arrangements by which the requisite surplus ("economic") was extracted from the peasant producers. Initially embodied in jurisdictional rights over the customary tenantry which sanctioned the extraction of a rent, these arrangements later took the form of property in office which gave rights to a share in centralized exactions, state taxation.

Furthermore, it is impossible to grasp the *evolution* of the feudal economy as a whole simply by means of the so-called "economic" formula proposed by Bois. According to this formula, the "structural contradiction of small-scale production and large-scale property" led inexorably towards the "fall in the rate of [the feudal] levy". In Bois's view, the very fact that the system of production was set in motion by small peasant possessors ("small-scale production") directly ("economically") determined that the system of surplus extraction by extra-economic compulsion ("large-scale property") would decay. It did so, specifically, by determining the long-term "disintegration" of the lords' ability to realize returns from the "various rent-paying holdings within the framework of the seigneurie". Nevertheless, this formulation is heavily one-sided and, for that reason, ultimately misleading.[24]

[24] Above, pp. 109–11, esp. n. 6. For a full discussion of Bois's approach, see below, pp. 242–6.

In particular, as I shall try to show, just as the feudal system of class relations was "politically" constituted, it tended to impose an extra-economic dynamic on the course of feudal economic evolution. Naturally, what the lords could extract was limited by what the peasants could produce, and in this sense peasant-based production profoundly shaped the feudal economy, as Bois says. But the fact remains that the system of surplus extraction tended to develop according to its own logic, so to speak, and, to an important degree, without reference to the requirements of peasant production – as a function, in particular, of the lords' growing needs for *politically motivated consumption*, arising from their needs both to maintain a dominant position *vis-à-vis* the peasantry and to protect themselves *vis-à-vis* one another. If it is true that lordly surplus extraction was ultimately restricted by peasant-based production, it was also the case that the system of lordly surplus extraction could limit, even govern, the development of peasant production itself. As a result, feudal economic development manifested a two-sided, conflictive interaction: between a developing system of production for subsistence through which the class of peasant possessors aimed to reproduce themselves and provide for the continuity of their families, and a developing system of surplus extraction by extra-economic compulsion for non-productive consumption, by which the class of feudal lords aimed to reproduce themselves as individuals and as a ruling class.

(II.1.2) Lords, Peasants and Declining Productivity

I would, therefore, begin by maintaining, as against Postan and Hatcher who appear to deny this, that the overall class structure of production (property structure) – based on extra-economic compulsion by feudal lords in relationship to peasant producers who possessed their means of subsistence – was at the root of declining productivity and, ultimately, the forms of feudal crisis. Instead, Postan and Hatcher assert that the causes of declining productivity are to be found in the "backwardness and stagnation of prevailing technology and, above all, the insufficiency of manorial investment".[25] But this is only to pose the question which, in my view, they do not fully face: what accounts for these inadequacies? Postan

[25] Above, p. 73.

and Hatcher attribute the lack of technological innovation to the "insufficient supply of new technological possibilities". But, if it were true, as they say, that capital-using technologies capable of increasing agricultural productivity were unavailable, then their complementary contention that agricultural investment was insufficient would not make sense. For, in that case, even a low level of investment would have been sufficient to maintain production at the highest *possible* level. This is, indeed, the position of J. Z. Titow, who argues that lordly investment, though low in proportion to their total income, was adequate to the low level of existing technology.[26] Nevertheless, it has been convincingly shown by Eleanor Searle and others that technologies capable of significantly raising agricultural productivity by means of relatively large-scale investments were indeed available in medieval Europe – and they included some of the main components of what was later to constitute the agricultural revolution of the early modern period. What is more, these technologies were actually *used*, on at least some occasions, during the thirteenth and fourteenth centuries, even in England. The question which needs to be asked, therefore, is why were they not *more widely applied*. The problem in other words was not, as Postan and Hatcher contend, the "insufficient supply of new technological possibilities", but rather the feudal economy's inability *to make use* of the possibilities which existed. Given the low capacity to apply existing capital-using technologies, the low level of investment in agricultural production is immediately understandable.[27]

How, then, did feudal property or surplus-extraction arrangements limit the capacity for the adoption of more productive methods and in this way reduce the potential for productive investment – thereby turning the economy towards extra-economic or "political" forms of development? To begin with, they did so (like other pre-capitalist economic arrangements) by making the direct producers, both lords and peasants, independent, to an important degree, from the imperative to respond to market opportunities by

[26] J. Z. Titow, *English Rural Society, 1200–1350* (London, 1969), pp. 49–50. As Titow puts it, "the technical limitations of medieval husbandry seem to me to have imposed their own ceiling on what could be usefully spent on an estate" (p. 50).

[27] Above, pp. 31–3; B. H. Slicher van Bath, *The Agrarian History of Western Europe, A.D. 500–1850* (London, 1963; repr. London, 1966), pp. 178–9; E. Searle, *Lordship and Community* (Toronto, 1974), pp. 147, 174–5, 183–94, 267–329. The quotation is from Postan and Hatcher, p. 77 above.

maximizing returns from exchange. The economy thus remained "patriarchal" in its central aspects. In general, peasant producers possessed (more or less) direct, *non-market* access to their means of subsistence (land, tools). This meant that they were not *compelled* to sell on the market to acquire the means to buy what they needed to subsist and to produce. In consequence, they did not *have* to deploy their means of production so as to compete most effectively with other producers. They could, instead, orient production directly to reproducing their family labour force. Similarly, since the lords had immediate access to their peasants' surplus, thus direct access to their means of reproduction, they were under no directly economic compulsion to produce competitively on the market and therefore were relieved of the direct pressure to cut costs.

This is not, of course, to deny that the development of trade created important incentives to increase output in order to increase returns from exchange so as to meet growing consumption needs; for of course it did – especially for the lords, who could potentially dispose of large surpluses. Nevertheless, even to the extent that the lords did attempt to maximize production for exchange, their relations with their tenants tended to induce them to try to do so, not through the application of fixed capital and increased skill to improve labour productivity, but through the intensification of peasant labour, the increase of levies in money or kind on the peasant producers, or the expansion of the area of cultivation.

Where feudal lords were able to retain significant direct, extra-economic controls over a dependent peasantry, as in early thirteenth-century England, it was only natural that, in so far as they tried to increase output through increasing demesne production, they turned to intensifying villein labour. Yet, in so doing, the lords had necessarily to eschew the application of new techniques and fixed capital. For labour by villeins, in possession of the means of subsistence, was necessarily forced labour; and such "non-dismissible" labour was notoriously difficult to adapt to methods of production requiring the careful application of fixed capital or high skill (or necessitated very high supervisory costs). Thus, the lords' reliance on their "costless" labour made economic sense, but this labour could not be combined with investment in new techniques to provide the basis for agricultural transformation.[28] Of course, as

[28] In my original essay, I implied that the lords did not improve production because

population increased (especially as the thirteenth century wore on) wages dropped so low and land prices rose so high that lords were induced to commute labour rents for money rents, and to cultivate their demesnes using wage labour or to lease them on the market (because they could profit by this shift). But low wages and high land prices also reduced the incentive to opt for capital-using, labour-saving innovations, while favouring the maintenance of the old labour-intensive, labour-squeezing methods – although now on the basis of hired labour rather than villein services – and the channelling of investment funds into land purchases (rather than capital improvements).

The demesnes' entanglement with village-organized agriculture posed further barriers to their improvement. Demesne parcels were often scattered throughout the open fields, and were, moreover, subject to community-regulated cultivation. Attempts by the lords to consolidate or engross could therefore meet significant barriers – the resistance of the peasant community as a whole, or the refusal of the individual peasant to sell his land. It is somewhat puzzling that Postan and Hatcher accuse me of implying that the "mass eviction of villeins was a practice in which landlords could regularly engage", when I referred, in this regard, precisely to "the difficult and costly processes of building up large holdings and investing, of removing customary peasants and bringing in new techniques".[29] In any case, to the extent that the strength of community controls or peasant possession limited the lords' ability to reorganize agricultural production, their attempts to increase revenues were, once again, channelled towards squeezing *rather than* improvement.

Where the lords tried, and succeeded, in increasing their income through increased levies on the peasants in money or kind (rather than in labour) they undercut the chances for development on lands possessed by peasants, through reducing the peasants' funds for investment. In England such levies appear to have increased during the thirteenth century. But it was also the case that the peasants'

they had the *alternative* of squeezing the peasants by extra-economic compulsion. This formulation is misleading. I believe it is more correct to say that, because the lords had no choice but to rely upon surplus extraction by extra-economic compulsion, they were largely prevented from improving, because the former could not be combined successfully with the latter. Above, pp. 31–2. Cf. M. Mate, "Profit and Productivity on the Estates of Isabella de Forz, 1260–92", *Econ. Hist. Rev.*, 2nd ser., xxxiii (1980).

[29] Above, pp. 76, 32.

potential for developing the forces of production was itself definitely limited. Given the small plots available to most of them and their limited investment funds, the peasants' possibilities for accumulation and innovation were sharply restricted. Given, in turn, the uncertainties of the harvest, the giant oscillations of food prices and the related vagaries of the market for cash crops, the peasants naturally wished to avoid the risk of dependence upon the market for sales or purchases. They attempted, therefore, to orient their production directly towards ensuring immediate subsistence needs. They diversified, in order, so far as possible, to produce on their own plots the full range of their necessities, and marketed only physical surpluses. This tendency to "production for subsistence" naturally constituted a strong barrier to commercial specialization and ultimately to the transformation of production, even when market opportunities developed. It also posed a major barrier to those rural accumulators, richer peasants and lords, who wished to collect land; for the peasants would not easily part with the plots which were the basis for their existence unless they had to. On the contrary, they tended to subdivide their holdings among their children. Indeed, the peasants' *morcellement* of parcels under population growth tended to overwhelm any counter-tendency to accumulation in the agricultural economy as a whole, further undermining the potential for development.[30]

(II.1.3) Forms of Feudal Development: From Colonization to Political Accumulation

The inability of both lords and peasants to improve labour productivity beyond a certain point, a consequence of feudal class-productive or property relations, thus imposed certain limits and possibilities, and conditioned specific overall patterns of feudal economic development – patterns which were, in the long run, typically non-productive and extra-economic. The major exception proves the rule. Major capital expenditures on production are to be found above all on new agricultural "plant" (on the infrastructural

[30] H. Neveux, "Déclin et reprise: la fluctuation biséculaire, 1330–1560", in G. Duby and A. Wallon (eds.), *Histoire de la France rurale*, 4 vols. (Paris, 1975–6), ii, pp. 20–9. Here there is an excellent discussion on the limits to peasant production, and to specialization and investment, in the medieval context.

conditions which formed the basis for the extension of existing forms of production) rather than on the equipment of labour with more and better means of production. Colonization, the opening up of new land to cultivation, was indeed the archetypal form of feudal development and feudal improvement. So long as new lands were available and population grew, lords could increase their income simply by establishing additional peasants on previously uncultivated land. *Potentially at least*, in this situation, output could grow and lords and peasants improve their condition, with a minimum of conflict. For lords might avoid the costs of coercion, while benefiting from the multiplication of tenures at, say, constant rents (which is not to argue that they would or could always choose this option).

Nevertheless, the potential for this form of development was obviously limited. For the possibilities of extending the cultivated area, and for supporting in this way additional rent-paying peasants, were clearly restricted by the finite supply of land. Beyond colonization, therefore, especially given the limited possibilities of increasing output via investment and improvement, feudal development tended to take inward-looking forms – forms of *redistribution* of wealth, rather than its creation.

Postan and Hatcher point out that there was a strong predilection on the part of feudal lords to purchase land, rather than invest in fixed capital improvements, and they attribute this to a "preference" which "was deeply rooted in the mode of life and scale of values of feudal nobility".[31] But this is only a partial answer. For the preference for land must itself be understood, at least in part, as an outcome of the established class-productive relations; it made sense from an economic point of view. Because investment in fixed or human capital to improve demesne production could, as noted, be expected to yield only the most limited returns, it was reasonable for the lords to use their surpluses simply to increase the size of their holdings, thus extending their control over rent-producing land and peasants. Moreover, because the barriers to improvement extended to the peasant sector as well, the peasants showed the same bias towards the purchase of land, partly as speculation, as well as to help further ensure subsistence. In other words, in the feudal context, land was a good investment. Indeed, it showed itself to be that much better an investment to the degree that population growth

[31] Above, p. 78.

propelled a long-term tendency towards rising land and food prices – and as the economy proved incapable of responding to these market signals by proportionally increasing output.

Beyond opening up new land or purchasing cultivated land, the lords, as a rule, could systematically increase their income only by taking from one another or by squeezing more from their peasants. Thus the long-term tendency, prevalent throughout the feudal epoch (from *circa* 1000–1100), to "political accumulation" – that is, the build-up of larger, more effective military organization and/or the construction of stronger surplus-extracting machinery – may be viewed as conditioned by the system's limited potential for long-term economic growth, and, to a certain extent, as an alternative to extending or improving cultivation. Given the difficulties of increasing production, the effective application of force tended to appear, even in the short run, as the best method of amassing wealth.

But to what extent *could* individual lords, or groups of them, gain access to more of the social surplus through political accumulation?[32] This problem was posed especially sharply because the very means of coercion (force/jurisdiction) maintained by every individual lord to ensure his reproduction (as a lord) *vis-à-vis* the peasants constituted a threat to the other lords. The result was a generalized tendency to intra-lordly competition and conflict, *and this made political accumulation a real necessity*, at least in the longer run. At the same time, this "parcellized sovereignty" had potentially anarchic effects, which had to be overcome if political accumulation was to be pursued successfully.

In the first instance, of course, military efficacy versus other lords or improved jurisdictional powers over the peasants required the collecting and organizing of followers – recruited, naturally, for the most part, from within the ruling class, normally from among its lesser elements. But to gain and retain the loyalty of their followers, the overlords had to feed and equip them, and in the long run reward them. Minimally, the overlord's household had to become a focus of lavish display, conspicuous consumption and gift-giving. But beyond this, it was generally necessary to provide the followers

[32] For the following paragraphs, see for example G. Duby, *The Early Growth of the European Economy* (Ithaca, 1974); P. Anderson, *Passages from Antiquity to Feudalism* (London, 1974); and O. Brunner, G. Duby, O. Hintze, J. F. Lemarignier and J. R. Strayer, in F. L. Cheyette (ed.), *Lordship and Community in Medieval Europe: Selected Passages* (New York, 1968).

with the *means to attain or maintain their status as members of the dominant class* – that is, a permanent source of income, requiring a grant of land with associated lordly prerogatives (or, later, an office). Naturally, if paradoxically, such grants tended to increase the followers' independence from the overlords, leading to a renewed potential for disorganization, fragmentation, anarchy. As a result, in the long run, further grants tended to be necessary. Successful political accumulation therefore required that increased military power and/or jurisdictional authority yield returns which *more than covered* their increased costs, and such costs tended to grow over time. In consequence, political accumulation tended to become self-perpetuating and escalating – the amassing of more land and men to more effectively exert force in order to collect the resources for the further application of power.

Political accumulation is, nevertheless, quite incomprehensible merely in such quantitative terms. It was, in addition, a *qualitative* process requiring the increasingly sophisticated self-organization of the feudal ruling class. In the first place, the lords needed broader, more elaborate forms of political co-operation in order to extract a surplus from increasingly well-organized peasant communities, and to counteract the effects of peasant mobility. Since the scope of peasant organization tended to be geographically limited to the village or region, the effectiveness of the lords' surplus-extracting administration tended to depend on the degree to which intra-lordly organization could be extended, and intra-lordly competition correspondingly reduced. Second, the lords required more developed political forms to facilitate the reciprocal protection of their property against one another, and this meant the establishment of rights through the promulgation and enforcement of law. Finally, intensified competition between groups of lords tended to require increasingly sophisticated forms of military organization and weaponry. Speaking generally, the organization of groups of lords around a leading warlord for "external" warfare (for defence or conquest) most often provided the *initial* source of intra-lord cohesion, and this served, in turn, as the basis for building more effective internal collaboration for the mutual protection of one another's property and for controlling the peasantry. Throughout the feudal epoch, then, warfare was the great engine of feudal centralization.

All this is merely to say that an essential long-term basis of feudal accumulation was the development of feudal states – by which is minimally meant the various forms of association for self-government of groups of feudal lords, each of whom maintained, in the last analysis, direct access to, or private property in, the means of applying force. This is not to say that a high level of lordly organization was always required. Nor is it to argue that state-building took place as an automatic or universal process. One might argue, for example, that at the frontiers of feudal society, to the east and the south, so long as colonization remained an easy option, there was relatively little (internally generated) pressure upon the lordly class to improve its self-organization – and that the opposite tended to be the case in the older, long-settled regions. At the same time, just because a strong feudal state might become "necessary" did not always determine that the lords could successfully avoid anarchy (witness western Germany after the twelfth century). What is being argued, however, is that to the degree that disorganization and competition prevailed within groups of feudal lords, they would tend to be vulnerable not only to depredations from the outside, but to the erosion of their own dominance over the peasants – to their decay as a ruling class. The economic success of individual lords, or groups of lords, did tend to depend on feudal state-building, and the long-term trend, overall, does appear to have been towards greater political centralization for political accumulation.

It seems to me, therefore, that those historians who have insisted upon a narrowly "political" definition of feudalism as a "form of government" and who have, in turn, focused upon the broad range of relationships of obligation and exchange which were constructed to bind man to man in feudal society (not only the relations of vassalage strictly speaking, but also the more loosely defined associations structured by patronage, clientage and family) have grasped an essential driving force of the system.[33] Yet, in the same way that some Marxists have failed to draw all of the necessary "economic" implications of the specifically extra-economic ("political") nature of the feudal surplus-extracting relationship, those historians who have stressed the heavily "political" nature of feudal dynamics have

[33] For a convenient summary of the arguments for a narrowly political definition of feudalism (Strayer, Coulborn, Lyon), see J. W. Hall, "Feudalism in Japan", in J. W. Hall and M. Jansen (eds.), *Studies in the Institutional History of Early Modern Japan* (Princeton, 1968), esp. pp. 24–6ff. Cf. R. H. Hilton, *A Medieval Society* (London, 1966; repr. Cambridge, 1983), ch. 2.

tended sometimes to forget that much of feudal government, feudal state-building, was about "economics", indeed "accumulation" – the extraction, circulation, redistribution and consumption of peasant-produced wealth.

In this context, trade expanded largely in relationship to growing ruling-class consumption needs, fuelled especially by the expanding requirements of political accumulation. It facilitated a circuit of production essentially involving the exchange of artisan-produced luxury and military goods for peasant-produced necessities (food) extracted by the lords. In the first instance, the growth of this social division of labour, founded on the rise of urban-based industry (concentrated classically in Flanders and northern Italy), further benefited the lords, for it reduced costs through increasing specialization, thus making luxury goods relatively cheaper. Nevertheless, in the long run, the growth of this form of social division of labour on a European scale was disastrous.[34] It meant a growing disproportion between productive and unproductive labour in the economy as a whole (for little of the output of the growing urban centres went "back into production" to augment the means of production or means of consumption of the direct peasant producers). Over time, moreover, the tendency to political accumulation was *intensified* by the growing need for conspicuous consumption (which went along with the growing availability of luxury goods) and by the increasing requirement for military supplies (which grew up with the escalation of the size of armies and the growing complexity of weapons). As the agricultural economy thus saw its foundations progressively sapped, the weight of the urban society upon it continued to grow, inviting serious disruption.

If it is true, then, that the effectiveness of lordly political accumulation was, in the last analysis, limited by the weakness of the underlying feudal-productive base, it is still the case that increasingly powerful, increasingly well-organized feudal class states could be, and were, constructed through concentrating energy and centralizing organization, even in the face of the declining capacity of the agricultural forces to support the population. As a result, the self-propelling tendency to increasing political centralization for political accumulation not only tended to accelerate the long-term tendency of the productivity of labour to decline; it also disrupted the

[34] Above, pp. 127–8.

"normal" Malthusian mechanism for bringing population into line with production. As the peasants' surplus tended to reach its limit, and indeed to decline with the drop-off of population, the lords' build-up of more powerful instruments to redistribute it via coercive extraction and warfare tended to quicken, thereby creating the conditions for catastrophic crises of the economy and society as a whole.

(II.2) DEMOGRAPHY AND DEVELOPMENT IN THE GROWTH PHASE OF THE ECONOMY *CIRCA* 1150–1300

Inability to come satisfactorily to terms with the "fusion" between the "political" and the "economic", that profoundly marked the feudal-productive system, is the central weakness of the approaches of both Bois and the demographic interpreters. This problem is, indeed, manifested in the analyses by *both* Bois *and* the demographic interpreters of the growth phase of the European medieval economy in the later twelfth and thirteenth centuries and, as we shall see, of the long period of crisis which followed. Their approaches are, of course, quite different. Nevertheless, their interpretations suffer from a similar difficulty – a failure adequately to take into account the divergent evolutions, in both character and strength, of those mechanisms of extra-economic compulsion improvised by the feudal lords in different regions to ensure the extraction of a surplus in the face of peasant opposition. By counterposing the analysis of Bois to that of the demographic interpreters, it is possible to see the force of this objection and to begin to indicate the sort of alternative required.

(II.2.1) The French Economy in the Thirteenth Century: A Falling Rate of Feudal Rent?

The guiding conception of Bois for his analysis of the feudal economy as a whole is what he terms "the tendency to a falling rate of feudal levy". In the up-phase of the twelfth and thirteenth centuries the feudal ruling class was able to take only a decreasing proportion of the total output, as compared to the class of peasants. This was, in the first instance, because the rents levied by the lords tended to be fixed in money, while population growth led to rising relative land prices, rents and food prices. This tendency of the rate of rent to decline, says Bois, facilitated a process of economic growth, for it allowed population to grow and peasant tenures to multiply, especially through the opening up of new lands (assarts). For a time population growth and new tenures gave the lords enough new income to compensate for declining returns from their established customary tenures. Still, the end point had to come sooner or later: the potential for colonization was used up, peasant productivity declined, and, with continually growing population, there was a quickening rise in prices. At a certain point, therefore, the absolute size of the rent going to the lords had to drop, for increases in the area under cultivation and a rising population could no longer make up for the accelerating decline in the rate of rent, and a crisis ensued.[35]

Now, there is no reason to dispute the foregoing trends, presented by Bois, as they apply to medieval Normandy. Indeed, as I observed in my original article, they seem to hold good beyond Normandy throughout much of northern France in the later twelfth and thirteenth centuries. By this time the *cens* were everywhere fixed and hereditary. Moreover, not only Normandy but the neighbouring provinces of Ile-de-France and Picardy also experienced the important trend towards fixing tallages, eliminating their arbitrary character, at least by the end of this period (1250–1300). The same tendency is evident in these provinces for entry fines: these also seem to have been generally set at a fixed and steady rate.[36] Finally, and of paramount importance, throughout most of this region the demesnes (where an adjustable, economic rent could be levied) were of very restricted scope in relation to the peasant sector (where rents were fixed in money). By Bois's survey, the demesnes seem to have covered 10 per cent or less of the cultivated surface in thirteenth-century Normandy. Guy Fourquin obtained an analogous result (10–12 per cent) for the area around Paris. And the findings are apparently similar throughout the region, although quantitative data is hard to come by.[37] Thus, through much of

[35] Bois, *Crise du féodalisme*, pp. 203–4, 354–60.

[36] Above, pp. 20–2, 56–7; G. Fourquin, *Les campagnes de la région parisienne à la fin du moyen âge* (Paris, 1970), pp. 175–9; R. Fossier, *La terre et les hommes en Picardie jusqu'à la fin du XIIIe siècle*, 2 vols. (Paris, 1968), ii, pp. 555–6, 714; Neveux, "Déclin et reprise", p. 36.

[37] Bois, *Crise du féodalisme*, p. 217. Bois's results for Normandy are supported by M. de Bouard, *Histoire de la Normandie* (Toulouse, 1970), p. 160. For the Paris region, see Fourquin, *Campagnes de la région parisienne*, pp. 138–9. For further

thirteenth-century France (particularly the north), the situation was as Duby has summarized it: labour services were inconsequential; there was a generally light incidence of customary rent from the *cens*, as inflation left money rents absurdly unadjusted. As a result, the lion's share of the lord's income was made up of returns from the demesne, since, unlike customary levies, these could be adjusted to prices.[38] But the inability, or the loss of ability, to dispose of the requisite powers to extract adequate (or even significant) rents from their customary lands (*cens*) seems to have left large sections of the French feudal class with an insufficient landed economic base. In consequence, first indebtedness, then widespread land sales, became endemic.[39] It is no wonder that historians of medieval France besides Bois have found declining rents leading to a crisis of seigneurial revenues from various points in the thirteenth century.[40] The question, however, is the source of this trend.

Why was there a falling rate of feudal levy in northern France in the thirteenth century? Bois tells us that it was built into the very structure of feudal production. The peasant, Bois asserts, "possessed, with the usufruct of the land and the control of the process of production, a trump card, while the seigneur, excluded from this process, exercised his levy only by virtue of acts of an extra-economic origin . . . There resulted, in the long run, an evolution of relations of economic forces favourable to the peasant and generative of an erosion of the rate of levy". This balance of forces was clearly manifest in the principle of *tenure chassée* – hereditary holding at fixed and customary charges.[41]

Nonetheless, the insufficiency of this reasoning should be evident. I have also of course argued that, in view of the peasants' possession of their means of production, the lords' ability to exact a rent through extra-economic compulsion was critical for their reproduction. But the question which must be asked of Bois is why such a set of arrangements should necessarily have been favourable

indications, see G. Fourquin, "Au seuil du XIVe siècle", in Duby and Wallon (eds.), *Histoire de la France rurale*, i, pp. 566–8.

[38] G. Duby, *Rural Economy and Country Life in the Medieval West* (London, 1968), pp. 210–11, 218–19, 224, 238–9.

[39] See Fossier, *Terre et hommes en Picardie*, ii, pp. 622–3; Fourquin, *Campagnes de la région parisienne*, pp. 151–2; Bois, *Crise du féodalisme*, pp. 196–7.

[40] See the summary of research in Neveux, "Déclin et reprise", especially the section on the "difficultés de la seigneurie", pp. 35–9.

[41] Bois, *Crise du féodalisme*, p. 355; also pp. 203–4.

to the peasants, as far as income shares is concerned, especially over the long term. Why could not the lords, in the face of peasant possession, have maintained, or even proportionally increased, their manifold charges (fines, tallages, labour rents and so forth) by coercive means?[42] We can agree that the lords might *at first* grant favourable conditions to peasants in order to induce them (and allow them) to open up new land for cultivation. But this would not explain what would have prevented the lords from subsequently adjusting established levies or introducing new ones in order to protect or improve their incomes. What is required, but missing, from Bois's account, is an explanation of the lords' ostensibly inherent, *long-term* structural weakness as surplus-extractors by extra-economic compulsion from peasant possessors.

This difficulty is made all the more acute since Bois points (somewhat contradictorily) to a *secondary* tendency within feudalism towards the *accumulation of land* by lords (and big peasants) at the expense of the mass of the peasantry, which he sees as characteristic of the growth phase of the feudal economy.[43] Yet Bois does not explain why this trend, which potentially opened the way to increasing economic rents from growing demesnes, could not have counteracted the tendency to a declining rate of feudal levy from the customary holding. For, especially under the conditions of increasing population, which would obviously have pushed up returns from each unit of demesne land, increasing land to the lords would have meant increased rents and thus a counter-trend in income distribution to the falling rate of feudal levy.

The question is, then, why the lords could not have expanded their demesnes enough to be able to counteract declining returns from the customary plots. They could have accomplished the latter either through appropriating newly assarted land to their demesnes, or through transforming old, customary tenures to leaseholds. It will be noted that this question is analogous to the first. For it poses, once again, in a different form, the problem of the distribution of property and of class power, and its determinants. The insufficiency of Bois's reasoning is indeed manifest when it is simply noted that there would have been no decline in the rate of feudal levy had the

[42] Bois is aware of this *possibility*, but in my view gives no satisfactory explanation as to why it could not be realized. See, for example, *ibid.*, pp. 203–4.
[43] *Ibid.*, pp. 167–8, 217, 342–6, 361ff.

lords been able to add sufficiently large new seigneurial levies to the old ones or to increase the relative size of their demesnes, or had they merely been capable of taking their rent in kind (rather than money) and/or extracting the levy as a proportion of the harvest (rather than as an absolute amount). In fact, Bois provides instances of all these phenomena in thirteenth-century France.

Finally, Bois speaks as if the lords were content to maintain a steady *absolute* income, and to allow the peasants to take an increasing *share* of the output. But this is to assume away the problem of the lords' *needs* as a ruling class in relationship to the income they were receiving. Without an analysis of the lords' changing consumption requirements, and the processes affecting these, we cannot determine the economic demands they would have wished to place upon the peasants, had they been able. But Bois fails to consider this problem and, as a result, he ends up by proceeding *as if* the lords' needs were constant.[44] This assumption cannot be justified empirically or conceptually. The requirements of the feudal lords, and their actual consumption, *undoubtedly rose* throughout the medieval period. Moreover, their growing consumption needs were not accidental, nor can they be dismissed as "superstructural". They expressed certain imperatives, deriving from the processes by which the lords were compelled to reproduce themselves as individuals and as a class – above all, the necessity to build up, increasingly, the means for political accumulation.

In sum, even were we to discover a universal tendency to a declining rate of feudal rent throughout the medieval period, we would still have to explain why the lords *allowed it* and/or *could not prevent it*.

(II.2.2) The English Economy in the Thirteenth Century: Demographically Determined Lordly Prosperity?

While the model of Bois seems to "fit" the French evidence, it

[44] Thus he tends, for example, to see the lords moving to intensify their surplus extraction only when there is an absolute decline in their incomes. It should be emphasized that the problem of evaluating the extent to which the income of the lords as a class is "adequate" – that is, the sufficiency of their income – is a very complicated one indeed, even leaving aside the question of their changing consumption needs. For one has to determine, first, the absolute amount going to the ruling class in relationship to its changing size and, second, the *distribution* of the surplus *within* the ruling class.

appears to be contradicted by the radically different English data for the same period. First, in the later thirteenth century (1279) a good third of the cultivated land in England was held in unfree tenure, and these villein holdings were subject to arbitrary and potentially increasing dues of all sorts.[45] By contrast, the French *cens* tenures, which yielded derisory returns by the middle of the thirteenth century, appear to have covered some five-sixths to nine-tenths of the cultivated surface (they should, indeed, be seen as somewhat analogous to the lightly taxed English freehold tenures, which covered about a third of the cultivated land). On average, according to Postan's estimates, some 50 per cent of the villein tenants' total produce was extracted by English lords, while, in comparison, Bois's conclusion is that the French lords secured only 9–10 per cent of their customary peasants' output.[46] In turn, English demesnes covered a third of the cultivated surface, perhaps three times the proportion covered by the demesnes of northern France (and naturally yielded increasing rents with the thirteenth-century population increases). Finally, and relatedly, villein labour services were very much alive in later thirteenth-century England. Duby has described the English situation at this point with respect to labour services as analogous to that on the Continent in the ninth century.[47]

Bois's response to this divergence is curious, but follows inexorably from his theory of the declining rate of feudal levy. He tells us that thirteenth-century England – with its large demesnes, its labour services, and arbitrary levies on customary land (villeinage) – "exhibits an evident backwardness" with respect to French development.[48] It was behind, having some catching up to do. In time, English developments would have gone the same way as the French, with an inevitable tendency to falling levies and shrinking demesnes; they simply required more time to do so.

Nevertheless, long-term trends in medieval England actually ran counter to Bois's interpretation. Not only did England fail to catch up with France, it sometimes travelled in the opposite direction. Indeed, the fact that income in England appears to have gone

[45] These results for England, based on the Hundred Rolls of 1279, are given in E. A. Kosminsky, *Studies in the Agrarian History of England in the Thirteenth Century* (Oxford, 1956), pp. 92–5, 203–6.
[46] Bois, *Crise du féodalisme*, p. 191.
[47] Duby, *Rural Economy and Country Life in the Medieval West*, pp. 210–11.
[48] Above, p. 113.

increasingly to the lords during much of the growth phase of the medieval economy has been used by the demographic interpreters Postan and Hatcher to argue against me that it was not feudal power, but increasing population, operating through the laws of supply and demand, which determined income distribution.[49] To complete this argument they feel obliged to assert once again that the strengthening of lordship which took place in England in this period was itself a function of population increase.[50] I would simply respond that it never occurred to me to deny that population growth leading to rising demand for land would have distributed income in favour of the lords – *if* they had established enough power to vary rents in accord with prices on customary lands and/or *if* they possessed ample demesnes.[51] But I do deny that population increase, in itself, could endow the lords with either of these.

As Postan and Hatcher themselves point out, even though population was increasing during the twelfth century, much of this period witnessed a trend towards fixed payments from the peasants to the lords, a tendency which favoured the peasants.[52] (This is perhaps what Bois's theory would lead us to expect.) Nonetheless, from the later twelfth and especially the thirteenth centuries there developed, with continuing population growth, a reversal of the previous trend. The lords successfully reasserted their rights to make increasing exactions from the peasants. This had its legal expression in the hardening of the lines between free and unfree peasants, with a large part of the rural population consigned to unfreedom. With unfreedom went liability to increasing payments and (very much contrary to what Bois would lead us to predict) this was especially the case, apparently, in the longest settled regions.[53]

[49] Above, pp. 72, 75–6, and *passim*.

[50] Thus they argue that the fact that rents were high for freely negotiated leases in the thirteenth century shows that the high and mounting payments on unfree customary lands reflected market forces, rather than "mere excesses of feudal power" (above, p. 72). See also p. 219, n. 3 above.

[51] Above, p. 22.

[52] Above, p. 68; Postan, "Medieval Agrarian Society in its Prime: England", pp. 585–6; R. H. Hilton, *The Decline of Serfdom in Medieval England* (London, 1969), pp. 15–16.

[53] "In much of 'the anciently settled core of medieval England' . . . the trend seems to have been for the outgoings of the customary tenants to rise . . . seigneurial charges were augmented": E. Miller and J. Hatcher, *Medieval England* (London, 1978), p. 151, and also pp. 111, 131, 213–24. See also Hilton, who speaks of "a counter-attack by estate owners . . . waging a successful battle against their

Finally, throughout the thirteenth century the lords seem to have expanded their demesnes, partly through assarts and partly through converting to demesne customary tenures upon which they found it difficult to raise levies.[54] Thus, although population rose consistently during the twelfth and thirteenth centuries, in England it could, in itself, determine no consistent pattern of income distribution. The latter depended on the changing character of the social-property relationships and the changing balance of class forces. These seem to have underpinned a reversal of mid-twelfth-century trends which were apparently favourable to the peasants, so as to shift the distribution of income during the thirteenth century in favour of the lords, over and against the unfree peasants (while leaving the free peasants in a relatively favoured position).

To clarify this point, it is necessary to take exception to the puzzling statement made by Postan and Hatcher, that "The close definition of villein status and obligations in the late twelfth and the thirteenth centuries may have . . . helped to protect the villeins against arbitrary exactions". They quote Bracton to the effect that the lords' authority over their peasants "once extended to life and death, but is now restricted by the civil law".[55] But this is beside the point. For the lords hardly required such untrammelled physical powers over their peasants to exercise economically effective lordship. What *was* unquestionably critical in this respect was the exclusion of the villeins from the protection of the royal courts against the lords' arbitrary exactions, and this result was precisely the upshot of the legal developments of this period. It was enough for the lord to establish the fact that his tenant was a villein (unfree) to have him denied legal protection; to have thrown out of court any appeal by the tenant that the lord's exactions were unjustified; and to force the peasant back upon his own and the community's resources in any conflict with the lord.[56]

customary or villein tenants": Hilton, *Decline of Serfdom in Medieval England*, p. 16.

[54] Hatcher, "English Serfdom and Villeinage", pp. 16–21.

[55] Above, p. 74.

[56] See Miller and Hatcher's own recent summary: "The unfree tenant . . . enjoyed a possession regulated by a private manorial court and held his land . . . merely in villeinage and at the will of his lord . . . To the extent that the villein in fact held at his lord's will, uncertainty did lie at the heart of villeinage – an uncertainty extending both to the security of his tenure and the terms on which he held his land. The king's courts would neither afford him protection against eviction nor

If we do not understand that villein tenure exposed the peasants to potentially arbitrary exactions, while free (or freer) tenure could give them legal protection and fixed dues, backed up by the king's courts, we cannot comprehend why there was such intense conflict in the later twelfth and thirteenth centuries between lords and peasants concerning the status of the tenure of individual peasants or groups of peasants. As Postan has elsewhere concluded, "In general it remains true that the enhanced power over tenants, which landlords acquired as land grew scarcer and dearer, lay lightly on the *censuarii* and lighter still on the freeholders. The chief sufferers from the twin process of growing land shortage and manorial reaction were again the villeins".[57]

It is therefore hard to see how Postan and Hatcher can argue as if certain cases which they cite – where unfree tenants (particularly heirs) inside the community were subjected to lower fines on taking over a plot than freemen from outside, or where unfree peasants paid lower dues on their customary plots than were paid for (similar) demesne leases – constitute evidence that "villein tenure in the thirteenth century could often provide a measure of protection".[58] For there was no legal basis for such protection. On the contrary, the instances they refer to would seem to provide evidence that the unfree peasants could sometimes *protect themselves* against their lords, *even in the absence of legal rights*. That the peasant community was often better prepared to defend its own members than strangers is what we would expect. Nor is it surprising that, on some occasions, the fact that land was held in customary tenure (even if

award him damages against his lord; the villein had no standing in the public courts against his lord unless the latter's actions went beyond all reason (e.g. maiming or killing) . . . The logical conclusion is that lords could regard the custom that governed villein tenures 'as but a revocable expression of their own wills' . . . ": Miller and Hatcher, *Medieval England*, pp. 116–17 and, in general, ch. 5.

57 For examples of conflict between lords and peasants over the status of peasant tenure, and of their critical economic effects on income distribution, the ability or inability of the lords to collect rents (in this case their inability, due to the peasants' successful proof of free legal status), see Searle, *Lordship and Community*, pp. 154–66. See also E. Searle, "Seigneurial Control of Women's Marriage", *Past and Present*, no. 82 (Feb. 1979), p. 17. For the quotation from Postan, see his "Legal Status and Economic Conditions in Medieval Villages", in his *Essays on Medieval Agriculture and General Problems of the Medieval Economy* (Cambridge, 1973), p. 289, and *passim*.

58 Above, pp. 74–6.

unfree) could provide a basis for peasant resistance to the lords' demands (whereas demesne land might be conceded to be outside the community's purview). Such resistance could, in turn, lead to lower payments for customary plots than for similar demesne lands subject to the market. But none of this means that *villein status* gave protection. It only points to the fact that the community of villein peasants could on occasion enforce its custom against the lords' rights to arbitrary levies (which is a very different thing). Indeed, such cases reveal once again the inadequacy of accounts like that of Postan and Hatcher which attempt to comprehend the rate of feudal levy as a function of market forces, and show the need to investigate the evolution of feudal rent in terms of the sources of class power, and as the outcome of class conflict.[59]

In light of the foregoing, it is difficult, finally, to understand how the observation of Postan and Hatcher, that in the thirteenth century increasingly "high fines seem to have been supported by market forces", undermines my view that the increase of these levies rested on feudal powers, as they seem to think. For what, after all, were such fines, but incidents of feudal lordship? Indeed, the point made by Postan and Hatcher that increased entry fines were sometimes used in this period as a substitute for increased tallages only emphasizes the connection with the lords' jurisdictional rights over their peasants.[60] Without such lordship, neither tallages, nor entry fines, nor the whole range of other feudal levies (labour dues, heriots, fines on marriage, and so on) could be exacted, let alone increased. Where lordship had been firmly sec-

[59] At the same time, we should perhaps be wary of exaggerating the effectiveness of peasant resistance or of underestimating the powers of lordship in thirteenth-century England. For example, it has recently been demonstrated that on the very ample estates of Westminster Abbey rents on villein holdings were systematically higher throughout the whole of the medieval period than those for contractual tenancies of any sort, in particular demesne leases. On the Westminster Abbey estates the monks succeeded throughout the thirteenth and into the fourteenth century in turning the screw more or less continuously against the villeins, using entry fines, tallages and ultimately a sophisticated method of commuting labour dues to money rents at increasingly high rates of conversion (money per work unit). B. H. Harvey, *Westminster Abbey and its Estates in the Middle Ages* (Oxford, 1977), pp. 236–8, and appendix 9. See also Edward Miller's observation that for the abbey's villeins, "total charges were higher than anything that could have been got for their land on the free market": E. Miller, review of *ibid.*, in *T.L.S.*, 3 Feb. 1978.

[60] Above, pp. 74–5.

ured, population pressure could perhaps at times make it easier for the lords to collect dues from unfree tenants (whose economic options were severely restricted by the scarcity of land). But, as we have seen, such demographic conditions could, in themselves, in no way establish such lordship, nor automatically make possible such levies (let alone endow demesne lands). It was, on the contrary, only because the English seigneurs succeeded, on the whole, in *imposing* and maintaining such lordship over and against the peasants, and in holding on to broad demesnes, that they were able to prosper from the apparently favourable, but potentially disastrous, market conditions of the later twelfth and thirteenth centuries.

To take the argument a small step further: without the powers that accrued to lordship – expressed in legal rights which allowed variable, indeed arbitrary, exactions – the lords were in danger of losing their property, in any meaningful sense, in their customary land.[61] In other words, by assuring that they could adjust levies (especially fines), feudal powers tended to give the English lords ultimate control over the land. Indeed, during the thirteenth century, English lords went a significant distance towards establishing their proprietorship of villein land. This helped enable them to maintain their position not only in the favourable conjuncture of the up-phase in the feudal economy, but, as we shall see, over the very long term.[62]

That population growth, in itself, could in no way ensure such powers is finally confirmed when we merely recollect developments in northern France at this time. Here, in the face of rapidly rising population, prices and rents per acre from the later twelfth and thirteenth centuries, the lords lost their prerogatives of lordship, as the peasants succeeded in getting their feudal dues fixed – tallages and fines, as well as rent. (As an indirect result, moreover, the lords' demesnes tended to contract.) By the early fourteenth century the peasants of northern France *had achieved effectively full property rights to the customary land* (fixed, minimal dues and the right to inherit). This outcome was in stark contrast to that in England in the

[61] For illustrations of the connection between rights accruing to lordship and effective control over property, and vice versa, see Searle, *Lordship and Community*, pp. 154–66, 184–94.

[62] On the English aristocracy's long-term ability to maintain control over the land, and the role of feudal powers in ensuring this, see pp. 291–9 below.

same period, and it too was to have important long-term consequences. In any case, in *this* French context, it is hardly surprising that Bois has discovered a tendency to "a declining rate of feudal levy". But, in the same way that the French developments charted by Bois (and others) highlight the shortcomings of the model of the demographic interpreters, so the English trends presented by the demographic interpreters (and others) highlight the shortcomings of the model of Bois. The evidence adduced by each undermines the theory of the other.

(II.2.3) Feudal States and Economic Evolution: England versus France

Now, Bois cautions us that the "various mechanisms by which the class struggle is dominant in the historical process are normally so complex and unpredictable that it is very rare that such a unilateral approach [as Brenner's] leads to anything other than ideological short-cuts".[63] But in light of the foregoing discussion we are perhaps entitled to ask whether the mechanisms by which class organization and class struggle have affected economic developments are not, at times at least, less obscure than Bois would have us believe. To what *else*, indeed, are we to attribute the divergent dynamics of distribution in French, as opposed to English, rural society of the thirteenth century, with their powerful, differential effects on ruling-class fortunes? The fact is that for quite some time historians of medieval France have been describing the period culminating in the latter part of the thirteenth century as one of "peasant conquests".[64] Meanwhile, historians of medieval England have been describing the same period as one of seigneurial or manorial reaction.[65] Whereas in thirteenth-century France the generally observed trend has been towards seigneurial revenue difficulties, in England the

[63] Above, p. 110.

[64] Neveux, "Déclin et reprise", p. 36; Fossier, *Terre et hommes en Picardie*, ii, pp. 708ff., section entitled "Les conquêtes paysannes"; Fourquin, *Campagnes de la région parisienne*, p. 190.

[65] Miller and Hatcher, *Medieval England*, p. 212; R. H. Hilton, "Freedom and Villeinage in England", *Past and Present*, no. 31 (July 1965), pp. 6, 9–13ff.; Hilton, *Decline of Serfdom in Medieval England*, pp. 16–19ff. Hilton explicitly notes the relative lack of success of peasant resistance in England, as compared to France, and alludes to its implications for analysing the balance of class forces, income distribution and so forth (above, pp. 128–9).

same period has come to be regarded as a golden age for the lordly class. Is there not at least an *apparent* basis for concluding that we are registering the effects of different balances of power, a consequence of divergent processes of class-political organization and class conflict? And is the attempt to pose the problem of this difference a retreat into historical "voluntarism", the inexplicable and lawless realm of "politics", as Bois asserts.[66] Or must we not recognize that to analyse the evolution of an economy in which the dominant class relies "economically" for its very existence (its reproduction as the dominant class) upon arrangements for extracting a surplus from the direct producers which are specifically extra-economic (that is, "political") it is necessary to offer a systematic account of the development of these arrangements, as they are conditioned by class conflict.

What may, therefore, be at issue in the divergent evolutions in England and France in the thirteenth century – there is at least a basis for the hypothesis – is not so much the backwardness of England's "economic" evolution relative to that of France, as Bois would have it, but rather England's relative advance in terms of feudal "political" ruling-class organization. What may have been responsible for the superiority of English lords as extractors of a surplus from their peasants was their superior self-organization – their superiority *vis-à-vis* French lords as feudal centralizers and feudal accumulators. Indeed, it seems to be a matter of a difference in the development of the feudal state. In this context we should perhaps be wary of using Bois's terminology of "unequal development", especially as he links this to the notion of the "age" of the system. This is not because these phrases are entirely inapplicable, but because they tend to lead Bois in the direction of unilineal evolutionary conceptions, whereby each region is *bound*, sooner or later, to experience the same developmental pattern as its neighbours (declining rate of rent), unaffected either directly or indirectly by previous evolution elsewhere.[67] In fact English feudal class self-government appears to have been "ahead" of the French in the twelfth and thirteenth centuries, not only because its starting-point was different, but because it built upon advances in this sphere

[66] Above, pp. 110, 115.

[67] Above, pp. 114–15. Bois is quite aware of such "external" interactions – indeed he charges me with neglecting them – but this does not, in my opinion, free his interpretation from a tendency to unilineality.

already achieved on the Continent, especially in Normandy. In turn, when French centralization accelerated somewhat later, it was influenced by English development, and was indeed, in part, a response to direct English politico-military pressure. But French feudal centralization did not follow the English pattern and, over time, radically diverged from it. Thus the development of the mechanisms of feudal accumulation tended to be not only "uneven" but also "combined", in the sense that later developers could build on previous advances made elsewhere in feudal class organization.

Thus the precocious English feudal centralization around the monarchy was, of course, no mere legacy of the Anglo-Saxon kings. It owed its strength in large part to the level of feudal "political" organization already achieved by the Normans in Normandy before the Conquest, which was probably unparalleled elsewhere in Europe. The emergence of this organization was undoubtedly associated with the Normans' vocation as warriors and conquerors. It was evidenced especially in the establishment of effective supremacy by the duke in settling disputes among his tenants, as well as in his ability to control the building of castles by his nobles and to confiscate their lands in the event of rebellion. Nevertheless, the efficacy of the duke's administration was not simply the result of the duke's imposition, but emerged largely as an expression of the high level of solidarity of the Norman aristocracy as a whole – and this set the pattern for subsequent feudal evolution in England.[68] Of course, the requirements of organizing the Conquest, occupying England and establishing their class rule there brought the Norman aristocracy's self-organization to an even higher pitch.[69] Feudal centralization in England was spectacularly expressed in the outlawing

[68] See, for example, F. M. Stenton, *English Feudalism, 1066–1166* (Oxford, 1932), ch. 1; D. C. Douglas, *William the Conqueror* (London, 1964), pp. 133–55. "It is misleading . . . to dissociate the resuscitation of ducal power in Normandy under Duke William from the rise of the feudal aristocracy at that time . . . the rapid increase of Norman strength . . . is not to be explained by reference to a continued opposition between the Norman duke and the Norman magnates . . . the interests of the greater Norman families were seen to be becoming ever more notably linked with those of the duke" (p. 137).

[69] J. Le Patourel, "The Norman Colonization of Britain", *Settimane di studio del Centro italiano di studi sull' alto medioevo*, xxvi (1969), pp. 412–13, 419–33. This article offers a superb synthesis on the developing cohesiveness of the Norman aristocracy over the process of conquest, its methods and goals, its underlying feudal dynamic; see esp. pp. 430–3. See also J. Le Patourel, *The Norman Empire* (Oxford, 1978).

of private warfare, a development previously inconceivable on the Continent. It was manifested, too, in the novel procedure whereby all undertenants were required to swear allegiance not only to their immediate overlords but also to the king, as well as in the more highly evolved system of military obligation and organization.[70] The monarch, as leading lord, was of course the focus for all these processes; but monarchical strength in this case was the expression of the breadth and depth of lordly collaboration.

Subsequent developments, especially during the reigns of Henry I and Henry II, by and large manifested the same centripetal tendency towards increasing the capacities of the crown. But growing monarchical power reflected growing aristocratic cohesion. This is not to dispute, of course, that the monarch, with his patrimony, played a critical initiating and constructive role in feudal centralization, or to deny that he could, for various reasons, find himself in serious conflict with his aristocratic followers, as individuals or as a group. Nor can the king's actions be understood, in any simple or direct way, to reflect the will of his aristocracy, which, in any case, was rarely united. It remains true, nonetheless, that the development of English feudal government, through a sort of homoeostatic mechanism, was made to conform closely with the interests of the English aristocracy. For in every area of governance the crown remained profoundly dependent upon the aristocracy's support. The feudal lords, led by the magnates, operated all levels of English royal administration, from the immediate entourage of the king (the Curia), on down through the perambulating courts, to the county sheriffs; they provided the core of the monarch's military organization; and they ultimately guaranteed the crown's financial wherewithal. As a result, the construction of an increasingly effective feudal state required the aristocracy's acquiescence and backing, and reflected their self-interest. For the king to build *his* power, it was necessary that he organize and unite his aristocracy around him; it was thus inevitable that he build *their* strength in the process.

As has often been recognized, it thus makes little sense systematically to counterpose the English monarch as chief lord to the

[70] Stenton, *English Feudalism, 1066–1166*, pp. 11–14, 23. In France, of course, the governing principle was "the vassal of my vassal is not my vassal". Correlatively, the elaborate attempts to *regulate* private warfare on the Continent attest to its acceptance as a fact of life.

barons who surrounded him, supported in turn by their own followers. An unusually strong monarchy reflected an unusually strong aristocracy, hierarchically organized in the most highly developed feudal state in Europe. Monarchical government was indeed a manifestation of the lords' more or less conscious recognition of the commonality of their interests, and of the need to regulate their mutual interrelations in order successfully to exploit the peasantry, as well as to profit handsomely, as they did, from exerting their military might against other aristocratic groupings on the Continent. *The growth of a powerful monarchical state in England, therefore, expressed no "merely political" evolution, but the construction of social-class relations which made possible the most effective "accumulation" in the economic realm.*[71]

Thus one of the initial results of the occupation of England by the highly cohesive Norman aristocracy appears to have been the tightening of feudal controls and the imposition of increased levies upon the peasantry. It is notable in this respect that from early Norman times the seigneurs "enjoyed the assistance of the royal administration and the royal courts to recover their 'fugitive' villeins".[72] In turn, it may be no accident that the temporary disorganization of the feudal class during the civil wars of King Stephen's reign was accompanied by the significant peasant gains of the middle of the twelfth century.[73] Finally, the restrengthening of the monarchy during the latter part of the twelfth century seems to have been reflected in the reconstruction of lordly power over the peasants from about the same time. The growth of monarchical authority found its highest expression in the development of royal justice and the common law. Especially with the legislation of Henry II, the feudal aristocracy registered its common interest in allowing the monarchical courts to adjudicate disputes among them over

[71] On feudal monarchical centralization under Henry I and Henry II, its aristocratic character and dynamic, see *ibid.*; also W. L. Warren, *Henry II* (London, 1973); J. C. Holt, *Magna Carta* (Cambridge, 1965; repr. Cambridge, 1969). Note also R. H. Hilton's comment that "there was no European aristocracy which, as a class, had the same power in the state as the English barons": Hilton, *Medieval Society*, p. 2.

[72] H. R. Loyn, *Anglo-Saxon England and the Norman Conquest* (London, 1962), pp. 327–8, 343; Hatcher, "English Serfdom and Villeinage", pp. 28–9; Miller and Hatcher, *Medieval England*, pp. 126, 114.

[73] Postan, "Medieval Agrarian Society in its Prime: England", p. 585; Hilton, *Decline of Serfdom in Medieval England*, p. 16.

privileges and property (although it goes without saying that the royal administration never escaped aristocratic control). In this way the ruling class secured the private rights of its individual members. On the other hand, the obverse side of precisely this legal advance – no less important because it was inexplicit – was the development in law which led to the restriction of access to the king's law to *freemen* and thereby *exclusion of the unfree peasantry*. In granting the monarchical administration the task of protecting their property (from one another), the English aristocracy in the process came to define that property to include their arbitrary rights over their peasants. The unfree peasants with their lands were consigned to the courts of their lords, so that in the eyes of the law[74] the lords could dispose "at will" of both peasants and lands. This provided the lords with an indispensable lever to raise dues arbitrarily on customary lands and tenants. The extraordinary intra-class cohesiveness of the English aristocracy was thereby manifested simultaneously in their formidable military strength, in their ability to regulate intra-lord conflict, and in their capacity to dominate the peasantry. The inextricable interdependence of "the political" and "the economic" in the course of feudal class-productive evolution could not have been clearer.

The foregoing development in England is in marked contrast to that in France during the same period, which was characterized by a multitude of conflicting feudal jurisdictions, dominated by *competing* feudal lords. Whereas late eleventh- and twelfth-century England witnessed the growth of monarchical centralization, most of France in these years was characterized by the extreme fragmentation of authority, expressed in the lack of effective political organization at the level of the monarchy or even the principality.[75] Through much of France in this era, power was effectively in the hands of the so-called "banal lords" or "castellans". The emergence of these potentates seems to have depended on the creation of relatively broad, if still localized, political organization – the build-up of a powerful following around the overlord and his castle, and the construction on this base of a wide-ranging and effective adminis-

[74] Miller and Hatcher, *Medieval England*, pp. 112–17; Hilton, "Freedom and Villeinage in England".

[75] E. M. Hallam, "The King and the Princes in Eleventh-Century France", *Bull. Inst. Hist. Research*, liii (1980), pp. 143–6; E. M. Hallam, *Capetian France, 987–1328* (London, 1980), pp. 27–63.

trative/judicial apparatus. Effective judicial authority, backed by the magnates' knightly military machine, appears to have provided the critical foundation for the successful extraction of what came to be understood as customary rent from the peasantry. Meanwhile, those whom Duby calls "domestic lords" (lacking banal powers) appear to have found it difficult to maintain feudal levies in the face of direct resistance by increasingly united peasant communities, while peasant mobility in the face of lordly competition made things worse. Their control over the peasants having been eroded from below, the domestic lords were wide open to attack from above by the castellans, who, in turn, absorbed lesser landlords into their administration.[76] Once again, therefore, the extra-economic forms of feudal development came to govern feudal economic evolution, though in a different way from England. As Duby puts it, the "dominant force influencing the direction in which the manorial economy developed came from the changed distribution of the powers of authority", which occurred with the rise of banal lordship.[77]

It may not, then, be unreasonable to attribute the relative weakness of French feudal lords as surplus-extractors during the growth phase of the medieval economy, to a significant extent, to their lack of political unity. If this is so, the trend towards declining seigneurial revenues in France in this period is incomprehensible in Bois's terms, as an inevitable outcome of a mechanical tendency towards a declining rate of feudal levy. It was rather the result of peasant conquests, achieved through the resistance of highly organized French peasant communities. What appears, however, to have made possible the French peasants' success was the relatively extreme disorganization of the French aristocracy. For although they were probably about as well organized and rebellious as their French counterparts, the English peasants could not make compar-

[76] G. Duby, *The Three Orders* (Chicago, 1980), pp. 151–9; Duby, *Rural Economy and Country Life in the Medieval West*, pp. 188–9. For observations on the effects of peasant mobility on lordly power, see T. Evergates, *Feudal Society in the Bailliage of Troyes under the Counts of Champagne, 1152–1284* (Baltimore, 1975), pp. 23–30.

[77] Duby, *Rural Economy and Country Life in the Medieval West*, pp. 173ff. Note Duby's contrast of French developments with those of the same period in England, where there were essentially no castellans and no banal lordships, and where the "king recognized the personal authority of lords of manors, and this helped to consolidate the 'domestic lordship' . . . " (p. 195).

able gains against an English ruling class which was considerably more unified than was the French.

The full significance of the process of class formation and class conflict specific to later medieval France can be seen particularly clearly in the Paris region during the first part of the thirteenth century. There the seigneurs, facing rising prices, moved sharply to reverse the prevailing trend towards the fixing of peasant dues by attempting to depress the peasants' condition back towards serfdom. They did so, in particular, by insisting upon the peasants' liability to *arbitrary* levies, notably the seigneurial *taille*, which was the acknowledged token of serfdom. But the lords were ultimately thwarted by peasant revolt. Less dramatic but equally effective processes of resistance have been charted through the villages of much of France in this same period.[78] Now, Bois taxes me for making the decay of serfdom – that is, the decline of the lords' ability to extract a surplus from peasant possessors by means of extra-economic compulsion[79] – central to my account of feudal evolution. But it seems clear, especially in comparative perspective, that it was precisely the French lords' inability to prevent the decay of serfdom (lordship) – expressed directly in the lords' loss of ability to impose arbitrary (that is, variable) levies and to adjust dues on customary land in the

[78] Fourquin, *Campagnes de la région parisienne*, pp. 166–8, for the slide towards serfdom in the region in the mid-thirteenth century, and its reversal. On successful peasant resistance elsewhere at this time, see also Fossier, *Terre et hommes en Picardie*, ii, pp. 555–60.

[79] Above, p. 109, n. 6. Bois at this point deepens the confusion when he speaks as if I have equated serfdom with labour services. In reality I went out of my way to deny this equation, to state that labour services were *not* of the essence, and to argue that it was the system of surplus extraction by extra-economic compulsion which was critical. "Serfdom denoted not merely, nor even primarily, labour dues as opposed to money dues, but, fundamentally, powerful landlord rights to arbitrary exactions and a greater or lesser degree of peasant unfreedom" (above, p. 26). On the other hand, when Bois says that the "economic bases of the system are in reality the various rent-paying holdings within the framework of the seigneurie" (above, p. 109, n. 6), he does nothing to clarify matters. For what was essential is that this (feudal) rent – whether high or low, arbitrary or fixed – was the consequence of extra-economic compulsion. When he speaks, therefore, of the disintegration of the system, he is referring precisely to the lords' decreasing ability to *adjust* rents on their customary holdings and the resulting decay in the value of fixed money payments in the face of inflation. This is the decline of serfdom. The weakened seigneurie may therefore be said to represent, still, lordship or serfdom, but in an attenuated form: its very existence is threatened, at least in tendency.

face of inflation[80] – which was responsible for the French aristocracy's declining feudal rents and, in turn, their declining incomes,[81] especially in the thirteenth century. It should be recollected, in contrast, that the late twelfth and thirteenth centuries were precisely the period in England when the aristocracy as a whole – also in part reacting to inflation – succeeded in excluding their villein tenants from the king's courts and assigning much of the customary tenantry to villein status, thus exposing much of the peasantry to arbitrary exactions.[82]

Finally, the same line of reasoning may be seen to support my original argument that the key *long-term* basis for the development and consolidation of effective centralized monarchy in France, especially from the later thirteenth century, was the relative superiority of its *centralized system of surplus extraction* (especially state taxation) over the decentralized, competitive lordship of the castellans and other great magnates. In this context, I emphasized the highly conflicted processes of monarchical development in France, its contradictory character, which stands in sharp contrast to the parallel evolution in England.[83] For the Capetian house began as one lordship among many, one feudal "political accumulator" among many. It emerged and established itself as a greater lordship over and against, *in competition with*, the more localized, more individualized lordships.[84] The distinctive character of this development was initially evidenced in the absence, indeed exclusion, of the greater French lords from the king's household and

[80] It should be noted that those relatively few French lords (generally to be found among the greatest) who did retain the requisite strength *vis-à-vis* the peasantry were able consciously to impose levies in a way which allowed them to counteract the effects of inflation. See J. R. Strayer, "Economic Conditions in the County of Beaumont-le-Roger, 1261–1313", *Speculum*, xxvi (1951), pp. 279–80.

[81] Note that the erosion of lordship (serfdom) with the resultant loss of revenues appears to have led, indirectly, to the lords' loss of land. Declining revenues from their customary tenants was, in turn, one of the forces which compelled the lords to sell off their lands throughout the period, shrinking their demesnes. Fossier, *Terre et hommes en Picardie*, ii, pp. 622–3; Bois, *Crise du féodalisme*, pp. 196–7; Fourquin, *Campagnes de la région parisienne*, p. 151.

[82] P. D. A. Harvey, "The English Inflation of 1180–1220", *Past and Present*, no. 61 (Nov. 1973), esp. pp. 21–3; Hilton, "Freedom and Villeinage in England", pp. 13–14; Miller and Hatcher, *Medieval England*, pp. 210–12ff., 242–3.

[83] Above, pp. 55–8. For problems, however, with the formulations I made there, see below, pp. 262–3 and n. 87.

[84] See, in general, J. F. Lemarignier, *La France médiévale* (Paris, 1970), pp. 227–30, 248–58ff.

administration – its staffing by lesser knights – which stands in sharp contrast to the Anglo-Norman government, led from the first by the magnates with their lesser lords around them.[85] The competitive process through which the monarchy evolved was also manifested in the development of royal justice as a mechanism to fill the royal coffers at the expense of the seigneurial courts, and above all in the rise of (arbitrary) royal taxation which threatened the collection of lordly dues of all sorts. It was, finally, tellingly expressed in the French crown's propensity to recognize peasant appeals against arbitrary levies by local seigneurs at a time (the later thirteenth century) when, in stark contrast, the English monarch was recognizing the lords' rights over their peasants' persons and property by refusing them access to the royal courts.[86] This divergent evolution of peasant legal status – towards property sanctioned by monarchy in France, towards serfdom backed by the crown in England – appears to provide a significant index of the divergent patterns of class formation and class conflict and of the divergent evolutions of the systems of property in the two regions at this period.

Nonetheless, although I believe this formulation to be essentially correct, I think that Bois, in his critique, has pointed to an important lacuna in my account, which could, as he says, open the way for misunderstanding. As Bois indicates, local lords were vulnerable to royal penetration of their territory in part because they had already experienced the erosion of their power to extract rents from their tenants. Weakened by the prior decline in their income, they were less able to fight the imposition of royal taxation. On the other hand, as Bois rightly emphasizes, it is also true that at least some of these very same lords could take up office in the new state machine.[87] They would, in this way, become its beneficiaries, and its

[85] Stenton, *English Feudalism, 1066–1166*, pp. 30–5; C. W. Hollister and J. W. Baldwin, "The Rise of Administrative Kingship", *Amer. Hist. Rev.*, lxxxiii (1978), esp. pp. 902–5; E. Bournazel, *Le gouvernement capétien au XIIe siècle, 1108–1180* (Paris, 1975). See also the review of Bournazel's book by G. T. Beech, in *Cahiers de civilisation médiévale, X^e–XIIe siècles*, xx (1977), pp. 269–70.

[86] Bois, *Crise du féodalisme*, pp. 203–4, 254–6, 364; G. Fourquin, "Le temps de la croissance", in Duby and Wallon (eds.), *Histoire de la France rurale*, i, pp. 381–2; Neveux, "Déclin et reprise", pp. 35–6; Lemarignier, *France médiévale*, pp. 227, 296–8; P. Chaunu, "L'état", in Braudel and Labrousse (eds.), *Histoire économique et sociale de la France*, i, pt 1, pp. 146–7.

[87] Bois, *Crise du féodalisme*, pp. 204, 264; above, p. 111. In this context, my reference to the state as an "independent", "class-like" surplus-extractor could, as Bois says, be misleading. I used the terminology to emphasize the *novelty* of

supporters. The monarchy's development thus occurred within the context of the disorganization of the French feudal aristocracy and, in important respects, in conflict with it. Yet, ironically, the long-term, unintended consequence was to reorganize and reconstitute the French ruling class on a stronger basis.

In sum, during the twelfth and thirteenth centuries the French monarchy gradually increased its power by means of conquest and alliance. But, especially from the later thirteenth century, the decline of seigneurial revenues – a result of lordly disorganization and peasant conquests – appears to have allowed for significant steps towards a *new form* of monarchical centralization. The lordly class began a long-term process by which many of their number would gravitate towards the royal administration, opening the way towards the construction of the tax/office state – with a concomitant strengthening of peasant property by the monarchy.[88] By the early fourteenth century this evolution had only just begun, and had a

the new form of centralized surplus extraction (tax/office) associated with the development of French absolutism and its *conflict* with the established decentralized form (serfdom or lordship) – and I still believe this emphasis is vital to grasp the specificity of the French socio-economic evolution. Nevertheless, the aforementioned phrases can lead to a one-sided formulation: overemphasizing the points of separation and conflict between the systems of surplus extraction and between the monarchy and the aristocracy, while passing over the points of interconnection and interpenetration – and the way that the rise of the one helped compensate for the decline of the other.

[88] In connection with the consolidation of the monarchy's original base in the Paris region, Fourquin concludes: "Between the middle and end of the thirteenth century, Ile-de-France was freed of serfdom . . . The 'French' rural community . . . was indisputably strengthened by the struggles of the thirteenth century to gain the fixing of the *taille* and other charges. Its power was already manifest when . . . it pressed the mother of St Louis to arbitrate the differences dividing the peasants from the seigneurs, and the death of serfdom in the Paris region represented its victory . . . From its side, the crown moved more and more to reinforce the cohesion of the rural groups. For the rural communities were a remarkable counterweight to seigneurial authority": Fourquin, *Campagnes de la région parisienne*, pp. 189–90. In turn, says Fourquin, from the end of the reign of St Louis, the seigneurs "no longer have enough revenue to live from their lands, the more so as the fixing of peasant taxes makes of the seigneur more and more a *rentier* of the soil. They make a massive entry into the royal administration in full expansion" (pp. 151–3). Fourquin here emphasizes rising expenditures, as well as declining incomes, as the source of seigneurial financial difficulties. In the Maçonnais it was also both peasant resistance eroding incomes and increased expenditures which undermined lordship and opened the way to monarchical penetration. See Lemarignier, *France médiévale*, p. 250, summarizing Duby's work. For the same processes in Picardy, see Fossier, *Terre et hommes en Picardie*, ii, pp. 598ff., 708ff., 732–5.

very long way to go towards completion. There was, of course, as yet nothing resembling a unified absolutist rule. Long-established banal potentates remained strong; the creation of new appanages further threatened unity. Nonetheless, in retrospect, the basic pattern of subsequent development had been established. *In the long run*, the growth of *centralized surplus extraction* served to reorganize the aristocracy: it brought the lesser lords into dependence on royal office and induced the greater ones to come to court and ally themselves with the monarchy.

By contrast, in England, the more advanced organization of the ruling class as a whole, the centralization of the barons around the monarchy, permitted the reintensification of seigneurial powers and institutional rights over and against the peasantry in the later twelfth and thirteenth centuries. In this way, lordly political cohesion ensured successful *decentralized* feudal surplus extraction – that is, serfdom. The lords thus secured their property, broadly conceived, in both the short and the long run. As a result, there is no sign in England of the crisis of seigneurial revenues evident in thirteenth-century France and, in turn, there is no tendency to substitute an emergent system of centralized surplus extraction for an eroding decentralized system – no embryonic rise of an absolutist form of rule.

(II.3) THE ONSET OF FEUDAL CRISIS AND ITS FORMS

Feudal class or property relations determined a long-term tendency to declining productivity,[89] and this formed, as it were, the basic structural limitation on the overall development of the feudal social economy. At the same time, in light of the foregoing discussion, it will perhaps be clearer why systematic reference to the divergent processes of feudal class formation which took place in different regions is required in order to understand the varying ways in which the feudal crisis actually manifested itself in those same regions from the later thirteenth to the mid-fifteenth century: its appearance at different points in time; its somewhat disparate *immediate* causes and characteristics; and its differing results.

[89] The tendency to declining productivity on which Bois and I are in agreement (cf. above, pp. 31–4) is not, of course, the same thing as a tendency to declining rate of feudal rent.

(II.3.1) The Output/Population Ceiling: Its Class-Relative Character in Pre-Plague Europe

Postan and Hatcher berate me for an exaggerated preoccupation with surplus-extraction relations between lords and peasants, and with a corresponding neglect of the economic limitations of production by small peasant producers. In particular, Postan and Hatcher point out that population growth leading eventually to poverty was a phenomenon not only of the regions of entrenched lordship, but those where the manor was weak or non-existent.[90] I must express a certain amazement at this charge, for a central concern of my essay was precisely the barriers posed to real economic development by an agriculture based on small parcellized peasants. This was hardly a subterranean theme, nor could it have been obscurely expressed, for (as we shall see) I have been attacked by several other critics on the grounds that I have underestimated the economic/productive potential of the small peasantry.[91]

On the other hand, although the peasant-based agriculture which characterized medieval and much of early modern Europe could not, in my view, sustain a qualitative breakthrough to economic development, it was certainly capable of supporting a substantial degree of quantitative economic growth. For this reason, *pace* Postan and Hatcher, I would argue that the *variable* strength of lord-peasant surplus-extraction relations could be a significant factor in limiting or increasing the potential for peasant-based economic and demographic expansion. Indeed, the facts cited by Postan and Hatcher actually serve to undercut their own argument. The regions of weaker lordship and dense population to which they refer could not, as they say, support *unending* demographic expansion. Continuing population growth had *eventually* to result in widespread poverty and famine. It is, nonetheless, notable that these freer regions could and did support levels of population which were far greater than those to be found in the highly manorialized areas in the same period. According to one recent survey of thirteenth-century conditions, "the density of population computed for Normandy [where lordship was very weak] . . . was very much higher than can possibly be ascribed to any major province in con-

[90] Above, pp. 70–2. [91] Above, p. 30. For these critics, see below, pp. 306ff.

temporary England [which was, of course, highly manorialized]".[92] Similarly, the figures given by Postan and Hatcher for the amount of land per person on the average plot in the *non-manorialized* English fenland region are something between two-thirds and one-half that considered to be the *subsistence minimum* in manorial England.[93] These results are perhaps understandable in view of the fact that the average villein peasants in the areas of established lordship normally gave up 50 per cent of their income on rent.

It is worth noting that the very historian whose results concerning peasant population and poverty are employed by Postan and Hatcher in order to play down the significance of feudal powers in relationship to economic and demographic development has gone rather far in drawing quite the opposite conclusions from theirs. H. E. Hallam argues, in fact, that the region of relatively "advanced agriculture . . . was also the region of heavy population and free institutions, where lordship was at a discount".[94] In other words, the peasants in the areas of weak lordship not only appear to have had greater consumption possibilities due to lower seigneurial levies. In turn, they seem to have achieved greater production per acre than their counterparts in the manorialized regions because they had significantly more of their surplus at their disposal to reinvest. It is therefore not surprising that their potential for demographic growth was also correspondingly greater. Indeed, in this light it does not seem far-fetched to interpret the relatively high population densities of much of thirteenth-century France compared to those of England precisely in terms of the relative weakness of French lordship and surplus extraction compared to that of England in this period.[95]

[92] N. J. G. Pounds, "Overpopulation in France and the Low Countries in the Later Middle Ages", *Jl Social Hist.*, iii (1969–70), p. 239.

[93] The minimum plot capable of providing subsistence for the average peasant family (4.5 members) is calculated by Titow to be from 13.5 to 10 acres (3 to 2.2 acres per person): Titow, *English Rural Society, 1200–1350*, pp. 78–83ff. Titow's minimum subsistence plot had to be doubled in size to cover an average rent assumed to confiscate 50 per cent of the peasant product (p. 81).

[94] H. E. Hallam, "The Postan Thesis", *Hist. Studies* [Melbourne], xv (1971–3), p. 222.

[95] As Neveux argues, "*The survival of an abundant peasantry thus flows also from village conquests, a positive weakening of the seigneurie* . . . [The decline of seigneurial exactions thus] diminished the peasants' costs and contributed to maintaining a relatively dense population in the countryside, despite the smallness of many plots. Consequently, the seigneurs submit to an economic impoverishment": Neveux, "Déclin et reprise", pp. 36, 39 (my italics).

(II.3.2) The Crisis of Seigneurial Revenues and its Results

The crisis of the feudal economy, when it came, did not take a simple Malthusian form. It does appear that almost everywhere in western Europe, at various points in the later thirteenth or fourteenth centuries, there was, eventually, an end to population growth. Indeed, the plagues of the mid-fourteenth century and after seem to have marked the catastrophic denouement to a process of demographic decline already well under way. According to strict Malthusian reasoning, this demographic downturn should have cured the system's ills by bringing population into line with resources, setting off another period of demo-economic growth. But instead there ensued a long period of economic and demographic decline – stagnation and, in some places, catastrophe.

The demographic interpreters are certainly aware of this difficulty. Nonetheless, despite the contention of Postan and Hatcher, it is difficult to see how it can be resolved within their basic framework, whether this be dubbed "Malthusian" or "Ricardian". Postan and Hatcher argue, "If we accepted that Ricardo's irreversible trend of diminishing returns operated only so long and so far as it remained unchecked by investment and innovation, then the absence of innovation and paucity of investment in medieval agriculture would go a long way to explain why the late medieval recovery was so slow and tardy".[96] Yet this seems to me to miss the point. For population drop-off should have brought cultivation back off the marginal on to the good lands and, *by this very process*, to have raised agricultural productivity. Correspondingly, the higher per capita income of the peasantry should have facilitated greater agricultural investment. Both of these mechanisms did take effect and did ultimately power a new demo-economic upsurge – but only in the very long run, after a lag of at least a century. The question is, why the delay?

This difficult problem is not yet fully resolved. Nonetheless, I would agree with Bois that the later medieval Europe-wide crisis of seigneurial revenues and its effects will have to be a central component of any adequate interpretation.[97] Declining aristocratic

[96] Above, pp. 69–70. Le Roy Ladurie does not make this argument, but simply refers to the factor of disease.

[97] The persistence of the plague through much of the fifteenth century must also be central to any attempt at explanation. But even accepting that the plague was

incomes, sooner or later, brought determined efforts everywhere on the part of the seigneurs to recoup their fortunes through aristocratic reorganization to squeeze the peasants and to wage intra-feudal warfare more effectively. This was the so-called "aristocratic reaction", to which I referred at length in my original article.[98] It tended to cause further disruption of the peasant productive forces, leading to additional demographic downturn – thus a downward spiral reflecting the disequilibrium between the conflicting needs of conflicting social classes, not just between population and resources.

On the other hand, the seigneurial crisis was not, as Bois claims, a simple and direct outcome of a more or less automatic and continuous process of declining rate of feudal levy, but was bound up with the divergent evolutions of class relations. In some places the crisis of seigneurial incomes preceded population decline and was a more or less immediate outcome of peasant conquests and the resultant decline in the rate of rent. But elsewhere, where seigneurial powers and property had remained intact or been strengthened, a declining rate of rent and the seigneurial incomes crisis occurred only after the downturn in population, which was itself the result partly of the tendency of productivity to decline and partly of the persistence of bubonic plague. At the same time, because feudal surplus-extraction systems had taken different forms and operated with differing degrees of effectiveness in different places, the methods to which the seigneurs could resort in order to counteract their income

undoubtedly one important factor in preventing the reflux of population, is it proper to regard it as wholly exogenous? This is at least questionable. For, as has often been pointed out, the outbreak of plague epidemics tended to be closely correlated with the onset of famines. In the fifteenth century, famine itself was generally the result of the ravages of war. The fact that the plague appears to have struck so lightly in fifteenth-century Flanders, which enjoyed unusually advanced agriculture and which largely avoided the disruptive effects of warfare, is one piece of prima-facie evidence for this connection. That the strength of the plague appears to have declined with the improved nutrition of the masses and the end of the disruption caused by warfare in later fifteenth-century France is another. On the other hand, it seems also to be true that the plague struck fiercely in certain places and on certain occasions where there appears to have been no particular sign of malnutrition. Bois, *Crise du féodalisme*, pp. 278–80; Le Roy Ladurie, "Masses profondes: la paysannerie", pp. 488–97, 511–14; Neveux, "Déclin et reprise", p. 91.

[98] Above, pp. 34–5, 109 n. 6. I do not fully understand why Bois accuses me of neglecting the decline of seigneurial incomes and insisting on a difference between us on this point (even if we are not fully in accord on the causes).

problems varied – with variable consequences for short-term production trends and long-term economic development.

In northern France the decline of seigneurial revenues began as early as the mid-thirteenth century, if not before.[99] From the end of the thirteenth century, this decay was paralleled by – and in part conditioned – the rapid rise of centralized monarchical taxation. The latter was radically accelerated with the onset of the Hundred Years War. War itself met with the approval of many of the seigneurs, both large and small, because it could, in various ways, offer a way out of their economic difficulties through office in the state apparatus, or from the fruits of battle, especially the ransoming of wealthy prisoners. Thus the state apparatus grew, became more effective and increased its exactions, with some of the revenues being used to offset the intensified seigneurial revenue crisis. Rising taxation, however, struck a peasant economy which was already stretched to the limit. By the early fourteenth century, precisely the weakness of seigneurial levies appears, as noted, to have allowed peasant population to approach what were close to the highest possible levels, given the landed resources and level of technique (in any case, levels not to be attained again, in some places, until the eighteenth century).[100] As a result, the rising centralized levies had the effect of disrupting production and undermining population. During the middle third of the fourteenth century, decline became precipitate, with the invasion of foreign troops, followed closely by plague, then further invasions leading to demographic devastation.

Nevertheless, demographic drop-off failed to restore equilibrium. For it meant fewer taxpayers, so lower overall revenues to the seigneurs, and thus an ever greater need to recoup. In some places, seigneurs attempted to respond after 1350 by tightening seigneurial controls and increasing decentralized levies – that is, by restrengthening serfdom.[101] But, in general, French lords did not

[99] See Neveux's comment that the "malaise of the seigneurie is long term . . . going back at least to the second quarter of the thirteenth century": Neveux, "Déclin et reprise", p. 35. See also Bois, *Crise du féodalisme*, pp. 200, 240; Fourquin, *Campagnes de la région parisienne*, p. 152.

[100] Le Roy Ladurie, "Masses profondes: la paysannerie", pp. 483–5. See also p. 266, n. 95 above.

[101] For seigneurial reaction in France via the intensification of decentralized lordship/serfdom, see references given above, p. 23, n. 26.

have this option. The basic response was therefore to encourage, and try to take advantage of, the interconnected development of intensified warfare, the growth of monarchical taxation, and the build-up of the state machine (offices). In consequence, during the latter part of the fourteenth century and the earlier part of the fifteenth century, increasing taxation and increasingly destructive military campaigns, in relationship to the shrinking peasant productive base, set off an "infernal cycle" of disequilibrium and decline, which repeated itself at intervals for a century, and reached catastrophic proportions in the 1430s and 1440s. The acceleration of political centralization for political accumulation thus short-circuited the needed Malthusian adjustment, and plunged the system instead into long-term and generalized crisis.[102]

In England, in contrast to France, signs that seigneurial revenues were under pressure, stagnating or falling, apparently began to appear only several decades into the fourteenth century, if then – another indication, perhaps, of the relatively well-entrenched position of English lords *vis-à-vis* their peasants.[103] This was about the same time that population seems to have reached its limit and begun to decline, and it is possible that the two phenomena are related. Even so, it is not certain that a broad threat to feudal incomes appeared before the plagues of the mid-fourteenth century and after, which brought a drastic population drop-off, and thus downward pressure on rents of all kinds. Not surprisingly, there is widespread evidence of attempts by the seigneurs to tighten their controls over the peasants at this point. Predictably, these took the form of endeavours to strengthen lordly political organization in order to use the already existing machinery of *decentralized* surplus extraction by extra-economic compulsion. Efforts were made to hold down peasant mobility, to set wage ceilings, and to control intra-lord competition for labour – in order to increase, or at least maintain, old rent levels.[104]

[102] Bois lays bare the foregoing interconnected processes superbly well in *Crise du féodalisme*, esp. chs. 10–13. I am greatly indebted to his account. See also Neveux, "Déclin et reprise", pp. 55ff.

[103] Above, pp. 129–30 and n. 18. The timing should once again be compared to that of France.

[104] Hilton, *Decline of Serfdom in Medieval England*, pp. 35–42. It should be noted that there was in England relatively little tendency to replicate the French development towards absolutist, centralized surplus extraction (taxes plus office). The French lords, having seen their ability to extract rents curtailed by peasant conquests, tended to be vulnerable to royal incursions. Given their

Thus, contrary to what the demographic interpreters might lead us to expect, population drop-off in England after 1349 did not in many places bring about an immediate, corresponding decline in levies. It is, indeed, by reference to increasing seigneurial extra-economic pressures on and controls over the peasants that historians have tended to account for the maintenance of rents at old, pre-plague levels, sometimes well into the 1380s on various estates around the country – despite the drastic demographic decline.[105] This partially successful attempt to maintain old rent levels in the face of rapidly declining population may have caused some dislocation of peasant production, undermining the peasantry's ability to recover economically or demographically despite the more favourable land/labour ratio. This may have set in motion, to some extent, the same sort of downward spiral as was charted in France, at least for a time.

Nevertheless, economic disruption appears to have been significantly less severe in England than in France. Population density had not in general reached such high levels as were attained in France: very likely, the high levels of seigneurial levy in the early fourteenth century prevented the same degree of demographic expansion. Nor did the rate of feudal levy (rents plus taxes) increase in England after 1350 to anything like the extent it appears to have done in France, and certainly not for any extended period. Nor did the English countryside suffer the devastations of war experienced in

revenue-raising problems, they might even welcome the expansion of royal taxation, if this enabled them to profit from the fruits of office. By contrast, English lords had been able to collect substantial rents from broad demesnes and to extract relatively high feudal dues from their villein tenures during the thirteenth century and beyond. In consequence, they had less need for royal taxation (as the basis for income from office) and tended, indeed, to oppose it, since the king's taxes tended to undermine the peasants' ability to pay them rents. See J. R. Maddicott, *The English Peasantry and the Demands of the Crown, 1294–1341* (*Past and Present* Supplement, no. 1, Oxford, 1975), esp. pp. 23–4, 49–50, 71. Correspondingly, to the extent that taxation grew in England, it tended to develop in connection with, and under the control of, a maturing English parliament, not in absolutist fashion as in France.

105 See, for example, J. A. Raftis, *Tenure and Mobility* (Toronto, 1964), pp. 139–44ff.; Hilton, *Decline of Serfdom in Medieval England*, pp. 35–42. In Harvey's words, "Many of the tenurial arrangements . . . defied the economic realities of their time. Rents did not fall equally with the demand for land on this estate after 1348, if indeed they fell at all; villeins continued to be asked for, and to pay, rents that the monks of Westminster had no hope of exacting from tenants holding on contractual terms": Harvey, *Westminster Abbey and its Estates in the Middle Ages*, p. 268, and also pp. 262–4.

France, since the Hundred Years War was fought on French soil.[106] Moreover, by the early part of the fifteenth century the seigneurial reaction had failed, broken by peasant resistance, as well as peasant mobility. (This is an indication perhaps of the inferiority of the English *decentralized* form of surplus extraction, however well organized and unified, in comparison with the newly emergent French *centralized* system of surplus extraction (tax/office) – especially under the conditions of relative depopulation of the later middle ages.) The lords could extract only much lower, now basically economic, contractual rents. There was no development of a centralized state tax machine. The ruling class as a whole were forced to recoup their incomes by other means – by foreign military interventions and ultimately (relatively small-scale) civil war. Ironically, it may have been the long-term *inability* of the English aristocracy to step up surplus extraction by extra-economic force *vis-à-vis* the peasantry by intensifying serfdom or by imposing absolutist taxation, combined with the English lords' short-term success in solving their financial crisis by military means abroad, which prevented the sort of economic catastrophes that were experienced in some places on the Continent in this period.

In east Elbian Germany there is still another pattern. Medieval demographic and economic development in this area appears to have been strongly influenced by west European trends, due to its heavy reliance on colonization from the west. As a result, the timing of the crisis in eastern Germany appears to have been somewhat delayed; it took a somewhat different form; and it had a very different outcome from that in the west. Demographic stagnation and ultimately downturn in eastern Germany seem to have followed upon the end of population growth in the west, and it manifested itself rather clearly in the later fourteenth century with the drying up of colonization.[107] This naturally posed a great threat to seigneurial

[106] Above, p. 113.

[107] F. L. Carsten, *The Origins of Prussia* (Oxford, 1954), pp. 101–2, 114 and, in general, ch. 8; Postan, "Economic Relations between Eastern and Western Europe", p. 149; M. Malowist, "The Economic and Social Development of the Baltic Countries from the Fifteenth to the Seventeenth Centuries", *Econ. Hist. Rev.*, 2nd ser., xii (1959–60), p. 181. It should not be assumed that population downturn was universal in north-eastern Europe in the later middle ages. For example, Poland, in contrast to eastern Germany (Mecklenberg, Pomerania, Brandenburg, Prussia), may not have experienced any serious break in its demographic growth right through the sixteenth century. I. Gieysztorowa, "Research into the Demographic History of Poland", *Acta Poloniae historica*, xviii (1968), pp. 10–11, and *passim*.

incomes. For, in the east, development had taken place on the basis of what was perforce a highly attenuated form of lordship. The problem for the lords was to make unsettled land yield a profit. They had little choice, therefore, but to offer peasant settlers favourable terms: fixed dues and free status (the so-called "Germanic Law"). Still, so long as population grew, both lords and peasants could benefit in a situation of plentiful land.[108] Under these conditions, there appears to have been little incentive for the development of the lords' self-organization, centralization for purposes of political accumulation. States remained, by and large, extremely weak and the nascent aristocracy was notoriously disorganized, disunited, undisciplined.

But from the later fourteenth century, population growth sharply decelerated. In contrast with the west, the explanation for this appears only to a slight extent connected with problems of declining productivity; for in the east there was still masses of unsettled land to colonize. It was in part the plagues, but apparently above all the sharp slow-down of immigration, consequent upon the generalized demo-economic downturn in the west, which set off in the east the same sort of cycle of decline which was already taking place in the west, with correspondingly disruptive economic and demographic consequences. Lords experienced declining revenues, and they attempted to respond by taking extra-economic measures. Lacking any well-developed centralized state apparatus to turn to (for enhanced income from offices and taxation), the lords of eastern Europe tried to increase their exactions from the peasantry by intensifying serfdom. At the same time, they stepped up their attacks upon one another, while largely dismantling what little there had been of monarchies or unified states (the decay of the Teutonic Order in the fifteenth century is only the most spectacular case in point). Finally, they organized for war externally, and the devastations of the military campaigns appear to have had particularly disruptive effects on production and population. Their revenues further threatened, the lords made renewed attempts to recoup at the expense of the peasants and one another – leading to the familiar downward spiral of eco-demographic disequilibrium and decline.[109]

[108] See M. Malowist, "Problems of the Growth of the National Economy of Central-Eastern Europe in the Late Middle Ages", *Jl European Econ. Hist.*, iii (1974), pp. 322–9. See also Carsten, *Origins of Prussia*.

[109] Carsten, *Origins of Prussia*, ch. 8; M. Biskup, "Polish Research Work on the History of the Teutonic Order State Organization in Prussia, 1945–1959", *Acta*

III THE OUTCOME OF FEUDAL CRISIS AND SUBSEQUENT PATTERNS OF DEVELOPMENT

From the middle of the fifteenth century, in much of western Europe, the conditions making for crisis finally receded, and there was a new period of economic upturn. Peasant cultivation had drawn back on to the better lands, making for the potential of increased productivity; the incidence and destructiveness of civil and external warfare seems to have abated somewhat, reflecting perhaps the exhaustion and temporary disarray of the nobility; the levels of ruling-class exactions from the peasants appear to have declined correspondingly, at least temporarily; and the impact of the plagues appears to have diminished. There occurred a new period of population increase and expansion of cultivation, leading to the growth of production with a concomitant increase in the incomes of both the lord and peasant classes. The consequent growth in demand provided the basis for a new era of expansion of European industry and commerce. The latter reached far beyond its previous limits, especially to the Americas and over the sea route to the east. In important respects, however, the European commercial economy of the early modern period retained much of its medieval character. It remained heavily focused on the production of high-quality textiles (now made especially in England and Holland), as well as wine (from France), supplemented by silks and spices brought in from the east. These goods, which were heavily, though not solely, oriented towards ruling-class consumption were, *grosso modo*, exchanged for basic food products, supplied by a radically expanding grain market, now profoundly involving the agriculture of eastern Europe.

It was my argument that the divergent economic responses, in different European regions, to the opportunities and dangers opened up by the new period of economic expansion were critically

Poloniae historica, iii (1960), pp. 96–9, where are summarized, in particular, the studies by Bronislaw Geremek on the question of the manpower shortage in Prussia in the fifteenth century. Geremek emphasizes the importance of warfare in causing the demographic decline in the early fifteenth century: B. Geremek, "Problem siły roboczej w Prusach w pierwszej połowie XVw." [The Manpower Problem in Prussia during the Early Fifteenth Century], *Przeglad historyczny*, xlviii (1957). I wish to thank Kasha Seibert for translating this article for me. See, to a similar effect, H. H. Wächter, *Ostpreussische Domänenvorwerke im 16. und 17. Jahrhundert* (Würzburg, 1958), p. 15.

conditioned by the agrarian property settlements, the systems of surplus extraction, which emerged from the crisis of seigneurial incomes of the later medieval period. These settlements themselves represented, to a significant degree, the outcome of divergent long-term processes of agrarian class formation and class conflict – processes in which the peasantry of the different regions of Europe had been able to limit, to a greater or lesser degree, the form and strength of the structures which could be developed by the ruling class to extract a surplus to ensure their reproduction. At the same time, it appears that in every case – the rise of serfdom in eastern Europe, the rise of absolutism in connection with the consolidation of peasant property in France, the development of classically capitalist relations on the land in connection with the emergence of a new form of unified state in England – the newly emergent system of surplus extraction was made possible by a significantly higher level of ruling-class self-organization, of self-centralization, than had previously been attained in that region – and may thus be seen, at least from one angle, to mark a continuation, if not a culmination, of the general feudal tendency in this direction. Finally, the different systems of property which were established were responsible, in my view, for structuring widely divergent patterns of economic evolution in the different regions – the impositions of different forms of agricultural involution and ultimately "general crisis" on most of the Continent, the critical breakthrough to self-sustaining growth in England.

(III.1) THE ROOTS OF THE DIVERGENCES

(III.1.1) The Rise and Decline of Serfdom: East versus West

For some reason Postan and Hatcher deny that the population drop-off, especially from the fifteenth century, and the accompanying threat to seigneurial incomes, was a critical inducement for the movement towards enserfing the peasants in east Elbian Germany – the use of extra-economic jurisdictional rights in order to extract a surplus in the face of demographically induced downward pressures on rents and upward pressure on wages.[110] Nonetheless, it is no coincidence that in Prussia, for example, the first in a long

[110] Above, p. 67; see also p. 221, n. 9.

series of governmental ordinances aiming to strengthen lordly controls over the peasantry (especially by limiting mobility in various ways), so as to buttress lordly rent exactions, was issued in the wake of the first sharp demographic losses that came with the wars of the first decades of the fifteenth century. These ordinances *explicitly* refer to the shortage of labour as their justification and explanation.[111]

Moreover, despite what Postan and Hatcher imply, there seems to be agreement among historians that during the second half of the fifteenth century the lords began to succeed in subjecting the Prussian peasants to more severe controls and heavier dues *in the face of, and despite, sharply reduced population levels*. Certainly, the rise of serfdom in eastern Germany did not depend upon a new period of population upturn; serfdom had been firmly established long before population began to rise again, towards the middle of the sixteenth century. Precise data are difficult to come by. But, for example, in the Samland, where the seigneurial offensive was pursued early and vigorously, we know that the population in 1525 remained approximately one-third below its level of 1400. Yet, in the intervening period, serfdom had been intensified and had become a fact of life for a large section of the peasantry of the region.[112] It was, of course, this installation of serfdom in eastern Germany under conditions of demographic slump which led me to call into question the widely held view that the corresponding popu-

[111] Carsten, *Origins of Prussia*, ch. 8; Geremek, "Problem siły roboczej w Prusach w pierwszej połowie XVw.".

[112] Heide Wunder, who in her critique is concerned to emphasize the *similarity* between east and west German developments at the end of the middle ages, nonetheless summarizes the evolution in the east from the later fifteenth century in a way which brings out its distinctiveness: "All groups [among the peasantry] saw themselves confronted by a social levelling of the previous rural social order, which brought with it social insecurity. *The tendency of this social levelling was downwards, the reverse therefore of the upward levelling tendency since the fourteenth century* . . . The peasants and freemen sought by means of their rebellion [1525] to reverse this levelling process": H. Wunder, "The Mentality of Rebellious Peasants", in B. Scribner and G. Benecke (eds.), *The German Peasant War of 1525* (London, 1979), p. 155 (my italics). For further material on population decline and the deterioration of the peasants' position in the later fifteenth century, see H. Wunder, "Zur Mentalität aufständischer Bauern", *Geschichte und Gesellschaft*, Sonderheft 1, *Der deutsche Bauernkrieg, 1524–1526* (1975), pp. 22, 32; H. Wunder, "Der samländische Bauernaufstand von 1525", in R. Wohlfeil (ed.), *Der Bauernkrieg, 1524–1526* (Munich, 1975), pp. 153, 162–3; Geremek, "Problem siły roboczej w Prusach w pierwszej połowie XVw.", pp. 231–2ff.

lation drop-off in western Europe could, in itself, have accounted for the accompanying decline of serfdom.

To begin to explain why the lords of late fourteenth- and fifteenth-century western Europe were unable to respond to the seigneurial revenue crisis by strengthening serfdom, *despite their attempts to do so*, while their counterparts in east Elbian Europe were indeed able to succeed in this, my account focused on the relatively recent development of the latter region, and especially its colonial character. The lords of north-eastern Europe – eastern Germany, as well as Poland – had led and controlled from the start a belated process of agrarian development, imposing "artificial", rationally laid-out forms of peasant settlement. By contrast, their counterparts in western Europe had to impose their power "from the outside", against peasant communities which were longer established and better organized – with established traditions of (often successful) struggle for their rights. As a result, eastern lords had the possibility of solving their revenue problems through enserfing the peasants, whereas this option was foreclosed to those in the west by the relatively greater strength of the western peasants. The eastern lords actually were able to accomplish this task largely by means of politically reorganizing themselves, especially through developing new forms of feudal state.[113]

Heide Wunder finds this account contradictory. If the east Elbian German peasants were, at the start, by my own admission, the freest in western Europe, how could they also be so ripe for enserfment? Wunder points especially to the fact that the east Elbian peasants received from their lords, upon their settling, very broad grants of liberties.[114]

There is in my view, however, nothing inconsistent about arguing that peasants could gain initially excellent conditions, yet remain essentially weak as a class over and against the lords. The lords were obliged to offer favourable terms to induce colonists to settle, and it was in their interest to do so. Indeed, so long as they could attract a steady flow of new settlers to open as yet uncultivated land, they could, over an extended period, take a relaxed approach to their peasants, benefiting from increased lands in production and perhaps improved productivity, while avoiding the costs of coercion. Yet this does not gainsay the fact that these conditions

[113] Above, pp. 40–6. [114] Above, p. 92.

were *granted* by the lords (for their own reasons), that the peasants *received* them from the lords. This was a very different process from that which occurred in many places in the west, where the peasants often *extracted* their gains from the lords by means of successful resistance, requiring the self-organization of the community over a very long term. In consequence, the peasants in the east were at a disadvantage when the lords changed their policy in the direction of greater exactions and controls,[115] in order to deal with their problem of labour scarcity.[116]

As to the long-term basis for the relatively weaker position of the peasants *vis-à-vis* the lords in eastern as compared to western Germany, Wunder has rightly pointed out that my reference to the spread in the east of the particular *Waldhufen* type of village community – in which peasant production was organized on a significantly more individualistic and less communally regulated basis than elsewhere – can provide at best only part of the explanation. For, as she states, these were far from universal in the region.[117] Nonetheless, Wunder does seem to agree that settlement in the west was far more dense than in the east. Nor does she appear to dispute the fact that in the west there was quite commonly a lack of correspondence between village and lordship, while, in contrast, a one-to-one lord-to-village relationship was the norm in the east. This disparity between lordship and village in the west led to divided authority and gave the western peasants certain potentials for

[115] For cases in the west where lords successfully made similar reversals in policy, see Searle, *Lordship and Community*, pp. 45–68; Duby, *Rural Economy and Country Life in the Medieval West*, pp. 113–14.

[116] In this connection, Wunder's reference (above, p. 93) to the *Handfeste* – the original settlement contracts which granted the east German peasants their freedoms – seems to miss the point; for it appears to confuse the question of *formal* rights (granted to attract settlers) with actual social and power relations. The *Handfeste* manifested the lords' initial need for labour, but they tell us little about the subsequent evolution of forces. A historian of the region has drily remarked of the *Handfeste*: "their content is of an almost barren similarity, and the last one that one reads says hardly more about the legal relationships of the village community than does the first one". By contrast, the granting of the peasant charters of the west, the *Weistümer*, reflect in general the outcome of a process of struggle, constituting direct evidence that the peasants had won their demands. H. Patze, "Die deutsche bäuerliche Gemeinde im Ordensstaat Preussen", in *Die Anfänge der Landgemeinde und ihr Wesen*, 2 vols. (Konstanzer Arbeitskreis für mittelalterliche Geschichte, Vorträge und Forschungen, vii–viii, Stuttgart, 1964), ii, p. 150.

[117] Above, pp. 93–4.

manoeuvre apparently unavailable to their eastern counterparts. The west European peasants could stand united as a village against a lord who could claim jurisdiction over only part of the village – or, to put it another way, against lords whose jurisdiction over the village was divided and perhaps competitive. In addition, the peasant could, and did, more easily develop solidarity across villages than could the various lords of these villages, who might be frustrated and disorganized by the maze of separate jurisdictions through which they, individually, dominated the villagers. These differences, which put the east European peasantry at a disadvantage relative to their west European counterparts, do seem to be connected with the later development of the region and its origins as a colonial area. Indeed, the lords' direct operation of the colonization process in the east appears to have allowed them, consciously or unconsciously, to establish a pattern of settlement which in the long run facilitated their domination over the region's economy.

I attempted to give further indications of the possible significance for subsequent development of the differential evolutions of lord/peasant relations in eastern as compared to western Europe by showing that the only area in eastern Germany where there was a significant peasant outbreak at the time of the great peasant wars in 1525 – that is, East Prussia – had experienced an agrarian evolution which distinguished both its lord and peasant classes from those of the rest of the region. The Teutonic Knights who settled East Prussia carried out a highly distinctive policy of colonization and development. As much as possible they aimed to build their regime directly upon peasant producers and to forestall the emergence of a lordly or knightly class which might prove competitive. It seems likely that this made for a peasantry in the Teutonic lands which was more strongly entrenched than those of the other regions of east Elbian Germany.[118] When, during the fifteenth century, the Teutonic Order gradually disintegrated and a new class of knightly landowners began to establish themselves in its place, this peasantry may have found some temporary room to manoeuvre unavailable to its counterparts elsewhere in eastern Germany.[119]

[118] Carsten, *Origins of Prussia*, pp. 54, 57–8, 60–1, 70–3; F.-W. Henning, *Herrschaft und Bauernuntertänigkeit* (Würzburg, 1964), pp. 36–7.

[119] Carsten, *Origins of Prussia*, pp. 89–148; Wunder, "Samländische Bauernaufstand", pp. 162–3; Wunder, "Zur Mentalität aufständischer Bauern", pp. 29–32; Henning, *Herrschaft und Bauernuntertänigkeit*, pp. 41–9ff.

Furthermore, *pace* Wunder, it appears to me no accident that the peasant revolt of 1525 in East Prussia was centred in the Samland, for this area was dominated by Prussian peasants, with cohesive communities which had a long history that preceded the Germans' colonization process, and which remained relatively unaffected by that process. Wunder does admit that the Prussian communities were the most densely populated in the east. However, she argues that they cannot be considered strong, for the political liberties granted to the Prussian peasants by the Teutonic Order were less far-reaching than those which were granted to the German settlers in the same territory. But this is again, in my view, to confuse *formal* rights with evidence of actual social relationships – of social power.[120] The Prussian communities retained some of their old solidarities at the communal and extra-communal level, and this gave them resources for resistance. In particular, there seems to be evidence that the older organizational forms were maintained by the Prussian peasants, not only the Prussian freemen (the "big peasant" élite between the Prussian peasants and Teutonic Knights to whom Wunder wishes to call special attention).[121] In any case all evidence, including that offered by Wunder, indicates that the German settlers barely penetrated the Samland region. As Wenskus concludes, "the German colonization had only very little influence, so that the old Prussian relationships were long able to remain undisturbed".[122]

Continuing her criticism along the same line, Wunder argues that "all sections of the peasantry in this multi-ethnic region [Samland] took part in the rising – German peasants, Prussian peasants, and also Prussian freemen".[123] But surely this is misleading. Wunder has elsewhere analysed the participants in the revolt. On her evidence, there seem to have been about 2,500 who took part in the peasants' army. It seems likely, she says, that almost all of the three hundred or so Prussian freemen resident in the Samland where the revolt was mostly based were active. On the other hand, she also points out that "the number of German peasants participating cannot have

[120] Above, pp. 95–6.

[121] R. Wenskus, "Kleinverbände und Kleinräume bei den Prussen des Samlandes", in *Anfänge der Landgemeinde und ihr Wesen*, ii, pp. 220, 227–32.

[122] *Ibid.*, p. 202. For Wunder's evidence to same effect, see her "Zur Mentalität aufständischer Bauern", p. 22 and n. 53.

[123] Above, p. 96.

been altogether that great, in that relatively few German new settlements were present, [and those] primarily in the easterly territorial area" (whereas the revolt was centred in the western part of the Samland).[124] This leads unavoidably to the conclusion that the majority of the activists in the revolt were mere Prussian peasants. I see no reason to contest Wunder's view that the Prussian freemen – who constituted a distinct layer in the population with unusually broad political and commercial connections beyond the villages – played a key organizing role in the rising. Nevertheless I do not see how the statement that the Prussian freemen apparently assumed a position of leadership in any way runs counter to my argument asserting the significance of relatively strongly organized Prussian communities; it seems to amplify it.

But the main point is that Wunder's critique fails almost entirely to come to terms with the central issues at stake. In 1525 there were massive peasant revolts throughout much of western Germany, but none in eastern Germany, with the one exception (the Samland) to which I referred. Why was there, relatively, so little opposition in the east, as compared to that in the west? Why did opposition develop in the Samland Prussian peasant communities, but virtually nowhere else? After all, at this time the free German peasants of the east Elbian region in general and Prussia in particular – the peasantry both big and small – were also undergoing a significant deterioration in their position.[125] Why did they not rebel? Finally, the key question: why was it that in western Germany the long-term trench warfare of peasant communities with the lords left the peasantry with some 90 per cent of the land and only minor dues owed to their immediate lords, while in the east the tables were turned and serfdom rose with a vengeance?

Wunder refers to the grain trade as the basic condition for the rise of serfdom in eastern Germany. She also points out that from the later middle ages the seigneurs' problems of declining revenues forced them to seek new solutions.[126] However, she does not explain why enserfing the peasants was a viable option for the east European lords, when it does not appear to have been one for their

[124] Wunder, "Zur Mentalität aufständischer Bauern", p. 22 and n. 53; Wenskus, "Kleinverbände und Kleinräume", pp. 202–3.
[125] Wunder, "Zur Mentalität aufständischer Bauern", p. 32; Wunder, "Samländische Bauernaufstand", p. 163.
[126] Above, pp. 97–8.

counterparts in the west, who had similar problems and similar incentives. After all, the opportunities arising from the developing grain market, as well as the problems of declining seigneurial revenues, presented the same powerful incentives from Normandy to Poland and beyond. Yet, despite their attempts, the lords of western Europe nowhere succeeded in re-establishing serfdom. Indeed, in some places it was the peasants, and not the lords, who consolidated their position and who thereby gained access to the expanding grain-export markets. It is odd that in their contribution Postan and Hatcher could also fall back upon the grain trade to explain the different developments in eastern and western Europe, since Postan has devoted so much of his own work to demolishing the notion of a direct correlation between the development of commerce and either the emergence or the decline of serfdom – and has indeed explicitly denied that the distinctive evolution in the east can be explained by the world commerce in grain.[127] Economic needs or desires cannot explain their own satisfaction, nor can opportunities account for the capacity to take advantage of them. As Postan writes, "The divergence between East and West . . . was not, however, the result of spontaneous economic change; it was brought about by the exercise of landlords' power".[128]

In fact, the lords of eastern Europe were, in the end, able to enserf the peasants only by means of stepping up the level of their own political organization. The crisis of seigneurial revenues had led, sooner or later, to the disintegration of even the strongest monarchies of medieval eastern Europe, leaving no potential for the growth of absolutism in the east. Instead, we find a dual development taking place throughout the region from the later medieval period. First, there was a long-term development of intra-lordly cohesion at the local and provincial levels. This was classically manifested in Poland, with the growing strength and importance of the local and provincial diets. Second, there was the consolidation of lordly power at the national level through the rise of the estates, a phenomenon which was nearly universal in eastern Europe. In creating these governing institutions, the lords of eastern Europe constructed a form of state peculiarly appropriate to their rather simple needs. It was a form in which they could represent them-

[127] See above, p. 221, n. 9, and below, n. 128.

[128] Postan, "Economic Relations between Eastern and Western Europe", pp. 170, 173–4.

selves in the most immediate and direct way, and through which they could make certain that their rights over their land and peasants were protected, while ensuring that the costs of any state administrative apparatus could be kept to a minimum (a task naturally complicated by their tendency to involvement in warfare).[129] It was, finally, a form of state which differed significantly from those which were emerging throughout most of western Europe. Nonetheless, it was similar to the states of the west in one crucial respect: it manifested a qualitative advance in the self-consciousness and self-organization of the aristocracy; such advances were apparently necessary throughout Europe to ensure the aristocracy's continuing dominance and capacity for reproduction, in the wake of the seigneurial crisis and peasant resistance of the later medieval period.

The eastern lords' political reorganization allowed them to benefit from the trans-European economic upturn of the sixteenth century. But their increased capacity for surplus extraction by means of extra-economic compulsion and for political accumulation created the potential, over the longer term, for economic disruption. Agricultural growth on the basis of expanding demesnes and increasing labour services offered only the most restricted possibilities for development. By the 1560s and 1570s Poland's national output appears to have reached its upper limit (not to be attained again until the eighteenth century). From this point onwards, the growth of the lords' product depended upon redistributive measures and was achieved largely by increasing the size of the demesnes directly at the expense of the peasants' plots, thereby eroding the system's chief productive forces (peasant labour and animals). Poland's experience, moreover, appears to have typified that of the north-east European region. Precipitately declining productivity everywhere called forth the familiar "political" remedies. Increased levies on the peasantry, intensified struggles within the ruling classes, and external warfare issued in economic regression and the east European version of the "general crisis of the seventeenth century".[130]

[129] J. Bardach, "Gouvernants et gouvernés en Pologne au moyen-âge et aux temps modernes", *Recueils de la Société Jean Bodin*, xxv (1965), esp. pp. 273–4; Carsten, *Origins of Prussia*, ch. 12.

[130] A. Maczak, "Export of Grain and the Problem of Distribution of National Income in the Years 1550–1650", *Acta Poloniae historica*, xviii (1968); J. Topolski, "La régression économique en Pologne du XVIe au XVIIIe siècle",

(III.1.2) The Rise of Capitalist Property Relations on the Land: England versus France

Bois, for all his disagreements, accepts my argument that the emergence of different class-productive structures in England and France lay behind their divergent patterns of economic evolution in the early modern era – and he accepts, in part, my account of the historical roots of these developments. Bois appears to agree that a successful drive towards undermining the possessing peasantry and establishing capitalist class relations lay behind the transformation of agriculture and rising agricultural productivity in early modern England. He also agrees that the consolidation of production based on small peasant possessors, especially in relationship to now-centralized surplus extraction by the absolutist state (as well, we should add, as the squeezing by landlords of tenants where the former owned the land), was responsible for continuing agricultural stagnation and eventually agrarian crisis in France.[131] The thrust of his criticism, however, is that these divergent evolutions become comprehensible only when interpreted in light of his overall schema for feudal development, centred on the tendency to a falling rate of feudal rent.

France. As I did in my article, Bois links the failure of French agriculture to respond more successfully to the rise of prices and of markets in the early sixteenth century largely to the entrenched position of the peasantry. But Bois's interpretation of the latter reveals, in my view, the mechanistic tendency of his overall approach. He says, "the peasants resisted expropriation here better than elsewhere, because the tenants were already beginning to appear as proprietors (*an effect, in the final analysis, of the long-term fall in the rate of levy*)".[132] It seems to me that Bois's causal chain is here set out back to front. The falling rate of feudal levy which the lords were unable to counteract in the first part of the sixteenth century *was the result, not the cause*, of the peasants' increasingly effective proprietorship in the land. This proprietorship was not, of

Acta Poloniae historica, vii (1962); L. Zytkowicz, "An Investigation into Agricultural Production in Masovia in the First Half of the 17th Century", *Acta Poloniae historica*, xviii (1968); E. Le Roy Ladurie and J. Goy, *Tithe and Agrarian History from the Fourteenth to the Nineteenth Century* (Cambridge, 1982), pp. 122–3.

131 Above, pp. 109–10; Bois, *Crise du féodalisme*, p. 347, and "Conclusion générale".

132 Above, p. 114 (my italics).

course, a new development in the sixteenth century, but represented the outcome of a long process whereby the lords' various levies were fixed and the peasants' tenure became hereditary. Indeed, already by the latter part of the thirteenth century, *cens* tenure had been recognized as tantamount to full property throughout much of the north of France.[133] And what of the sources of this proprietorship? Bois professes disdain at my accounting for it, in part, through reference to the long history of struggles of peasant communities on the Continent against an initially disorganized feudal ruling class. Yet can he really propose a "falling rate of feudal levy" apart from this history of struggle and its effects?

Bois implies that the security of tenure of the French peasantry in the sixteenth century may be explained further by a certain laxity on the part of the lords, attributable, in turn, to the benefits some of them could derive from the absolutist state. He says that "the lords, who had found some measure of salvation in the service of the state, were less *inclined* than elsewhere to explore new economic avenues".[134] Nonetheless, this formulation is misleading. For the lords' "inclinations" were structured by their class position – in particular, by their *limited capacity* to exert class power against the peasants.

Whatever their access to revenues from state office, the French lords would, *in any case*, certainly have *wished* to expropriate their peasant tenants. For this was the only way they could position themselves to raise rents from their land. As it was, powerful peasant tenure determined hereditarily fixed dues, thus exiguous and, in the face of inflation, declining customary rents – "a declining rate of feudal levy". As Bois himself points out, during the early sixteenth century the lords made systematic and powerful *attempts* to evict their tenants. Yet, as a rule, they were unable to succeed, in large part because of the strength of the peasantry, sometimes manifested in successful peasant revolts.[135]

133 G. Fourquin, *Lordship and Feudalism in the Middle Ages* (London, 1976), pp. 189–92; Fourquin, *Campagnes de la région parisienne*, pp. 175–6, 179.

134 Above, p. 114 (my italics).

135 Cooper is therefore wrong to attempt to use evidence gathered by Bois to prove that lords could indeed expel their tenants. He confuses the *desire* to do so with the *ability* to do so. Above, p. 157. As Bois states, "What I was able to observe in Normandy fully accords with his [Brenner's] analysis: from 1520–30 one can see the beginnings of a tendency towards the expulsion of tenant farmers (a faint echo of the British enclosure movement), which in the end encountered fierce

It was precisely the ensconced position of the peasantry which *compelled* the lords to turn to the state for revenues. Many of them had only small demesnes. And they could not, locally and individually, successfully raise levies on customary tenures. To extract a surplus from the customary peasantry, the lords had to turn to the concentrated power of the state apparatus (tax/office).

The lords' involvement with state office and taxation had, however, further important implications for the strength of the peasantry in the localities (especially the security of peasant tenures), thus for the lords' abilities to expel them from the land, and ultimately for the economic potential of peasant production. For as the lords turned to state office and state taxation, they tended through that process to strengthen the overall power of the monarchical administration, and thus monarchical jurisdiction. The result was to clip the wings of the lords' local jurisdiction, further reducing their ability to move against peasant possessors. As Bois is obliged to admit, although the "state remains, for the most part, the instrument of feudalism", it is also the case that the "use to which this instrument was actually put served in the long run to weaken feudalism by competing with direct seigneurial extraction".[136] This was, of course, the point I tried to make (and for which I was nevertheless chastised by Bois).

Now, Croot and Parker deny that the French monarchy was a significant force for peasant protection and go so far as to deny that French peasants had stronger property rights than their English counterparts. But rather than offering evidence for their position, they content themselves with pointing out that, in the long run, royal taxation of the land had the effect of ruining part of the French peasantry. This is just what I myself asserted.[137] But it simply does not follow that, because monarchical taxation undermined peasant property (especially in the long run), monarchical judicial intervention did not also enforce peasant rights, thus protecting peasant property.

In fact, Croot and Parker never begin to come to terms with the various ways in which the state intervened to support peasant prop-

peasant resistance . . . This is the same class struggle as occurred in England, but the result is different because the peasantry in France proved to be very strong" (above, p. 109). For a nearly identical statement, see Bois, *Crise du féodalisme*, p. 347.

[136] Above, p. 111, n. 11. [137] Above, pp. 82–4, 88–9, 60–2.

erty in France (which is odd, in view of their willingness to believe implicitly in the state's action to support the peasantry in England). In the first place, throughout the medieval period, notably during the epoch of demographic devastation and land desertions of the fifteenth century, the monarchy appears to have played a powerful role in affirming the integrity of the *cens*. Great masses of customary land were left unoccupied at this time. But it was difficult for the lords to absorb them to their demesnes, for the monarchy would, in effect, stand up for the rights even of long-absent peasants who could prove that they had once been occupants of the tenures, or even legitimate heirs of former occupants. Indeed, the crown had to pass a series of acts in the fifteenth century merely to provide enough assurance to the lords to allow them to resettle the land – as before on the basis of fixed hereditary *cens* tenures (the so-called *reaccessments*).[138] In the period of reconstruction the peasants' position as holders of *cens* tenure was further consolidated, as for the first time there was a *cens* contract which was universally set in writing, thus providing for even stronger protection in the courts.[139]

Second, in the fifteenth and sixteenth centuries the state moved to abolish the remnants of serfdom, and in particular the seigneurial *taille*, thus preventing the exaction of arbitrary rents. By this time, of course, such burdens were in many parts of France a thing of the past. Nevertheless, the monarchy did have a real impact where serfdom survived strongly into the fifteenth century, notably in the centre (for example, Nivernais) and the east. Here, the monarchy played a significant part by recognizing and thus consolidating gains won by direct peasant action.[140]

Third, from the mid-fifteenth century, the monarchy issued a series of ordinances supporting local customs and, in particular, published for province after province the so-called "customs". The latter fixed peasant rights and gave them full backing in law, defini-

[138] For the complex and extended procedure of *criées* necessary for the lords to recover land vacated by the peasants and, more generally, for the lords' difficulties *vis-à-vis* the land in this period, see Fourquin, *Lordship and Feudalism in the Middle Ages*, pp. 218–22; Fourquin, *Campagnes de la région parisienne*, pp. 430–2ff.; A. Plaisse, *La baronnie du Neubourg* (Paris, 1961), pp. 366–8.

[139] Neveux, "Déclin et reprise", p. 136.

[140] Chaunu, "L'état", pp. 146–7; Neveux, "Déclin et reprise", pp. 135–6; A. Bossuat, "Le servage en Nivernais au XVe siècle, d'après les registres du parlement", *Bibliothèque de l'Ecole des Chartes*, cxvii (1959), pp. 115–20; Le Roy Ladurie, "Masses profondes: la paysannerie", pp. 526–8.

tively consolidating peasant property through much of France. It also became a good deal easier in this period to make appeals from the seigneurial to the monarchical courts, as the royal administration effectively invaded the countryside – a trend manifested, for example, in the establishment from the 1550s of a new layer of royal courts, the *presidiaux* courts.[141]

Finally, and perhaps most symptomatic of the overall evolution, the monarchy moved to place full responsibility for the collection of the royal *taille* in the hands of the peasant villages. It thus reinforced the community over and against its old rival, the seigneurie. But, of course, as it did so, it prepared the ground for the increasingly effective imposition of increasingly heavy royal, centralized surplus extraction, in place of the decaying decentralized seigneurial levies.[142]

The fact is that despite the enormous incentives provided by rapidly rising prices in the early sixteenth century, which drastically devalued returns from fixed rents from the *cens* tenures, there is little evidence of an effective seigneurial reaction. The seigneurs simply did not have sufficient feudal powers at their disposal – expressed especially in rights to make arbitrary levies – to allow them to establish their ownership of the land in order to charge economic rents.[143]

The absolutist state, based on taxation and office, thus developed to a significant degree in conflict with, and at the expense of, the old decentralized forms of seigneurial extraction, and many individual feudal lords were losers in this process. As a result, the rise of absolutism provoked systematic, though sporadic and ultimately ineffectual, opposition from the seigneurial class. The seigneurial reactions against the monarchy which periodically inter-

[141] Chaunu, "L'état", pp. 91–3ff.; Neveux, "Déclin et reprise", pp. 135–6; J. Jacquart, *La crise rurale en Ile-de-France, 1550–1670* (Paris, 1974), pp. 102–3; Le Roy Ladurie, "Masses profondes: la paysannerie", pp. 526–8.

[142] Lemarignier, *France médiévale*, p. 318; Neveux, "Déclin et reprise", pp. 135–6.

[143] See Le Roy Ladurie's comment on this period: "The very popular notion of 'seigneurial reaction' or refeudalization has for neither the sixteenth century nor the eighteenth century any real significance": E. Le Roy Ladurie, "Les paysans français du XVIe siècle", in *Conjoncture économique, structures sociales: Hommage à Ernest Labrousse* (Paris, 1974), p. 346. As Jacquart points out, the *saisie féodale* for failure of *hommage* was practised, but it never brought about the confiscation of the fief: Jacquart, *Crise rurale en Ile-de-France*, p. 102. See also p. 109 above.

rupted the long-term expansion of French absolutist state organization are the most obvious expression of the real *competition* which prevailed between the old and the new modes of extraction.[144] On the other hand, French absolutism could develop *more or less* continuously, because it could absorb into state office many of those very same lords who were the casualties of the erosion of the seigneurial system.[145] Meanwhile, through its entire development, the absolutist monarchy had no choice but to ally with, and simultaneously incorporate, the greatest feudal lords – magnates who kept their autonomy right into the seventeenth century, even as they penetrated the heart of the state machine, especially the army.[146] If the absolutist state machine thus helped to erode the old *structure* of surplus extraction, it also benefited many of the *personnel* who had lived off that structure.

In sum, the absolutist state was no mere guarantor of the old forms of property based on decentralized seigneurial extraction. Rather, it came to express a *transformed* version of the old system. It should be emphasized, however, that as the French monarchy built up its absolutist organization, it could not but, in that very process, reconstruct ruling-class power, if on a very different basis. It was officers of the crown, many of them "new men", who most assiduously went about building up the monarchical state. But, in turn, actually to consolidate *its* power, the crown had to ensure the allegiance of these servants. This could only be done in what was, in its essentials, the old manner: the crown had no choice but to secure service and loyalty by granting assured private property rights in part of the surplus extracted from the peasantry. This had been classically accomplished in the medieval period through the endowment of a fief (although many other sorts of grants were also made to the same purpose in that epoch). Now, archetypically, there was the grant of an office, at first for life, later hereditarily[147] (although, again, other sorts of endowments, such as pensions and land, were also given). In short, a more effective system of surplus extraction against the peasantry required a more effective, tightly-knit political association of the ruling class, a stronger state. This was, in fact,

[144] Chaunu, "L'état", pp. 136, 144, 166ff.
[145] Bois, *Crise du féodalisme*, pp. 257, 364.
[146] R. Mousnier, *Etat et société en France aux XVIIe et XVIIIe siècles* (Paris, 1969), pp. 89–92.
[147] *Ibid.*, pp. 46–51.

constructed in large part through the re-creation of "private property in the political sphere" for the benefit of the crown's servants – and this meant, paradoxically, the renewal of the crown's ultimate dependence upon a (reconstructed) independent ruling class (largely, though only partially, based in office). The office-holders' independence was consolidated with the declaration of the full heritability of office in 1604 (which went along with the imposition of the *paulette*, or tax on office). Their increasing autonomy was manifested throughout the early modern period in the growing self-assertiveness of their *parlements* and, in turn, in their periodic resistances and revolts.[148]

This new crystallization of class relationships was to prove disastrous for economic development. Peasant possession was further strengthened, and its old limitations remained in force: the failure to specialize or to improve and the tendency to subdivision rather than accumulation. To make matters worse, the new system of surplus extraction was more effective than the old and was oriented even more single-mindedly to conspicuous consumption and war. It developed to an even greater extent without reference to the requirements of the peasants' productive forces and was, in the long run, more fully at odds with them.

From the second half of the fifteenth century, the French middle peasants assumed powerful control over the land and set in motion the developmental pattern familiar from the medieval period: demographic growth leading to the pulverization of holdings, accompanied by declining productivity, leading ultimately to stagnation and decline. For a time the lords could benefit from this process: their incomes could grow merely through the reopening of deserted land and the multiplication of peasant tenures (even with fixed rents). But after a while, as cultivation was spread to more marginal lands, and as productivity began to fall in the face of rising population, accelerating inflation began to eat away at fixed rents. This signalled the beginning of the end for the period of growth, and the onset of economic problems of all sorts – not only for the peasantry, but for the local lords, who once again found their incomes failing to keep up with growing needs.[149]

During the second half of the sixteenth century, France appears

[148] *Ibid.*, p. 51.
[149] Le Roy Ladurie, "Masses profondes: la paysannerie", pp. 555–76.

to have reached the old ceilings of population and production that it had attained in the early fourteenth century.[150] Correspondingly, as in the later medieval period, one witnesses the outbreak of every sort of struggle to redistribute by extra-economic means the relatively fixed national income. But now the tendencies to political accumulation through taxation and warfare were realized to an unprecedented degree.

Before 1550 taxes had not risen as a proportion of peasant output. But the situation was then transformed. Taxes on a family of four rose from an equivalent of seven days' output per year in 1547 to the equivalent of fourteen days' output per year in 1607 and to the equivalent of thirty-four days' output per year in 1675.[151] Meanwhile, the depredations accompanying the wars of religion directly undermined production to a disastrous degree. From the stagnation and decline which were already evident in the middle of the sixteenth century, the French economy descended by fits and starts into the general crisis of the seventeenth century. After decades of destruction by troops and taxation, the sixteenth century "ended in catastrophe marked above all by a fall in population and production".[152] After a brief period of subsequent recovery, there was after 1630, once again, near perpetual disruption of the economy, resulting from external war (the Thirty Years War), compounded by civil war (the Fronde) and the continuing build-up of the absolutist tax state. As in the fourteenth and earlier fifteenth centuries, the intensification of every form of political accumulation had undermined the operation of the classic Malthusian mechanisms of adjustment and forced the economy as a whole into protracted, systemic crisis.

England. To explain the emergence of capitalist property relations on the land in England, Bois asserts that the nobility "was faced with a peasantry whose rights had been too well established for a return to serfdom to be possible, but not sufficiently established to enable it to maintain control of the land when faced with seigneurial pressure". The lords could, therefore, proceed over time to undermine and eliminate the peasant possessors. This was

[150] *Ibid.*, pp. 576–85.
[151] M. Morineau, "La conjoncture ou les cernes de la croissance", in Braudel and Labrousse (eds.), *Histoire économique et sociale de la France*, i, pt 2, pp. 978–80.
[152] *Ibid.*, p. 994.

precisely my analysis. On the other hand, Bois once again *accounts* for this situation in terms of his unilineal "declining rate of rent" schema. As he argues, "the relative backwardness of England's social evolution as compared to that of France was to prove its trump card in the transition from feudalism to capitalism". In his view the falling rate of feudal rent had not played itself out in (backward) England to the extent that it had in (advanced) France, so that the English lords remained well enough placed to recover their positions.[153]

I have already stated my reservations concerning this approach. In contrast, I have argued that precisely the *advanced* self-organization of the English ruling class in the medieval period had allowed them to make their decentralized forms of feudal surplus extraction work well during the growth phase of the feudal economy; that, with the collapse of population in the mid-fourteenth century, they had naturally attempted to fall back on these tried and true forms in order to recoup, initiating the seigneurial reaction after 1350; but that these decentralized methods of surplus extraction had proved inadequate in the long run to counteract peasant resistance and mobility, to prevent the decline of serfdom or to stop a long-term fall in rents, especially from the later fourteenth century. The English aristocracy may, for a certain period, have compensated to some extent through war overseas, benefiting perhaps for the last time from its superior feudal class organization and cohesion.[154] But once war ceased to pay when waged against an ever more united French aristocracy and French state, they were thrown back on their own resources.

As a result of the class-wide crisis of seigneurial revenues, neither the crown in relation to its magnate followers, nor the magnates in relation to their lesser landed class followers, possessed the economic resources, the necessary "glue", to cement the old intra-aristocratic alliances which had formed the basis for aristocratic and, ultimately, monarchical strength and stability in England. For

[153] Above, p. 114. One should recall in this regard that Bois also explains the greater success of English lords *vis-à-vis* their peasants in the twelfth and thirteenth centuries in terms of English "backwardness".

[154] On aristocratic profits from war, see the conflicting views of K. B. McFarlane, "War, the Economy and Social Change", *Past and Present*, no. 22 (July 1962), and M. M. Postan, "The Costs of the Hundred Years War", *Past and Present*, no. 27 (April 1964).

the heightened demands made upon financially straitened overlords by needy followers with collapsing rents were simply too great. The result was the rise of faction, aristocratic disorganization and the intra-class conflict which led to the breakdown of government and the descent into civil war which marked the middle part of the fifteenth century.[155]

It was the English lords' inability either to re-enserf the peasants or to move in the direction of absolutism (as had their French counterparts) which forced them in the long run to seek novel ways out of their revenue crisis. With the decline of their own self-discipline and self-organization under the pressure of the later medieval crisis of seigneurial revenue, the English ruling class was impelled, for a time, to turn the instruments of feudal political accumulation in upon itself.[156] But the resulting zero-sum game *within the ruling class*, in the context of declining overall ruling-class incomes, could not constitute a stable solution. Lacking the ability to reimpose some system of extra-economic levy on the peasantry, the lords were obliged to use their remaining feudal powers to further what in the end turned out to be capitalist development. Their continuing control over the land – their maintenance of broad demesnes, as well as their ability to prevent the achievement of full property rights by their customary tenants and ultimately to consign these tenants to the status of leaseholders – proved to be their trump card. This control of landed property was, above all, an expression of their feudal powers, the legacy of the position the lords had established and maintained throughout the medieval period on the basis of their precocious self-centralization. They would consolidate these powers by carrying their self-centralization to an even higher level, using somewhat different forms, in the subsequent era.

Now here again Croot and Parker demur: just as they think that I have overstated the security of the French peasants' possession, they believe I have underrated the hold of the English customary peasants on the land. In particular, they raise the question of the security of the tenure enjoyed by the English copyholder, implying

155 R. L. Storey, *The End of the House of Lancaster* (London, 1966), introduction.

156 See Storey's comment: "Baronial revolts abroad were provoked by the increasingly despotic nature of royal government, but here [in England] civil war came for the very opposite reason, for what contemporaries called 'the lack of politic rule and governance' . . . " (*ibid.*, p. 28).

I have underestimated it.[157] This is an important question. But the security of copyhold was only one of a whole series of factors which affected the hold on the land which could be exerted by the English peasants in the early modern period, and it needs to be evaluated, therefore, within a broader context.

First, it is necessary to recall that, already by the end of the thirteenth century, English lords held outright in demesne a much greater percentage of the cultivated land than did their French counterparts, something like one-third as compared to one-eighth or one-tenth. Second, and equally important, another third of the land in England was in villein tenure, thus subject to arbitrary levies from the lords (tallages, fines and so forth), with the (unfree) tenants having recourse only to themselves to protect their rights to it. (In the eyes of the king's courts, this was the lords' land, whatever the varying realities of local custom and the local balance of power.) By contrast, in France (at least in the north) some 85–90 per cent of the land was under *cens* tenure, thus effectively free from arbitrary levies and essentially owned by the peasants.

The period of population drop-off only accentuated this difference. In France, as noted, the peasants' unoccupied customary lands were largely protected from take-over by the lords. As a result, around 1450–1500, just about the same (restricted) amount of land remained under demesne, subject to economic rents, as in the thirteenth century.[158] In England, by contrast, the lords often could assimilate customary (unfree) lands to their demesnes (there was certainly no law to prevent it). It is difficult to make quantitative estimates, but in study after study there is evidence that at least a significant proportion of formerly customary (villein) land – considered by the lords to be theirs (especially because the law said it was and because no one was present to challenge them) – was simply added to the demesnes, that is to the leasehold, economic rent sector.[159]

[157] Above, pp. 82–3.

[158] Bois, *Crise du féodalisme*, pp. 281, 319; Fourquin, *Campagnes de la région parisienne*, pp. 474–5. In the area around Paris studied by Jacquart, seigneurial demesnes covered some 12 per cent of the *cultivated* surface in the later fifteenth century: Jacquart, *Crise rurale en Ile-de-France*, p. 110.

[159] R. H. Hilton, "A Study in the Pre-History of English Enclosure in the Fifteenth Century", in *Studi in onore di Armando Sapori*, 2 vols. (Milan, 1957), i; J. P. Genêt, "Economie et société rurale en Angleterre au XVe siècle d'après les comptes de l'hôpital d'Ewelme", *Annales E.S.C.*, xxvii (1972), pp. 1464–71; Howell, "Stability and Change, 1300–1700", p. 473; R. A. Lomas, "Develop-

This brings us to the question of the evolution of the (formerly villein) land which *remained* in customary tenure into the later fifteenth century – the issue of copyhold *per se*. We now see that at the beginning of the early modern period a good deal less of the surface was held in the form of customary tenure in England than in France, and a good deal more was fully in the hands of the lords (demesne). What was the future of the customary land which was left? Did it, like the French customary tenure (*cens*), evolve into virtual freehold? Or did it revert eventually to the lords, so that they could charge economic rents?

This problem ultimately boils down to the question of what rights of the copyholder the courts were prepared to back up, assuming now that the copyholder *could* get recognized in court (as both Kerridge and Gray agree they could from the early decades of the sixteenth century).[160] This seems in turn to come down to the question of the customary conditions under which the peasants held their land. Where they had established heritability and fixed fines as the custom, they could become essentially freeholders. But, as Kerridge points out, over significant areas of the country the peasants had established no such customs. They held for a given number of years or lives, subject to arbitrary fines. According to Kerridge, copyholders could be charged with arbitrary fines particularly in the west of England and on the northern borders, where especially insecure tenures prevailed. A further proportion of the land was thus subject to essentially demesne conditions – that is, copyhold under these conditions was equivalent to economic leasehold of landlord property, since the adjustable fines could be used as economic rents. Finally, there is the ambiguous case which has aroused so much controversy, where copyholders did hold by inheritance, but where fines were arbitrary. These conditions were prevalent especially in East Anglia, the midland plain, the fens, the South Downs and south-coast regions.[161] Croot and Parker present evidence that *by the early years of the seventeenth century* the courts

ments in Land Tenure on the Prior of Durham's Estate in the Later Middle Ages", *Northern Hist.*, xiii (1977); R. B. Dobson, *Durham Cathedral Priory, 1400–1450* (Cambridge, 1973), pp. 282–3; H. P. R. Finberg, *Tavistock Abbey* (Cambridge, 1959), pp. 250–2, 256–7; and above, pp. 160–1 and n. 80.

[160] Cf. E. Kerridge, *Agrarian Problems in the Sixteenth Century and After* (London, 1969), with C. M. Gray, *Copyhold, Equity and the Common Law* (Cambridge, Mass., 1963).

[161] Kerridge, *Agrarian Problems in the Sixteenth Century and After*, pp. 38–9.

had begun to resolve this anomaly by setting fines at "reasonable" rates.[162] But this fact actually *undercuts* their case. For it shows that protection for copyholders by inheritance without fixed fines began to be established only very late in the day – after a century of rising prices and rents. During that time there appears to have been no legally established limit to which fines could be raised, and be supported in court on appeal. Those copyholders who had survived to this late date must very often have been rather substantial figures, capable of paying the rising rents (in the form of higher fines) or buying up the property themselves.

In sum, it seems hard to deny that the direct feudal rights and powers, maintained by the English lords throughout the whole of the medieval epoch, gave them a powerful basis for establishing, holding on to and extending their control over the land in the subsequent period – and that, in this respect, they enjoyed a far stronger position *vis-à-vis* their peasants than did their French counterparts. Of course, the English lords' property in the land gave them only the right to lease their holdings at competitive rates; and at the start, in the fifteenth century, rents must have been very low. Nonetheless, so long as there was the potential for increased competition for the land, the market in leases provided the basic condition for both the restoration of landlord incomes and the economic differentiation of the tenants.

The initial processes of differentiation, resulting in the rise of larger capitalist tenant farmers, were perhaps facilitated, in the fifteenth century, by the maintenance of wool exports (in either raw or manufactured form) at roughly fourteenth-century levels, in the face of a 50 per cent drop-off in population – that is, half the number of farmers in England were now producing the same amount of wool as before. This differentiation was probably given an impetus by the generalized commercial upturn, marked by the rapid growth of cloth production for export from the third quarter of the fifteenth century, and accelerating rapidly from the 1520s.[163] Ultimately, the

[162] See Croot and Parker, p. 82 above, who base themselves upon A. W. B. Simpson, *An Introduction to the History of the Land Law* (London, 1964), p. 161. The same point is made by R. H. Tawney, *The Agrarian Problem in the Sixteenth Century* (New York, 1967), pp. 296 (and n. 3), 297, and Kerridge, *Agrarian Problems in the Sixteenth Century and After*, p. 40.

[163] On the early phases of differentiation, see T. H. Lloyd, *The Movement of Wool Prices in Medieval England* (*Econ. Hist. Rev.* Supplement, no. 6, London, 1973), pp. 24–30; Hilton, "Study in the Pre-History of English Enclosure in the Fifteenth Century"; F. R. H. Du Boulay, "Who were Farming the English

growing shift of population into industrial employments, supplemented by a powerful demographic upturn, determined a long-term increase in the demand for agricultural products, leading to a rise in food prices, which called forth the growth of agricultural production and productivity.[164] Agricultural development took place through characteristically capitalist processes conditioned by the new system of social relations in which the organizers of production and the direct producers (sometimes the same persons) no longer possessed their full means of reproduction (especially the land) and were therefore compelled to produce systematically for the market. The resulting competition among tenants for the land and among landlords for tenants stimulated cost-cutting, thus specialization and improvement, leading over time to the replacement of small, relatively inefficient peasant tenants by larger capitalist tenants, thus underpinning an agricultural transformation.

As opportunities in agricultural production and commercial landlordship grew and the economic potential of the old feudal affinities and their marauding activities declined, the balance of forces was tipped increasingly against any sort of successful attempt at feudal reorganization for political accumulation. Growing numbers of landlords and tenants thus turned to the monarchy to guarantee the peace and stability they required for ongoing commercial productive activity. During the early modern period the long-term tendency towards the increasing *self-centralization* of the English landed classes was thereby extended, although now in a qualitatively different form which corresponded to the transformed character of the property or surplus-extraction relations through which the landed classes were coming to reproduce themselves. An increasingly centralized state, rooted ever more firmly in broad landed layers, could thus more effectively undermine the disruptive behaviour of those decreasing numbers of landed elements whose economies still depended upon the application of extra-economic methods (at this point focused mainly upon banditry, raiding and the spoliation of monarchical administration and justice). In turn, as even the greatest magnates saw their localized political strength

Demesnes at the End of the Middle Ages?", *Econ. Hist. Rev.*, 2nd ser., xvii (1964–5); F. R. H. Du Boulay, *The Age of Ambition* (London, 1970), pp. 55–8; Genêt, "Economie et société rurale en Angleterre au XVe siècle", pp. 1464–71.

164 See Bowden, "Agricultural Prices, Farm Profits, and Rents"; D. C. Coleman, *The Economy of England, 1450–1750* (Oxford, 1977), esp. chs. 2, 3, 7.

eroded by the state, many of them were obliged to turn to economic landlordship.[165]

The affirmation of absolute private property by the landlords over and against peasant possession went hand in hand, therefore, with the gradual rise of a different sort of state, one which attained a monopoly of force over and against the privatized powers of feudal potentates. The state which emerged during the Tudor period was, however, no absolutism. Able to profit from rising land rents, through presiding over a newly emerging tripartite capitalist hierarchy of commercial landlord, capitalist tenant and hired wage-labourer, the English landed classes had no need to revert to direct, extra-economic compulsion to extract a surplus. Nor did they require the state to serve them indirectly as an engine of surplus appropriation by political means (tax/office and war).

What they needed, at least on the domestic front, was a cheap state, which would secure order and protect private property, thus assuring the normal operation of contractually based economic processes. This goal they were able to achieve in the course of the sixteenth and seventeenth centuries (through processes far beyond the scope of this essay to describe) by means of the strengthening of parliament as their special instrument of centralized control over the government and through an increasing stranglehold on state office, above all at the local level. Two experiments in royal absolutism were aborted, and no tax state came to prey on a developing English economy. Characteristically, although the new state was operated at all levels by the landed class, it offered only restricted opportunities for the fruits of office, and local administration was typically not paid at all. In turn, although it monopolized force, the new state levied only minimal taxes. It is indeed symptomatic that when taxes did begin to be raised significantly from the later seventeenth century onwards, they were levied *upon its own members* by a landlord class now unambiguously in control of the state, thanks to its victories over the crown. This is in contrast to the situation in France, where one mark of membership of the ruling class was exemption from state taxation – and naturally so, since the state was centrally conceived as a political, wealth-generating mechanism for the aris-

[165] See L. Stone, "Power", in his *The Crisis of the Aristocracy, 1558–1641* (Oxford, 1965), ch. 5; M. E. James, *Change and Continuity in the Tudor North* (Borthwick Papers, no. 27, York, 1965); M. E. James, "The First Earl of Cumberland and the Decline of Northern Feudalism", *Northern Hist.*, i (1966).

tocracy. In England the landlord class, having uprooted the peasantry, could depend largely upon the operation of "impersonal", "economic" processes – the exploitation by capitalist tenants of free wage-labourers and, in turn, the operation of intra-capitalist competition, especially among tenants in the agricultural sector, but also in the economy as a whole.

To sum up: by the end of the seventeenth century the English evolution towards agrarian capitalism had brought about the end of the age-old "fusion" of the "economic" and the "political", and the emergence of an institutional separation between state and civil society. With the breakthrough of economic development, manifested above all in the increasing productivity of labour, the achievement of wealth ceased to be essentially the zero-sum game it had been under feudal social-productive relations. In turn, the amassing and direct application of force in order to redistribute a strictly limited social product ceased to be the *sine qua non* for the success of the ruling class. English development had distinguished itself from that in most places on the Continent in two critical, inter-related aspects. It was marked by the rise of a *capitalist aristocracy* which was presiding over an *agricultural revolution*.

(III.2) RESULTS OF THE DIVERGENCES: LORDS, PEASANTS AND CAPITALIST AGRICULTURE 1450–1750

Just as my account of the *roots* of the divergent evolutions of property or surplus-extraction relations in different European regions in the wake of the later medieval crisis of seigneurial revenues has been called into question, so has my understanding of the *implications* of these property settlements for the subsequent course of economic development. This is particularly the case with regard to my view of the different significances, for the distribution of wealth and the development of the productive forces, of the consolidation of peasant proprietorship in relationship to the rise of absolutism – classically in France – in comparison with the rise of the classic landlord / capitalist tenant / wage-labourer relationship – above all, in England.

(III.2.1) Property Forms and the Evolution of Landownership

To begin with, Croot and Parker contend that, even if the peasantry did emerge in later medieval France with far stronger rights to the soil than did their counterparts in England, this could have had little real significance; for "economic" forces, most especially the market, must have been determinant in the long run. As they state, "in both France and England economic rather than legal considerations were instrumental in determining the pattern of landholding". They maintain that "the rights of the French peasantry were an obstacle to more rational farming . . . but these would not have been an insuperable obstacle if the economic incentives and determination to override them had existed". According to Croot and Parker, the general problem with my approach is specifically manifested in my failure to come to terms with the "lack of any equivalent in France to the celebrated class of English yeomanry, which was itself the product of a process of [economic] differentiation within the ranks of the peasantry, a process not experienced by their French counterparts".[166]

But Croot and Parker beg the central question. There is no disagreement between us as to the special significance for economic development in England of "the rise of the yeoman" – that is, the emergence of a class of larger commercial farmers out of a process of economic differentiation of the peasantry, in contrast with the pulverization and levelling of the peasantry which was the predominant trend in early modern France. The problem is to *explain* these different trends. The point is that the purely "economic" starting-point for these divergent processes was roughly the *same* in both England and France. In the later fifteenth century, in both countries, a middle peasantry on relatively quite large holdings appears to have held a strong position. The difficulty arises because, despite what Croot and Parker imply, the peasantry – and especially peasant property – subsequently underwent radically different evolutions in the two countries, *even though market forces, above all rising food prices, made themselves strongly felt in both places throughout the early modern period, creating more than ample incentives to try to make a profit through the accumulation of land leading to differentiation*. It is to explain these diverging evolutions that it is indispensable to make reference to the different property systems[167] in which the peasantries were enmeshed in France and

[166] Above, pp. 84, 83, 85.

[167] Cf. Genêt, "Economie et société rurale en Angleterre au XVe siècle", pp. 1468–9, with Neveux, "Déclin et reprise", p. 107. I should emphasize that my argument is for the primacy of *social-property relationships* and *not* – as I may not have made clear enough – the size of farms *per se*. Different forms of social-property

England. For these allowed and/or compelled the peasantry in each country to respond to roughly similar economic (market) conditions in different ways.

The differentiation of the English peasantry was thus critically conditioned by the fact that, under the newly emergent social-property relations, they had *no choice* but to respond to the rising market by competing with one another as effectively as possible – by cost-cutting, and thus by specializing, accumulating their surpluses, and innovating. But this compulsion to compete was only the *result* of the fact that *they were separated from possession of the land*, thus deprived of direct (non-market) access to their means of subsistence, correlatively consigned to leasehold status, and, as a result, subjected to the system of *competitive rents*.[168] In this system the larger farmers, who could produce more efficiently and more profitably on the market, could use their competitive edge to accumulate land directly at the expense of the smaller farmers – superseding them when their leases ran out by offering a higher and more secure rent or outbidding them for those tenancies which came on to the market. In turn, the landlords had to compete for the best tenants if they wished to get the maximum rent from leasing their land – in particular, by offering larger, consolidated holdings, sometimes enclosed and improved. It was not, as Croot and Parker imply, the rise of the market in itself which made for the rapid differentiation of the peasantry in England and the rise of the yeoman (almost always larger commercial *tenants*), but rather the social-property relationships which made the English agricultural producers fully dependent upon competitive production.[169]

By contrast, as virtual owners of their plots, French peasants did not face the falling-in of their leases, rising fines or direct com-

relationship made different forms of economic behaviour rational, possible and necessary for the individual economic actors and, in this way, conditioned different overall patterns of economic development/non-development. See R. Brenner, "The Social Basis of Economic Development", in J. Roemer (ed.), *Analytical Marxism* (Cambridge, 1985).

168 As Genêt explains, during the fifteenth century the "position of the peasants was strengthened . . . But . . . the seigneurs . . . preserved the rights they had on their lands and . . . the means of taking a profit from them": Genêt, "Economie et société rurale en Angleterre au XVe siècle", pp. 1468–9.

169 Paradoxically, Croot and Parker on several occasions refer to precisely these competitive processes as lying behind the economic differentiation of the peasantry which took place in England, but they do not make the appropriate comparison with the quite different situation in France. See above, pp. 82–3, 85–6.

petition for their tenures. So long as they held a plot which could produce enough to feed their families and pay their taxes, they were not, as a rule, compelled to sell and compete effectively on the market to survive. Most had little possibility of accumulating. They had little choice but to follow the familiar pattern of producing with the aim of directly supporting themselves and their children, and of subdividing their land on inheritance. Croot and Parker should not be surprised that in this context of social-property relations any tendency to differentiation leading to the rise of a yeoman class was overwhelmed by the tendency to morcellation.

It was thus from the latter part of the fifteenth century that the institutionalization of different social-property systems in England and France began to condition a definitive parting of the ways for their respective economies. This was manifested first of all in a dramatic divergence in the subsequent evolutions of the distribution of landed property in the two countries. The latter was the result, first, of an apparent difference in the demographic regimes which came to prevail in each country and, second, of the new rise of the market, which, though powerfully felt in both countries, had different effects in each. The operation of each of these causes was traceable back, in turn, to the different institutionalized property arrangements.

In France, from various points after 1450, there was a sharply accelerated upturn in population, as in the twelfth and thirteenth centuries. Indeed, already by the mid-sixteenth century, in some regions a little later, French population had already equalled and in some places actually exceeded the record levels of the early fourteenth century.[170] The contrast with England is remarkable. There, population stagnated until perhaps the 1510s. Moreover, even when it began to grow, its pace appears to have been significantly slower than that of France, reaching fourteenth-century levels only in the middle of the seventeenth century, or perhaps only by 1700.[171]

It is hard to avoid the temptation to see in this demographic contrast an initial and definitive effect of the divergence in property sys-

[170] Le Roy Ladurie, "Masses profondes: la paysannerie", pp. 355–61; Neveux, "Déclin et reprise", pp. 101–3.

[171] J. Cornwall, "English Population in the Early Sixteenth Century", *Econ. Hist. Rev.*, 2nd ser., xxiii (1970); I. Blanchard, "Population Change, Enclosure and the Early Tudor Economy", *Econ. Hist. Rev.*, 2nd ser., xxiii (1970); Coleman, *Economy of England, 1450–1750*, pp. 12–13ff.

tems, as well as a critical cause of the divergent evolutions in the distribution of property. In France the reaffirmation, even the strengthening, of peasant property from the mid-fifteenth century made possible a renewal of the old peasant-based demographic regime. This was apparently set in motion by the (relatively) early age of marriage, rooted in turn in the easy and early accession to a plot, based finally on strong peasant property which allowed for the subdivision of holdings. The rapid demographic advance which was thereby made possible led to the extreme parcellization of property. In England, by contrast, we can at least hypothesize that, due to the loss of firm possession by the direct cultivators and the correspondingly enforced rise of commercial tenantry, holders of plots (leasehold farmers) had little choice but to treat their holdings as commercial investments, as a source of profit (if they wished to keep them), and could no longer view them as the *directly* self-sufficient basis for a continuing family. This tended to preclude subdivision, for smaller plots were uneconomic. As a result, children could no longer count on receiving a plot on coming of age. On the contrary, the number of children in the family, so far as possible, had to be adapted to the economic-productive requirements and potentials of the commercial holding. The result appears to have been later marriages, smaller families, and the sending of children outside of the household into other occupations. The interrelated outcomes were slower population growth and, in general, the prevention of the subdivision of holdings.[172]

In this same period of generalized, Europe-wide commercial upturn the impact of the market upon different social-property systems constituted a second powerful force conditioning the divergent evolutions of the distribution of property in England and France. This can be brought out especially well by comparing developments in the most commercialized areas of France with those in England in the period from the mid-fifteenth to the second half of the sixteenth century. For these purposes, the Paris region is exemplary, for it would be difficult to specify an area of France where market forces had a greater impact. The city itself grew rapidly in this period, and exercised a huge pull on its hinterland. Moreover, population increased in the agricultural region around Paris at a tremendous

[172] This paragraph is derived from Bois, *Crise du féodalisme*, pp. 353–4, and Howell, "Stability and Change, 1300–1700".

pace. The result was especially fast rising prices, particularly for food and land. Not only the incentives for accumulation but the potential accumulators (in the persons of local lords, courtly office-holders, city merchants and well-off peasants) were present. Those who failed to accumulate land missed an enormous opportunity to profit; those landholders who stayed with their customary tenures saw their rents, in real terms, dwindle into insignificance.[173]

What were the actual results? We can get a remarkably good idea on the basis of Jacquart's massive study, which encompasses seven seigneuries covering some 4,699 cultivated hectares in the Paris region. Even in this area, by 1550–60 – after close to a century of urban development, demographic growth, expansion of the market and sky-rocketing prices – some 2,567 proprietors, each with a holding of less than 60 acres, still held 69 per cent of the cultivated land, in comparison with 17 proprietors with more than 60 acres (including the seven seigneurs on the large, ancient demesnes) who held 31 per cent of the cultivated surface (the demesnes themselves covering 18 per cent). Presenting the same results slightly differently: 2,516 proprietors with holdings of less than 24 acres owned 55 per cent of the land, while 75 proprietors with 25 acres or more held 45 per cent of the land.[174] There had clearly been some significant build-up of properties; but very few proprietors benefited from accumulation, and a massive peasantry remained seated on the land.

The limited undermining of peasant property which had taken place in the Paris region had been conditioned by processes *beyond the market*. By 1550 population growth and *morcellement* had already led to a situation in which 88 per cent of the properties (2,273 holdings) were under 6.2 acres, thus too small to support a family without supplementary sources of income. Pressured by rapidly rising prices, which meant higher subsistence costs and lower wages, and the weight of taxation, many peasants were forced to sell out.[175]

Even where some accumulation of *property* took place, the

[173] See Fourquin, *Campagnes de la région parisienne*; Jacquart, *Crise rurale en Ile-de-France*.

[174] Calculated from the chart in Jacquart, *Crise rurale en Ile-de-France*, p. 118, with clarifying information in ch. 3.

[175] J. Jacquart, "Immobilisme et catastrophes, 1560–1660", in Duby and Wallon (eds.), *Histoire de la France rurale*, ii, p. 265.

basically peasant organization of *production* remained as yet unaffected. Indeed, the pattern of ownership fails to reveal just how restricted were the potentials for accumulation *for the purpose of* more effective production, for market farming and for improvement. For the units of property were themselves broken up into many, many parcels of cultivation, scattered through the fields, miniscule in size – an unambiguous testimony to the continuity of the peasant-dominated system. On one of the seven seigneuries studied by Jacquart, not a single parcel reached 12.5 acres in size! Indeed, if we exclude the seigneurie of Trappes (where both units of ownership and cultivation were exceptionally concentrated), there was a total of only ten parcels in all which exceeded 12.5 acres in the entire area covered by the survey. Engrossment thus proceeded apart from, indeed often in conflict with, the needs of production. Ironically, larger units of property might mean smaller units of cultivation.[176]

The contrast between the evolution of even this most precociously developed French region and that of England is, it seems to me, clear. For in many areas of England – by no means all, of course – there occurs a continuous process of build-up of larger holdings and units of cultivation at the expense of smaller ones, at least from the second part of the fifteenth century. In the closely studied community of Chippenham (Cambridgeshire), in the thirteenth century, the half-virgate holding (15 acres) was predominant, as almost everywhere else. By the second third of the fifteenth century, still only a fifth of the holdings were more than 30 acres. By 1540, however, 22 out of 42 holdings were 27 acres or more. Indeed, 12 of these holdings (including the demesne) were 50 acres or more, and they constituted 1,560 acres (of which the demesne counted 780 acres) out of a total of 2,265 cultivated acres, or some 64 per cent.[177] In the Wiltshire chalk lands, moreover, we learn that already by "the early 16th century most of the land was in the hands of capitalist

[176] Jacquart, *Crise rurale en Ile-de-France*, pp. 123–4. For the pulverization of the units of cultivation as a fundamental barrier to agricultural progress in France, see J. Meuvret, "La vaine pâture et le progrès agronomique avant la Révolution", in his *Etudes d'histoire économique* (Paris, 1971), pp. 195–6. For increasing pulverization of holdings even in the face of engrossment, see G. Cabourdin, *Terre et hommes en Lorraine, 1550–1635*, 2 vols. (Nancy, 1977), ii, pp. 640–1.

[177] M. Spufford, *Contrasting Communities* (Cambridge, 1974), ch. 3. Spufford, however, denies that the peasants' lack of property rights was at all important in determining their loss of the land.

farmers, and by the middle of the 17th century capitalist farms occupied most of the farmland".[178] In the west midlands it has been found that from the fifteenth century the "trend . . . toward the diminution of the small-holding group and the increase in the number of large holdings [30–100 acres of arable] seems fairly certain".[179] Even in Leicestershire, ostensible bastion of English peasant farming, the *average* and *typical* unit was already 45 acres in the second half of the sixteenth century.[180] This is almost four times the size of the representative peasant holding in the medieval period or the representative French holding of the sixteenth century. As early as 1500, half-yardlanders were already becoming rare in Leicestershire.[181]

Now, Cooper appears to argue that agrarian structures in France and England were not, by the later sixteenth century, significantly different.[182] By contrast, I would conclude that while the pattern of agrarian evolution in France from 1450 did not break fundamentally with that of the medieval period because it was, as before, dominated by peasant possessors, that of England did experience a breakthrough. This difference had, moreover, profound implications for the development of production.

(III.2.2) Property Relations and Productivity

The foregoing divergence in property settlements in England and France was, by the latter part of the sixteenth century, conditioning not only distinctive patterns in the evolution of property distribution, but different paths of development of the agricultural productive forces. Croot and Parker, as well as Cooper and Le Roy Ladurie, argue that I underestimate the capacity of the peasantry to increase agricultural productivity when I insist that the productive systems based on small peasants in possession of their means of subsistence were a barrier to the qualitative agricultural development required for sustaining economic growth in the early modern

[178] E. Kerridge, "Agriculture, *c.*1500–*c.*1793", in *V.C.H. Wiltshire*, iv, p. 57.

[179] R. H. Hilton, *The English Peasantry in the Later Middle Ages* (Oxford, 1975), p. 40, quoted by Cooper, p. 154, n. 57 above.

[180] W. G. Hoskins, "The Leicestershire Farmer in the Sixteenth Century", in his *Essays in Leicestershire History* (Liverpool, 1950), pp. 137–8. However, this figure does not include either the many cottagers' farms or the demesnes.

[181] Howell, "Stability and Change, 1300–1700", p. 474.

[182] Above, esp. pp. 164–8.

period, while the "English system" provided the ground for a definite breakthrough in this era. Nevertheless, it appears to me that these propositions are well supported by the economic experiences of both England and France throughout the early modern period, as well as that of western Europe as a whole.

(III.2.2.a) Peasant Possession in France versus Capitalist Tenantry in England

In the face of the massive growth of demand, expressed in rising food prices which affected broad areas of France, especially the north, from the early sixteenth century, the peasant grip on production was clearly responsible for stifling the growth of output. As we learn from case studies of Normandy and Cambrésis, areas exposed to especially heavy pressures from the market, the high point of production for the market, both local and overseas, came early to the region – in the first decade or two of the sixteenth century.. After this point, as population grew, peasants with increasingly smaller plots were forced to devote greater and greater proportions of their land to production for immediate subsistence to ensure their survival. We find, therefore, a decrease in the production of such commercial crops as hemp, flax and the like. Animal production was, moreover, continuously cut back in favour of production for the peasants' own consumption. By the 1540s in both regions not more but less grain was actually being sent to market, even though grain prices were rising precipitately. Meanwhile, the potential for improving agricultural productivity, dependent upon increased animal production, was definitely undermined.[183]

There is no sign whatsoever of innovation or advance in peasant farming in the sixteenth century, or at any time through to the end of the seventeenth century. Productive techniques stagnated throughout France, no less in the north than elsewhere. As Jacquart summarizes earlier local research throughout the various regions of the country, "one finds no trace of decisive technical progress and the results of peasant activity remained virtually the same in their mediocrity".[184] In consequence, almost everywhere in France, pro-

[183] H. Neveux, *Les grains du Cambrésis* (Lille, 1974), pp. 692–3, 697–8; Bois, *Crise du féodalisme*, pp. 337–40.

[184] Jacquart, "Immobilisme et catastrophes", p. 239; see also pp. 213, 216–21, 224–5, 237–9. For similar findings, see Le Roy Ladurie, "Masses profondes: la paysannerie", pp. 568–78.

ductivity per head was declining significantly by the early decades of the sixteenth century, leading to new subsistence crises, skyrocketing prices and, as noted, absolute ceilings on agricultural output (not to be reached again until the eighteenth century).[185] *Well before the onset of the devastations of the religious wars*, therefore, French peasant-based agriculture had in the course of its own unimpeded development sunk into stagnation and decline.

The contrast with England is clear. There, over the course of the early modern period, one witnesses an agricultural revolution. Given the technology available to the mixed agricultural production of medieval and early modern Europe, qualitative improvement which would make for significant cheapening in basic food production required that animal and arable husbandry be more tightly bound together and made more mutually reinforcing; in particular, animal production had to increase in relation to arable in order to provide manure and ploughing to counter the tendency to declining fertility of the soil. Peasant production for subsistence tended to make animal and arable production mutually competitive because it put a premium on food production for immediate consumption and discouraged specialization in fodder crops and animal-raising. It thereby constituted an immediate barrier to the foregoing sort of transformation, whereas the rise of the capitalist property system facilitated it – not only by conditioning a tendency to specialization and improvement enforced by competition, but by giving rise, via the aforementioned processes of differentiation (instead of morcellation), to a class of capitalist farmers who could take the risks, make the investments and carry out the larger-scale farming which was required.

These mechanisms are laid bare in Eric Kerridge's close study of agricultural arrangements and developments in early modern Wiltshire. Here there was a system of capitalist farms in operation from the early sixteenth century. The impact of the market was also felt from very early on. There ensued a process of economic differentiation, with concomitant specialization and improvement. Everywhere grain farming came to predominate on the chalk soils,

[185] See Le Roy Ladurie, "Masses profondes: la paysannerie", pp. 576–85. Bois found that production reached its height in Normandy by 1540, if not before: Bois, *Crise du féodalisme*, p. 337. Jacquart also put the output ceiling at around 1540–50, for Ile-de-France: Jacquart, *Crise rurale en Ile-de-France*, pp. 49–50.

where it was particularly appropriate. Moreover, by the mid-seventeenth century, large farms had entirely taken over specialized grain production, for the small farmer could not compete in the application of the favoured sheep-and-corn methods. On the other hand, if they wished to survive, the smaller farmers, as tenants, were themselves forced to specialize for the market. They had to abandon grain production, but in the so-called Cheese Country, which was quite suitable for dairy farming, they were able to hold their own. For in this the large producer enjoyed relatively little competitive edge.[186]

The developments in Wiltshire represent a microcosm of the processes which occurred in England as a whole in the early modern period. Joan Thirsk refers to "the predominance of large farmers in the specialized corn-growing areas" and concludes that, "In specialized corn-growing areas, the successful men were always yeomen farmers or gentlemen with substantial fortunes" – "As for the small farmer in arable areas, he had little hope for survival".[187] The reasons for this are not far to seek. In the first place, in grain production there were significant economies of scale to be had in the use of basic infrastructure and of farm animals and implements, as well as in the application of labour. Second, especially with the requirements for large sheep-folds, a great deal of capital was required. Third, the cost of perhaps the most potent innovation applicable to the traditional sheep-and-corn area, the floating of the water-meadows, was beyond the reach of the small farmers.[188]

Similarly, where lands were turned from arable to the revolutionary system of "up-and-down" husbandry – which allowed for the interdependent growth of both animal and arable output – it was nearly always capitalist farmers who were responsible. As Kerridge puts it, "Making an up-and-down farm was not a thing anyone could

[186] Kerridge, "Agriculture, *c.*1500–*c.*1793", pp. 61, 49, 54, 57–9, 63–4.

[187] J. Thirsk, "Seventeenth-Century Agriculture and Social Change", in J. Thirsk (ed.), *Land, Church and People: Essays Presented to Professor H. P. R. Finberg* [Supplement to *Agric. Hist. Rev.*, xviii (1970)], pp. 151, 166; J. Thirsk, "The Peasant Economy of England in the Seventeenth Century", *Studia historiae oeconomicae*, x (1975), p. 8. Thirsk defines yeomen as "substantial farmers with large acreage, who relied on a hired labour force" (*ibid.*, p. 7).

[188] Thirsk, "Seventeenth-Century Agriculture and Social Change", pp. 151, 153, 155, 166; Thirsk, "Peasant Economy of England", pp. 8, 10; Kerridge, "Agriculture, *c.*1500–*c.*1793", pp. 52, 54, 55–7; E. Kerridge, *The Farmers of Old England* (London, 1973), pp. 75–7, 81.

do. It took boldness, patience, and plenty of capital". This was because big changes were required in the layout of the farm, in its equipment, and in the time required to yield returns. Not surprisingly, therefore, in those areas where farmers adopted up-and-down husbandry during the early modern period – and they did so especially from the later part of the sixteenth century in the midland plain, the vales and the north-east lowlands – these developments were accompanied by the massive decline of small producers.[189]

It appears that small farmers were also at a disadvantage in cattle-rearing. The graziers, it seems, tended to be big capitalists who had plenty of investment funds and could afford to wait. This was, at any rate, the case on those lands which were turned over to permanent grass from permanent arable, a specialization carried out to bring the husbandry into closer accord with the suitability of the soil. In these areas a great deal of capital was applied for enclosure and restructuring of the farms.[190]

On the other hand, small men could and did survive in particular fields where they could be as efficient as large – above all in dairying, but also in market gardening near the towns. The small farmers maintained a strong hold in the pastoral regions, where they carried on a multiplicity of small commercial-agricultural (for example, hemp, flax) and industrial activities. Even so, the restricted range of agricultural possibilities open to these highly commercialized small farmers must be emphasized. In turn, they owed their very existence to the increases in productivity of the grain-producing areas, which allowed those areas to export their growing food surpluses and to supply the increasing import needs of the pastoral/commercial areas.[191]

[189] Kerridge, *Farmers of Old England*, pp. 106, 127, 128, and in general ch. 4.

[190] Thirsk, "Seventeenth-Century Agriculture and Social Change", pp. 155, 157; Thirsk, "Peasant Economy of England", p. 11; Kerridge, *Farmers of Old England*, pp. 62, 90–1.

[191] In the foregoing context, national averages of farm sizes like those put in evidence by Cooper hide more than they reveal about the transformation of agricultural production in England; for, as we have seen, this was the opposite of a homogeneous process. It was, on the contrary, characterized by the greatest variation in farm size, by region, terrain and crop. The survival of numerous small farmers – leading to a relatively low national average size of farms – is explained in ways which in no way contradict my argument: by the competitiveness of small farmers in pastoral regions and in horticulture; by the disinterest of big farmers in areas of poor soils; by the security of tenure enjoyed by peasants in a few regions. It should be noted, moreover, that the weight of small farming in agriculture is exaggerated when it is measured in terms of the proportion of small farms

Finally, it needs to be emphasized that the advantages of the system of capitalist agriculture, in comparison with a system based on peasant possessors, is not merely a question of the advantages of larger versus smaller farmers in particular agricultural lines, their superior capacity to make this or that "once and for all" specialization or improvement. Perhaps most significant is the tendency of capitalist property relations to enforce, by way of competition, a systematic drive towards specialization and improvement as an ongoing process in the *economy as a whole* – to a social and geographic division of labour. Thus we find in England not only the early development of a complex system of interdependent regional specialization, in which the development of one specialized area fed off and fed into the development of the next, but a continuing evolution and transformation of this system as new techniques became available. This is exemplified with the rise of the very potent systems of "mixed farming" in which, schematically speaking, the increased cultivation of fodder crops was used to support the production of animals, which in turn fed back into ongoing grain production, with fallows abolished. This system was much more adaptable to the light sandy soils than to the heavy clayey ones which had hitherto provided England with much of its grain. As a result, during the seventeenth century one witnesses a wholesale transformation of formerly grain-producing areas, particularly midland England, towards animal production. The accompanying "depopulation" and freeing of labour opened the way for the rise of new industries in the neighbouring vicinities, among them leather goods (connected with animal-raising in the area), lace, hosiery and clothmaking. Meanwhile, the light-soil areas of the southern part of the country became even more fully devoted to grain. Consequently, demand for agricultural labour in the arable areas intensified, and industrial production in these areas tended correspondingly to decline. Instead, these regions exported grain to support industry and non-food commercial agriculture elsewhere.[192]

out of the total number, rather than the proportion of the total cultivated surface covered by small farms – or better still, the proportion of good corn-producing land covered by such farms. See above, pp. 144–5. Cooper makes many of these same points himself.

192 E. L. Jones (ed.), *Agriculture and Economic Growth in England, 1660–1815* (New York, 1967), pp. 9–11, 36–7; E. L. Jones, "Agriculture and Economic Growth in England, 1660–1750: Agricultural Change", *Jl Econ. Hist.*, xxv (1965), pp. 10–18.

(III.2.2.b) Large Tenant Farms in France and England
What, then, is to be said about the fact, brought against me by both Croot and Parker and by Cooper, that large tenant farms using wage labour did ultimately become preponderant in some regions in France, especially in the later seventeenth century, yet do not appear to have been associated with improvement or to have brought progress to their regions? Does this invalidate the interpretation? In my original article I pointed to the same phenomenon and advanced an explanation: that, despite its similarity in outward form, the system of production characterized by large demesnes which emerged in parts of France in the early modern period reflected in reality the existence of very different social-productive relations from those which prevailed in England.[193] The underlying point I tried to make was that to analyse the productive potentials associated with a given system of property relations – indeed, to fully *define* that system – it is not enough to focus on individual units of production; their place within the economic system as a whole must be specified. One needs, in this case, to comprehend the larger individual units in their interrelations with the other agricultural-productive units, as well as with those in industry. In fact the large tenant farm in seventeenth-century France tended to *function* very differently from its English counterpart, not only because it represented the outcome of a very different historical evolution, but especially because it operated within a very different overall property system – one which remained in its basic dynamic *peasant-dominated*.

Thus larger tenant farms as a rule represented the outcome of processes whereby French landlords were able *for the first time* to assert their property over what had formerly been peasant land. Just as the original process of dispossessing the peasantry in England had depended to a large degree upon the operation of the system of surplus extraction *by extra-economic compulsion* (in particular, the feudal right to levy variable fines), so it did in France. In France, however, it was growing royal levies of taxes, combined with the devastating direct effects of military conflict on the villagers' properties, which made it possible for accumulators of the land to undermine the peasants' position (often already weakened by the extreme

[193] Above, pp. 61–2 and n. 111.

fragmentation of holdings). The first significant wave of expropriations came during the wars of religion, and they were concentrated especially in areas directly exposed to fighting, notably Burgundy and the Paris region. A second significant wave of engrossment accompanied the internal and external conflicts of the second third of the seventeenth century, especially the years of the Fronde. Again, it was the undermining effect of rising fiscal pressures, exacerbated by military depredations, which forced peasants into debt and ultimately to sell out to local proprietors.[194]

The large units of property which emerged in France from the foregoing processes appeared similar to those of England. However, they arose within an environment in which they remained surrounded – in their immediate environs and throughout France – by a massive, albeit semi-landless, peasantry. As a result, they took on an economic dynamic very different from that of their English counterparts. The appropriation of peasant land by village engrossers – which only exacerbated the effects of the subdivisions of holdings, consequent on peasant population growth – left masses of peasants on holdings too small to provide subsistence, having to seek leases and supplementary employment to make ends meet.[195] Meanwhile, the weakness of agricultural productivity, bound up with peasant-based production, restricted the French home market and the industrial sector, leaving few alternative employments outside agriculture. In the last analysis, it was *the demand for land for subsistence by peasants confined to the countryside which thus continued to determine the level of rents*, despite the rise of large units of property and production.[196] This was manifested in the secular rise

194 N. Fitch, "The Demographic and Economic Effects of Seventeenth Century Wars", *Review* [Fernand Braudel Center, S.U.N.Y. Binghamton], ii (1978–9); P. de Saint-Jacob, "Mutations économiques et sociales dans les campagnes bourguignonnes à la fin du XVIe siècle", *Etudes rurales*, i (1961); Jacquart, *Crise rurale en Ile-de-France*, pp. 213–27, 248–53, 691–707, 723ff.

195 For the large numbers of mini-peasant producers alongside the great farms, see Jacquart, *Crise rurale en Ile-de-France*, pp. 721, 724–7, 741–2; E. Le Roy Ladurie, "De la crise ultime à la vraie croissance, 1660–1789", in Duby and Wallon (eds.), *Histoire de la France rurale*, ii, pp. 414, 428.

196 For the upward pressure on rents from small, often sub-subsistence peasants who would pay significantly higher rates per acre than big tenants, see J. Jacquart, "La rente foncière, indice conjoncturel?", *Revue historique*, ccliii (1975), pp. 372–4. See also B. Veyrassat-Herren and E. Le Roy Ladurie, "La rente foncière autour de Paris au XVIIe siècle", *Annales E.S.C.*, xxiii (1968), pp. 549–55; above, pp. 170–1.

in rents during much of the seventeenth century, as the continuing erosion of the peasants' share of the surface determined a continuing growth in demand for land, even after population had reached its peak.[197]

In the foregoing economic context, the best returns could obviously be made simply by squeezing the tenants (directly, by raising rent). Correlatively, it made sense for the proprietors to desist from investment in fixed capital and to plough their receipts back into the purchase of more land. This squeezing sometimes took place directly through leasing the demesne in small parcels to peasant tenants. Very often, however, the demesne was taken over by a large farmer. But these big tenants tended to play more the role of financial intermediaries between the lords and the mass of the peasantry than that of independent capitalists. They did provide some investment funds, especially for ploughs and for animals. But other capital expenditures appear to have been restricted, and labour-intensive techniques favoured. The big tenants appear to have been, in the last analysis, the lords' dependents: more or less bound to the land, they had few economic alternatives and were allowed relatively little scope to accumulate surpluses. They relieved the lords of direct responsibility for managing the lands, while carrying out myriad seigneurial administrative tasks such as collections and justice for them.[198] In turn the lords, recruited increasingly from the ranks of the high officials and urban bourgeoisie, appear to have adopted a largely passive approach to their estates, making few improvements while buying ever more land. But this "*rentier* mentality" had a good and sufficient material basis – the profitability of rent-squeezing methods of surplus extraction in the face of endemic peasant land hunger.

I did indeed argue that a more productive and more collaborative relationship had by this time emerged between landlord and tenant in significant areas of England, helping to underwrite continuing

[197] For the fluctuations in rent in the north of France – its rise through the period of the religious wars; its fall-off after that; its recovery to its old high levels rather early in the seventeenth century; and its accelerated increase from around 1640 – see Jacquart, "Immobilisme et catastrophes", pp. 251–2; Jacquart, "Rente foncière, indice conjoncturel?", p. 365.

[198] See Jacquart's comment: the labourers "were never anything but the *mandataires* [representatives], at the heart of the rural world, of those who held the true reins of power": Jacquart, *Crise rurale en Ile-de-France*, pp. 756–7.

development. Cooper considers that in so doing I have somehow attributed distinctively charitable motives and productive intentions to English landlords ("Brenner sounds like a Tory defender of the Corn Laws").[199] But no such thing is contained in my argument (nor do I imply that French lords were somehow backward or anti-entrepreneurial). My point is simply that the different social-productive conditions which had come to prevail in England and France by the later seventeenth century made for different strategies to best protect and improve landlord incomes. In England, especially in the grain-growing regions, capitalist farmers controlled a highly capital-intensive husbandry, and the numbers of landholding peasants had declined drastically. In this situation, landlord incomes depended upon the tenants' ability to farm effectively on the basis of capital investment. Capitalist profits were, in short, a condition for landlord rents. To the degree that landlords attempted to squeeze tenants, preventing them from making a reasonable profit on their investment, the latter might cease to invest, and ultimately give up their leases, moving to another farm or perhaps even another field of production. On the other hand, there existed no mass of semi-proletarianized peasantry on the land – let alone one which could afford to pay a rent equivalent to that paid by the capitalist tenants. Economic success, in brief, depended on accumulation and innovation and, in this context, when the tenant was short of funds it was at times in the interest of the landlord to take over, to some degree, the function of capital investment (in which case the landlord would take part of his return in the form of profit). Thus the sort of landlord/tenant symbiosis to which I referred had a good economic rationale and tended to condition a dynamic agricultural development. Cooper is in the end obliged to acknowledge that its existence has been verified again and again for the later seventeenth and eighteenth centuries.[200]

The qualitative difference between the anatomically similar English and French large farms is strikingly evidenced in their manifestly different functioning in the period of low grain prices of the later seventeenth century. Excellent profits could still be made in

[199] Above, pp. 177, 179–80.

[200] Above, pp. 178–9 and n. 139. See Jones, "Agriculture and Economic Growth in England, 1660–1750: Agricultural Change", as well as the sources cited by Cooper himself. See also Coleman, *Economy of England, 1450–1750*, pp. 122–3.

English agriculture in this period, provided that the appropriate steps were taken to make farms more efficient. On lands suitable for grain this meant an intensification and expansion of the advanced forms of sheep-and-corn husbandry – the greater use of fodder crops, enclosure, the build-up of larger farms. On formerly arable lands appropriate to pasture, good returns were possible by conversion to permanent grass, or to up-and-down husbandry, usually requiring enclosure and the construction of essentially new farm operations. The build-up of productive units, the input of capita and the acceleration of innovation were what was required in both cases. That this was, indeed, what took place provides convincing evidence for the grip of capitalist production relations on English agriculture in this period, as well as the superiority of these relations.[201]

The response of French proprietors to the low food prices of the period from the 1660s onwards was in marked contrast to that of their English counterparts, as Cooper himself points out.[202] In the face of a declining market for agricultural products, a market which "indicated" that rents "should" be lowered to correspond to lowered prices, they insisted on raising them. As a result, a great number of their tenants, including their larger tenants, were caught in a squeeze between high rents and low prices, were pushed into debt and ultimately were forced to yield up their farms to their lord, as well as much of their accumulated property, including farm implements and even household furnishings.[203] This did not, however, indicate that French landlords were more or less rational, more or less charitable than their English counterparts; they simply faced a different situation. When the bad times came after 1660, it made sense for French lords to shift the burden to their tenants, because they could get away with it and still profit handsomely. Rents appear to have been kept up by the demand from semi-landless peasants, who were apparently willing to intensify their labour to be better able to pay more to the lords. The big tenants

[201] Thirsk, "Seventeenth-Century Agriculture and Social Change", pp. 155–7; and above, pp. 177–81. Thus the fact that many landlords adopted a draconian policy towards their *small* tenants does not controvert my argument, as Cooper suggests, but further supports it.

[202] Above, pp. 170–1, 175–6, 178–80.

[203] Jacquart, *Crise rurale en Ile-de-France*, pp. 742, 744–8; Jacquart, "Immobilisme et catastrophes", pp. 254–5, 261–5.

appear to have been unable to avoid continuing to pay these high rents because they had nowhere else to go. They ended up, in many cases, handing over to the lords every last bit of their accumulated capital in order to hold on to their leases, before finally going under. Jacquart thus refers to the "lamination" of farmers and rural merchants in this period.[204] Of course, in the end, market forces were bound to assert themselves. But they did so only in the long term. In many cases, landlords were able to maintain high rents in the face of low prices for a generation. But while rents were thus kept up in the north of France until 1700,[205] the French agricultural base continued to be eroded.

(III.2.2.c) Agricultural Production: The Long-Term Results in England versus France

The long-term outcome of the operation of these very different systems of social-property relations in England and France was only to intensify the sharp disparity in their respective agricultural performances. This conclusion has been disputed by a revisionist school (apparently supported, although inconsistently, by Cooper), which has sought to deny what was for long an accepted orthodoxy. Thus Cooper implies that it was the greater exposure to the devastations of warfare which explains any weakness of French agriculture relative to English agriculture in the sixteenth and seventeenth centuries.[206] Other historians have argued in turn that especially from the early eighteenth century, with the end of the worst excesses of absolutism, French agriculture experienced an impressive growth which compared quite favourably with that of England.[207]

The revisionist case depends, however, on the findings of J.-C. Toutain, contained in a large-scale macro-study of French national income. Toutain's data have been largely discredited.[208] Certainly,

[204] Jacquart, *Crise rurale en Ile-de-France*, pp. 747–8.
[205] Jacquart, "Rente foncière, indice conjoncturel?", p. 365.
[206] Above, pp. 183–4. It seems to me that Cooper's position on this question in this article is profoundly contradictory, and I have made use of the evidence he himself offers to oppose this view.
[207] See especially P. K. O'Brien, "Agriculture and the Industrial Revolution", *Econ. Hist. Rev.*, 2nd ser., xxx (1977); also R. Roehl, "French Industrialization", *Explorations in Econ. Hist.*, xiii (1976), p. 260.
[208] E. Le Roy Ladurie, "Les comptes fantastiques de Gregory King", *Annales E.S.C.*, xxiii (1968); D. Landes, "Statistics as a Source for the History of Economic Development in Western Europe", in V. Lorwin and J. Price (eds.), *The Dimensions of the Past* (New Haven, 1972), p. 74; E. L. Jones, "Introduc-

they are accepted by few students of French agricultural history of the eighteenth century. On the basis of their studies of tithe returns – as well as less direct evidence – almost all have concluded that *agriculture stagnated at least until 1750*.[209]

The evidence for England is less direct than that for France, but the results are fairly clear. English population was about 2.2 million in 1450; it exceeded 5 million by 1700. At the same level of population in the fourteenth century there had been chronic famine and crisis. By 1700 subsistence crisis had already been, for a long time, a thing of the past. The last even relatively severe one had occurred in 1597, but even this was not serious by Continental standards. Meanwhile, by 1700, perhaps up to half the population was in non-agricultural pursuits, having to be supported by agricultural producers. At the same time, England had become one of Europe's largest grain-exporters.[210]

What about the eighteenth century? For this period approximations of English and French agricultural growth have been based largely on an assumed *constant per capita consumption of grain*. On

tion: Industrial Patterns and their Rural Backgrounds", in the Italian edition of *Agricultural History and Industrial Development* (typescript). I wish to thank E. L. Jones for allowing me to consult this manuscript prior to publication.

209 Le Roy Ladurie thinks that I do not in my essay sufficiently appreciate French agricultural progress in the pre-industrial period, but for present purposes I would accept his own summary: "On the whole, from the fourteenth century to the first part of the eighteenth century, the agricultural product was without doubt agitated by fluctuation . . . but it was not animated, in the very long run, by a durable movement of growth . . . A true growth takes form . . . only after 1750, and then often in a hesitant fashion": Le Roy Ladurie, "Masses profondes: la paysannerie", p. 575. See also Le Roy Ladurie, "De la crise ultime à la vraie croissance", p. 395. For arguments that agricultural productivity in France did not begin to grow significantly until after 1840, see G. Grantham, "The Diffusion of the New Husbandry in Northern France, 1815–1840", *Jl Econ. Hist.*, xxxviii (1978).

210 On the mildness of English subsistence crises, even in the sixteenth century, in comparison with the French, see A. Appleby, "Grain Prices and Subsistence Crises in England and France, 1590–1740", *Jl Econ. Hist.*, xxxix (1979). On English grain exports, see D. Ormrod, "Dutch Commercial and Industrial Decline and British Growth in the Late Seventeenth and Early Eighteenth Centuries", in F. Krantz and P. M. Hohenberg (eds.), *Failed Transitions to Modern Industrial Society* (Montreal, 1975), pp. 37–40; J. A. Faber, "The Decline of the Baltic Grain-Trade in the Second Half of the 17th Century", *Acta historiae Neerlandica*, i (1966), pp. 125–6; A. H. John, "English Agricultural Improvement and Grain Exports, 1660–1765", in D. C. Coleman and A. H. John (eds.), *Trade, Government and Economy in Pre-Industrial England: Essays Presented to F. J. Fisher* (London, 1976), pp. 47–64.

this assumption, population growth can provide, in gross terms, a good indicator of the rate of growth of the food supply. As Cooper explains, the case of the revisionists that English agricultural growth in the first part of the eighteenth century was not relatively greater than the French is based on outmoded demographic data (the Brownlee-Rickman estimates). More recent figures supplied by the Cambridge Group, on the basis of data from parish registers, show that (while food prices were relatively stable) English population was growing much faster than earlier estimates indicated. This suggests a much more rapid growth in agricultural output for the later seventeenth and early eighteenth centuries than had previously been thought. Cooper ends up by concluding that "there probably was appreciable growth of agricultural output in the late seventeenth and early eighteenth centuries when French output was stagnant or falling, and the English rate of growth would have been much faster than the French until 1750". "By 1760", he says, "the differences between English and French agriculture were certainly much greater than in 1560, even if the comparison is restricted to the predominantly arable regions of open-field France".[211]

(III.2.2.d) French and English Agriculture in European Comparative Perspective

The development of agriculture elsewhere in Europe in the early modern period tends to confirm the foregoing relationships and patterns.

The Dutch Case. Le Roy Ladurie refers me to the rise of progressive Dutch agriculture in the sixteenth and seventeenth centuries as if it exemplifies his argument that a peasant-dominated agricultural economy could, in the early modern period, provide the foundation for agricultural breakthrough.[212] Yet what is most significant about the Dutch agrarian structure at the start of the early modern period is its *systematic difference* from the typical west European feudal-peasant pattern. There had never been a

[211] Above, pp. 141–2, 183. Looking at the eighteenth century as a whole, and using analogous methods, E. L. Jones has come to similar conclusions. He finds that whereas in England and Wales in 1700 one person employed in farming fed 1.7 persons, in 1800 one person fed 2.5 persons, an increase of 47 per cent. In France the equivalent calculation is that in 1701 one person fed 1.2 persons, and in 1789 one person fed 1.3 persons, an increase of only 8 per cent: Jones, "Introduction: Industrial Patterns and their Rural Backgrounds", pp. 27–9.

[212] Above, p. 105.

strongly rooted lordly class capable of extracting a surplus by means of extra-economic compulsion, and by 1500 the landed class received exclusively economic rents. Equally significant, there had never been a traditional "patriarchal", "possessing" peasantry with direct, non-market access to its means of subsistence.[213] Agriculture could be established, apparently, only on the basis of small dairy and livestock production; as a result, from the start, farmers had little choice but to specialize output for exchange, for they had to buy grain in the market in order to subsist.[214] From very early on, moreover, tenantry appears to have been widespread, further enforcing the tendency to competitive market production.[215]

Given this non-feudal, non-peasant social-property structure, it is perhaps not surprising that, from the sixteenth century onwards, Dutch agriculture experienced no tendency towards a demographically powered evolution on the basis of ensconced peasant possessors – the familiar Malthusian pattern leading to morcellation, declining productivity, and crisis.[216] Instead, under pressure from the urban markets there took place a process of economic growth based on competition and differentiation: highly specialized market production led to the supersession of smallholders and the build-up of large farms, on the basis of capital investment, technical change and the introduction of wage labour.[217]

The Flemish Case. Finally, both Cooper and Le Roy Ladurie point to the precocious improvement of Flemish agriculture in the early modern period, which was indeed operated by very small agriculturalists.[218] Does this case prove that peasants could and did

[213] J. de Vries, "On the Modernity of the Dutch Republic", *Jl Econ. Hist.*, xxxiii (1973), pp. 194–5ff.; J. de Vries, *The Dutch Rural Economy in the Golden Age, 1500–1700* (New Haven, 1974), pp. 24–41.

[214] De Vries, "On the Modernity of the Dutch Republic", p. 194. Note the huge role of grain imports in making possible specialization in livestock as well as industry: De Vries, *Dutch Rural Economy in the Golden Age*, pp. 169–73; H. van der Wee, "The Agricultural Development of the Low Countries as Revealed by the Tithe and Rent Statistics, 1250–1800", in H. van der Wee and E. van Cauwenberghe (eds.), *Productivity of Land and Agricultural Innovation in the Low Countries* (Louvain, 1978), p. 12.

[215] De Vries, *Dutch Rural Economy in the Golden Age*, p. 33.

[216] It is notable that De Vries explicitly conceptualizes the specificity of Dutch agrarian development as following a *specialization* as opposed to a *peasant* model: *ibid.*, *passim*.

[217] J. de Vries, *The Economy of Europe in an Age of Crisis, 1600–1750* (New York, 1976), p. 71.

[218] Above, pp. 105, 149–50 n. 40, 160, 188 n. 163.

provide the basis for a breakthrough to agricultural and, in turn, economic development in the early modern period? It needs to be noted at the outset that the small Flemish agriculturalists generally did not possess their means of subsistence. It appears, in fact, that an important phase in separating the peasants from the "possession" of the land – and thus in conditioning agricultural development – took place during the reconstruction of the countryside in the wake of the late medieval population drop-off, when landlords turned customary tenures to leasehold. In any case, in the early modern period Flemish agriculture was primarily carried out either by commercial tenants or by mini-freeholders whose farms were too small to produce "for subsistence". Both had to produce for the market and to specialize in order to survive.[219]

What made it not only necessary for these small producers to specialize and improve for the market, but also possible to do so successfully, was first of all the easy availability of grain brought in from eastern Europe. Massive grain imports from eastern Germany and Poland gave Flemish cultivators relative freedom from the usual pressures to orient production to the variety of subsistence needs, in order to avoid dependence on the market for survival. Such security of supply in basic necessities was not, of course, available to most of Europe's peasantry, who were in general obliged to be self-reliant.[220] Correlatively, the Flemish peasants' immediate access to the great Flemish industrial centres – they were located in the shadows of the Flemish towns – gave them ready and reliable markets, and made specialization that much less risky.[221] Finally, and indispensably, the Flemish farmers' proximity to the cities gave them access to the big urban supplies of fertilizer (human and animal). Fertilizer from the towns was the linchpin of their entire

[219] H. van der Wee and E. van Cauwenberghe, "Histoire agraire et finances publiques en Flandre du XIVe au XVIIe siècle", *Annales E.S.C.*, xxviii (1973), pp. 1056–8; F. M. Mendels, "Agriculture and Peasant Industry in Eighteenth-Century Flanders", in E. L. Jones and W. N. Parker (eds.), *European Peasants and their Markets* (Princeton, 1975), pp. 194, 198–9; and above, pp. 160–1.

[220] A. Verhulst, "L'économie rurale de la Flandre et la dépression économique du bas moyen âge", *Etudes rurales*, x (1963), pp. 76–7; A. van der Woude, "The *A. A. G. Bijdragen* and the Study of Dutch Rural History", *Jl European Econ. Hist.*, iv (1975), p. 235; B. H. Slicher van Bath, "The Rise of Intensive Cultivation in the Low Countries", in J. S. Bromley and E. H. Kossman (eds.), *Britain and the Netherlands* [i] (London, 1960), p. 149.

[221] Slicher van Bath, "Rise of Intensive Cultivation in the Low Countries", pp. 145–6.

productive enterprise, which would have been very difficult without it.[222]

It must be emphasized that these mini-farmers did not, by and large, produce basic food crops. They specialized, rather, in all sorts of industrial crops, in dairy products and in market gardening.[223] It was not, therefore, the small Flemish agriculturalist who supported the expanding Flemish industrial centres. On the contrary, neither the specialized, Flemish small peasant agriculture, nor the advanced Flemish industry, could have flourished had it not been for grain imports from the east.

In view of all its special features, it is hardly surprising that Flemish-type agriculture barely spread at all beyond the regions in which it originally found a home. Are we to suppose that the neighbouring peasants of northern France were somehow too conservative to copy their Flemish brethren? Did the Enlightenment come early to the Catholic peasants of Flanders, while it eluded their less favoured counterparts not too many miles away in Normandy, Cambrésis and Picardy? Le Roy Ladurie himself, writing elsewhere, is careful to describe the Flemish agricultural developments as "aberrant" and to point out that they "seem to develop in isolation" (in a "vase clos") – precisely because of the peculiar, urbanized, grain-importing conditions of the region.[224] Is it not clear that this is the exception that proves the rule?

One qualification to conclude these considerations on the potentials of pre-industrial peasant agriculture: what was "the rule" in medieval and early modern Europe cannot be taken to hold good for all times and all places. For the relationships between certain property systems and certain paths of economic evolution, especially of the development of the productive forces, are not governed by trans-historical laws. In particular, once breakthroughs to ongoing capitalist economic development took place in various regions, these irrevocably transformed the conditions and character of the analogous processes which were to occur subsequently elsewhere. Over time, and especially in the course of the

[222] "The model functions fully only near cities . . . which furnish the necessary complements of fertilizer": Le Roy Ladurie, "De la crise ultime à la vraie croissance", p. 414.

[223] Mendels, "Agriculture and Peasant Industry in Eighteenth-Century Flanders".

[224] Le Roy Ladurie, "Masses profondes: la paysannerie", pp. 511–14, esp. p. 514; also quoted by Cooper, p. 160 above; Le Roy Ladurie, "De la crise ultime à la vraie croissance", pp. 414–16.

nineteenth century, the significance for economic advance of agriculture based on small owner-operators was altered. The incentives for production for the market grew; the pressures to orient production to subsistence declined; and the technological potential of the small family farm was expanded. As the rise of industry made available an ever wider range of commodities at low costs, there were tremendous inducements for the peasants to give up the home production of necessities and to specialize, and buy what they needed on the market. With ever-expanding world supplies in basic food and improved transportation to make these accessible, there was decreasing risk in specialization. Finally, with the development of artificial fertilizers and the growth of biological knowledge towards the end of the nineteenth century, the small family farm obtained positive advantages in certain types of production. Especially in the new forms of animal (combined with fodder crop) production ("polyculture-élevage"), the best techniques were as applicable to small as to large farms and required little capital. Moreover, the small family farmer could apply a quality and care in labour necessary for animal production which was usually unattainable on capitalist farms using wage labour.[225] These developments naturally made much more likely a smooth transition from peasant to essentially capitalist farming, without the need for extra-economic processes to separate the direct producer from the means of subsistence – the continuity of the family farm.

CONCLUSION: INDUSTRY, AGRICULTURE AND ECONOMIC DEVELOPMENT

It was the growth of agricultural productivity, rooted in the transformation of agrarian class or property relations, which allowed the English economy to embark upon a path of development already closed to its Continental neighbours. This path was distinguished by *continuing industrialization* and overall economic growth *through* the period when "general crisis" gripped the other European economies, and into the epoch of the industrial revolution.

[225] C. Servolin, "L'absorption de l'agriculture dans le mode de production capitaliste", in Y. Tavernier, M. Gervais and C. Servolin (eds.), *L'univers politique des paysans* (Paris, 1972), pp. 44–5, and *passim*; M. Gervais and C. Servolin, "Réflexions sur l'évolution de l'agriculture dans les pays développés", *Cahiers de l'Institut économique appliqué*, ser. Ag 3, no. 143 (1963), pp. 102–6.

Now, quite possibly, the spectacular rise of English cloth production for export from the later fifteenth century – powerfully supplemented by population growth a bit later – was what *set off* the overall process of English economic development in the early modern period. It may well have provided the *initial* pressure of demand which set in motion the highly responsive agricultural-productive system. Nevertheless, it is critical to emphasize that the English cloth export industry, like its Continental counterparts, was characterized by its *continuity with* and *similarity to* the great medieval cloth industries of Flanders and northern Italy: it responded to the same feudal dynamics, was subject to the same feudally based limitations, and could not therefore provide the foundations for continuing growth. It grew up on the basis of its ability to capture a large segment of a growing European demand for essentially luxury products, rooted in growing upper- and middle-class incomes, based finally on the growth phase of the European economy extending from the later fifteenth century. But like its predecessors of the medieval period, the growth of the English cloth industry for export was strictly limited by the restricted size of the European market, ultimately bounded by the system's inability to transform agricultural production. Thus the English cloth export industry, like all of its Continental counterparts, inevitably began to falter as population and production on the Continent reached a ceiling and began to descend into crisis in the later sixteenth and seventeenth centuries. The intensified competition experienced not only by the English cloth export industry, but by *all* of the major Continental cloth export industries, was an indication that the market had reached a point of saturation. Beyond that point, there might be some redistribution of market shares among the national cloth export industries, but industry as a whole could not grow significantly.[226] Henceforth, every Continental

[226] Coleman, *Economy of England, 1450–1750*, pp. 48–55, 61–5; F. J. Fisher, "London's Export Trade in the Early Seventeenth Century", *Econ. Hist. Rev.*, 2nd ser., iii (1950–1); B. Supple, *Commercial Crisis and Change in England, 1600–1642* (Cambridge, 1959); D. Sella, "The Rise and Fall of the Venetian Woollen Industry", in B. Pullan (ed.), *Crisis and Change in the Venetian Economy, 1550–1630* (London, 1968); P. Deyon, "La concurrence internationale des manufactures lainières aux XVIe et XVIIe siècles", *Annales E.S.C.*, xxvii (1972); C. Wilson, "Cloth Production and International Competition in the Seventeenth Century", *Econ. Hist. Rev.*, 2nd ser., xiii (1960–1).

region sank, sooner or later, into the interrelated agricultural and industrial crisis of the seventeenth century.

What, therefore, *marks off* the English economy from those of all its European neighbours in the seventeenth century was not only its capacity to maintain demographic increase beyond the old Malthusian limits, but also its ability to sustain continuing industrial and overall economic growth in the face of the crisis and stagnation of the traditionally predominant cloth export industry. Although perhaps originally activated by cloth exports, the continuing English industrial expansion was founded upon a growing domestic market, rooted ultimately in the continuing transformation of agricultural production. It was, by contrast, the restricted and declining home market – undermined by decaying agricultural productivity – which was at the root of the widespread drop-off in manufacturing production throughout France, western Germany and eastern Europe.

The fact that the industrial development of Continental Europe continued to be fettered by its feudal agrarian base throughout the early modern period is finally confirmed by the constricted developmental path of even its most advanced region, the United Provinces. By the early seventeenth century, Dutch shipping dominated the European carrying trade and may have constituted the economy's most dynamic sector. There was also an impressive cloth industry for export, located especially at Leiden. Furthermore, important paper, brewing, bleaching, baking, and brick- and tile-making industries, at least partly for export, grew up in this period. Meanwhile, a vital agricultural sector developed rapidly by carrying specialization by region, and especially in relationship to the European economy, to an extremely high pitch.

The problem was, however, that all of these developments were spurred by and dependent upon the general growth of the European economy during the sixteenth and into the seventeenth century. The industrial and agricultural sectors were heavily dependent upon grain imports from eastern Europe for their existence. Even more significant, both shipping and cloth, as well as a number of other leading Dutch industries, were dependent upon overseas export markets, and thus overseas production. This was eventually true also of Dutch agriculture. In sum, Dutch production hardly constituted an economy in its own right; it grew up as an integral part of the overall European economy and naturally shared its fate.

It was predictable, then, that as the European economy as a whole moved into stagnation and crisis at various points in the seventeenth century, the Dutch economy would be profoundly affected. The carrying trade was perhaps most sensitive to the general European crisis, stagnating after 1650. Cloth, too, could not help but be hurt, the output of Leiden falling by one-third between 1650 and 1700. Because it was so deeply rooted in the European economy, the Dutch economy could not turn back in upon itself when the crisis came. The Dutch had simply built too great an edifice on shaky foundations. The region's advanced economic organization had allowed it to dominate the growing markets of Europe's economy in "phase A". But when these markets inevitably reached their limit, the Dutch economy was bound to fall back. Enmeshed in what remained an essentially feudal circuit of production, the Dutch economy was slowly strangled, as that circuit gradually constricted with the onset of "phase B".[227]

By contrast, the English economy of the early modern period witnessed the gradual construction of mutually interdependent, mutually self-developing agricultural and industrial sectors at home. That English production had already begun to orient towards a developing home market by the second quarter of the seventeenth century appears to be evidenced in the relatively small degree to which the dramatic crisis of the traditional cloth export trade in this period disrupted the economy as a whole. The economic crisis was largely confined to the areas directly involved in cloth production for export, and was manifested in high levels of unemployment in these areas.[228] But at the very same time (1615–40) there was a significant growth of all sorts of import trades: not only luxury goods for the upper classes but a wide range of consumer goods, such as fruits from Spain, currants from the Levant, spices from the Indies,

[227] For the foregoing paragraphs, see especially Van der Woude, "*A. A. G. Bijdragen* and the Study of Dutch Rural History", pp. 227–41. Schöffer comments: "To a certain degree, we can call the economic prosperity of the Dutch Republic parasitical . . . [It] was bound to Europe in all its fibres . . . Holland's prosperity waned after 1660, the Republic was also enmeshed in the B-phase of European economic development": I. Schöffer, "Did Holland's Golden Age Co-incide with a Period of Crisis?", *Acta historiae Neerlandica*, i (1966), pp. 100–1.

[228] Supple, *Commercial Crisis and Change in England, 1600–1642*.

tobacco from America.[229] This seems to indicate the existence of a substantial middle-class, even lower-class, market at home. The appearance of an actual glut in grain production in these years, with accompanying lower prices, seems to have eased the effects of the cloth crisis and provided the basis for continuing growth.[230]

The continuing dynamism of the English economy in the second half of the seventeenth century bore witness to the transformation which had occurred. During this period, as Thirsk explains, there was a rapid growth of a whole range of industries which had their beginnings in the Tudor period (including stocking-knitting, lace-making, linen-weaving and so forth), as well as a host of other "consumer industries" (knives, edge tools, hats, pots and the like).[231] It is difficult to assign quantitative weight to these developments. Nevertheless, the macro-economic trends seem to confirm the impression that there was a significantly growing home market for industrial goods. Demographic growth continued through the end of the seventeenth century and into the eighteenth, and population continued to shift from agriculture into industry and from the rural towards the urban areas, as there was a big growth not only of London, but also of Liverpool, Manchester and Birmingham. Even so, grain prices ceased to rise. This allowed real wages to increase, a new golden age for working people. With agriculture providing growing discretionary incomes and increasing purchasing power not only to the middle but to the lower classes, the home market continued to grow. Industry fed on agriculture and stimulated in turn further agricultural improvement – an upward spiral that extended into the industrial revolution.[232]

[229] H. Taylor, "Trade, Neutrality and the 'English Road', 1630–1648", *Econ. Hist. Rev.*, 2nd ser., xxv (1972); A. M. Millard, "The Import Trade of London, 1600–1640" (Univ. of London Ph.D. thesis, 1956), appendices.

[230] J. Thirsk, *Economic Policy and Projects* (Oxford, 1978), p. 161. I wish to thank Joan Thirsk for allowing me to consult her manuscript in advance of publication.

[231] *Ibid.*, ch. 5, and conclusion.

[232] For the continuing development, see Coleman, *Economy of England, 1450–1750*, chs. 6, 7, 9, 11; A. H. John, "Agricultural Productivity and Economic Growth in England, 1700–1760", *Jl Econ. Hist.*, xxv (1965); D. E. C. Eversley, "The Home Market and Economic Growth in England, 1750–1780", in E. L. Jones and G. E. Mingay (eds.), *Land, Labour and Population in the Industrial Revolution* (London, 1967).

Index

Ábbreviations:

Boh.	Bohemian	Eng.	English	Germ.	German
C	Century	Fr.	French		

Past and Present Publications

General Editor: PAUL SLACK, *Exeter College, Oxford*

The Brenner Debate: Agrarian Class Structure and Economic Development in Pre-Industrial Europe, edited by T. H. Aston and C. H. E. Philpin*
Eternal Victory: Triumphal Rulership in Late Antiquity, Byzantium, and the Early Medieval West, Michael McCormick*†
East-Central Europe in Transition: From the Fourteenth to the Seventeenth Century, edited by Antoni Mączak, Henry Samsonowicz and Peter Burke†
Small Books and Pleasant Histories: Popular Fiction and its Readership in Seventeenth-Century England, Margaret Spufford*
Society, Politics and Culture: Studies in Early Modern England, Mervyn James*
Horses, Oxen and Technological Innovation: The Use of Draught Animals in English Farming 1066–1600, John Langdon
Nationalism and Popular Protest in Ireland, edited by C. H. E. Philpin
Rituals of Royalty: Power and Ceremonial in Traditional Societies, edited by David Cannadine and Simon Price*
The Margins of Society of Late Medieval Paris, Bronisław Geremek†
Landlords, Peasants and Politics in Medieval England, edited by T. H. Aston
Geography, Technology, and War: Studies in the Maritime History of the Mediterranean, 649–1572, John H. Pryor*
Church Courts, Sex and Marriage in England, 1570–1640, Martin Ingram*
Searches for an Imaginary Kingdom: The Legend of the Kingdom of Prester John, L. N. Gumilev
Crowds and History: Mass Phenomena in English Towns, 1780–1835, Mark Harrison
Concepts of Cleanliness: Changing Attitudes in France since the Middle Ages, Georges Vigarello†
The First Modern Society: Essays in English History in Honour of Lawrence Stone, edited by A. L. Beier, David Cannadine and James M. Rosenheim
The Europe of the Devout: The Catholic Reformation and the Formation of a New Society, Louis Châtellier†
English Rural Society, 1500–1800: Essays in Honour of Joan Thirsk, edited by John Chartes and David Hey
Lordship, Knighthood and Locality: A Study in English Society c. 1180–c. 1280, P. R. Coss
English and French Towns in Feudal Society: A Comparative Study, R. H. Hilton
An Island for Itself: Economic Development and Social Change in Late Medieval Sicily, Stephan R. Epstein

Epidemics and Ideas: Essays on the Historical Perception of Pestilence, edited by Terence Ranger and Paul Slack

The Political Economy of Shopkeeping in Milan, 1886–1922, Jonathan Morris

* Published also as a paperback

† Co-published with the Maison des Sciences de l'Homme, Paris